Third Edition

LLOYD D. BROOKS, Ed.D.

MEMPHIS STATE UNIVERSITY

MEMPHIS, TENNESSEE

 EMCParadigm

Developmental Editor: Cynthia Miller

Copyeditor: Carol Kennedy

Text/Cover Design: Queue Publishing Services

Desktop Production and Illustrations: Tim Heitman

Acknowledgments: We wish to thank the following instructors and technical experts who contributed to this book:

Mr. Leo Gafney
Consultant
Lakeville, CT

Ms. Debbie West
Draughons Junior College
Nashville, TN

Ms. Donna McFalls
West Tennessee Business College
Jackson, TN 38302

Library of Congress Cataloging in Publication Data

Brooks, Lloyd D.
      Business math / Lloyd D. Brooks. -- 3rd. ed.
         p.   cm.
      Rev. ed. of: College business mathematics. c1988.
      Includes index.
      ISBN 1-56118-657-0
      1. Business mathematics.   I. Brooks, Lloyd D.
      College business mathematics.   II. Title.
      HF5691.B764   1996
    650'.01'513--dc20
                                  94-21341
                                     CIP

Published by: EMC/Paradigm
               300 York Ave.
               St. Paul, MN 55101
               800-535-6865

E-mail questions or comments regarding this text may be sent to PUBLISH@emcp.COM.

Printed in the United States of America

10 9 8 7 6 5 4 3 2 1

CONTENTS

Page	Photo Credits
1	International Stock Photography/Bill Tucker
2	International Stock Photography/Roger Markham Smith
44	International Stock Photography/Wayne Sproul
60	International Stock Photography/Kachaturian
103	International Stock Photography/Frank Maresca
104	International Stock Photography/Russell Clemens
116	International Stock Photography/Richard Hackett
130	International Stock Photography/Michael Phillip Manheim
156	Image Bank/HMS Images
190	International Stock Photography/Peter Russell Clemens
212	International Stock Photography/Jeff Greenberg
252	International Stock Photography/Peter Russell Clemens
274	International Stock Photography/Peter Langone 3486
310	International Stock Photography/Richard Hackett
333	International Stock Photography/Frank Maresca
354	Photo Edit/David Young-Wolf
396	International Stock Photography/JG Mason
415	International Stock Photography/Bill Stanton
472	International Stock Photography/Hal Kern

PREFACE

Interest, insurance, mortgage, sales tax—you have probably heard these terms; but do you know what they mean? Which of these are a consideration in your life?

Whether it's reconciling a bank statement, making payments on a car, or buying stocks from a major corporation, business math is prevalent in almost everyone's life. Therefore, it is important to learn the principles of business math in order to make informed decisions about your personal and professional life.

This text has been developed to make the study of business math comprehensive and interesting. It combines real-life applications of business math with easy-to-comprehend instruction and analysis. The best way to learn business math is to solve problems, and this text has been structured to provide ample practice with a wide variety of problems. For each concept presented, a model problem demonstrates how the solution is reached. Then you are asked to apply your skills to solve a similar problem on your own. There are several of these problems throughout each chapter to provide immediate practice and feedback. By working these problems, as well as the applications at the end of each chapter, you will discover the basics of business mathematics and how to apply the concepts in this book to your life.

FEATURES

This text contains several features and tools to help you learn business math:

Unit Introduction

A brief introduction presents the topics that will be covered within the unit. The units are broken down into different types of business mathematics, such as marketing mathematics, and accounting and financial mathematics.

Chapter Performance Objectives

Each chapter begins with objectives that state the learning benchmarks and standards established for each chapter.

Marginal Notes

Terms and concepts that may be unfamiliar are explained in the margin to help build vocabulary and conceptual understanding

Model Problems

Following each concept within a chapter, a model problem is worked out to illustrate how the solution is reached.

Apply Your Skills

Following the Model Problems within a chapter, Apply Your Skills exercises provide an immediate opportunity to solve problems related to each topic.

Performance Applications

At the end of each chapter, drill-and-practice problems provide ample practice solving the chapter problems.

Chapter Practice Tests

At the end of each chapter is a sample test to provide additional practice solving the chapter problems.

Connections

Connections exercises ask questions about real-life documents, such as USA Today charts, to demonstrate everyday uses for business math.

Decisions

Decisions exercises require you to make effective business and financial decisions.

Chapter Reviews and Quick References

A review appears at the end of each chapter that highlights key points, formulas, examples, and page references.

Communications

Communications exercises appear at the end of each unit and teach you how to communicate and comprehend the language of business math.

Unit Self Tests

At the end of each unit is a sample test to provide additional practice solving the problems contained in the unit.

STUDENT SUPPLEMENTS

Student Solutions Manual

Solutions to end-of chapter Performance Applications, and Connections, Decisions, and Communications problems are given for student reinforcement.

Electronic Calculator

An electronic calculator is included with the textbook for use when solving business math problems

The Net Effect

The Net Effect is a software program designed to provide authentic practice in business math. You are invited to complete real-life business math tasks as an employee in a retail music store. The tasks take place in several areas of the business and involve a variety of business documents. This program is available on 3.5" disks and CD-ROM.

UNIT 1

Basic Mathematic Operations

Even when we were small children, as we became aware of the world around us, it was apparent that basic mathematics provides the foundation for much of our daily activity. Some of our earliest experiences with mathematics involved making simple purchases and saving and spending money. Can you remember the first time you were paid for a job you did?

Included in this unit are the basic skills of addition, subtraction, multiplication, and division. These skills are enhanced using applications such as sales invoices, bank reconciliation statements, and wage computations. These applications relate to real-life situations you will encounter throughout your lifetime.

Chapter 7

ADDITION AND SUBTRACTION

Performance Objectives

1. Determine the place value of numbers.
2. Round whole numbers in a verbal format.
3. Group digits to increase computational speed.
4. Read numbers and estimate solutions to increase accuracy.
5. Add digits in vertical and horizontal formats.
6. Subtract digits in vertical and horizontal formats.

The growth of microcomputers has made the processing of numerical data even more important than in the past. This equipment can process millions of values in a few seconds. Ironically, however, the electronic equipment in use today makes the study of business mathematics more essential than ever. To use the equipment effectively, you must first understand business mathematical procedures.

Although business mathematics applications require very precise results, computations are often logical and fairly easy to learn. Most problems result not from a lack of knowledge, but from a lack of attention to details, which then causes errors. Several factors can contribute to increased accuracy, as illustrated in Figure 1.1.

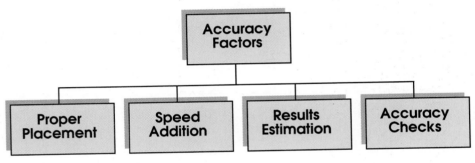

Figure 1.1 Accuracy Factors

PLACE VALUE

From prehistoric times to the present, people have used symbols to represent quantities. The Romans used seven letters to express numerical values, whereas the Egyptians used symbols. Most modern countries use the decimal number system, which is based on the ten digits 0, 1, 2, 3, 4, 5, 6, 7, 8, and 9.

Electronic calculators and computers use the decimal system to process numerical values. The value of each digit depends on its place in relation to the decimal point. Each number place has a value ten times greater than the number place to its right. For example, 40 is ten times greater than 4, and 400 is 10 times greater than 40.

Number place determines a number's actual value. Figure 1.2 shows the values of various positions to the left and right of the decimal point.

Place value is a system whereby the position of the digit determines its value.

The value is determined by the position relative to the decimal point.

BILLIONS			MILLIONS			THOUSANDS			UNITS				DECIMALS		
HUNDRED BILLIONS	TEN BILLIONS	BILLIONS	HUNDRED MILLIONS	TEN MILLIONS	MILLIONS	HUNDRED THOUSANDS	TEN THOUSANDS	THOUSANDS	HUNDREDS	TENS	ONES	DECIMAL POINT	TENTHS	HUNDREDTHS	THOUSANDTHS
												.			

Figure 1.2 Place Value Chart

READING VALUES

Numbers are read according to their position in the place value chart.

Whole numbers should be separated into groups of three digits, with a comma separating each group. Name each group, such as millions, thousands, hundreds, units, and so forth. Begin at the left of the number and then read the numerals in each group, indicating the name as the group is read. However, the group name *units* is not stated.

The decimal point is used to separate units from decimal portions of the number. The word *and* is used to indicate the decimal point in reading the number. For example, the number **2,456,208.45** is read as **two million, four hundred fifty-six thousand, two hundred eight, and forty-five hundredths.** Commas are used to separate digits into groups of three placed from left to right. Other examples are shown in Model 1.1.

Reading numbers is especially important when communicating by telephone. For example, a customer requesting an account balance will be misinformed if an amount is read incorrectly.

Reading numbers

7	read *seven*
214	read *two hundred fourteen*
12,716	read *twelve thousand, seven hundred sixteen*
7,204,000	read *seven million, two hundred four thousand*
4.2	read *four and two-tenths*
18.35	read *eighteen and thirty-five hundredths*
0.421	read *four hundred twenty-one thousandths*
$12.45	read *twelve dollars and forty-five cents*
18%	read *eighteen percent*

Apply Your Skills

Indicate how each of the following numbers should be read.

(a) 345 _____

(b) 1,382 _____

(c) 425.84 _____

(d) $27.53 _____

(e) 14.2% _____

INCREASING SPEED BY GROUPING

Speed is important in making mathematical computations by hand. One way to add numbers quickly is to identify groupings of two or more numbers that total 10, because addition in groups of 10 is relatively fast. See Model 1.2.

Addition in groups of 10

Apply Your Skills

Which values should be grouped to speed addition for the following addition problem?

7
4
3
6
2

(a) _____

(b) _____

Practice makes grouping values easier and increases speed in manual addition. When a calculator or computer is used, the numbers should be entered in order without grouping because the values are recorded into memory as they are entered from the keyboard.

In Model 1.3, group the numbers from top to bottom as you add. To check the accuracy of your answer, add the numbers again by grouping the values from bottom to top. If you obtain the same answer twice, you can be reasonably certain that the answer is correct. Even when using a calculator, performing the addition twice is always recommended.

MODEL 1.3

Add the digits two times to assure the same answer for accuracy.

Checking the accuracy of addition

788	763
272	124
835	343
125	768
988	132
3,008	2,130

Apply Your Skills

Check the accuracy of the following addition problem. What is the correct answer? _____

1,243
302
3,428
8,319

Compare the estimated answer with the computed answer.

INCREASING ACCURACY BY ROUNDING

A second way to increase accuracy is to estimate the answer first and then compare the estimated answer with the computed answer to see if they are similar. To estimate, round the numbers to a specific digit, such as the hundreds place or the tenths place.

In *rounding* to the hundreds place, for example, if the digit that was in the tens place is 5 or more, increase the digit in the hundreds place by 1. Otherwise, the digit in the hundreds place is unchanged. Then convert all digits to the right of the hundreds place to zeros. Model 1.4 illustrates typical rounding of numbers.

Rounding is designed to make it easier to estimate or approximate the actual answer. The procedure for rounding values is fairly easy, as illustrated below.

Step 1   Choose the digit for rounding.

Step 2   If the digit to the right of the digit chosen for rounding is **5** or greater, increase the chosen digit by **1**. If the digit to the right of the digit chosen for rounding is **4** or less, do not increase the chosen digit.

Step 3   Unless rounding involves decimal values, change digits to the right of the digit chosen to zeros.

To see how these rounding procedures work in practice, the value 4,867 is rounded to the thousands position.

Step 1   Decide on the digit for rounding—thousands position in this example, 4,867.

Step 2   Since the digit (**8** in this example) to the right of the digit chosen is 5 or greater, the digit **4** is increased by **1**. The value 4 is changed to a **5**. This is called rounding up.

Step 3   The remaining digits are then changed to zeros to provide the following value: **5,000.** Therefore, the value 4,867 has been rounded to 5,000.

For an example involving a decimal value, assume that the value 4.638 is rounded to the tenths position. The rounding procedures used above can be repeated.

After rounding, zeros to the far right of the decimal point are usually dropped. For example, 8.65 rounds to 8.7.

Step 1   Decide on the digit for rounding—tenths position in the example, 4.**6**38.

Step 2   Since the digit to the right of the chosen digit (**3** in this example) is 4 or less, the digit chosen for rounding (tenths) is not changed.

Step 3   The remaining digits are then dropped to provide the following value: **4.6.** Therefore, the value 4.638 has been rounded to 4.6.

**MODEL
1.4**

Rounding values

46	rounded to tens	50
342	rounded to hundreds	300
562	rounded to hundreds	600
3,728	rounded to thousands	4,000
8.65	rounded to tenths	8.7
29.42	rounded to tenths	29.4
9.236	rounded to hundredths	9.24
8.923	rounded to hundredths	8.92
5.34%	rounded to tenths	5.3%
$4.55	rounded to dollars	$5.00

Apply Your Skills

Round each of the following numbers as indicated.

(a) 379   rounded to hundreds   _____

(b) 2,701   rounded to thousands   _____

(c) 8.28   rounded to tenths   _____

(d) 4.2519   rounded to hundredths   _____

(e) $27.58   rounded to dollars   _____

Perform the exercise in Model 1.5 to determine if your answer equals the answer given. First, compute the exact answer. Then compute the estimated answer to see if they are close.

Model 1.5 shows that the estimated answer is close to the exact answer. If the estimated answer is much different from the computed exact answer, the numbers should be added again.

Rounding answers: Whole numbers

Exact	Rounded to hundreds
345.28	300
450.38	500
2,562.36	2,600
650.00	700
4,008.02	4,100

Apply Your Skills

Estimate the following solution by rounding each of the values to hundreds. What are the (a) exact and (b) estimated solutions?

348	_____
2,479	_____
620	_____
570	_____

(a) _____   (b) _____

MODEL 1.5

Rounding procedures:

1. Identify digit for rounding.

2. Round up if digit to the right is 5 or more. Otherwise, do not change.

3. All digits to right of identified digit are changed to zeros (except for decimal values).

Rounding can also be used to estimate the answer in adding decimal values, as shown in Model 1.6.

The estimated answer is reasonably close to the exact answer. This comparison is another way to ensure that computations are accurate.

Rounding answers: Decimals

Exact	Rounded to hundreds
4.35	4.4
10.57	10.6
5.26	5.3
20.18	20.3

Apply Your Skills

What are the (a) exact and (b) estimated (rounded to tenths) solutions for the following addition problem?

5.76	_____
2.23	_____
14.21	_____
10.79	_____

(a) _____   (b) _____

MODEL 1.6

ADDING FIGURES HORIZONTALLY

Numbers are often arranged horizontally on business reports.

In hand calculations, horizontal addition is more difficult because the numbers are not aligned vertically for ease of reading. As in vertical addition, add the digits in the ones place first, then the digits in the tens place, and so on. With a calculator, of course, horizontal addition is as easy as vertical addition. Model 1.7 demonstrates horizontal addition.

MODEL 1.7

Horizontal addition is best performed with a calculator.

Horizontal addition

145 + 25 + 68 = ____ ____ **8** (carry 1 to tens place)

145 + 25 + 68 = ____ **3** **8** (carry 1 to hundreds place)

145 + 25 + 68 = **2** **3** **8**

Apply Your Skills

Compute the solutions to the following addition problems. Check your answers by adding values vertically and horizontally.

234 +		75 +		204 =	(a) _____
27 +		102 +		82 =	(b) _____
103 +		87 +		102 =	(c) _____
(d) _____ +		(e) _____ +		(f) _____ =	(g) _____

The accuracy of horizontal addition can be checked by adding the values horizontally and vertically as shown in Model 1.8. The sum of the vertical totals and the sum of the horizontal totals should be the same if all individual sums have been added correctly.

MODEL 1.8

Checking horizontal addition

42 +		36 +		45 =	· 123
32 +		18 +		19 =	69
35 +		16 +		32 =	83
109 +		70 +		96 =	**275**

You may now complete Performance Applications 1.1 and 1.2.

SUBRACTION

Finding the difference between two values is often necessary in business and personal applications. As shown in Model 1.9, the number subtracted is called the *subtrahend*, the number subtracted from is the *minuend*, and the resulting answer is the *difference*.

Components of subtraction

$4,274.45	Minuend
- 1,121.28	Subtrahend
$3,153.17	Difference (Remainder)

Apply Your Skills

Donald Quinn's account with the bank had a $2,519.45 balance. He withdrew $57.37 from the account. What was the balance after the withdrawal?

PROOF IN SUBTRACTION

Subtraction is the opposite of addition. Therefore, you can check or prove the accuracy of subtraction by adding the difference to the subtrahend to see if the resulting sum equals the minuend. You can check the subtraction in Model 1.9 by adding $1,121.28 + 3,153.17 = $4,274.45.

HORIZONTAL SUBTRACTION

Accounting records, journals, invoices, and charge account statements are often written in a horizontal format, as in 24 - 13 = 11. This horizontal arrangement makes it more difficult to align decimal points, as in 2.189 - 1.2 = .989, but the method used for horizontal subtraction is the same as for vertical subtraction.

ROUNDING ANSWERS IN SUBTRACTION

Estimating answers is also useful in subtraction. The procedure for rounding is like the one used for addition, discussed in Chapter 1. The subtrahend and minuend should be rounded to the same place, for example, tens or hundreds, as shown in Model 1.10.

Notice that the estimated answer is reasonably close to the actual answer. This is another safeguard to obtain the correct answer. Estimating becomes even more important when using a calculator because merely striking a wrong key can result in an error. Estimating fairly simple computations can be done mentally.

**MODEL
1.10**

Rounding answers in subtraction

Actual	Estimated
4,269	4,300
-1,138	-1,100
3,131	3,200

Apply Your Skills

City Furniture offered a $495 discount on a bedroom normally selling for $1,802. What were the (a) actual and (b) estimated prices after deducting the discount?

(a) $ _____

(b) $ _____

PERFORMANCE APPLICATION 1.1

1. Add the following numbers. Group by tens when possible.

(a) 859
     941
     228
     _____

(b) 894
     786
     323
     _____

(c) 983
     817
     272
     _____

(d) 972
     728
     282
     _____

(e) 899
     381
     528
     _____

(f) 895
     385
     928
     _____

(g) 937
     862
     121
     _____

(h) 426
     319
     208
     _____

(i) 419
     364
     237
     _____

(j) 764
     589
     405
     _____

(k) 282
     673
     652
     _____

(l) 143
     679
     187
     _____

(m) 587
     368
     783
     _____

(n) 547
     428
     913
     _____

2. Add the following numbers. Check the accuracy of your addition.

(a) $128.37
     26.45
     389.71
$ _____

(c) $126.84
     832.67
     289.85
$ _____

(e) $727.18
     107.40
     87.98
$ _____

(g) $62.85
     47.63
     52.52
$ _____

(i) $35.89
     43.67
     18.34
$ _____

(b) $ 38.72
     142.19
     321.86
$ _____

(d) $168.01
     78.15
     5.89
$ _____

(f) $ 30.57
     105.41
     52.18
$ _____

(h) $306.75
     42.18
     5.67
$ _____

(j) $176.88
     14.62
     934.22
$ _____

3. Add the following numbers. Check the accuracy of your addition.

(a) $248.62
     381.28
     429.74
     384.36
$ _____

(c) $481.65
     328.25
     526.72
     815.18
$ _____

(e) $387.43
     285.09
     683.11
     748.67
$ _____

(g) $245.78
     246.74
     467.28
     9,217.86
$ _____

(i) $837.49
     18,768.48
     87,987.53
     43,816.76
$ _____

(b) $368.45
     52.18
     327.53
     426.17
$ _____

(d) $144.62
     68.76
     15.63
     757.49
$ _____

(f) $1326.43
     248.67
     425.68
     7,328.47
$ _____

(h) $693.23
     35.48
     768.16
     9,783.67
$ _____

(j) $87,286.19
     89,286.37
     68,394.83
     73,837.51
$ _____

4. Round each of the following values to hundreds. Compute the exact and estimated answers for each problem.

	Exact	Rounded		Exact	Rounded		Exact	Rounded
(a)	146		(c)	850		(e)	762	
	258			745			2,569	
	1,267	___		874	___		4,287	___
	___	___		___	___		___	___

	Exact	Rounded		Exact	Rounded		Exact	Rounded
(b)	258		(d)	2,562		(f)	896	
	490			6,729			509	
	589	___		3,896	___		845	___
	___	___		___	___		___	___

5. Round each of the following values to tenths. Compute the exact and estimated answers for each problem.

	Exact	Rounded		Exact	Rounded		Exact	Rounded
(a)	2.456		(c)	3.51		(e)	4.239	
	3.609			12.58			5.89	
	3.781	___		6.55	___		4.247	___
	___	___		___	___		___	___

	Exact	Rounded		Exact	Rounded		Exact	Rounded
(b)	0.578		(d)	12.4		(f)	3.591	
	3.528			0.583			6.249	
	9.446	___		5.68	___		2.009	___
	___	___		___	___		___	___

6. Frank McKenzie estimates that one manufacturer's microcomputer will cost $2,489 and a second manufacturer's will cost $1,986. Round each price to hundreds and compute the estimated cost of purchasing both.

   $ _____

7. Concord Lighting Company sells three lamps for the following prices: $79.87, $59.23, and $24.15. Round each price to tens and compute the estimated total cost of the three lamps.

   $ _____

8. The Kilgore Pet Shop sells three dogs for the following prices: $189.45, $134.50, and $89.50. Round each price to tens and compute the estimated total cost of the three dogs.

   $ _____

9. The Cycle Store had the following total sales for the past three days: Monday, $2,422.55; Tuesday, $1,254.18; and Wednesday, $2,450.25. Round each daily sales total to hundreds and compute the estimated total sales for the three days.

   $ _____

PERFORMANCE APPLICATION 1.2

1. Add the following values vertically and horizontally. The grand totals of the vertical and horizontal totals should agree.

(a)	4 +	13 +	3 +	7 =	_____
(b)	27 +	33 +	87 +	13 =	_____
(c)	18 +	22 +	46 +	34 =	_____
(d)	78 +	12 +	43 +	87 =	_____
(e)	43 +	57 +	97 +	89 =	_____
(f)	41 +	75 +	38 +	59 =	_____
(g)	52 +	48 +	96 +	87 =	_____
(h)	86 +	74 +	39 +	38 =	_____
(i)	37 +	41 +	16 +	23 =	_____
(j)	_____ + (k) _____	+ (l) _____	+ (m) _____ = (n)	_____

2. The following chart lists the number of units produced by six employees in a manufacturing plant. Compute the number of units produced each day, the number of units produced by each employee, and the total number of units produced.

Employee Number	Units Produced Each Day					Totals
	Monday	Tuesday	Wednesday	Thursday	Friday	
101	184	216	198	180	191	_____
102	176	204	213	197	184	_____
103	204	188	216	182	232	_____
104	162	175	183	175	184	_____
105	189	182	178	194	177	_____
106	173	190	192	166	196	_____
Totals	_____	_____	_____	_____	_____	_____

3. The following chart lists sales made by each salesperson for each day of the week. Indicate the total sales for each salesperson, total sales for each day, and total sales for all salespersons during the week.

Day	Salesperson						Totals
	Abel	Collins	Hayes	Kendel	Munson	Rowe	
Monday	$623.14	$537.48	$462.37	$389.72	$518.37	$487.36	$ _____
Tuesday	587.56	489.72	523.87	417.69	507.20	518.27	$ _____
Wednesday	586.41	473.68	529.43	428.47	534.28	398.41	$ _____
Thursday	602.43	525.18	763.31	581.45	369.71	406.41	$ _____
Friday	368.45	415.32	602.10	513.47	423.87	523.62	$ _____
Totals	$ _____	$ _____	$ _____	$ _____	$ _____	$ _____	$ _____

4. Find the sum for each of the following problems. Then copy the addends as neatly as possible and find the sum a second time. Analyze the neatness of your figures and compare the results to ensure that the sums are the same for both solutions of each problem.

                          Copy   **Copy**   **Copy**

(a) 53
    45
    37
    82
    26

(c) 40
    97
    88
    20
    32

(e) $34.81
    73.28
    16.90
    96.96
    $ _____ $ _____

(b) 86
    75
    12
    48
    97

(d) $13.82
    4.67
    3.89
    98.25
    $ _____ $ _____

(f) $26.89
    74.83
    18.32
    92.78
    $ _____ $ _____

PERFORMANCE APPLICATION 1.3

1. Find the difference and check answers for each of the following problems.

(a)   68
      - 29
   _____

(b)   207
      - 89
   _____

(c)   88
      - 53
   _____

(d)   87
      - 48
   _____

(e) 8,520
     - 3,245
   _____

(f) 76,712
     - 53,891
   _____

(g) 1,008,235
     - 609,487
   _____

2. Find the difference for each of the following problems.

(a) 15 - 7 = _____

(b) 82 - 15 = _____

(c) 57 - 29 = _____

(d) 87 - 49 = _____

(e) 123 - 18 = _____

(f) 187 - 138 = _____

(g) 383 - 178 = _____

(h) 357 - 289 = _____

(i) 1,762 - 835 = _____

3. Compute the markup (the difference between the cost price and the selling price) for each of the following problems. Then compute totals for each column.

First Period				Second Period			
Item	Selling Price	Cost Price	Markup	Item	Selling Price	Cost Price	Markup
A	$ 6.73	$ 5.49	_____	AA	$ 13.52	$ 11.76	_____
B	8.26	6.84	_____	BB	19.89	13.52	_____
C	7.35	4.79	_____	CC	17.81	15.49	_____
D	6.40	5.38	_____	DD	38.89	32.92	_____
E	8.49	5.75	_____	EE	162.71	153.89	_____
F	9.28	7.67	_____	FF	165.98	139.52	_____
TOTALS	$ _____	$ _____	$ _____		$ _____	$ _____	$ _____

4. Estimate the sums of each of the following problems.

	Actual	Estimated		Actual	Estimated		Actual	Estimated
(a)	56	60	(b)	31	30	(c)	528	500
	78	___		22	___		763	___
	42	___		46	___		581	___
	54	___		53	___		730	___
	___	___		___	___		279	___
							___	___

5. A desk can be purchased at Midtown Furniture Center for $898.23 or at Denver Furniture Company for $913.35. How much can be saved by buying the desk at Midtown Furniture Center?

$ _____

CHECK No.	DATE	CHECK ISSUED TO	BALANCE BROUGHT FORWARD	✓	6,389	72
341	1/3/--	To Lucky Seven Beauty Shop / For personal services	AMOUNT OF CHECK OR DEPOSIT / BALANCE		17	21
342	1/3/--	To Lotus Restaurant / For lunch for client – Collins	AMOUNT OF CHECK OR DEPOSIT / BALANCE		37	25
343	1/4/--	To Lance and Associates / For consulting services	AMOUNT OF CHECK OR DEPOSIT / BALANCE		300	00
___	1/4/--	To Deposit – #43 / For weekly receipts #53	AMOUNT OF CHECK OR DEPOSIT / BALANCE		2,640	75
344	1/4/--	To Lorenz Photography / For office photography	AMOUNT OF CHECK OR DEPOSIT / BALANCE		175	80
345	1/4/--	To Luellen Building Supplies / For building materials	AMOUNT OF CHECK OR DEPOSIT / BALANCE		463	17
346	1/5/--	To City Nursing Home / For donation	AMOUNT OF CHECK OR DEPOSIT / BALANCE		100	00
347	1/5/--	To Kaye Furniture Store / For office furniture	AMOUNT OF CHECK OR DEPOSIT / BALANCE		898	72
___	1/5/--	To Service charge / For statement #12	AMOUNT OF CHECK OR DEPOSIT / BALANCE		10	22
348	1/6/--	To Easy Care Lawn Center / For lawn services	AMOUNT OF CHECK OR DEPOSIT / BALANCE		82	95
349	1/6/--	To Norris Office Supply / For office supplies	AMOUNT OF CHECK OR DEPOSIT / BALANCE		114	23
350	1/7/--	To Hunt, Hunt & James / For attorney fees	AMOUNT OF CHECK OR DEPOSIT / BALANCE		420	00
351	1/7/--	To Moran Insurance Agency / For policy #31306	AMOUNT OF CHECK OR DEPOSIT / BALANCE		179	24

6. One basic application of addition and subtraction is maintaining a checkbook balance. Deposits are added, and checks written and service charges are deducted from the balance. Compute the balance after each transaction in the check register shown here.

Ending balance

$ _____

PRACTICE TEST FOR CHAPTER 1
ADDITION AND SUBTRACTION

Complete each of the following problems and then compare your answers with the ones on page 645.

1. Add the following numbers. Check the accuracy of your addition. What is the total? _____

    $348.95
    27.62
    148.97
    207.40

2. Round each of the following values to tenths. Compute the (a) exact and (b) estimated answers.

    30.589
    8.07
    40.249

    (a) _____ (b) _____

3. City Computer Center sold three microcomputers for the following amounts: $1,845.56, $1,382.56, and $1,212.43. What were the (a) exact and (b) estimated (rounded to hundreds) totals for the sale?

    (a) $ _____ (b) $ _____

4. Juan Perez earned the following salary during each of the past four years: $32,452.28, $32,672.89, $31,872.32, and $30,176.89. Round each salary to thousands and compute his estimated total earnings for the four years.

    $ _____

5. Landscape Creations computes the following costs for a proposed job: Labor, $2,279.52; Materials, $764.82; and Plants, $945.68. Round each amount to hundreds and compute the estimated total for the job.

    $ _____

6. City Motors offered a particular automobile for $18,375. A competing firm offered the same automobile for $17,824. How much can be saved by making the purchase at the competing firm?
    $ _____

1.1 The chart shown below indicates the amount of residential fencing that was built in the United States of America during a period of one year. What were the (a) exact and (b) estimated (rounded to the nearest thousand miles) number of miles of fencing for the year?

(a) _____

(b) _____

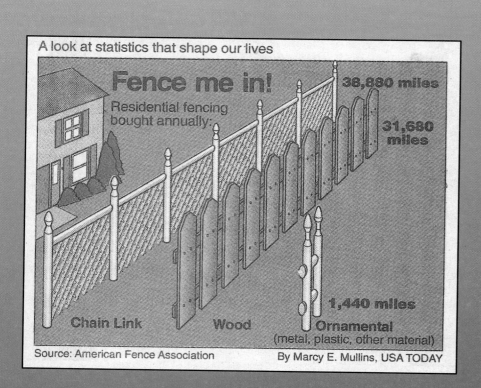

A look at statistics that shape our lives

Fence me in!
Residential fencing bought annually:

38,880 miles

31,680 miles

1,440 miles

Chain Link   Wood   Ornamental
(metal, plastic, other material)

Source: American Fence Association   By Marcy E. Mullins, USA TODAY

CONNECTIONS

1.2 The chart shown below indicates the number of people taking paid vacations during summer weeks. Assume that there are four weeks in each of the months. How many people were on paid vacation during the three months?

_____

A look at statistics that shape the nation

Vacation time is here!

On average, 2.3 million people are on paid vacation in any week. How that skyrockets in summer:

(millions per week)

5.9

5.7

3.3

June

July

August

Source: Bureau of Labor Statistics

By Stephen Conley, USA TODAY

DECISIONS

1.1 Assume that you are considering the possibility of building a new house containing 3,000 square feet of heated space. Several people must be hired to help build the house. (a) What is your estimated individual labor cost for each of the following groups of personnel: Carpenters, plumbers, electricians, architects, roofing specialists, brick masons, landscape technicians, wallpaper specialists, and flooring specialists? (b) What is the total estimated cost for these personnel? (c) What is the estimated total cost required to build the house, assuming that the cost per square foot is $80? Phone a building contractor in your city to determine the estimated cost for building a house in your city.

(a) $ _____

(b) $ _____

(c) $ _____

1.2 Assume that you have been requested to represent your school at a professional meeting in New York City. A local company has agreed to donate $1,500 or an amount equal to your expenses, whichever is greater. Estimate your individual and total expenses for the trip.

Airline fare   _____

Hotel   _____

Food   _____

Entertainment   _____

Taxi   _____

Airport parking   _____

What amount will be donated by the local company?

_____

ADDITION AND SUBTRACTION
Chapter Review and Quick Reference

Topic	Main Point	Typical Example	Text Page
Place value	A numeral's value depends on its position relative to the decimal point.	23 = Twenty-three 2,300 = Twenty-three hundred 23,000 = Twenty-three thousand	3
Reading whole numbers	Commas are used to separate digits into groups of three, placed from right to left.	230 = Two hundred thirty 2,182 = Two thousand one hundred eighty-two 3.8 = Three and eight tenths	4
Grouping	Digits can be grouped in tens to speed addition.	6 4 group 6 and 4 = 10 7 3 group 7 and 3 = 10	5
Rounding	Round to identified digit. Round up if digit to the right is 5 or more. Round down if digit to the right is 4 or less.	2,345 rounded to hundreds = 2,300 2,355 rounded to hundreds = 2,400 15.55 rounded to tenths = 15.6	7
Estimation	Numbers can be rounded to provide an estimated answer to improve accuracy.	**Exact:** 2,355 + 5,448 = 7,803 **Estimation:** 2,400 + 5,400 = 7,800	9
Horizontal addition	Numbers can be added horizontally as well as vertically. A calculator is helpful for this format.	23 + 45 + 7 = 75 23 45 7 75	10
Subtraction	Subtraction represents the difference between two values.	Minuend: $100 Subtrahend: 85 Difference: $ 15	11

Chapter 2

MULTIPLICATION AND DIVISION

Performance Objectives

1. Determine the basic steps required for problems requiring multiplication and division operations.
2. Determine procedures for improving accurateness by use of estimation of results.
3. Determine ways to proof solutions to improve accurateness.
4. Determine appropriate alignment for operations requiring multiplication and division operations.

Many people apply mathematics every day. Their uses of mathematics range from computing the cost of lunch to computing the monthly payment on a home mortgage. Even complex formulas for making business decisions require accuracy in addition, subtraction, multiplication, and division. Addition was discussed in Chapter 1. This chapter covers subtraction, multiplication, and division.

Fundamental operations include addition, subtraction, multiplication, and division, as shown in Figure 2.1. Many mathematical applications of a high order include a combination of these operations.

```
          Fundamental
           Operations
               |
   ┌───────┬───────┬───────┐
 Addition Subtraction Multiplication Division
```

Figure 2.1 Fundamental Operations

MULTIPLICATION

Multiplication is used to compute taxes, interest on loans, discounts on sales, insurance rates, and other business applications. The number that is multiplied is called the *multiplicand*, the number by which one multiplies is called the *multiplier*, and the resulting answer is called the *product*. As shown in Model 2.1, in the computation 23 × 8 = 184, the multiplicand is 23, the multiplier is 8, and the product is 184.

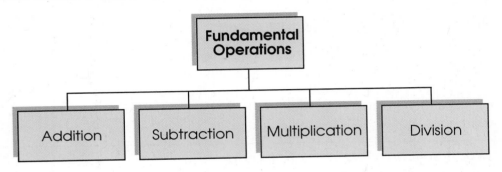

Multiplication terminology: Multiplicand, multiplier, and product.

Multiplication

```
      23            238          235  ◄──── Multiplicand
   ×   8          ×  135        ×  11  ◄──── Multiplier
     184          1 190          235  ┐
                   7 14          2 35  ├── Partial products
                  23 8          2,585  ◄──── Product
                  ──────
                  32,130
```

Apply Your Skills

Perez Computer Shoppe sold 12 microcomputer systems for $1,790 each. What was the total selling price for the microcomputers?

$ _____

MODEL 2.1

*Multiplicand
× Multiplier
= Product*

Align partial products directly below the corresponding digit in the multiplier.

Notice that the multiplicand and the multiplier are written so that their figures are aligned at the right. In the second problem, the multiplicand is first multiplied by the digit of the multiplier farthest to the right (238 X 5). The multiplicand is then multiplied by the second digit from the right in the multiplier (238 X 3). This process is continued until the multiplicand has been multiplied by each digit in the multiplier.

Also notice that the result of each individual multiplication is aligned under the digit in the multiplier, as shown in Model 2.1. These results are called *partial products*. The sum of the partial products equals the product.

ROUNDING ANSWERS IN MULTIPLICATION

In multiplication, even a small error in one step can result in a large error in the product. To estimate the answer to a multiplication problem, round the multiplicand and the multiplier to the same place (tens, hundreds, thousands, etc.) and then multiply. The numbers in Model 2.2 have been rounded to the nearest ten.

MODEL 2.2

Rounding answers in multiplication

Exact:	55.34	x	44	=	2,434.96
Estimated:	60	x	40	=	2,400

Apply Your Skills

Ed's Camera Center sold 21 cameras for $89.25 each. What were the (a) actual and (b) estimated total incomes for the cameras?

(a) $ _____

(b) $ _____

Round each number to the same place value position when estimating.

Multiplication accuracy check:
Product ÷ Multiplier = Multiplicand

Comparing the exact and estimated answers will show whether any gross errors have been made. In this chapter, the number of decimal places to the right of the decimal point will be two. More advanced problems that involve placing the decimal point are presented in Chapter 8.

CHECKING THE ACCURACY OF MULTIPLICATION

To check the accuracy of multiplication, divide the product by either the multiplicand or the multiplier. The answer to that division should equal the third number in the calculation as shown in Model 2.3.

Checking the accuracy of multiplication

Problem:	25	x	5	=	125	
Check:	125	÷	5	=	25	
or	125	÷	25	=	5	

MODEL 2.3

Division terminology: Dividend, divisor, quotient, and remainder.

Apply Your Skills

Harry Jones worked 38 hours last week for $7 per hour. The payroll clerk computed $266 total pay. Was this the correct amount?

_____ Yes

_____ No

You may now complete Performance Application 2.1.

DIVISION

Division is used in many mathematical computations, such as computing the average daily sales of a department store. Division is the process of determining how many times one number can be divided into another number. Four terms apply to the numbers involved in basic division. The number to be divided is the *dividend*, the number the dividend is divided by is the *divisor*, and the answer is the *quotient*. If the divisor does not divide into the dividend evenly, the part that is left is the *remainder*. Model 2.4 illustrates different formats that can be used for division problems. In Model 2.4, 18 is the dividend, 3 is the divisor, and 6 is the quotient; there is no remainder.

Division: Dividend ÷ Divisor = Quotient As with other operations, proper alignment is critical for division problems.

Division

$$18 \div 3 = 6$$

or 18/3 = 6

or $3\overline{)18}$ with quotient 6

MODEL 2.4

Division accuracy check: Quotient x Divisor + Remainder = Dividend

Apply Your Skills

Belinda Musso earned $480 while working 40 hours. What was her pay rate per hour?

_____

In division, always remember to keep the numbers properly aligned. Model 2.5 shows a division problem with a remainder.

MODEL 2.5

As with other operations, proper alignment is critical for division problems.

Alignment in division

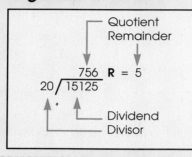

```
            756  + remainder of 5
      20 / 15125
          140
          112
          100
          125
          120
            5    (remainder)
```

- -

Apply Your Skills

Divide 18,274 by 25. After dividing to the last whole number, what is the remainder?

_____

ROUNDING ANSWERS IN DIVISION

To estimate the answer to a division problem, round off both the divisor and the dividend to the same place, as shown in Model 2.6.

MODEL 2.6

Estimating answers in division

Step 1   Round each number to the same place value.

Step 2   Divide in the usual way.

Actual: 4218 divided by 69 equals 61 with a remainder of 9

Estimated: 4200 divided by 70 equals 60

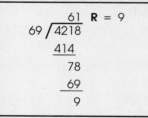

```
            61  R = 9
      69 / 4218
          414
           78
           69
            9
```

- -

Apply Your Skills

Hamilton Furniture recorded $148,143.60 in sales by 12 salespersons. What were the (a) actual and (b) estimated average sales per salesperson?

(a) $ _____

(b) $ _____

CHECKING THE ACCURACY OF DIVISION

To verify the accuracy of division, multiply the quotient by the divisor and then add any remainder. The result should equal the dividend. Model 2.7 illustrates checking the accuracy of division.

Checking the accuracy of division

Step 1 Multiply the quotient by the divisor.

Step 2 Add the remainder, if any.

Problem:	$675 \div 25$	=	27
Check:	25×27	=	675
Problem:	$191 \div 2$	=	95 with a remainder of 1
Check:	$(95 \times 2) + 1$	=	191

MODEL 2.7

Division accuracy check: Quotient x Divisor + Remainder = Dividend

Apply Your Skills

Harriet McAliffe divided 729 by 25. Her computed answer was 29 with a remainder of 3. Was this solution correct?

_____ Yes   _____ No

DIVISION APPLICATIONS

Although division is not used as often in business as addition, subtraction, and multiplication, it is frequently used in statistical computations to compute means, profit-and-loss ratios, and standard deviations.

To find the mean or average of a group of numbers, first find the sum of that group of numbers and then divide by the number of numbers in the group. For example, assume that Rita McGuire had scores of 75, 85, 92, and 88 on 4 tests. Model 2.8 illustrates how to find her average score.

**MODEL
2.8**

Finding the average of four test scores

Step 1 Find the sum of the group of numbers.

75 + 85 + 92 + 88 = 340

Step 2 Divide the sum by the number of values in the group.

340 ÷ 4 = 85

Sum: 75 + 85 + 92 + 88 = 340

Average: 340 ÷ 4 = 85

Thus, Rita McGuire's average score for the four tests was **85**.

Apply Your Skills

Dennis Jones worked 6 hours on Monday, 8 hours on Tuesday, 10 hours on Wednesday, 6 hours on Thursday, and 10 hours on Friday. What was the average number of hours worked each day?

_____

PERFORMANCE APPLICATION 2.1

1. Compute the actual and estimated products of each of the following problems.

Actual	Estimated	Actual	Estimated	Actual	Estimated

(a) 93
     x 27
     _____   _____

(c)   27
     x 18
     _____   _____

(e) 198
     x 92
     _____   _____

(b) 86
     x 13
     _____   _____

(d) 121
     x 54
     _____   _____

(f) 316
     x 302
     _____   _____

2. Multiply the unit price by the quantity to determine the total price for each item on the following invoice.

Quantity	Item Stock Number	Unit Price	Total
89	101-B	$14.00	$ _____
73	102-X	38.00	$ _____
27	819-A	17.25	$ _____
35	723-Z	24.16	$ _____
27	814-P	32.50	$ _____
32	916-F	16.82	$ _____
			$ _____

3. A secretary has an average typing speed of 53 words per minute. How many words can the secretary type in 17 minutes?

   _____

4. Bill Jones makes $8.85 per hour. How much will he earn for working 23 hours?
   $ _____

5. A certain machine can produce 37 items per minute. How many items will be produced in (a) 42 minutes? (b) 3 hours?

   (a) _____

   (b) _____

6. A car is driven 13,128 miles during the first year. How many miles will the car be driven in 7 years if it is driven the same number of miles each year?

   _____

7. A man drives a car at an average speed of 55 miles per hour. How many miles will he travel in 9 hours?

   _____

8. A carton contains 24 cans of tomato juice. How many cans will 38 cartons contain?

   _____

9. A secretary can take shorthand dictation at 120 words per minute. How many words can the secretary take in 37 minutes?

   _____

PERFORMANCE APPLICATION 2.2

1. Find the quotient for each of the following problems.

(a) $4\overline{)196}$

(b) $5\overline{)175}$

(c) $3\overline{)192}$

(d) $8\overline{)248}$

(e) $3\overline{)561}$

(f) $9\overline{)2,502}$

(g) $7\overline{)3,948}$

(h) $8\overline{)37,456}$

(i) $132\overline{)6,996}$

(j) $128\overline{)73,728}$

(k) $218\overline{)14,606}$

(l) $231\overline{)92,862}$

(m) $102\overline{)38,862}$

(n) $231\overline{)27,951}$

2. Compute the unit cost for each of the following items.

Item	Total Cost	No. of Units	Unit Cost
A	$ 28.75	23	$
B	33.04	14	$
C	31.50	18	$
D	26.35	31	$
E	412.32	16	$

3. Compute the actual and estimated quotients for each of the following problems.

Actual   Estimated   Actual   Estimated   Actual   Estimated

(a) $22\overline{)638}$

(d) $306\overline{)11,934}$

(g) $29\overline{)928}$

(b) $38\overline{)1,976}$

(e) $42\overline{)2,478}$

(h) $198\overline{)8,316}$

(c) $294\overline{)14,994}$

(f) $898\overline{)35,920}$

PERFORMANCE APPLICATION 2.3

1. Compute the quotient for each of the following problems. Check the accuracy of your division by multiplying the quotient by the divisor, and then adding any remainder.

(a) $37\overline{)1,665}$

(b) $30\overline{)600}$

(c) $18\overline{)1,118}$

(d) $16\overline{)370}$

(e) $38\overline{)1,599}$

(f) $26\overline{)1,204}$

(g) $121\overline{)4,235}$

(h) $206\overline{)31,518}$

(i) $316\overline{)64,780}$

2. Sarah Dower received the following scores in accounting class: 88, 79, 94, 80, 84. What is her average score?

   _____

3. Jerry Caldwell drives his car 1,404 miles and uses 39 gallons of gasoline. On the average, how many miles can he drive per gallon?

   _____

4. Don Roberts earns gross pay of $1,408 for 22 working days. What is his average daily pay?

   $ _____

5. Dorothy Ling drove 468 miles in 9 hours. What was her average miles per hour?

   _____

6. Carol Poulo's annual salary is $19,476. What is her monthly salary?

   $ _____

7. Jim Baker drove the following miles during a 5-day period: 420, 430, 418, 413, and 434. How many average miles per day did he drive?

   _____

8. Sales at Barney's Fitness Center for 3 months were as follows: $21,680.20, $22,819.62, and $23,736.68. Find the average monthly sales for the 3-month period.

   $ _____

9. Four candidates received the following numbers of votes: 22,100, 28,450, 24,600, and 25,862. What was the average number of votes received by the 4 candidates?

   _____

PRACTICE TEST FOR CHAPTER 2
MULTIPLICATION AND DIVISION

Complete each of the following problems and compare your answers with the ones on page 645.

1. Barbara Heinz earned $11 per hour while working 39 hours. What were her (a) actual and (b) estimated total earnings?

   (a) $ _____

   (b) $ _____

2. Brent Musberger found that he can average 57 miles per hour. On a recent vacation trip, he traveled for 18 hours. How many miles did he travel during the trip? _____

3. Employees at Dinzmore Electric Co. had combined earnings of $12,795 last week. If there were 15 employees, what was the average earnings per employee? $ _____

4. Ted Mertz ordered 21 radios for a $31.25 per item cost. What were the (a) actual and (b) estimated total costs for the order?

   (a) $ _____

   (b) $ _____

2.1 The chart shown below indicates average SAT scores in the United States for the years 1967 to 1993. (The SAT is the dominant admissions test used by colleges.)

(a) How much did the total verbal score in 1973 exceed the total verbal score in 1993?

_____

(b) Which year provided the highest total verbal score?

_____

(c) Which year provided the highest total math score?

_____

(d) In how many years was the total math score lower than the score in 1993?

_____

CONNECTIONS

	Averages, by year					
	Avg. verbal scores			**Avg. math scores**		
	Men	**Women**	**Total**	**Men**	**Women**	**Total**
1967	463	468	466	514	467	492
1968	464	466	466	512	470	492
1969	459	466	463	513	470	493
1970	459	461	460	509	465	488
1971	454	457	455	507	466	488
1972	454	452	453	505	461	484
1973	446	443	445	502	460	481
1974	447	442	444	501	459	480
1975	437	431	434	495	449	472
1976	433	430	431	497	446	472
1977	431	427	429	497	446	470
1978	433	425	429	494	444	468
1979	431	423	427	493	443	467
1980	428	420	424	491	443	466
1981	430	418	424	492	443	466
1982	431	421	426	493	443	467
1983	430	420	425	493	445	468
1984	433	420	426	495	449	471
1985	437	425	431	499	452	475
1986	437	426	431	501	451	475
1987	436	425	430	500	453	476
1988	435	422	428	498	455	476
1989	434	421	427	500	454	476
1990	429	419	424	499	455	476
1991	426	418	422	497	453	474
1992	428	419	423	499	456	476
1993	428	420	424	502	457	478

Source: The College Board

2.2 The chart shown below indicates the calories, fat, and sodium content for selected foods sold at popular fast food restaurants.

(a) If John ate a roast chicken salad at Arby's, a hamburger at Hardee's, and baked fish at Long John Silver's, what were his total calories from these three meals?

_____

(b) Maurice decides to have lunch at Burger King. He narrows his choices to a broiled chicken sandwich and a chunky chicken salad. How many calories will he save by choosing the chunky chicken salad?

_____

(c) Bill, Dan, Carl, and Carla decided to have lunch at McDonald's. Bill and Carla had McLean deluxe sandwiches. Dan had a chicken fajita. Carl had a chunky chicken salad. What was the average number of calories for the group?

_____

Healthiest Fast Foods			
Food	**Calories**	**Fat**	**Sodium**
Arby's			
Light Roast Chiken Sandwich	276	7	777
Roast Chicken Salad	204	7	508
Burger King			
Chef Salad	178	9	568
Broiler Chicken Sandwich	267	8	728
Chunky Chicken Salad	142	4	443
Hardee's			
Hamburger	260	10	510
Long John Silver's			
Baked Chicken, Light Herb	130	4	630
Baked Fish, Lemon Crumb (3)	150	1	370
McDonald's			
McLean Deluxe	320	10	670
Hamburger	255	9	490
Chef Salad	170	9	400
Chicken Fajita	190	8	310
Chunky Chicken Salad	150	4	230

CONNECTIONS

2.1 Banks Furniture Center offered a bedroom suite for $3,478 plus a $75 delivery charge. Center City offered the same furniture for $4,612 less a $75 discount for cash payment. Their delivery charge is $50. National offered the same furniture for $3,512 with no delivery charge or discount. Which company offered the best price?

_____

2.2 Karl Heinz is requested by the purchasing department manager to determine the lowest bid for 100 electronic typewriters. Company A bid $23,900 for the order. Company B bid $260 per typewriter for the first 50 ordered and $220 per typewriter for the next 50 ordered. Company C bid $236 per typewriter, but added a $200 delivery charge for the order. Which companies offered the (a) lowest and (b) highest bids?

(a) Lowest bid: _____

(b) Highest bid: _____

2.3 Norman McDougal maintains achecking account with Coppertown National Bank. He had a $12,572 beginning balance, 3 deposits totaling $3,765.89, 4 payroll deposits for $375.50 each, and 2 withdrawals totaling $7,718.95. Deposits are added to the beginning balance and withdrawals are deducted from the balance to compute the ending balance. What were the (a) total deposits, (b) total withdrawals, and (c) ending balance?

(a) Total deposits: $ _____

(b) Total withdrawals: $ _____

(c) Ending balance: $ _____

DECISIONS

MULTIPLICATION AND DIVISION
Chapter Review and Quick Reference

Topic	Main Point	Typical Example	Text Page
Multiplication	Multiplication determines the product of two or more numbers.	Multiplicand: 45 Multiplier: x 10 Product: 450	27
Division	Division determines the number of times one value is represented in another value.	Quotient ⟶ 4 Divisor ⟶ 15/60 Dividend	29
Remainder	A remainder is the number that remains when the divisor does not divide evenly into the dividend.	3 remainder of 1 2/7 6 1	29

Chapter **3**

MERCHANDISE
RECORDS

Performance Objectives

1. Obtain an introductory understanding about typical merchandise sales records.
2. Determine computations needed to complete cash sales slips.
3. Determine basic inventory card mathematics.
4. Determine computations needed for completion of sales invoices.

Merchandise is defined as products that businesses purchase for resale to consumers or other businesses. The size and type of business determine the way that it maintains merchandise and sales records. For example, an automobile agency that sells relatively few large items each day will maintain a record for each automobile sold, but a department store that sells hundreds of small items each day will need more detailed records. All businesses need to maintain records to keep track of what merchandise has been sold. A separate record may be kept for each item (such as an automobile), or a summary record may be kept on total sales (such as total sales of fruit in a supermarket).

Merchandise records can be used to determine which items are selling well or which items are not selling as well as other items. Records are important to the business selling merchandise as well as the person or business purchasing the merchandise. All essential information about the transaction must be maintained using records such as those illustrated in Figure 3.1. During earlier times records were prepared manually and stored in large filing cabinets. In today's modern business environment, the computer serves as the heart of record development and maintenance systems. For example, many products have a bar code that can be easily read by special sensing devices connected to a computer.

Merchandise: *Products that are purchased for the purpose of resale.*

Inventory: *A listing of merchandise available for sale.*

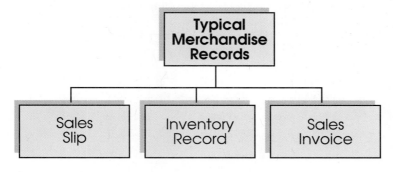

Figure 3.1 Merchandise Records

SALES RECORDS

Many retail stores issue sales slips to provide a record of the sale. This slip normally indicates the quantity, description, price, sales taxes, and amount due for items sold. A handwritten sales slip is shown in Model 3.1.

**MODEL
3.1**

*Sales slips are
used by
department and
other retail stores
to provide a
record of the
sale.*

Sales Slip

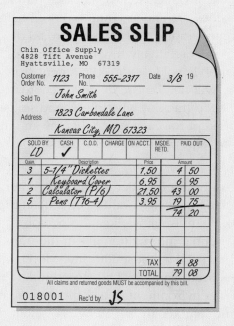

Apply Your Skills

Perform the computations needed to complete the sales slip shown below.

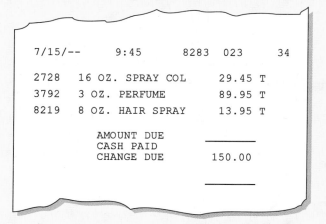

*Although
computer and
manual
computational
procedures are
similar, almost all
records are now
maintained on
computers.*

Many stores continue to use handwritten sales slips, but some stores now use computerized cash register slips. The sales clerk can simply enter the product number, and the computer then records the description and price of the item sold on the cash register tape. The computer can also monitor the number of products in stock and notify the store to reorder products when needed. Figure 3.2 illustrates a computerized sales slip.

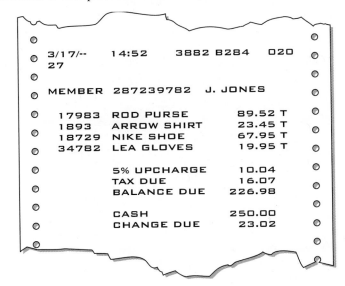

```
3/17/--      14:52      3882 B284    020
27

MEMBER  287239782   J. JONES

  17983   ROD PURSE        89.52 T
  1893    ARROW SHIRT      23.45 T
  18729   NIKE SHOE        67.95 T
  34782   LEA GLOVES       19.95 T

          5% UPCHARGE      10.04
          TAX DUE          16.07
          BALANCE DUE     226.98

          CASH            250.00
          CHANGE DUE       23.02
```

Figure 3.2 Computerized Sales Slip

INVENTORY RECORDS

Stores must maintain a record of merchandise purchased and sold in order to know when to reorder merchandise and to determine which items are selling fast and which are selling slowly. This record is called an *inventory* and may be kept in computer memory or on handwritten cards. The record must indicate sales, purchases, and balances for each item. Model 3.2 is a typical inventory record.

Inventory record

RENYO WATCH		PRODUCT No. RW726-89		
COST PRICE: $ 69.45				
SALE PRICE: $139.99				
DATE	TRANSACTION	INCREASE	DECREASE	BALANCE
03/01	Beg. Balance			18
03/07	Sale		3	15
03/08	Sale		2	13
03/21	Purchase	8		21
03/26	Sale		4	17

Most large stores use computers to maintain sales and inventory records.

Government requirements and business practice require accurate recordkeeping.

MODEL 3.2

Information about the product—such as price and description—can be stored electronically on the product label.

Apply Your Skills

Review the inventory card shown below. Provide the amounts for the **Balance** column.

Sales are
deducted from
and purchases
are added to
inventory.

PARAMOUNT PENS — PRODUCT No. YU387-35 COST PRICE: $ 69.00 SALE PRICE: $139.95				
DATE	**TRANSACTION**	**INCREASE**	**DECREASE**	**BALANCE**
1/1	Beg. Balance			50
1/4	Sale		5	
1/5	Sale		8	
1/6	Purchase	12		
1/7	Sale		3	

Notice that each purchase of merchandise by the store increases the inventory or number of items available for resale to customers. Similarly, each sale to a customer is deducted from the store's inventory, and fewer items are then available for resale.

SHIPPING MERCHANDISE

Many stores operate catalog departments that ship products to the customer. A *sales invoice* shipped with the merchandise states the product description, price, quantity, and other information about the order. This invoice must be much more complete than a sales slip because it also serves as a bill. Manufacturers and wholesalers that regularly ship merchandise to retailers usually use sales invoices. Model 3.3 illustrates a typical sales invoice.

Sales invoice

INVOICE							INVOICE No. 25702

SOLD TO
Barcelona & Cofer, Attorneys
290 53rd Street
Brooklyn, NY 11232

SHIP TO
Same

Customer's Order No. 6729	Sold By Smith	Terms C.O.D.	Ship Via Truck	F.O.B.	Date 3/17/--	

QUANTITY ORDERED	QUANTITY SHIPPED	DESCRIPTION	UNIT PRICE	AMOUNT
12	12	Single-Strike Ribbon (43872 REM)	9.10	109.20
5 doz.	5	Pocket Secretary Refills (3462 TAZ)	6.25	31.25
7	7	Stationery Cabinet (8BC-BW-1 LIT)	40.95	286.65
--	--	**Total		427.10

The sales invoice is often sent with the merchandise shipment; otherwise, it follows by mail in a few days.

Apply Your Skills

Complete the section of the sales invoice shown below, including computation of the total amount. What is the invoice total?

$ _____

	F.O.B.	Date 3/17/--	

QUANTITY ORDERED	UNIT PRICE	AMOUNT
8	12.45	
12	24.95	
9	7.95	
	**Total	

PERFORMANCE APPLICATION 3.1

1. The following items were sold on account to Robert Newport, 925 Carpenter Crossing, Folcroft, PA 19032. Complete the sales slip, including both the price and amount columns. Use the current date.

3 pairs shoes	@	42.75
4 shirts	@	13.95
2 ties	@	8.50
6 pairs socks	@	4.99
Sales tax		10.37

SALES SLIP

Customer Order No. _____	Phone No. _____			Date _____	19 ____

Sold To _____

Address _____

SOLD BY	CASH	C.O.D.	CHARGE	ON ACCT.	MSDE. RETD.	PAID OUT
Quan.	Description			Price	Amount	
					TAX	
					TOTAL	

All claims and returned goods MUST be accompanied by this bill.

018002   Rec'd by

2. The following items were sold cash on delivery to Roberta Rawls, 716 North Wells Street, Chicago, IL 60610. Complete the sales slip, using the current date.

7 cases diskettes	@	8.75
5 printer ribbons	@	8.25
2 computer cables	@	29.95
3 books	@	19.95
1 type cleaner	@	8.50
Sales tax		10.11

SALES SLIP

Customer Order No. _____	Phone No. _____			Date _____	19 ____

Sold To _____

Address _____

SOLD BY	CASH	C.O.D.	CHARGE	ON ACCT.	MSDE. RETD.	PAID OUT
Quan.	Description			Price	Amount	
					TAX	
					TOTAL	

All claims and returned goods MUST be accompanied by this bill.

018003   Rec'd by

3. Compute exact and estimated amounts (estimate by rounding to the nearest dollar) for each of the following items.

Item No.	Quantity	Price	Exact Amount	Estimated Amount
1	23	$ 1.35	_____	_____
2	45	2.49	_____	_____
3	12	0.85	_____	_____
4	17	12.45	_____	_____
5	15	8.47	_____	_____

4. Compute and estimate the amounts (by rounding to the nearest dollar) for each of the following items.

Product	Price	Quantity	Exact Amount	Estimated Amount
Golf Balls	$ 0.45	48	_____	_____
Binoculars	39.95	6	_____	_____
Jackets	79.95	3	_____	_____
Candles	1.25	50	_____	_____
Watches	39.95	2	_____	_____

5. The Slumber Rest Co. sells bedspreads for $41.37 each. What amount would an invoice for 12 bedspreads show?

$ _____

6. Newson Appliances sells washing machines for $399.95 each. What amount would an invoice for 3 machines show?

$ _____

7. Newson Appliances sells table lamps for $59.99 each. What amount would an invoice for 5 lamps show?

$ _____

8. The Best Discount Store sells electronic calculators for $29.95 each. What amount would an invoice for 36 calculators show?

$ _____

PERFORMANCE APPLICATION 3.2

1. Compute the amounts in each line and the total for the following invoice. Assume that no sales tax is charged.

INVOICE					INVOICE No. 25701

SOLD TO	SHIP TO
International Importers	Same
744 Western Avenue	
Boston, MA 02135	

Customer Order No. 30741	Sold By Upton	Terms C.O.D.	Ship Via Truck	F.O.B.	Date 8/28/--

QUANTITY ORDERED	QUANTITY SHIPPED	DESCRIPTION	UNIT PRICE	AMOUNT
12	12	Memo Holders (1373-1 ELD)	6.59	
15	15	Diskette Cleaning Kit (11250 DEE)	9.59	
8	8	Rotary Card File (SR48C-DE)	34.95	
6	6	Ledger Sheets (K2E FR)	16.05	
13	13	Computer Labels--4 x 1 7/16 (2044 RVE)	13.25	
15	15	Staple Gun (80007 HFH)	16.59	
37	37	Weekly Appointment Books (340-53-5 COL)	3.75	
125	125	Looseleaf Desk Calendar (P34-00 JJ)	7.95	
--	--	***Total		

ORIGINAL   THANK YOU

2. Martina Meade sold 40 items at $12.35 each. Sarah Rasch sold 38 items at $12.55 each. Who made the larger sale?

3. Tim Brandon sold 12 items at $14.95 each. Brenda Miller sold 14 items at $14.75 each. Who made the larger sale?

_____

4. The Town and Country Furniture Center normally sells a ceramic table lamp for $69.99. During a special sale, the lamps are offered for $59.95 each if 3 or more are purchased. What is the cost of 3 lamps?

$ _____

5. The Buy-Rite Food Store can purchase dinner rolls for $9.59 per case. What is the cost of 17 cases?

$ _____

6. The Computer Center normally sells a dot matrix printer for $289.59. During a sales promotion, the price of each printer is reduced by $30.00. If 5 printers are sold, what are the (a) regular and (b) reduced total sales amounts for the 5 printers?

(a) $ _____

(b) $ _____

7. For each mile driven, City Car Rental charges $0.27. Michelle Hanson rented a car for an 837-mile trip. What amount was she charged?

$ _____

8. The Arco Sports Center sells one brand of basketball for $23.95 each. What is the cost of 7 basketballs?

$ _____

9. The Brandon Discount Center sells calculators for $24.95 each. What is the cost of 4 calculators?

$ _____

PRACTICE TEST FOR CHAPTER 3
MERCHANDISE RECORDS

Complete each of the following problems and then compare your answers with the ones on page 645.

1. Steinberg Shoe Store made the following sale: 3 pairs of shoes @ $69.75 and 5 pairs of socks at $7.95. Sales taxes were $12.35. How much was due for the sale?

   $ _____

2. The Crafts Center sells homemade quilts for $229.95 each. What is the amount of the invoice for 12 quilts?

   $ _____

3. A bonus is being given to the salesperson with the highest total sales for the day. Timothy Brumberg sold 43 items for $37.95 each. Beverly Collins sold 38 items for $39.95 each. Which salesperson had the larger sale?

   $ _____

4. The Computer Center normally sells a popular brand laser printer for $899.99. During a special promotion, the price was reduced by $45. What were the total (a) regular price and (b) discounted price for 5 printers?

   (a) $ _____   (b) $ _____

5. Reddy Computing Service sells a popular brand notebook computer for $1,795 with a $50 delivery charge per order. Martin and Sons sells the same computer for $1,775 with free delivery, but charges a $27.95 warranty charge per computer. What is the total cost for 5 computers purchased from each company?

   (a) Reddy Computing Services: $ _____

   (b) Martin and Sons: $ _____

3.1 The chart shown below indicates the amount of frozen treats consumed by the average person in the United States. Survey three persons to determine their ages and their estimates about the amount of frozen desserts consumed during their lifetimes. Compute the consumption amount based on the chart. Then complete the diagram shown below to show the number of gallons for each person.

Name	Age	Consumption Estimate	Consumption Computation
		Ice cream:	Ice cream:
		Sherbet:	Sherbet:
		Frozen yogurt:	Frozen yogurt:
		Ice milk:	Ice milk:

A look at statistics that shape our lives

Frozen treats

A person eats, on average, about 5 gallons of frozen desserts per year. How that breaks down by type:

Ice cream 63%

Ice milk 24%

Sherbet 3%

Frozen yogurt 10%

Source: USDA, 1992 data

By Julie Stacey, USA TODAY

3.2 The chart shown below indicates the percentage of surgeries that are performed on an inpatient basis and on an outpatient basis. Assume that 7,000 operations were performed in 1980 and 7,000 operations were performed in 1991. What number were performed on an (a) inpatient and (b) outpatient basis during these two years? What reasons can you give for the increase in outpatient and decrease in inpatient surgeries during the time shown on the chart?

1980 (a) _____ (b) _____

1991 (a) _____ (b) _____

Reasons: _____

_____

_____

_____

_____

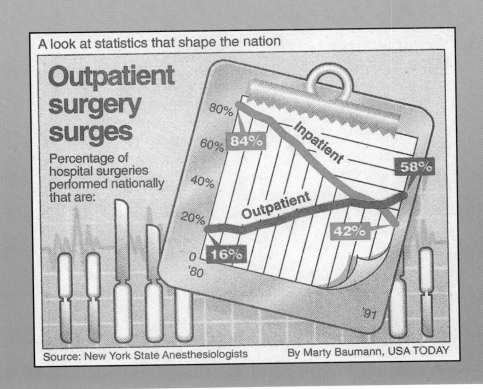

A look at statistics that shape the nation

Outpatient surgery surges

Percentage of hospital surgeries performed nationally that are:

Inpatient
84%
58%

Outpatient
16%
42%

80%
60%
40%
20%
0
'80
'91

Source: New York State Anesthesiologists   By Marty Baumann, USA TODAY

CONNECTIONS

3.1 Toys-4-Fun, a small wholesale toy firm, carries a doll called Space Cadet that has a $59.95 wholesale price. At the beginning of the month, there were 2,300 dolls on hand. The firm purchased 5,000 dolls and sold 4,350 dolls during the month. Someone broke into the warehouse during the month, which resulted in an unknown number of dolls being stolen. A count at the end of the month indicated that there were 2,000 dolls on hand. For insurance purposes, what were (a) the number of dolls stolen and (b) the value of the dolls stolen?

(a) _____   (b) $ _____

3.2 Business units maintain various merchandise records, such as inventory records, sales records, and purchase records. Visit a retail store (such as a supermarket, department store, or clothing store) in your area. Write a one-page report to describe how the business maintains inventory records. Include in your report the degree of dependence on computers for maintaining the records. You may also attach copies of records, if available, from the business.

DECISIONS

MERCHANDISE RECORDS
Chapter Review and Quick Reference

Topic	Main Point	Typical Example	Text Page
Merchandise	Merchandise is goods that a business purchases for resale.	A department store purchases sporting goods equipment for resale.	45
Sales record	Businesses must have evidence of a sale.	Retail stores normally issue a sales slip or cash register receipt as evidence of a sale.	45
Computerized records	Many records are generated by using computers in today's business environment.	Information from a cash register tape can be used to record sales, maintain inventory, and order merchandise that is low in inventory.	47
Inventory record	Computer or manual records must be maintained to track merchandise.	Beginning balance: 35 + Purchases: 20 - Sales: 10 = Ending balance: 45	47
Sales invoice	The sales invoice provides a record of the sale to the buyer.	Quantity: 38 Price: $19.95 Total: $758.10	49

BANK STATEMENT RECONCILIATION

Performance Objectives

1. Define and identify the need for checking account records.
2. Prepare deposit slips, checks, and other checking account forms.
3. Maintain a check register.
4. Identify the need for bank statements.
5. Be able to read a bank statement.
6. Identify the purpose of electronic funds transfer.
7. Prepare a bank statement reconciliation based on a comparison of the bank statement with the check register.

Bank depositors place money into an account that permits withdrawing funds from the account by writing checks against the balance. This type of account is called a *checking account*. Periodically, the bank sends a statement that reflects deposits, withdrawals, charges, and other transactions affecting the account. The depositor also keeps a record of these transactions in a checkbook. *Reconciliation of the bank balance* involves comparing the transactions recorded in the bank statement with those recorded in the checkbook. Adjustments are made and/or errors are corrected to make the balances equal. This chapter presents information about banking records and shows you how to reconcile your checkbook record with the bank's record of your account.

A typical bank statement is shown in Figure 4.1.

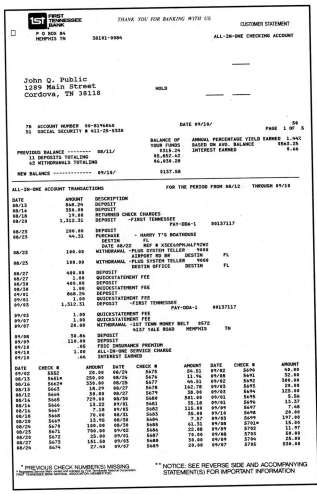

Figure 4.1 Bank Statement

Payer: *The person or business issuing a check.*

Payee: *The person or business receiving funds from the check.*

Banks and other financial institutions provide checking accounts for customers. Records and procedures required to operate a checking account are similar for both business and consumer accounts. **Depositors** are customers of the bank who place funds in checking accounts. Checks can be used like money to order the financial institution to make payments. Use of checks means that you do not have to carry lots of cash around or worry about keeping up with it. The person or business issuing a check is called the **payer**. The bank that is ordered to make the payment is called the **drawee**. The person or business receiving funds from the check is called the **payee**. Steps required to operate an account are shown in Figure 4.2.

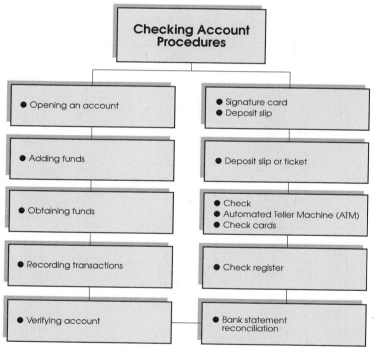

Figure 4.2 Checking Account Procedures

MAKING A DEPOSIT AND WRITING A CHECK

Deposit slip: *A form used to add funds to an account.*

To write checks to pay bills and to obtain cash, bank customers must have funds in their checking accounts. Bank customers deposit and withdraw funds periodically during the month as money is available or needed. A typical deposit slip and check are shown in Models 4-1 and 4-2.

Making a Deposit

**CHECKING
ACCOUNT
DEPOSIT**

DATE _____ *March 6* _____ 19 _____
DEPOSITS MAY NOT BE AVAILABLE FOR IMMEDIATE WITHDRAWAL.

SIGN HERE ONLY IF CASH RECEIVED FROM DEPOSIT

TCF BANK *fsb* TCF Bank Minnesota fsb
Edina, MN

⑈599913501⑈ 6078005786⑈

CURRENCY		120	00	
COIN				
C H E C K S	LIST CHECKS SINGLY			17-7000/2910 BRANCH 7
	#8910	876	25	
	#2411	92	45	
TOTAL FROM OTHER SIDE				**DEPOSIT TICKET**
SUB-TOTAL		1,088	70	PLEASE ITEMIZE ADDITIONAL CHECKS ON REVERSE SIDE
TOTAL ITEMS	LESS CASH RECEIVED			
	TOTAL DEPOSIT	1,088	70	

Apply Your Skills

Assume that $178.95 in currency and the following checks were deposited today: #3219 for $79.25 and #1903 for $95.89. Complete the deposit slip shown below to record this deposit.

**CHECKING
ACCOUNT
DEPOSIT**

DATE _____ 19 _____
DEPOSITS MAY NOT BE AVAILABLE FOR IMMEDIATE WITHDRAWAL.

SIGN HERE ONLY IF CASH RECEIVED FROM DEPOSIT

TCF BANK *fsb* TCF Bank Minnesota fsb
Edina, MN

⑈599913501⑈ 6078005786⑈

CURRENCY				
COIN				
C H E C K S	LIST CHECKS SINGLY			17-7000/2910 BRANCH 7
TOTAL FROM OTHER SIDE				**DEPOSIT TICKET**
SUB-TOTAL				PLEASE ITEMIZE ADDITIONAL CHECKS ON REVERSE SIDE
TOTAL ITEMS	LESS CASH RECEIVED			
	TOTAL DEPOSIT			

MODEL 4.2

Check: A piece of paper ordering the bank to pay funds to someone.

Writing a Check

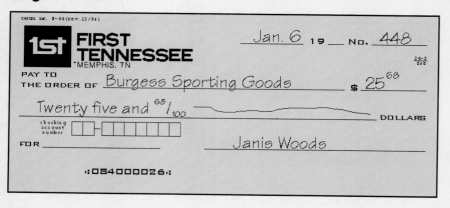

Apply Your Skills

Assume that check number 2315 needs to be written today, payable to Village Shops, for $27.13. Use the form shown below to write the check.

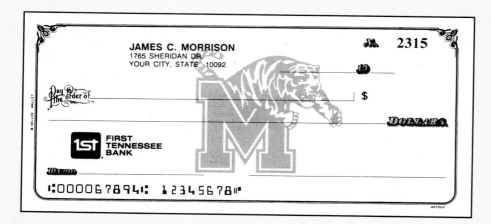

The Federal Reserve Board has established regulations about where endorsement can be placed on the back of checks. The endorsement must be placed within 1 1/2 inches from the left edge of the check. The remainder of the back of the check is reserved for bank endorsements. The payee can simply sign the back of the check to create an endorsement. However, the endorsement can be **restricted** by adding "for deposit only" to the endorsement, which designates that the full amount of the check must be deposited into the endorser's account.

MAINTAINING A RECORD OF CHECKS AND DEPOSITS

Bank customers maintain check registers or check stub records to show deposit and withdrawal transactions and a running balance. Charges made by the bank, such as service charges, check purchases, and return check charges and additions, such as interest earned on the account, should also be shown on the check register or check stub record. A typical check register is shown in Model 4.3.

Check register:
A written record of checks, deposits, charges, and other items affecting the account.

Maintaining a Check Register

MODEL 4.3

CHECK NO.	DATE	CHECK ISSUED TO	BALANCE BROUGHT FORWARD	✔	784	16
15	1/1	To Joe M. Smith / For supplies	AMOUNT OF CHECK OR DEPOSIT / BALANCE		18 / 765	32 / 84
16	1/2	To Martin, Inc. / For delivery	AMOUNT OF CHECK OR DEPOSIT / BALANCE		20 / 745	36 / 48
—	1/3	To Deposit / For Account 2416	AMOUNT OF CHECK OR DEPOSIT / BALANCE		260 / 1,005	00 / 48
		To / For	AMOUNT OF CHECK OR DEPOSIT / BALANCE			
		To / For	AMOUNT OF CHECK OR DEPOSIT / BALANCE			
		To / For	AMOUNT OF CHECK OR DEPOSIT / BALANCE			

Apply Your Skills

Assume that you are maintaining the check register shown below. The balance brought forward was $3,135.89. Check #1201 and #1202 were written yesterday for $125.98 and $385.27 respectively. A $523.75 deposit was made today. Checks #1203 and #1204 were written today for $120.80 and $75.82 respectively. Make the needed entries in the check register.

CHECK NO.	DATE	CHECK ISSUED TO	BALANCE BROUGHT FORWARD	✔		
		To / For	AMOUNT OF CHECK OR DEPOSIT / BALANCE			
		To / For	AMOUNT OF CHECK OR DEPOSIT / BALANCE			
		To / For	AMOUNT OF CHECK OR DEPOSIT / BALANCE			
		To / For	AMOUNT OF CHECK OR DEPOSIT / BALANCE			
		To / For	AMOUNT OF CHECK OR DEPOSIT / BALANCE			
		To / For	AMOUNT OF CHECK OR DEPOSIT / BALANCE			

Banks offer a variety of checking account plans. Some charge a fee if the balance falls below a specified level and others charge a fee (such as 20 cents) for each check written during the month. Some banks do not charge a fee, and some banks may pay interest on all or a portion of the account balance. These items will be shown on the bank statement and should be used to adjust the check stub balance while reconciling the bank balance.

RECONCILING THE BANK STATEMENT

The balance shown on the bank statement is reconciled (made to agree) with the check stub balance by adjusting each balance or by correcting errors. Reconciliation simply involves making adjustments to one balance for transactions that have already been reflected in the other balance. For example, a recent deposit may not be reflected on the bank statement but may have been added to the check stub balance on the day of the deposit. This adjustment will require the late deposit to be added to the bank balance. Except for correcting errors, this process is repeated for each item that is reflected in one balance but not in the other. Of course, the late deposit will eventually be added to the bank balance and reflected on a future statement. Typical items that may need to be adjusted are discussed below and illustrated in Figure 4.3.

Reconciliation: A process to match depositor records with bank records.

Many banks provide a reconciliation form on the back of the bank statement.

The adjusted bank and check stub balances should match after reconciliation.

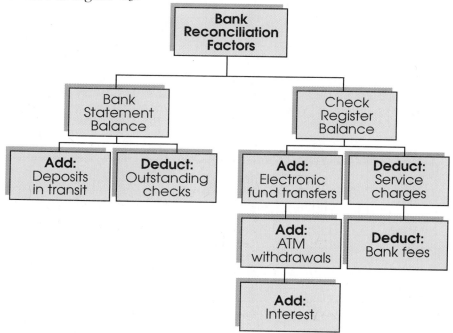

Figure 4.3 Bank Reconciliation Factors

A form for bank reconciliation such as the one depicted in Figure 4.4 is sometimes provided by the bank to help customers make their check stub balance equal to the bank statement balance.

RECONCILIATION OF BANK STATEMENT			
Bank statement balance	$ _____	Check stub balance	$ _____
Add late deposits	_____	Add interest	
		Total	$ _____
Total	$ _____	Deduct printing charges	_____
		Deduct service charges	_____
Deduct outstanding checks	_____	Deduct returned check	_____
Adjusted bank balance	$ _____	Adjusted stub balance	$ _____

Figure 4.4 Bank Statement Reconciliation Form

SUBTRACTIONS FROM THE BANK STATEMENT BALANCE

Subtract these from the bank statement balance:

1. *Outstanding checks*—checks that were written and recorded on the check stub but have not yet been paid by the bank and are thus not shown on the bank statement.

2. Any *withdrawal* from an automatic teller machine that was made too late to be reflected on the bank statement but was deducted from the check stub.

3. Any *electronic funds transfer* to another account that was made too late to be reflected on the bank statement but was deducted from the check stub.

ADDITIONS TO THE BANK STATEMENT BALANCE

Add to the bank statement balance:

> *Deposits in transit*—deposits that were made too late for inclusion on the statement. These must also be accounted for in reconciling the bank statement.

SUBTRACTIONS FROM THE CHECK STUB BALANCE

Subtract these from the check stub balance:

1. *Bank service fees* based on the number of checks written, account balance, or overdrafts. These charges will be shown on the statement.

2. The *bank charge* for printing new checks.

3. *Rejected or returned checks*—checks that cannot be paid to your account because the party who gave the check to you stopped

Bank statement:
A monthly form sent by the bank to list all transactions affecting the account.

Evaluate each item correctly to determine additions and subtractions from bank statement balance.

Deposits in transit:
Deposits that were made too late to appear on the statement.

Some banks charge fees based on average balance and number of checks written.

payment on the check or does not have sufficient funds to cover the amount of the check. Such checks must also be accounted for in reconciling the statement.

ADDITIONS TO THE CHECK STUB BALANCE

Add these to the check stub balance:

1. *Electronic funds transferred* from another account (such as a payroll check) into the checking account.

2. *Interest* earned on the account balance during the period.

3. The amount of any *note collected* by the bank that was credited to your account.

Remember that the bank statement and check stub amounts should be carefully studied to determine entries on one record that should be reflected on the other record as either subtractions or additions to the balance. After this is completed, the new balances of the two records should be the same. In other words, the bank balance and check stub balance must be in agreement so that the reconciliation is complete.

Assume that the bank statement shows a balance of $379.50 and a service charge of $3.50. A review shows outstanding checks (No. 113 for $15 and No. 115 for $10) amounting to $25 and a deposit in transit for $20. The check stub balance is $378.00. The reconciliation of the bank balance for this situation is shown in Model 4.4.

Notice that the adjusted bank balance and the adjusted check stub balance must be equal.

After reconciliation, you are ready to begin a new period with a "clean slate," knowing that your check stub balance correctly reflects your checking account balance.

Check stub: A blank form attached to a check to record transactions and maintain a running balance.

The bank statement should be reconciled each month.

MODEL 4.4

Reconciliation of bank balance

Bank Balance	$379.50		Check stub balance	$378.00
Deduct:			Deduct:	
Check No. 113	$15.00		Service charge	3.50
Check No. 115	$10.00	25.00		
		$354.50		$374.50
Add:			Add:	
Deposit in transit		20.00		0.00
Adjusted bank balance		$374.50	Adjusted check stub balance	$374.50

Apply Your Skills

You received your bank statement today showing a $1,225.50 balance, a $5.00 service fee, and $12.25 interest earned. A review of the check book showed a $1,315.27 balance. A comparison shows that there was a $300.25 deposit in transit and two outstanding checks for $85.25 and $117.98. Use the form shown below to reconcile the bank statement.

RECONCILIATION OF BANK STATEMENT		
Bank statement balance $ _____	Check stub balance	$ _____
Add late deposits _____	Add interest Total	$ _____
Total $ _____	Deduct printing charges	_____
Deduct outstanding checks _____	Deduct service charges Deduct returned check	_____
Adjusted bank balance $ _____	Adjusted stub balance	$ _____

DEBIT CARDS

Writing checks to withdraw funds from the account remains the most widely used method. However, cards like the one shown can be used to provide electronic procedures for withdrawing funds. Also, some companies such as Exxon provide debit cards to permit immediate withdrawal from the account. These methods will become more popular as the country moves closer to a cashless society.

Figure 4.5 Debit Card

PERFORMANCE APPLICATION 4.1

1. Checks and deposits made during the month are listed below with a summary of the bank statement for Alicia Caesar. Find the check stub balance after each entry and reconcile the bank statement.

Check Stub

Beginning balance			$945.45
Deposit			100.50
Balance	(a)	$	
Check #101			30.00
Balance	(b)	$	
Check #102			75.50
Balance	(c)	$	
Check #103			125.40
Balance	(d)	$	
Check #104			67.35
Balance	(e)	$	
Deposit			300.50
Balance	(f)	$	
Check #105			50.25
Balance	(g)	$	

Bank Statement

Beginning balance:			$945.45
Checks:	#101	$30.00	
	#105	50.25	
	#103	125.40	
	#104	67.35	
Deposits:		$100.50	
Service charge:		7.50	
Ending balance:			$765.45

RECONCILIATION OF BANK STATEMENT

Bank statement balance	$	Check stub balance	$
Add late deposits		Add interest	
Total	$	Total	$
		Deduct printing charges	
		Deduct service charges	
Deduct outstanding checks		Deduct returned check	
Adjusted bank balance	$	Adjusted stub balance	$

2. Use the following information to reconcile the bank statement for June O'Brien.

Bank balance:	$3,675.82
Check stub balance:	$2,358.62
Checks outstanding:	#1801 for $540.20
	#1803 for $75.20
	#1804 for $80.30

Bank service charge: $3.50
Note collected by bank and credited to account: $750.00
Deposit in transit: $50.00
Check #1795 for $75.00 was omitted from the check stub but was included on her bank statement.

RECONCILIATION OF BANK STATEMENT

Bank statement balance	$_____	Check stub balance	$_____
Add late deposits	_____	Add note collected	_____
Total	$_____	Total	$_____
		Deduct service charges	_____
Deduct outstanding checks	_____	Deduct check #1795	_____
Adjusted bank balance	$_____	Adjusted stub balance	$_____

3. Use the following information to reconcile the bank statement for Michelle Oliver:

Bank balance:	$760.50
Check stub balance:	$729.42
Checks outstanding:	#314 for $50.80
	#315 for $75.25
	#316 for $60.48
Interest credited to account on bank statement:	$8.50
Service charge:	$5.00
Check deposited and returned by bank:	$50.45
Deposit in transit:	$100.00
Charges for printing checks:	$8.50

RECONCILIATION OF BANK STATEMENT

Bank statement balance	$_____	Check stub balance	$_____
Add late deposits	_____	Add interest	_____
Total	$_____	Total	$_____
		Deduct printing charges	_____
Deduct outstanding checks	_____	Deduct service charges	_____
		Deduct returned check	_____
Adjusted bank balance	$_____	Adjusted stub balance	$_____

PERFORMANCE APPLICATION 4.2

1. A list of checking account transactions is given below. Write a, b, c, or d in the blank to show whether the transaction requires an adjustment that (a) subtracts from the bank balance, (b) subtracts from the check stub balance, (c) adds to the bank balance, or (d) adds to the check stub balance in order to reconcile the bank statement.

   (a) A check that was deposited after the date of the bank statement. _____

   (b) A note that was collected by the bank and credited to the account. _____

   (c) An electronic funds transfer of the payroll check that was credited to the account. _____

   (d) An outstanding check that was written by the customer but was written too late to be reflected on the bank statement. _____

   (e) A bank service charge made because the balance fell below $500 during the month. _____

   (f) A check that was deposited into the account but was returned because the person who wrote the check did not have sufficient funds to cover it. _____

   (g) Interest earned on the average daily balance in the account.

   _____

   (h) A charge made by the bank for printing a new supply of checks.

   _____

   (i) A check for $8.97 that was incorrectly entered in the check stub as $8.79. _____

2. Study the check register transactions shown below. Enter the correct balance after each transaction.

CHECK NO.	DATE		CHECK ISSUED TO		BALANCE BROUGHT FORWARD	✓	4,869	50
579	4/6	TO FOR	Haysmith Clock Shoppe grandfather clock	AMOUNT OF CHECK OR DEPOSIT BALANCE			1,309	89
580	4/6	TO FOR	Elliott's Supermarket groceries	AMOUNT OF CHECK OR DEPOSIT BALANCE			108	16
――	4/7	TO FOR	Deposit #92 weekly payroll	AMOUNT OF CHECK OR DEPOSIT BALANCE			583	93
581	4/7	TO FOR	Hathaway Glassware china	AMOUNT OF CHECK OR DEPOSIT BALANCE			207	10
582	4/8	TO FOR	Midland Telephone phone bill	AMOUNT OF CHECK OR DEPOSIT BALANCE			59	39
――	4/8	TO FOR	Service charge returned check	AMOUNT OF CHECK OR DEPOSIT BALANCE			15	00

Ending balance $ _____

3. Doyle Whitherspoon received a bank statement that shows an ending balance of $1,814.37. His check stub balance shows a balance of $1,796.92. A review of his records indicates that the adjustments shown below are needed. Reconcile the bank statement on the form provided. Use the last day of last month as the date.

Interest added to the account	$7.45
Outstanding check #1103:	$30.00
Deposit in transit	$15.00
Bank service charge	$5.00

Doyle Whitherspoon RECONCILIATION OF BANK STATEMENT				
Bank statement balance	$ _____	Check stub balance	$ _____	
Plus late deposits	_____	Plus interest	_____	
Total	$ _____	Total	$ _____	
Less outstanding checks	_____	Less service charge	_____	
Adjusted bank balance	$ _____	Adjusted stub balance	$ _____	

4. Dennis Bower received a bank statement that shows an electronic funds transfer deposit of $1,728.15. If this is the only adjustment needed to his check stub balance of $2,609.24, what is the amount of his adjusted check stub balance?

$ _____

5. Clara Robertson forgot to record check #908 for $38.76 in her check register. If this is the only adjustment needed to her check stub balance of $748.25, what is the amount of her adjusted check stub balance? $ _____

PRACTICE TEST FOR CHAPTER 4
BANK STATEMENT RECONCILIATION

Complete each of the following problems and then compare your answers with the ones on page 645.

1. Should outstanding checks be (a) deducted from the bank statement balance or (b) added to the check register balance?

    (a) _____   (b) _____

2. A review of bank records revealed a $1,200 bank statement balance, $300 in outstanding checks, a $3 service fee, and a $75 deposit in transit. What was the bank statement adjusted balance? $ _____

3. A review of bank records revealed a $1,700 check register balance, $400 in outstanding checks, and a $4 service fee. What was the adjusted check register balance?

    $ _____

4. DeNaro Novelties received a notice of a $950 electronic funds transfer from a customer in Japan. If this is the only adjustment needed to the $2,700 check register balance, what is the amount of the adjusted check register balance?

    $ _____

5. Maria Retzlaff received a bank statement showing a $225.50 charge to her Exxon debit card. If this is the only adjustment needed to the $8,500 check register balance, what is the amount of the adjusted check register balance?

    $ _____

4.1 Review the chart shown below showing costs for borrowing money under three sets of conditions. John opened a 5-year loan. Belinda opened a 15-year loan. (a) How much additional interest did Belinda pay over the life of the loan? (b) What are two reasons that may have encouraged Belinda to opt for the loan with the higher interest payments?

(a) $ _____

(b) _____

_____

_____

_____

_____

CONNECTIONS

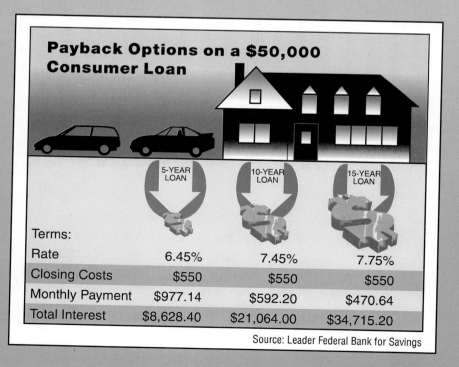

Payback Options on a $50,000 Consumer Loan

Terms:	5-YEAR LOAN	10-YEAR LOAN	15-YEAR LOAN
Rate	6.45%	7.45%	7.75%
Closing Costs	$550	$550	$550
Monthly Payment	$977.14	$592.20	$470.64
Total Interest	$8,628.40	$21,064.00	$34,715.20

Source: Leader Federal Bank for Savings

4.2 Review the survey results reported in the chart shown below indicating worst dating turnoffs. (a) Assuming that 500 persons responded to the survey, how many indicated "No sense of humor" as the worst dating turnoff? (b) Rank the categories relative to the way that you view them as the worst dating turnoffs, with the worst one being listed first.

(a) _____

(b) _____

      _____

      _____

      _____

      _____

A look at statistics that shape our lives

Worst dating turnoffs

74% Vulgar language

63% No sense of humor

56% Poor conversational skills

50% Poor table manners

41% Chronic lateness

Source: Pfaltzgraff survey by ICR Research Group

By Bob Laird, USA TODAY

CONNECTIONS

DECISIONS

4.1 The financial analyst for Johnson and Harris, Attorneys, reviewed the checking account records, which revealed the following items: checking account balance, $12,000; check register balance, $11,090; outstanding checks, $900; deposits in transit, $500; an electronic funds transfer into the account, $500; interest earned, $50; and service charge, $40. What is the adjusted bank statement and check register balance?

$ _____

Reconciliation of Bank Statement

Bank statement balance	$ _____
Add late deposits	_____
Total	$ _____
Deduct outstanding checks	_____
Adjusted bank balance	$ _____
Check stub balance	$ _____
Add funds transfer	_____
Add interest	_____
Total	$ _____
Deduct service charge	_____
Adjusted stub balance	$ _____

4.2 Call or visit a local bank in your area to determine the requirements for opening a checking account. What forms must be completed? What types of accounts are available? What charges are incurred for various accounts? Are debit cards available? Can the account be accessed by an automatic teller machine (ATM)? Does the bank permit electronic transfers (such as payroll earnings) into the account? Write a one-page report to summarize your findings.

BANK STATEMENT RECONCILIATION
Chapter Review and Quick Reference

Topic	Main Point	Typical Example	Text Page
Bank statement	This form includes transactions relative to checking accounts.	The statement contains a listing of checks, deposits, and charges recorded by the bank during the month.	61
Deposit slip or ticket	A form is used to record deposits of currency and checks.	An example of this form is shown on page xxx.	62
Check	A check is a direction to the bank to make a stated payment from an account.	An example of this form is shown on page xxx.	64
Payee	The payee is the person to receive payment from the check.	John Doe is the payee if the check is made payable to him.	64
Check register	The check register is used to maintain a record of transactions.	A depositor uses this form to maintain a listing of deposits and withdrawals.	65
Reconciliation	Reconciliation involves procedures that match bank records with check stub or register records.	Outstanding checks deduct from and deposits in transit add to the bank balance. Service fees deduct from and funds transfers add to the check register balance.	66
Outstanding check	A check that has been written but not submitted to the bank for payment is outstanding.	A check written on Monday will be outstanding until Wednesday, if submitted on that day for payment.	67
Electronic funds transfer	Funds can be transferred electronically from one account to another.	A debit card is used in a department store to pay for a merchandise purchase.	67

FRACTIONS

Performance Objectives

1. Determine the parts of a fraction.
2. Convert a mixed number to an improper fraction.
3. Convert an improper fraction to a mixed number.
4. Reduce a fraction to lowest terms.
5. Add and subtract values containing fractions and mixed numbers.
6. Multiply and divide values containing fractions and mixed numbers.

Mathematical calculations are simplified when only whole numbers are involved. However, only a portion, or part, of a whole number (fraction) may be necessary for some computations. For example, a person may purchase a piece of meat in the supermarket that weighs one and one-half pounds or candy that weighs three-fourths of one pound. This chapter provides background information, applications, and practice needed to understand how to make computations involving fractions.

PARTS OF A FRACTION

A *fraction* is used to represent a part of a whole number, such as one-half (1/2) or two-thirds (2/3) of the whole number. A fraction consists of two numbers separated by either a horizontal bar ($\frac{2}{3}$) or a slanted bar (2/3). The number on the top or left is called the *numerator* and the number on the bottom or right is called the *denominator*. Traditionally, fractions have been expressed by use of the horizontal bar. However, use of computers and electronic calculators have made the use of the slanted bar more popular as a format for expressing fractions. Both formats are illustrated below.

$$\frac{2}{3} = \frac{numerator}{denominator} \quad \text{or} \quad 2/3 = numerator/denominator$$

The denominator indicates how many parts there are in the unit. The numerator indicates how many of the parts are to be used in the computation. The fraction 2/3 indicates that the unit has been divided into three parts and that two of these parts are represented by the fraction, as shown in Figure 5.1.

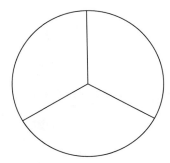

Figure 5.1 Example of a Fraction

TYPES OF FRACTIONS

A fraction that represents less than one unit, such as 1/2 or 3/4, is called a *proper fraction*. In all proper fractions, the numerator is less than the denominator.

A fraction that represents a whole unit, such as 1/1 or 5/5, or a fraction that represents more than a whole unit, such as 5/4 or 12/9, is called an *improper fraction*. For this type of fraction, the numerator is equal to or greater than the denominator.

A value that contains both a whole number and a fraction, such as 1 1/2 or 3 7/8, is called a *mixed number*.

Most computations involving fractions are made with proper fractions or improper fractions. Therefore, a mixed number, if used, can be converted to an improper fraction before the computation is made. However, the final answer (if it is an improper fraction) is converted to a mixed number. Examples are discussed below.

MIXED NUMBER CONVERTED TO AN IMPROPER FRACTION

A mixed number is changed to an improper fraction by multiplying the whole number by the denominator of the fraction and then adding the numerator. The mixed number 2 3/4 is changed to an improper fraction in the following model.

MODEL 5.1

Converting a mixed number to an improper fraction

Step 1 Multiply the whole number by the denominator of the fraction.
$4 \times 2 = 8$

Step 2 Add the numerator to the result obtained in Step 1.
$8 + 3 = 11$

Step 3 Place the result obtained in Step 2 over the denominator of the fraction in the mixed number. (Note that the denominator stays the same.)
$$\frac{11}{4}$$

Therefore, the mixed number 2 3/4 equals the improper fraction 11/4.

IMPROPER FRACTION CONVERTED TO A MIXED NUMBER

An improper fraction is changed to a mixed number by dividing the numerator of the improper fraction by the denominator of the improper fraction. The number of times the denominator can be completely divided becomes the whole number in the resulting mixed number. The remainder becomes the numerator in the fraction part of the mixed number, with the denominator of the improper fraction remaining the denominator. This is illustrated as follows. The improper fraction 11/4 is changed to a mixed number in this example.

Converting an improper fraction to a mixed number

Step 1   Divide the numerator by the denominator.
$11 \div 4 = 2$ (remainder of 3)

Step 2   Place the remainder of the division in Step 1 over the denominator of the improper fraction.
3/4

Step 3   The resulting mixed number is the whole number obtained in Step 1 and the fraction obtained in Step 2 (2 3/4 in this example).

LOWEST TERMS OF FRACTIONS

A fraction is *reduced to its lowest terms* when there is no number that can be divided equally into both numerator and denominator. To reduce a fraction to its lowest terms, divide both the numerator and the denominator by the same common number until further even division is not possible. The common number, or factor, is often apparent. For example, it is apparent that the factor 2 can be divided into both numerator and denominator for the fraction 4/10 as follows.

Reducing a fraction to lowest terms

$$4/10 = \frac{4 \div 2}{10 \div 2} = 2/5$$

Therefore, the fraction 4/10 reduced to its lowest terms becomes the fraction 2/5. In real value, 4/10 equals 2/5. However, the fraction is usually stated in its lowest terms when reporting an answer to a problem. Some large fractions may require more than one division to reduce to the lowest terms.

HIGHER TERMS OF FRACTIONS

Computations involving a series of fractions require that each fraction have the same denominator. A fraction can be *raised to higher terms* by multiplying both numerator and denominator by the same number. To determine the number to be used, determine the number of times the denominator is contained in the higher denominator. For example, 1/2 can be changed to 12ths by multiplying both numerator and denominator by 6 ($12 \div 2$) or 2/3 can be changed to 9ths by multiplying both numerator and denominator by 3 ($9 \div 3$). These conversions are illustrated below.

<table>
<tr><td>MODEL
5.4</td><td>

Raising a fraction to higher terms

$$1/2 \times 6/6 = 6/12 \qquad 2/3 \times 3/3 = 6/9$$

In other words, 1/2 equals 6/12 and 2/3 equals 6/9. This procedure is opposite to the procedure for reducing fractions to lower terms. These procedures will be useful in succeeding sections of this chapter, where addition, subtraction, multiplication, and division of fractions are illustrated.

</td></tr>
</table>

Addition or subtraction of fractions requires that the fractions have a common denominator. Problems in this chapter will provide additional practice with determining the lowest common denominator and practice with addition and subtraction of fractions and mixed numbers.

ADDITION OF FRACTIONS

Addition of a set of fractions containing common denominators is completed simply by computing the sum of the numerators of the fractions. If the set of fractions does not have a common denominator, each fraction must be converted to the lowest common denominator prior to computing the sum of the numerators of the set of fractions. Each of these situations is illustrated below. Notice that in reporting the answer, when the answer is an improper fraction, it should be converted to a mixed number, and each fraction should be reduced to its lowest terms.

<table>
<tr><td>MODEL
5.5</td><td>

Addition of fractions

1/12	1/2 becomes 3/6
5/12	2/3 becomes 4/6
+ 7/12	+ 1/6 remains 1/6
13/12 (or 1 1/12)	8/6 (or 1 1/3)

</td></tr>
</table>

ADDITION OF MIXED NUMBERS

An addition problem may contain one or more mixed numbers in the set. When mixed numbers are included, compute the sum of the fractional parts and add this sum to the sum of the whole number portions. This is illustrated on the next page by computing the sum of   1 1/3, 3 7/15, and 4 3/5.

Addition of mixed numbers

Step 1 Find the sum of the fractional parts. Reduce the sum to lowest terms.

1/3	becomes	5/15
7/15	remains	7/15
3/5	becomes	9/15
		21/15 = 1 6/15 = 1 2/5

Step 2 Add the result obtained in Step 1 to the whole number portions.
1 + 3 + 4 + 1 2/5 = 9 2/5

The sum of 4 1/2, 3 1/6, and 2 7/12 is computed as follows.

Step 1	1/2	becomes	6/12
	1/6	becomes	2/12
	7/12	remains	7/12
			15/12 = 1 3/12 = 1 1/4

Step 2 4 + 3 + 2 + 1 1/4 = 10 1/4

SUBTRACTION OF FRACTIONS

As in addition, fractions must have common denominators before subtraction. The subtraction process essentially involves determining the difference between the numerators of the two fractions. The smaller fraction is subtracted from the larger fraction. The following examples illustrate subtraction of fractions.

Subtraction of fractions

2/3	becomes	8/12		3/4	becomes	9/12
- 1/4	becomes	3/12		- 1/12	remains	1/12
		5/12				8/12 = 2/3

If needed, the result should be reduced to lowest terms.

SUBTRACTION OF MIXED NUMBERS

When one or both fractions are mixed numbers, the smaller number is subtracted from the larger number. The process involves first subtracting the whole number portion and then subtracting the fractional portion. This procedure is shown on page 86 for finding the difference between 15 4/5 and 4 1/2.

MODEL 5.8

Subtraction of mixed numbers

Step 1 Arrange the numbers in order, so that the smaller number is subtracted from the larger number.

15 4/5 - 4 1/2

Step 2 Find the lowest common denominator and convert the fractional portion.

15 4/5	becomes	15 8/10
4 1/2	becomes	4 5/10

Step 3 Subtract the whole number portion and the numerators of the fractional portions to compute the difference.

$$
\begin{array}{r}
15\ 8/10 \\
-\ 4\ 5/10 \\
\hline
11\ 3/10
\end{array}
$$

In some instances, the larger number may contain the smaller fraction. If this is the case, subtract 1 from the whole number and add it to the fractional portion. Remember that 1 equals 2 halves, 3 thirds, 4 fourths, and so forth. This type of problem is illustrated by finding the difference between 15 1/2 and 3 3/4.

MODEL 5.9

Subtraction of mixed numbers when the larger number contains the smaller fraction

Step 1 Subtract 1 from 15 to increase the numerator of the fractional portion after converting the fractional portion to the lowest common denominator.

15 1/2	becomes	15 2/4	becomes	14 6/4
3 3/4	remains	3 3/4	remains	3 3/4

Step 2 Find the difference between the whole number portion and the numerators of the fractional portion. If needed, the answer should be reduced to lowest terms.

14 6/4
3 3/4
11 3/4

You may now complete Performance Application 5.1

MULTIPLICATION OF FRACTIONS

The basic process for multiplication of fractions involves a fairly simple technique of multiplying the numerators and multiplying the denominators of the fractions. The answer, if needed, is then reduced to lowest terms. The four examples shown below illustrate this technique.

MODEL 5.10

Multiplication of fractions

$$\frac{2}{3} \times \frac{1}{2} = \frac{2}{6} = \frac{1}{3}$$

$$\frac{3}{7} \times \frac{1}{2} = \frac{3}{14}$$

$$\frac{1}{3} \times \frac{1}{4} \times \frac{2}{5} = \frac{2}{60} = \frac{1}{30}$$

$$\frac{3}{5} \times \frac{2}{7} \times \frac{1}{2} = \frac{6}{70} = \frac{3}{35}$$

Any number common to both numerator and denominator can be used to cancel the numbers to make them smaller and easier to use in computations. In other words, any common number that can be divided evenly into both numerator and denominator of any fraction in the series can be used to cancel or reduce the size of the fractions for easier computation. The number can be divided into the denominator of one fraction and into the numerator of an entirely different fraction, as illustrated below.

MODEL 5.11

Multiplication of fractions with cancellations

$$\frac{\overset{1}{\cancel{2}}}{7} \times \frac{3}{\underset{2}{\cancel{4}}} = \frac{3}{14}$$

$$\frac{\overset{1}{\cancel{3}}}{\underset{1}{\cancel{6}}} \times \frac{7}{\underset{3}{\cancel{9}}} \times \frac{\overset{2}{\cancel{10}}}{13} = \frac{14}{39}$$

MULTIPLICATION OF MIXED NUMBERS

Mixed numbers can be changed to improper fractions and multiplied in the manner described previously. This is often easier when using small numbers, as shown in the following computation.

3 1/2 x 2 1/4 becomes 7/2 x 9/4 = 63/8 = 7 7/8

A second method is used when there are large whole numbers to be multiplied. The first step is to multiply the whole numbers. The next whole number of the mixed number is then multiplied by the fractional part of the second mixed number followed by multiplying the second whole number by the fractional part of the first mixed number. Finally, the two fractions are multiplied. The products are then added to obtain the answer. This process is illustrated by multiplying 48 1/2 by 16 1/4.

**MODEL
5.12**

Multiplication of mixed numbers

Step 1 Multiply the whole numbers.
48 x 16 = 768

Step 2 Multiply each whole number by the fraction of the other mixed number.
48/1 x 1/4 = 12
16/1 x 1/2 = 8

Step 3 Multiply the fractions.
1/4 x 1/2 = 1/8

Step 4 Add the four products obtained in Steps 1 to 3.
768 + 12 + 8 + 1/8 = 788 1/8

Notice in Step 2 that a whole number such as 48 becomes 48/1 when used with multiplication of fractions.

DIVISION OF FRACTIONS

Division of fractions requires that the numerator and denominator of the divisor be inverted. The fractions are then multiplied as described above. The problem, 4/5 divided by 1/2, is solved as follows.

Division of fractions

4/5 divided by 1/2 becomes 4/5 x 2/1 = 8/5 = 1 3/5

Notice that the divisor 1/2 becomes 2/1 after the numerator and denominator are inverted. As an additional illustration, the problem, 3/8 divided by 3/4, is sovlved as follows.

3/8 ÷ 3/4 becomes
$$\frac{\overset{1}{\cancel{3}}}{\underset{2}{\cancel{8}}} \times \frac{\overset{1}{\cancel{4}}}{\underset{1}{\cancel{3}}} = \frac{1}{2}$$

Division of Mixed Numbers

Division of mixed numbers follows the same rule as division of fractions if the mixed numbers are changed to improper fractions. For example, the following illustration shows how to divide 5 3/4 by 2 1/8.

Division of mixed numbers

Step 1 Change the mixed numbers to improper fractions.
5 3/4 ÷ 2 1/8 becomes 23/4 ÷ 17/8

Step 2 Invert the divisor.
17/8 becomes 8/17

Step 3 Multiply the two fractions.

$$\frac{23}{\underset{1}{\cancel{4}}} \times \frac{\overset{2}{\cancel{8}}}{17} = \frac{46}{17} = 2\frac{12}{17}$$

A second example, 8 2/7 divided by 4 1/4, is shown below.

Step 1 58/7 ÷ 17/4

Steps 2 and 3 58/7 x 4/17 = 232/119 = 1 113/119

You may now complete Performance Application 5.2.

PERFORMANCE APPLICATION 5.1

1. Change each of the following mixed numbers to improper fractions or vice versa.

   (a) 3 1/4   = _____   (k) 55/7   = _____

   (b) 5 1/2   = _____   (l) 75/8   = _____

   (c) 6 1/8   = _____   (m) 95/3   = _____

   (d) 5 3/4   = _____   (n) 89/12   = _____

   (e) 6 7/8   = _____   (o) 125/9   = _____

   (f) 8 11/12 = _____   (p) 139/3   = _____

   (g) 9 13/16 = _____   (q) 147/5   = _____

   (h) 12 1/4 = _____   (r) 269/6   = _____

   (i) 13 2/3 = _____   (s) 409/8   = _____

   (j) 14 5/6 = _____   (t) 293/5   = _____

2. Reduce the following fractions to their lowest terms.

   (a) 2/6   = _____   (k) 60/380 = _____

   (b) 2/10   = _____   (l) 85/120 = _____

   (c) 4/10   = _____   (m) 96/128 = _____

   (d) 8/12   = _____   (n) 72/108 = _____

   (e) 9/15   = _____   (o) 75/195 = _____

   (f) 8/18   = _____   (p) 88/220 = _____

   (g) 8/26   = _____   (q) 81/135 = _____

   (h) 48/64 = _____   (r) 156/252 = _____

   (i) 52/76 = _____   (s) 85/135 = _____

   (j) 75/180 = _____   (t) 270/285 = _____

3. Add the following fractions and mixed numbers.

(a) 1/2
     2/3
     _____

(b) 3/4
     7/8
     _____

(c) 1/3
     2/7
     _____

(d) 5/6
     7/8
     2/3
     _____

(e) 5/7
     1/5
     3/10
     _____

(f) 1/4
     7/12
     1/2
     7/8
     _____

(g) 5/16
     1/4
     9/24
     _____

(h) 4 1/2
     2 2/3
     _____

(i) 9 3/4
     7 7/8
     _____

(j) 5 7/8
     2 1/3
     _____

(k) 12 1/6
     13 1/4
     _____

(l) 8 1/3
     5 5/6
     13 5/8
     19 9/16
     _____

4. Subtract the following fractions and mixed numbers.

(a) 1/2
     1/4
     _____

(b) 3/4
     1/8
     _____

(c) 4/9
     1/3
     _____

(d) 5/8
     1/3
     _____

(e) 5/12
     1/8
     _____

(f) 2/3
     1/16
     _____

(g) 6/7
     2/3
     _____

(h) 11/16
     5/12
     _____

(i) 8 3/4
     2 1/4
     _____

(j) 7 1/2
     2 1/4
     _____

(k) 15 2/3
     7 1/8
     _____

(l) 32 3/5
     7 3/8
     _____

(m) 63 5/6
     17 7/16
     _____

(n) 13 1/2
     8 3/4
     _____

(o) 29 1/3
     13 3/8
     _____

(p) 37 2/9
     21 1/3
     _____

(q) 41 2/7
     6 9/10
     _____

PERFORMANCE APPLICATION 5.2

1. Multiply the following fractions

    (a) 2/3   x   5/12   = _____

    (b) 5/9   x   4/8   = _____

    (c) 3/16   x   4/5   = _____

    (d) 7/8   x   2/3   = _____

    (e) 7/12   x   18   = _____

    (f) 5/9   x   21   = _____

2. Multiply the following mixed numbers.

    (a) 3 1/2   x   8 1/4   = _____

    (b) 9 3/8   x   11 5/6 = _____

    (c) 15 4/7   x   6 5/14 = _____

    (d) 2 1/2   x   3 2/3   x   2 5/6   = _____

    (e) 6 1/8   x   5 1/4   x   3 3/16 = _____

    (f) 5 2/3   x   3 1/4   x   8 7/12 = _____

3. A man purchased a microcomputer for $3,000. The company charges 1/5 of the purchase price for an annual maintenance fee. How much is the annual maintenance fee for this microcomputer?

    $ _____

4. There were 10,240 persons attending a rock concert. If 2/5 of the audience was female, how many females attended the concert?

    _____

5. A jigsaw puzzle contains 5,240 pieces. Ralph estimates that the puzzle is 5/8 completed. How many pieces have been put in place in the puzzle?

    _____

6. Divide the following mixed numbers and fractions.

(a) 3 1/2 ÷ 3/4 = _____

(b) 2 1/3 ÷ 5/6 = _____

(c) 5 1/4 ÷ 3/8 = _____

(d) 6 7/8 ÷ 5/16 = _____

(e) 5 1/2 ÷ 2 = _____

(f) 16 5/9 ÷ 3 = _____

(g) 3 1/2 ÷ 1 3/4 = _____

(h) 15 7/8 ÷ 5 9/16 = _____

(i) 24 2/3 ÷ 5 1/12 = _____

7. An automobile travels 240 miles in 5 1/2 hours. How many miles per hour does the automobile travel?

_____

8. An automobile travels 210 6/10 miles and uses 16 2/10 gallons of gasoline. How many miles per gallons is travelled?

_____

9. A student is able to transfer 84 3/4 credits and 271 1/5 quality points into another school. What is the student's grade point average based on the transfer of credit into the new school?

_____

10. An auditorium has 31,437 square feet of seating space. Each seat will take 3 1/2 square feet. How many seats will fill the seating space?

_____

PRACTICE TEST FOR CHAPTER 5

FRACTIONS

Complete each of the following problems and then compare your answers with the ones on page 646.

1. Change each of the following mixed numbers to improper fractions or change each improper fraction to a mixed number, as appropriate.

(a) 2 1/8 = _____

(b) 4 1/4 = _____

(c) 9 7/8 = _____

(d) 30 1/8 = _____

(e) 42 1/2 = _____

(f) 52 3/4 = _____

(g) 29/4 = _____

(h) 35/8 = _____

(i) 47/9 = _____

(j) 89/3 = _____

(k) 136/7 = _____

(l) 219/4 = _____

2. Reduce or raise the following fractions as indicated.

(a) 16/28 = _____ /7

(b) 9/27 = _____ /3

(c) 8/32 = _____ /4

(d) 2/3 = _____ /9

(e) 7/8 = _____ /24

(f) 4/5 = _____ /20

3. Reduce the following to their lowest terms.

(a) 3/9 = _____

(b) 2/8 = _____

(c) 3/18 = _____

(d) 4/12 = _____

(e) 6/32 = _____

(f) 75/180 = _____

(g) 96/128 = _____

(h) 81/135 = _____

(i) 85/136 = _____

4. Find the lowest common multiple of the following numbers.

(a) 2, 4, 8, 16 _____

(b) 3, 6, 12, 18 _____

(c) 2, 6, 10, 15 _____

(d) 2, 3, 8, 16 _____

(e) 3, 7, 21 _____

(f) 5, 8, 20 _____

(g) 10, 15, 18, 30 _____

(h) 6, 8, 9, 12 _____

5. Add the following fractions.

(a) 2/3 + 1/2 = _____

(b) 1/4 + 1/8 = _____

(c) 3/12 + 1/3 = _____

(d) 1/3 + 1/7 = _____

(e) 8/9 + 3/4 = _____

(f) 5/24 + 19/32 = _____

(g) 2/13 + 1/2 = _____

(h) 4/5 + 5/6 = _____

(i) 1/6 + 7/8 = _____

6. Add the following mixed numbers.

    (a) 3 1/2   +   2 1/3   = _____

    (b) 8 1/3   +   5 5/6   = _____

    (c) 6 5/8   +   17 7/16 = _____

    (d) 61 5/12 +   27 5/8   = _____

    (e) 16 3/8   +   3 1/3   = _____

    (f) 12 3/4   +   13 1/3   = _____

7. Multiply the following fractions.

    (a) 1/3   x   1/2   = _____

    (b) 3/8   x   2/9   = _____

    (c) 5/6   x   3/10   = _____

    (d) 2/9   x   5/12   = _____

    (e) 8/21   x   7/8   = _____

    (f) 2/3   x   15   = _____

    (g) 5/6   x   30   = _____

    (h) 14/15 x   45/56   = _____

    (i) 27/56 x   8/17   = _____

8. Multiply the following mixed numbers.

    (a) 5 1/2   x   7 1/4   = _____

    (b) 7 1/8   x   5 1/3   = _____

    (c) 15 5/7   x   5 3/5   = _____

    (d) 18 3/5   x   15   = _____

    (e) 3 1/2   x   2 1/3 x 3 1/7 = _____

    (f) 2 7/9   x   5 2/5 x 7 1/5 = _____

COMMUNICATIONS

Read the following dialogue between a store owner and her assistant manager and answer the questions below.

"Randy, what kind of numbers did we produce today?"

"Well, we had a pretty good day. Rang up $2,583.22 in sales."

"Good. Can you give me a breakdown by product grouping?"

"Sure. Let's see, receipts show we sold $970.80 in beverages, $784.34 in snack foods, $447.59 in candy, and $380.49 in newspapers and magazines."

"Great. Seems like our beverages sales are really picking up. Do you realize that over the last six weeks we have sold $29,000 worth of soda alone?"

"Lot of thirsty people out there. I better check our stock to make sure we're covered for tomorrow."

1. Assuming the store was open every day for the last six weeks, compute the daily average for soda sales. _____

2. Randy looked in the storeroom and discovered he needs to order to replenish soda stock. He'd like enough to handle at least one week's worth of sales. Based on the average daily soda sales (at .75 cents per can) and 24-can cases, how many cases should Randy order? _____

3. The owner checked the cash drawer and found $1,748.38 in currency and $844.84 in coin. Does the dollar amount line up with the sales reported by Randy? If not, what is the discrepancy?

_____

_____

_____

UNIT 1 SELF-TEST
BASIC MATHEMATIC OPERATIONS

1. Joe Chang made the following purchases: $128.45, $236.77, $17.89, and $173.23. What was the total amount of his purchases?

   $ _____

2. The Melrose Heating Company sells 3 heaters for the following prices: $24.56, $37.28, and $48.75. Round each price to tens and compute the estimated total cost of the 3 heaters.

   $ _____

3. Store A had total sales of $43,387.53. Store B had total sales of $52,173.12. By how much did Store B's sales exceed Store A's sales?
   $ _____

4. Joe Vocca had a beginning balance of $789.45 in his checking account. He made a $239.45 deposit. He wrote checks for the following amounts: $23.78, $89.34, and $75.04. What was his ending balance?
   $ _____

5. The Connie Forde Auto Center sold 207 automobiles with an average price of $3,818. Round all figures to hundreds and compute the estimated total sales amount.

   $ _____

6. Carl Dickerson drives his car at an average speed of 55 miles per hour. How many miles will he drive in 7 hours?

   _____

7. Brenda Everett earned $289.40 for 5 days of work. What were her average earnings per day?

   $ _____

8. A secretary needs to type a report containing 837 words. If the secretary can type 65 words per minute, how many minutes will be required to type the report? (Round to one decimal place.)

   _____

9. The following items were sold to a customer. Compute the amount per item and the total cost.

Item	Quantity	Price	Amount
A	13	$ 8.98	$ _____
B	9	14.95	$ _____
C	7	8.59	$ _____
D	9	19.98	$ _____
Total Cost			$ _____

10. Jim Brock's check stub balance was $789.14. His bank statement balance was $786.89. A review of his banking records showed a $5.00 bank charge that had not been recorded in the check stub. There were two outstanding checks ($20.50 and $17.25) and a late deposit ($35.00) that were not recorded on the bank statement. What was the reconciled balance of his account?

$ _____

11. Clara Fuller forgot to record check #723 for $137.89 in her check stub. If this is the only adjustment that needs to be made to her check stub balance of $625.30, what is her adjusted check stub balance?

$ _____

12. Roy Jones received a bank statement that included an electronic funds transfer deposit of $1,353.78. If this is the only adjustment that needs to be made to his check stub balance of $3,721.53, what is his adjusted check stub balance?

$ _____

UNIT 2

Decimal Amounts in Business

How much simpler is it for you to add 22.5, 80.7, and 15.3 than it is to add 22 1/2, 80 7/10, and 15 3/10? Using decimal representation for numeric values has become standard practice with the increased use of calculators and computers. Even determining the number of hours you work on a job can be simplified by using decimal representation for time periods, such as 7.75 hours instead of 7 hours and 45 minutes.

To work successfully with decimals requires understanding alignment of values at the decimal point and the concept of rounding off numbers. These principles are included in this unit along with basic addition, subtraction, multiplication, and division activities using decimal values.

CONVERSION OF DECIMALS

Performance Objectives

1. Determine place values of decimals.
2. Read decimal values.
3. Convert decimals to fractional equivalents.
4. Convert fractions to decimal equivalents.

As computers and electronic calculators become increasingly common and necessary business tools, most figures are stated in decimal form because computations performed with this equipment must be in decimal form. This chapter provides background knowledge needed to perform the fundamental processes of addition, subtraction, multiplication, and division using decimal values.

DECIMAL VALUES

Many values in business and everyday use are stated in decimal form. Examples include product prices, interest rates, discounts, speedometer readings, and measurements. The *decimal places* to the right of a decimal point (period) represent one or more tenths, hundredths, thousandths, and so forth of a single number, such as 0.1 or 0.15. A mixed decimal is a decimal number that combines a whole number and a decimal fraction, such as 5.1 or 5.65.

Place value with fractions, as with whole numbers, is important. The chart in Figure 6.1 is similar to the one used in Chapter 1 to show place value for whole numbers. Notice that the first place to the right of the decimal point is the tenths place, and each position to the right is a power of 10 (hundredths, thousandths, ten thousandths, and so forth). The value of each number place decreases as it appears further to the right of the decimal point. For example, 0.8 is greater than 0.08, and 0.2 is greater than 0.02 because of place value.

The wide use of computers has led to most values being expressed in a decimal format.

Decimal fraction *(commonly called a decimal) is the value to the right of the decimal point.*

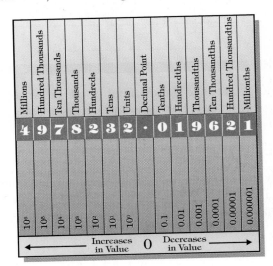

Figure 6.1 Place Value Chart

Model 6.1 shows how decimals are read. The fractional equivalents of the decimals are also indicated. Reading a decimal correctly helps to write it correctly.

**MODEL
6.1**

Reading Decimals

Decimal Value	Place Value	Pronounced	Fractional Value
0.5	Tenths	Five-tenths	5/10
0.06	Hundredths	Six-hundredths	6/100
0.072	Thousandths	Seventy-two thousandths	72/1,000
0.0002	Ten-thousandths	Two ten-thousandths	2/10,000
0.00003	Hundred-thousandths	Three hundred-thousandths	3/100,000
0.000008	Millionths	Eight-millionths	8/1,000,000
3.15	Hundredths	Three and fifteen-hundredths	3 15/100
114.7	Tenths	One hundred fourteen and seven-tenths	114 7/10
5.08	Hundredths	Five and eight-hundredths	5 8/100

Practice and applications for use with fractions are included in the appendix. If a review of fractions is needed, refer to this appendix prior to completing applications in this chapter.

Apply Your Skills

Write the pronunciation and fractional value for each of the following decimal values.

Decimal Value	Place Value	Pronounced	Fractional Value
0.7	_____	_____	_____
0.08	_____	_____	_____
0.075	_____	_____	_____
0.0075	_____	_____	_____
3.4	_____	_____	_____

Some people prefer to pronounce the decimal point. For example, 2.67 is read "two point sixty-seven," and 0.07 is read "zero point zero seven."

EQUIVALENT DECIMALS AND FRACTIONS

*Convert a fraction to its **decimal equivalent** by dividing the denominator into the numerator.*

Fractions can be converted to decimal equivalents and decimals can be converted to fractional equivalents. Model 6.2 shows how to convert the decimal .34 to a fraction.

Converting the decimal .34 to a fraction

Step 1 Read the decimal.

Read .34 as thirty-four hundredths.

Step 2 Write the decimal as a fraction by placing its digits in the numerator. The denominator is 1 followed by as many zeros as the number of places to the right of the decimal point.

34/100

Step 3 Reduce the fraction to its lowest terms.

34/100 = 17/50

Therefore, .34 equals 34/100 or 17/50.

Apply Your Skills

Convert each of the following decimal values to their fractional equivalents.

Decimal Value	Fractional Value
0.4	_____
0.25	_____
0.75	_____
0.62	_____

MODEL 6.2

Remember to read the fraction to determine its fractional denominator, such as .25 = 25/100.

*A **pure decimal fraction** has no whole number, such as 0.25.*

Mixed decimals can be changed to mixed numbers using the same procedure. Model 6.3 shows how to change 10.250 to its mixed number equivalent.

Converting the decimal 10.250 to a fraction

Step 1 Ten and two hundred fifty thousandths

Step 2 10 250/1,000

Step 3 10 250/1,000 = 10 1/4

Apply Your Skills

Convert each of the following mixed decimal values to their fractional equivalents.

Mixed Decimal	Fractional Equivalent
3.25	_____
25.35	_____
5.450	_____

MODEL 6.3

Mixed decimals have both a whole number and a decimal fraction, such as 10.25 or $1.25.

Mixed numbers have both a whole number and a fraction, such as 10 1/4.

Notice that the whole number in the mixed decimal remains the same when converted to a mixed number.

A fraction can be changed to a decimal by simply dividing the numerator by the denominator of the fraction. For example, 1/4 becomes 0.25 as shown in Model 6.4. Zeros are added to the right of the decimal until the division ends or until it appears that the denominator cannot be divided into the numerator evenly. In that case, the remainder is placed as a numerator over the divisor, and this fraction is placed to the right of the quotient. A *terminating decimal* occurs when conversion from a fraction to a decimal results in no remainder, such as 3/4 = 0.75. A *nonterminating, repeating decimal* occurs when conversion from a fraction to a decimal does not divide evenly and results in a remainder, such as 2/3 = 0.66 2/3. Both of these situations are shown in Model 6.4.

MODEL 6.4

*A **complex decimal** is one that contains a fraction, such as 0.333 1/3.*

Converting a fraction to a decimal

$$1/4 = 0.25 \qquad 4\overline{)1.0} \;\; \begin{array}{r} 0.25 \\ \hline \end{array}$$

$$\begin{array}{r} 0.25 \\ 4\overline{)1.0} \\ \underline{8} \\ 20 \\ \underline{20} \end{array}$$

$$1/3 = 0.333\ 1/3 \qquad \begin{array}{r} 0.333\ 1/3 \\ 3\overline{)1.000} \\ \underline{9} \\ 10 \\ \underline{9} \\ 10 \\ \underline{9} \\ 1 \end{array}$$

Apply Your Skills

Convert each of the following fractional values to its decimal equivalent.

Fractional Value	Decimal Equivalent
3/5	_____
3/4	_____
13/65	_____

PERFORMANCE APPLICATION 6.1

1. Evaluate each of the following pairs of decimal values and indicate which of the two numbers in each pair is larger.

   (a) .2 or .3   _____

   (b) .25 or .125   _____

   (c) .367 or .28   _____

   (d) .725 or .81   _____

   (e) 4.8 or 4.08   _____

   (f) 3.11 or 3.2   _____

2. Indicate the place value of the digit on the extreme right in each of the following numbers.

   (a) 0.2   _____

   (b) 0.25   _____

   (c) 0.3451   _____

   (d) 0.000001   _____

   (e) 3.289   _____

   (f) 4.8   _____

3. Write out in words how the following decimal values are read or pronounced.

   (a) 0.3   _____

   (b) .08   _____

   (c) 0.85   _____

   (d) 0.003   _____

   (e) 0.0017   _____

   (f) 0.00001 _____

   (g) 3.2   _____

   (h) 4.25   _____

4. Convert the following fractions to decimals or decimals to fractions:

	Decimal	Fraction			Decimal	Fraction
(a)	0.25	_____		(f)	0.375	_____
(b)	2.5	_____		(g)	0.875	_____
(c)	_____	3/10		(h)	0.025	_____
(d)	_____	1/8		(i)	_____	2/3
(e)	_____	3/4		(j)	_____	3/8

PRACTICE TEST FOR CHAPTER 6
CONVERSION OF DECIMALS

Complete each of the following problems and then compare your answers with the ones on page 646.

1. Write the pronunciation of the following fraction: 0.37.

   _____

2. What is the place value of the digit on the extreme right of the following decimal value: 0.473?

   _____

3. Which of the following decimal values is the largest, (a) 0.35 or (b) 0.035?

   _____ (a)   _____ (b)

4. Convert the decimal value 0.35 to its fractional equivalent.

   _____

5. Convert the fractional value 7/8 to its decimal equivalent.

   _____

CONNECTIONS

6.1 The following chart shows the increase in major household expenses over a five-year period. Write the pronunciation for each of the values shown in the chart. Note: The word "percent" is added after each value.

Clothes/Entertainment _____

Housing _____

Food _____

Transportation _____

A look at statistics that shape the nation

How much major household expenses have increased

(1986-91)

Clothes/Entertainment	28.3%
Housing	26.7%
Food	23.7%
Transportation	4.8%

Source: Bureau of Labor Statistics "Consumer Expenditure Survey"

By Marcia Staimer, USA TODAY

6.2 The newspaper analysis shown below describes market highlights for selected stocks. Convert each of the mixed fractions to equivalent mixed decimal values.

Merck	$33 1/4	_____
Schering-Plough	$66 3/8	_____
Bristol-Myers Squibb	$55 1/8	_____
Pfizer	$63 1/2	_____
American Home Products	$64 1/8	_____
Eli Lilly	$48 1/2	_____

Market Highlights

Drug stocks were a hot spot. Merck added $1\frac{1}{8}$ to **33\frac{1}{4}$** after it reported second-quarter operating profit of 15 cents a share after a charge, vs. 56 cents a year earlier. The results were in line with analysts' estimates. Merck also announced a restructuring aimed at cutting costs. Other drug stocks rallied after Wertheim Schroder recommended the group. Rising: Schering-Plough, $1\frac{1}{2}$ to **66\frac{3}{8}$**; Bristol-Myers Squibb, 7/8 to **55\frac{1}{8}$**; Pfizer, $\frac{1}{2}$ to **63\frac{1}{2}$**; American Home Products, $1\frac{1}{4}$ to **64\frac{1}{8}$**; Eli Lilly, $2\frac{1}{8}$ to **48\frac{1}{2}$**.

CONNECTIONS

6.1 Complete the following chart by supplying entries for the blanks.

Decimal	Fraction
0.75	_____
_____	5/8
12.25	_____
_____	$12 1/4

6.2 Review newspapers and/or magazines in your school library to find ten examples where decimals are being used. Provide a listing that illustrates each of the examples.

DECISIONS

CONVERSION OF DECIMALS
Chapter Review and Quick Reference

Topic	Main Point	Typical Example	Text Page
Place value	The value of a number depends on its relationship to the decimal point. Movement further to the left increases the value while movement further to the right decreases the value of the number.	30. is greater than 3.1. 0.3 is greater than 0.03. Whole numbers appear to the left of the decimal point. Decimal values appear to the right of the decimal point.	101
Reading decimal values	The word *and* is used in place of the decimal point. The place values of the numbers are also pronounced.	0.3 is read as three-tenths. 1.3 is read as one and three-tenths. 24.05 is read as twenty-four and five-hundredths.	102
Conversion of a decimal to a fraction	The decimal is placed as the numerator and the lowest place value is placed as the denominator of a fraction. Then the fraction is reduced to lowest terms.	$0.4 = \dfrac{4}{10} = \dfrac{2}{5}$ $0.25 = \dfrac{25}{100} = \dfrac{1}{4}$ $0.28 = \dfrac{28}{100} = \dfrac{7}{25}$	103
Conversion of a fraction to a decimal	Divide the denominator into the numerator.	$\dfrac{1}{4} = 4\overline{)\begin{array}{r}.25\\ 1.00\\ \underline{8}\\ 20\\ \underline{20}\\ 0\end{array}}$	104

Chapter 7

ADDITION AND SUBTRACTION OF DECIMALS

Performance Objectives

1. Add values containing decimal values.
2. Subtract values containing decimal values.
3. Round decimal values to the appropriate place value.
4. Align values in a format appropriate for problems requiring addition or subtraction.

Many applications require the addition and/or subtraction of decimals, such as deducting payments on account, computing statement balances, determining a customer's account balance, and computing payrolls. In this chapter, you will practice adding and subtracting decimal values and solving appropriate problems.

ADDITION OF DECIMALS

Adding decimal values is similar to adding whole numbers except that when adding by hand the alignment of the decimal point must be considered. Review Figure 7.1, which outlines specific rules for adding and subtracting decimals.

In other words, the decimal point must be aligned for each value, as shown in Model 7.1 when adding 1.23, 1.456, 16.71, and 293.1. Notice that zeros can be added to the extreme right of the decimal point to help you add decimal values without affecting the value. For example, 1.23 equals 1.230 or 1.2300. Some people prefer to add sufficient zeros so that the values, or addends, align evenly on the right side as shown in Model 7.1.

If you are using a calculator, however, it will automatically align the decimal point.

Addition: Finding the sum of two or more values.

1.23, 1.230, and 1.2300 all have the same value.

Rules for Addition and Subtraction of Decimals

Arrange the numbers in columns with the decimal points aligned in a vertical line.

Add or subtract each column, from right to left.

For subtraction problems, add enough extra zeros so that both values have the same number of decimal places.

Figure 7.1 Rules for Addition and Subtraction of Decimals

MODEL 7.1

The decimal points must be aligned in a vertical line.

Add zeros as needed to make each value have an equal number of places to the right of the decimal point.

Aligning the decimal point aligns the place values.

A calculator with a floating decimal will align the decimal point automatically.

Dollar values are normally rounded to two decimal places.

Alignment of decimals

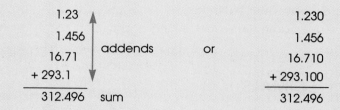

```
  1.23    ↑              1.230
  1.456   | addends  or  1.456
 16.71    |             16.710
+293.1    ↓            +293.100
_____                _____
312.496  sum            312.496
```

Apply Your Skills

Align the decimal points in a vertical column for each of the following addends and then compute the sum: 4.2, 17.435, 8.2, and 8.91. Do not round the sum for this problem. What is the sum?

_____

Decimal values can be added in the same manner as whole numbers if the decimal point in the answer is placed in the same vertical line as the other decimal points. Most computers and electronic calculators will align the decimal point automatically if the decimal point is keyboarded (entered) in the proper place along with each decimal place. While using the equipment, decimal values can be arranged in either horizontal or vertical column order. However, manual addition (or subtraction) of decimal values is easier to perform if the values are arranged in vertical order with the decimal points properly aligned. If an electronic calculator or computer is used, most problems in this and other chapters should first be solved manually and then with equipment in order to gain practice unless your instructor directs otherwise.

ROUNDING NUMBERS

Any number can be rounded to the desired number of places. As a general rule, addition or subtraction of dollar values should be carried to three places to the right of the decimal point and rounded to two places to the right of the decimal point. Note that rounding to two decimal places is normally done only after the final answer has been obtained.

A general rule for problems in this text and for making business calculations that involve multiplication or division is to round off numbers to four decimal places and then round off the answer to two decimal places. See Figure 7.2 and Model 7.2.

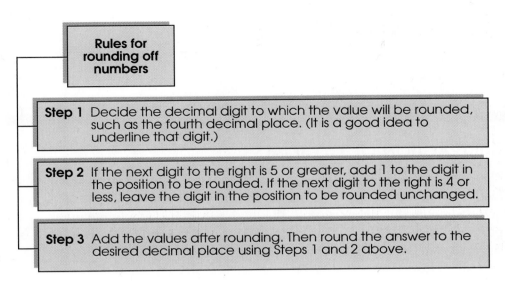

Figure 7.2 Rules for Rounding Off Numbers

Rounding up of all values is performed by many retail stores. For example, a department store or supermarket may round the value $9.372 to the value $9.38. The rule here is to round up to the next whole cent. Although this practice is followed in many stores, the general rule presented above will be followed for problems in this text.

If the original values had *not* been rounded, the actual sum would have been 29.308989. In this instance, the actual sum rounded to two decimal places would have been 29.31, which is the same as the sum obtained by rounding off. There may be a few instances in which the final sums will be inaccurate due to rounding of addends, but if the above rules for addition and subtraction problems are followed, the rounding usually balances out.

A dollar value such as $29.3090 is impossible, so round it to $29.31.

Rounding of decimal values (four places, with the answer to two places)

Step 1	14.32587
	6.425851
	3.28942
	5.267848
Step 2	14.3259
	6.4259
	3.2894
	+ 5.2678
	29.3090
Step 3	29.3090 = 29.31

MODEL 7.2

Money computations are treated like decimal problems. The decimal point separates the dollars and cents.

Apply Your Skills

Round each of the addends to four decimal places: 3.45676, 7.321938, 9.39565. Compute the sum. Then round the sum to two decimal places. What is the sum, rounded to two decimal places?

_____

SUBTRACTION OF DECIMALS

The rule for aligning the decimal point in addition of decimals also applies to the subtraction of decimals. However, adding zeros to the right of the decimal point is required in subtraction so that both values have the same number of places to the right of the decimal point. This is illustrated in the examples shown in Model 7.3, in which 8.112 is subtracted from 11.238, 1.243 is subtracted from 8.380, and 3.20 is subtracted from 7.25.

In the middle example, notice that the value 1 can be "borrowed" from the left digit to add 10 to the value. For example, 1 was borrowed from the value 8 (making the 8 a 7) to add 10 to the value 0. Then, 3 was subtracted from 10 to produce the value 7 in the answer.

After sufficient zeros have been added to right-justify (make even on the right side) the two values and the decimal point has been properly aligned, subtraction is performed in the same manner as subtraction with whole numbers. Because correct placement of the decimal point in the answer is so important, estimation and verification of answers are essential when making computations with decimals.

Subtraction: Finding the difference between two values.

Borrowing 1 from the hundredths position is required since 3 cannot be subtracted from 0, as indicated below.

$$\begin{array}{r} 8.3\overset{7}{\cancel{8}}\overset{10}{\cancel{0}} \\ -\ 1.2\ 4\ 3 \\ \hline 7.1\ 3\ 7 \end{array}$$

MODEL 7.3

Minuend: 11.238
Subtrahend: 8.112
Difference: 3.126

Borrowing is necessary when the subtrahend digit is less than the corresponding minuend digit.

Subtraction of decimals

$$\begin{array}{r} 11.238 \\ -\ 8.112 \\ \hline 3.126 \end{array} \qquad \begin{array}{r} 8.380 \\ -\ 1.243 \\ \hline 7.137 \end{array} \qquad \begin{array}{r} 7.25 \\ -\ 3.20 \\ \hline 4.05 \end{array}$$

Apply Your Skills

What are the differences for the following problems (do not round the differences)? (a) 14.582 subtracted from 26.89 and (b) 109.543 subtracted from 273.3972.

(a) _____ (b) _____

PERFORMANCE APPLICATION 7.1

1. Before adding the amounts for each problem, rewrite each value vertically with the decimal points properly aligned. (Do not round off.)

   (a) 27.2, 31.41, 32.192

   _____

   (b) 148.3, 16.075, 63.7052

   _____

   (c) 214.3789, 109.0003, 63.1

   _____

   (d) 807.2, 19.00901, 16.143

   _____

   (e) 167.1, 819.202, 16.8009

   _____

   (f) 15.81765, 189.7624, 1.81

   _____

   (g) 90.009, 45.25, 76.1124

   _____

   (h) 814.04, 782.009, 484.4, 21.8

   _____

   (i) 975.87, 0.50906, 3.6145, 3.12

   _____

   (j) 87.007, 70.0081, 134.83, 8.8

   _____

(k)   0.608, 913.21, 4.0098

_____

(l)   164.29, 14.009, 62.137, 18.423

_____

2. A person bought the following items at the grocery store: bread, $1.07; produce, $6.27; cheese, $4.19; and meat, $8.83. Determine the total amount due for the merchandise.

$ _____

3. A family spent the following amounts on various items in the family budget: rent, $480.00; food, $395.87; clothing, $162.37; miscellaneous, $405.95; and savings, $275.14. Determine the family's total expenses.

$ _____

4. Round the following numbers as indicated:

(a)   384 to the nearest ten _____

(b)   426 to the nearest ten _____

(c)   3,062 to the nearest hundred _____

(d)   452 to the nearest hundred _____

(e)   87,653 to the nearest thousand _____

(f)   87.521 to one decimal place _____

(g)   1,214.253 to one decimal place _____

(h)   16.895 to two decimal places _____

(i)   142.314 to two decimal places _____

(j)   16.21894 to two decimal places _____

(k)   162.21936 to three decimal places _____

(l)   14.89567 to four decimal places _____

(m)   6.89501 to three decimal places _____

(n)   152.155 to two decimal places _____

(o)   52.0504 to one decimal place _____

(p)   23,762.8951 to two decimal places _____

PERFORMANCE APPLICATION 7.2

1. Rewrite each of the following values with the decimal points correctly aligned, then subtract. (Do not round.)

   (a) 12.32 - 4.1   = _____

   (b) 28.6 - 9.42   = _____

   (c) 516.382 - 28.197   = _____

   (d) 472.4 - 36.817   = _____

   (e) 73.001 - 28.73   = _____

   (f) 0.216 - 0.1725   = _____

   (g) 0.8783 - 0.527   = _____

   (h) 1.0 - 0.264   = _____

   (i) 25.006 - 13.7268   = _____

   (j) 7.6 - 0.01254   = _____

   (k) 86,412.8 - 0.0739   = _____

   (l) 1.009 - 0.6873   = _____

2. Juan Rodriquez had a beginning checking account balance of $1,623.81. He then wrote checks for the following amounts: $14.67, $37.14, $289.34, $56.78, and $4.23. What was his ending balance after deducting these checks?

   $ _____

3. Barry Diaz budgeted $100 for supplies. He made the following purchases: clock, $23.45; folders, $11.49; planner pads, $17.45; and microcassette recorder, $57.95. Was the expenditure over the budget?

   _____ Yes   _____ No

4. An account statement for medical services for Albert Schaefer for the past month is shown below. Complete the statement by adding charges to the balance and subtracting payments made to the account.

Day	Charge	Payment	Balance
	STATEMENT: Albert Schaefer 3989 Poplar Avenue Memphis, Tennessee 38111		
1			$143.14
3	24.23		$ _____
7	62.37		$ _____
9		39.82	$ _____
15	27.89		$ _____
19		26.39	$ _____
21		14.26	$ _____
25		17.82	$ _____

5. Constance Rosetti had $647.13 at the beginning of the day. After counting her money at the end of the day, she had $378.26. How much did she spend during the day?

   $ _____

6. Avron Goldsmith drove his car for one month. At the beginning of the month, his odometer read 26714.6 miles. At the end of the month, his odometer read 27638.3. How many miles did he drive during the month?

   _____

7. Marla Smithson purchased a new car for $13,898.18 last year. This year, a new car with similar equipment costs $15,149.01. How much did the price of the car increase this year?

   $ _____

8. The promoter of a rock concert sold 13,750 tickets for $16.65 each for a total income of $228,937.50. Total expenses were $189,989.14. How much profit did the promoter make?

   $ _____

PRACTICE TEST FOR CHAPTER 7
ADDITION AND SUBTRACTION OF DECIMALS

Complete each of the following problems and then compare your answers with the ones on page 646.

1. Satish Mehra worked 7.25 hours on Monday, 8.2 hours on Tuesday, and 7.8 hours on Wednesday. How many hours did he work during the three days? _____

2. Five autos at the Lane Auto Center required the following gallons of gasoline to fill the tanks: 17.3, 12.8, 8.9, 15.4, and 12.2. How many gallons were purchased for the five cars?

   _____

3. A truck for Dan's Asphalt Paving carried 10.3 tons of asphalt. Paving a shopping center parking lot required 8.7 tons. How much remained on the truck after paving the parking lot?

   _____

4. A jeweler had 12.5 ounces of gold in stock. Creation of a bracelet required 1.8 ounces. How much remained in stock after the bracelet was made? _____

5. Carter Schoolfield earned $725.78 last week. Payroll deductions totaled $169.47. How much remained after payroll deductions? $ _____

CONNECTIONS

7.1 The chart shown below indicates the amount of money, in millions of dollars, spent on various operations paid with financing from Medicare, a government-sponsored health care program. Review the chart and answer the following questions.

(a) How much was spent on knee arthroplasty and prostatectomy operations combined?
$ _____

(b) How much was spent on all operations combined, with the exception of cataract removal/lens insertion operations? $ _____

(c) How much more was spent on cataract removal/lens insertion operations than all other operations combined? $ _____

(d) How much more was spent on coronary angiography operations than on prostatectomy operations? $ _____

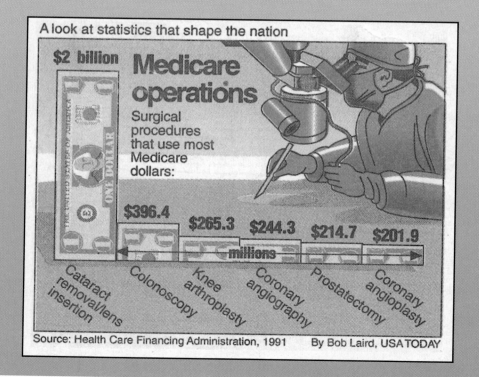

A look at statistics that shape the nation

$2 billion

Medicare operations

Surgical procedures that use most Medicare dollars:

$396.4 $265.3 $244.3 $214.7 $201.9

millions

Cataract removal/lens insertion   Colonoscopy   Knee arthroplasty   Coronary angiography   Prostatectomy   Coronary angioplasty

Source: Health Care Financing Administration, 1991   By Bob Laird, USA TODAY

7.2 The chart shown below indicates the percentage of various age groups who were absent from work for at least part of the week during a recent year, 1992. Review the chart and answer the following questions.

(a) What are the sum of the percentages for the 16–19 and 20–24 age groups? _____

(b) Which two age groups showed the highest percentage of absenteeism? _____

(c) Which age group showed the lowest percentage of absenteeism? _____

(d) In your opinion, are the figures reported for 1992 still valid for workers of today?

_____ Yes _____ No

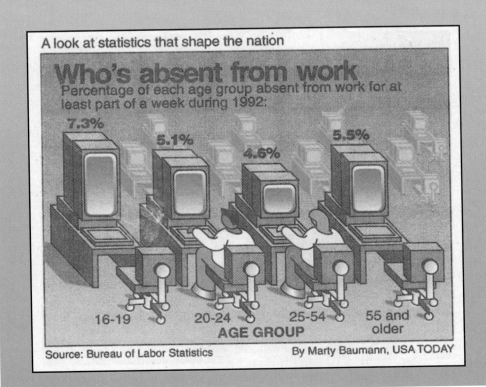

A look at statistics that shape the nation

Who's absent from work
Percentage of each age group absent from work for at least part of a week during 1992:

7.3%   5.1%   4.6%   5.5%

16-19   20-24   25-54   55 and older

AGE GROUP

Source: Bureau of Labor Statistics   By Marty Baumann, USA TODAY

CONNECTIONS

7.1 Royal Furniture Center made the following sale to a customer in Chicago: sofa, $1,950.75; wing chair, $454.95; desk, $725.85; curio, $1,350.50; and end table, $99. The customer was given an $85 discount due to a small scratch on the curio cabinet. An additional $50 special promotional discount was given for each piece of furniture with a price above $1,000. Shipping charges were $75. What was the final amount due for the furniture sale?

$ _____

7.2 The Computer Center store offers a $1,799 original price for a microcomputer system. A $50 delivery charge is required. This system is currently offered for a $125 discount. A laser printer has a $799 price. The Hardware Warehouse offers an equivalent microcomputer system for an $1,899 original price. This store does not require a delivery charge for local deliveries. A $175 discount is offered during a promotional sale campaign. A laser printer has an $819 price. Which store offers the best price for the microcomputer system and printer?

_____ Computer Center

_____ Hardware Warehouse

DECISIONS

ADDITION AND SUBTRACTION OF DECIMALS
Chapter Review and Quick Reference

Topic	Main Point	Typical Example		Text Page
Decimal alignment for addition	Decimal points should be in a vertical line for addition problems.	3.725 + 5.8 + 1.34 = 10.865		114
Decimal alignment for subtraction	Decimal points should be in a vertical line for subtraction problems.	8.24 - 3.1 = 5.14		114
Rounding values	General rule: Round values to four decimal places. Round the answer to two decimal places.	4.27341 + 3.78246 = 8.05587	**Rounded** 4.2734 + 3.7825 = 8.0559 = 8.06	115
Adding zeros for subtraction problems	Add zeros, as needed, to right-justify subtraction problems so that each factor has the same number of decimal places.	2.73 - 1.6128	2.7300 - 1.6128 = 1.1172	116

MULTIPLICATION AND DIVISION OF DECIMALS

Performance Objectives

1. Align the decimal point appropriately in the product and quotient.
2. Complete applications using multiplication.
3. Round values to the appropriate number of decimal places.
4. Complete applications using division.

Business applications in areas such as accounting, finance, statistics, real estate and data processing require a thorough knowledge of multiplication and division of decimal values because many business computations deal with decimal values. This chapter provides skill and knowledge needed to solve problems that involve decimal values.

MULTIPLICATION OF DECIMALS

Multiplication of decimal values is performed in much the same way as multiplication of whole numbers. A difference is that in multiplication of decimal values the decimal point must be placed at the proper position in the answer. The rules for multiplying and dividing decimal values are outlined in Figure 8.1. The rule for determining where the decimal point should be placed in the product is to count from right to left the number of decimal places in the multiplier and multiplicand combined. This is illustrated in Model 8.1, where 4.231 is multiplied by 4.5.

The electronic calculator will automatically place the decimal point.

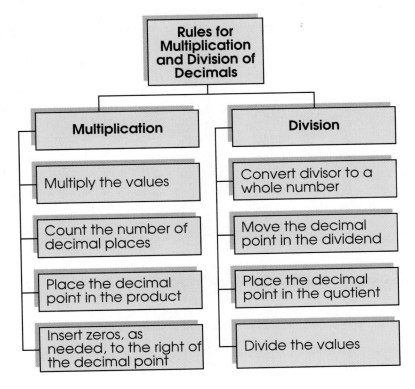

Figure 8.1 Rules for Multiplication and Division of Decimals

MODEL 8.1

Multiply, ignoring the number of decimal places.

Count the total number of decimal places.

Start at the right and count the number of decimal places.

Rule for placing the decimal point in the product

Step 1 Multiply the decimal values as whole numbers.

$$
\begin{array}{r}
4.231 \quad \longleftarrow \text{ multiplicand} \\
\times \quad 4.5 \quad \longleftarrow \text{ multiplier} \\
\hline
21155 \\
16924 \\
\hline
190395 \quad \longleftarrow \text{ product}
\end{array}
$$

Step 2 Count the number of decimal places in the multiplicand and multiplier combined.

4.231 (3 places) + 4.5 (1 place) = 4 decimal places

Step 3 Place the decimal point at the number of places (counting from right to left) in the product that corresponds to the sum obtained in Step 2.

19.0395

Apply Your Skills

4.3753 multiplied by 3.2. What is the product? _____

Whole numbers have an assumed decimal point at the right of the ones place. In Model 8.2, one of the factors is a whole number.

MODEL 8.2

Multiplying a decimal and a whole number

$$
\begin{array}{r}
4.231 \quad \text{multiplicand} \\
\times \quad 23 \quad \text{(0 decimal places)} \\
\hline
12693 \\
8462 \\
\hline
97.313 \quad \text{(3 + 0 = 3 decimal places)}
\end{array}
$$

Apply Your Skills

Georgio Romez earned $10.75 per hour while working 28 hours last week. What were his earnings?

$ _____

Model 8.3 shows how to count decimal places when small decimals are multiplied.

The method in Model 8.3 also applies when several decimal values are multiplied. As shown in Model 8.4, the number of places to the right of the decimal point in the product equals the sum of decimal places in all factors.

Multiplying small decimal nubmers

```
        .003     (3 decimal places)
    x   .0004    (4 decimal places)
    ─────────
    .0000012     (3 + 4 = 7 decimal places)
```

MODEL 8.3

Add zeros, as needed, to count enough places to the right of the decimal point.

Apply Your Skills

A piece of metal is 0.0008 inches in thickness. How thick is a stack of 25 pieces of the metal?

_____

Multiplying a series of decimal factors

```
        2.52     (2 decimal places)
    x    1.2     (1 decimal place)
    ─────────
        504
        252
    ─────────
       3024

    x    2.5     (1 decimal place)
    ─────────
      15120
       6048
    ─────────
     7.5600      (4 decimal places)
```

Note: This product can also be shown as 7.56 to omit the zeros without changing the value of the product.

MODEL 8.4

Zeros are omitted in this example without changing the value of the product.

Apply Your Skills

Three employees each worked 30 hours while earning $12.75 per hour. How much did the 3 employees earn?

$ _____

Electronic calculators will automatically place the decimal point correctly in the product.

ROUNDING NUMBERS

There is no universally accepted rule for deciding how far to carry out a decimal product or quotient. The preceding chapter indicated that computations involving dollars and cents should be carried to five decimal places and rounded to four decimal places and the final answer rounded to two decimal places. That is a good rule for multiplication and division computations as well.

For decimals other than money amounts, a general rule is to carry out the product to the total number of decimal places contained in the two largest factors. For example, the problem 2.34 x 3.583 x 2.3 will have a product rounded to five decimal places, but the problem 2.3 x 1.4 will be rounded to two decimal places. Answers to these problems will be 19.28371 and 3.22 respectively.

A general rule for division is to carry out the decimal place in the quotient to four places or to the number of decimal places in the divisor and the dividend combined, whichever is greater. For example, the problem 0.13 ÷ 0.7 will be rounded to three decimal places, and the quotient will be 0.186.

The rules in this chapter and the preceding chapter for rounding numbers should be used for rounding all problems in this text unless directions indicate otherwise.

You may now complete Performance Application 8.1.

DIVISION OF DECIMALS

Division of decimal values is similar to the division of whole numbers except that correct placement of the decimal in the divisor, dividend, and quotient is essential. Placement of the decimal point is outlined in Model 8.5.

MODEL 8.5

Move the decimal point to make the divisor a whole number.

Move the decimal point the same number of places in the divisor and dividend.

Correct placement of the decimal point in division

Problem: $1.5\overline{)3.525}$

Solution: **Step 1**   If the divisor is not a whole number, move the decimal point to the right of the divisor and move it the same number of places in the dividend.

$$15\overline{)35.25}$$

Step 2   Place a decimal point in the quotient directly above the decimal point in the dividend and then perform the division.

$$
\begin{array}{r}
2.35 \\
15\overline{)35.25} \\
\underline{30} \\
52 \\
\underline{45} \\
75 \\
\underline{75}
\end{array}
$$

Apply Your Skills

Where will the decimal point be placed in the dividend for each of the following problems? Do not perform the division.

(a) 34.892 divided by 2.3 _____

(b) 27.823 divided by 0.75 _____

(c) 3.4 divided by 0.852 _____

Remember that the decimal point in the quotient must be directly above the decimal point in the dividend. Also remember that the decimal point must be moved the same number of places in the dividend as in the divisor (unless the divisor is a whole number). See Figure 8.2.

(a) $.35 \div 7 = .05$

$$
\begin{array}{r}
.05 \\
7\overline{\smash{).35}} \\
\underline{35}
\end{array}
$$

(c) $11.25 \div 5 = 2.25$

$$
\begin{array}{r}
2.25 \\
5\overline{\smash{)11.25}} \\
\underline{10} \\
12 \\
\underline{10} \\
25 \\
\underline{25}
\end{array}
$$

(b) $75 \div .5 = 150$

$$
\begin{array}{r}
150.0 \\
5\overline{\smash{)750.0}} \\
\underline{5} \\
25 \\
\underline{25} \\
00 \\
\underline{00}
\end{array}
$$

(d) $10 \div .3 = 33.33\ 1/3$

$$
\begin{array}{r}
33.33\ 1/3 \\
3\overline{\smash{)100.00}} \\
\underline{9} \\
10 \\
\underline{9} \\
10 \\
\underline{9} \\
10 \\
\underline{9} \\
1
\end{array}
$$

Figure 8.2 Placement of Decimal Point in Division

The decimal point in the quotient should align with the one in the dividend.

Notice that in Figure 8.2 (d) the dividend cannot be divided evenly by the divisor. This is an *infinite number* because the quotient will continue to contain a remainder. In this case, the decimal should be rounded off or shown with the quotient expressed as a decimal combined with a fraction. The final remainder is shown as the numerator and the divisor as the denominator of the fraction. Depending on how many places the quotient

Round money amounts to two decimal places.

was carried, the quotient could have been 33.3 1/3, 33.33 1/3, 33.333 1/3, 33.3333 1/3, and so forth. Zeros can be added to the right of the decimal in the dividend, as needed, to carry the quotient the desired number of places. When calculators are used, the answer must be rounded because the display will not show fractions.

An electronic calculator will automatically place the decimal at the appropriate place in the quotient. The quotient that a calculator would display is underlined in the example below.

$$75 \div .5 = \underline{150}$$

Most problems and examples in the text are formatted to be solved using electronic calculators. Unless your instructor directs otherwise, problems should be solved manually to develop the thought process even if electronic calculators are also used. If calculators are available, problems can be solved both manually and with equipment to provide practice and check accuracy.

There are shortcut procedures that can be used when dividing or multiplying decimal values by multiples of 10. This is an important shortcut since many values are multiples of 10 in a decimal system. If dividing by a multiple of 10, move the decimal place to the left according to the number of zeros in the divisor, as shown in Model 8.6. If multiplying by a multiple of 10, move the decimal point to the right according to the number of zeros in the multiplier.

MODEL 8.6

Multiplying by multiples of 10

563.87 divided by 10 equals 56.387 (one place to the left)
563.87 divided by 100 equals 5.6387 (two places to the left)
42.8372 multiplied by 10 equals 428.372 (one place to the right)
42.8372 multiplied by 100 equals 4,283.72 (two places to the right)

Apply Your Skills

Use shortcut methods to solve each of the following problems.

(a) Howard Steiner worked 36.25 hours while earning $10 per hour. What were his earnings? $ _____

(b) Brenda Garland earned $1,076 last month while working 100 hours. What were her earnings per hour? $ _____

PERFORMANCE APPLICATION 8.1

1. Multiply each of the following problems. Rewrite each problem in vertical columns before completing the multiplication.

(a) 2.4 x 4.2 =

_____

(b) 3.54 x 2.4 =

_____

(c) 14.231 x 3 =

_____

(d) $14.26 x 1.50 =

$ _____

(e) $128.60 x 1.25 =

$ _____

(f) 0.6052 x 5 =

_____

(g) 0.0026 x 4 =

_____

(h) 0.0072 x 7 =

_____

(i) 0.0091 x 16 =

_____

(j) 0.0906 x 1.5 =

_____

(k) 316 x 0.25 =

_____

(l) $40.00 x 0.75 =

$ _____

(m) 0.5 x 0.25 =

_____

(n) 0.26 x 0.48 =

_____

(o) 272 x 0.201 =

_____

(p) 162 x 0.003 =

_____

(q) 297 x 0.0025 =

_____

(r) 318 x 0.000037 =

_____

(s) 0.002 x 0.004 =

_____

(t) 0.08 x .0012 =

_____

2. Multiply each of the following problems. Round off each product to the proper number of places using the general rules presented in the text.

   (a) 3.41 x 6.231 x 1.52 = _____

   (b) 3.54 x 2.5 x 3.2 = _____

   (c) 4.27 x 3.417 x 3.25 = _____

   (d) 4.516 x 2.1 x 3.5 = _____

   (e) 12.578 x 0.05 x 0.025 = _____

   (f) 128.42 x 0.54 x 0.25 = _____

3. Claudia Akins made 257 silk flowers during the week. She is paid 85¢ for each one. What were her total earnings?

   $ _____

4. Will Bernstein worked 40 hours during the week and was paid $9.78 per hour. What was his gross pay?

   $ _____

5. Marcell Perez typed 428 pages of manuscript material for a client. He charged $4.65 per page. How much did he earn for typing the manuscript?

   $ _____

PERFORMANCE APPLICATION 8.2

1. Divide each of the following problems. Rewrite each problem with the decimal point properly placed. Where rounding is needed, round problems to the proper place. Round problems involving money to two places.

(a) $54.25 \div 35 =$

_____

(b) $14.875 \div 3.5 =$

_____

(c) $10.44 \div 7.2 =$

_____

(d) $49.3125 \div .25 =$

_____

(e) $85 \div 2.5 =$

_____

(f) $96 \div 3.2 =$

_____

(g) $68 \div 5.2 =$

_____

(h) $79 \div 4.6 =$

_____

(i) $82 \div 0.5 =$

_____

(j) $75 \div 1.04 =$

_____

(k) $36.24 \div 8 =$

_____

(l) $96.48 \div 75 =$

_____

(m) $63.28 \div 8 =$

_____

(n) $0.69 \div 0.75 =$

_____

(o) $0.144 \div 0.03 =$

_____

2. Bowery Enterprises had a net profit of $12,627.75 for the year. The profit was divided equally among 3 partners. How much did each partner receive?

   $ _____

3. Joe Cobb had to travel 1,786.6 miles in 4 days. On the average, how many miles did he travel each day?

   _____

4. Jewell Gross drove 16,471 miles and used 1,470.6 gallons of gasoline. How many miles per gallon did she travel?

   _____

5. Bob Randolph assembled 3,800 pieces in 4.75 days. If he assembled an equal number of pieces each day, how many did he assemble each day?

   _____

6. Rochelle Lawson, a television performer, signed an annual contract for $360,565.25. For each of the 365 days in the year, how much will her daily earnings be?

   $ _____

7. A professional baseball player in Japan hit 361 home runs in 9.5 years. On the average, how many home runs did he hit each year?

   _____

8. Boxwood, Inc. employed 720 employees during the year. They missed a total of 5,940 days due to illness. On the average, how many days did each employee miss due to illness?

   _____

9. Roger Whittaker earned $371.64 for working 38 hours. How much did he earn per hour?

   $ _____

PRACTICE TEST FOR CHAPTER 8
MULTIPLICATION AND DIVISION OF DECIMALS

Complete each of the following problems and then compare your answers with the ones on page 646.

1. What is 27.437 multiplied by 3.2? _____

2. What is 160.75 divided by 0.25? _____

3. A recent study at Marz Corporation indicated that each letter produced in the office cost $6.78. What was the cost of 53 letters produced last week? $ _____

4. Ed Harris, an attorney, worked 5.25 hours on a case. His partner, Carla Cliff, worked 6.5 hours. They were paid $1,880 for the job. What were the earnings per hour for the job?

    $ _____

5. A major league baseball player signed a $780,000 one-year contract. An estimate was made that he will bat an average of 4.25 times in each of 152 games. Based on this estimate, how much will he earn (rounded to the nearest cent) for each time at bat? $ _____

CONNECTIONS

8.1 The following ad appeared in a newspaper during a special promotion by a hotel discount chain. What was the daily rate per person (a) if 2 persons stayed in the room and (b) if 3 persons stayed in the room and (c) if 4 persons stayed in the room?

(a) $ _____

(b) $ _____

(c) $ _____

Get a great room for just a few clams.

FROM $29* PER ROOM 1-4 PEOPLE

8.2 The following chart shows taxes levied on a pack of cigarettes (20 cigarettes per pack) by selected states. What were the taxes per cigarette in the following states (a) Massachusetts, (b) Minnesota, (c) Kentucky, and (d) Virginia? (Do not round.)

(a) $ _____

(b) $ _____

(c) $ _____

(d) $ _____

A look at statistics that shape the nation

Cigarette taxes vary wildly

Massachusetts
Minnesota
Connecticut

N. Carolina
Kentucky
Virginia

Highest state taxes on pack of cigarettes...[1]

51¢

48¢

45¢

1. New York's new budget calls for a 56¢ tax.

...lowest

Source: The Associated Press

By Cliff Vancura, USA TODAY

CONNECTIONS

143

8.1 Jake Hawkins, an accounting clerk, was offered a job with an option of making $15.65 per hour. He was also offered a second job that paid $524 per week with an opportunity for an annual bonus. Assuming that Jake works 40 hours per week for the full year (52 weeks), what annual bonus is needed in the second job in order to match annual earnings in the first job?

$ _____

8.2 Review a newspaper and/or business-related periodical in the library of your institution to determine ways or situations in which decimal values are being used in a business environment. Provide a list of examples for decimal values being used.

_____

_____

_____

_____

_____

_____

_____

_____

_____

DECISIONS

MULTIPLICATION AND DIVISION OF DECIMALS
Chapter Review and Quick Reference

Topic	Main Point	Typical Example	Text Page
Decimal placement: Multiplication	Decimal placement in the product equals the total decimal places in the multiplicand and multiplier.	Multiplicand 3.65 Multiplier x 2.5 Product 9.125	128
Rounding: Multiplication	Round to the sum of the number of decimal places in the two largest factors.	3.45 x 1.255 x 3.5 = 15.154125 rounded to 15.15413	129
Rounding: Division	Round to the greater of four places or the sum of the decimal places in the divisor and dividend.	2.45 ÷ 1.3 = 1.8846153 rounded to 1.8846	129
Rounding: Dollars	Round individual factors to four places and the final answer to two places.	$37.27 times 27.5 = $1,024.925 rounded to $1,024.93	129
Decimal placement: Division	The divisor is converted to a whole number. The decimal point is then moved an equal number of places in the dividend.	65.17 ÷ 3.5 becomes 651.7 ÷ 35	130

COMMUNICATIONS

Read the following memorandum and answer the questions.

```
                        Memorandum

To:    C. Ellsworth

From:  L. Swenson

Date:  March 19, 19XX

Re:    Payment Plan for Current Payables

As of today we have $5,920.43 in payables due and just
$4,880.28 in available cash. I have prioritized our
obligations and propose that we pay Simms Co. and Myers
Brothers in full; Overland Express and Evanrud Associates
three-quarters now and the balance in 30 days; and Vision
Advertising one fourth now and the balance in 30 days. We
will be able to pay the balances and get back on track
when we receive the $18,900.00 due from the Geffen project
in two weeks.

I am confident that the various vendors will agree to the
payment arrangements. Please let me know if you agree with
the plan and I will authorize the checks.

        Vendor                  Amount Due

    Simms Co.                   $2,825.14
    Myers Brothers                 684.25
    Overland Express               905.82
    Evanrud Associates             218.86
    Vision Advertising           1,286.36
```

1. How much does L. Swenson propose to pay to each vendor now?

2. What will be due to each vendor in 30 days?

3. Assume that you know Simms Co. and Vision Advertising (due to a contract clause) must be paid in full but that the other vendors will tolerate partial payment. Write a memo to L. Swenson to explain the modified payment plan. Supply amounts to pay now. Remember that total payments cannot exceed available cash.

UNIT 2 SPREADSHEET APPLICATION 1:
WORD PROCESSING CHARGES

The spreadsheet shown below is used to determine word processing charges. Customers are charged a rate per line that depends on the type of document. The amount charged is computed by multiplying the number of lines produced by the cost per line. Show these amounts in Column F. Show the sum of the amounts charged in Cell F19.

	A	B	C	D E	F	G
1	Clark Steno Service			**WORD PROCESSING CHARGES**		
2	--					
3	Job	Type of	Lines	Cost	Amount	Call
4	Number	Document	Produced	Per Line	Charged	761-2047
5	--					for
6	P23	Memo	120	0.10		Prompt
7	P24	Letter	175	0.09		Service
8	P25	Memo	128	0.10		*********
9	P26	Table	95	0.14		Please
10	P27	Letter	185	0.09		pay
11	P28	Letter	173	0.09		within
12	P29	Memo	145	0.10		15 days.
13	P30	Table	115	0.14		*********
14	P31	Manuscript	745	0.12		Thanks
15	P32	Letter	165	0.09		for your
16	P33	Memo	125	0.10		business.
17	P34	Memo	132	0.10		*********
18	--					
19	Amount Due					

Complete the spreadsheet and answer the following questions:

1. How many lines were produced for Job P26? _____

2. How many lines were produced for Job P34? _____

3. How many jobs were included on the report? _____

4. What type of document was completed for Job P28?

_____

5. What amount was charged for Job P27? $ _____

6. What amount was charged for Job P31? $ _____

7. What amount was charged for Job P33? $ _____

8. For what type of document is the highest cost per line charged?

_____

9. For which job was the highest amount charged?

_____

10. What was the total amount billed for all the jobs?

$ _____

UNIT 2 SPREADSHEET APPLICATION 2:
MILEAGE ANALYSIS

The spreadsheet shown below is used to determine the miles per gallon (called the *mileage* or *MPG*) and fuel cost for a fleet of automobiles. Divide the miles driven by the gallons of fuel used to compute the number of miles per gallon (round to one decimal place). Multiply the fuel used by the fuel cost per gallon to compute the fuel cost (round to two decimal places). Show the miles per gallon in column D. Show the fuel cost in column F. Show the sum of each column in Row 19.

	A	B	C	D	E	F	G	H
1	City Fleet Service			**MPG ANALYSIS**				
2	--							
3	Vehicle	Miles	Fuel	Miles per		Fuel		**********
4	ID	Driven	Used	Gallon		Cost		**********
5	--------------------------------------							**********
6	A41D8	876.8	48.3					Fuel cost
7	B44B7	759.7	45.7					per gallon
8	D4513	762.5	42.6					$0.869
9	G44N36	763.3	40.1					**********
10	H23H51	812.9	43.6					**********
11	JJ345A	805.2	45.7					**********
12	M142M3	653.4	38.7					
13	P33P35	746.8	42.3					
14	P45N2	800.5	42.7					
15	U7610	783.7	40.2					
16	V44F5	752.4	39.5					
17	Y6522	812.1	42.7					
18	--------------------------------------							
19	Totals			********				

Complete the spreadsheet and answer the following questions:

1. What was the MPG for Vehicle D4513? _____

2. What was the MPG for Vehicle P45N2? _____

3. What was the fuel cost per gallon? $ _____

4. What was the fuel cost for Vehicle H23H51? $ _____

5. What was the fuel cost for Vehicle U7610? $ _____

6. Which vehicle has the lowest MPG? _____

7. Which vehicle had the highest fuel cost? _____

8. How many vehicles had MPGs greater than 18.0?

    _____

9. What was the amount of total fuel used by the fleet?

    _____

10. What was the cost of total fuel used? $ _____

UNIT 2 SELF-TEST DECIMAL AMOUNTS IN BUSINESS

1. Write the following fractional values out in words to show how they are read or pronounced.

    (a) 0.5   _____

    (b) 0.08   _____

    (c) 0.013   _____

    (d) 0.0018   _____

    (e) 0.00007   _____

    (f) 4.02   _____

    (g) 5.0071   _____

    (h) 17.123   _____

2. Convert the following fractions to decimals or decimals to fractions as indicated. (Reduce fractions to lowest terms.)

	Decimal	Fraction
(a)	0.3	_____
(b)	0.25	_____
(c)	2.75	_____
(d)	5.8	_____
(e)	_____	7/10
(f)	_____	4/5
(g)	_____	1/2
(h)	_____	5/8

3. Add the following decimal amounts with the decimal points correctly aligned. (Do not round off.)

    (a) 17.2 + 6.3   = _____

    (b) 25.15 + 16.08   = _____

    (c) 13.001 + 25.08 + 6.27 = _____

(d) 6.17 + 0.07 + 3.0098   = _____

(e) 1.81 + 807.2 + 16.018   = _____

(f) 8.121 + 2.13 + 301.01   = _____

4. Round the following numbers to the places indicated.

(a) 567 to the nearest ten   _____

(b) 3,492 to the nearest thousand   _____

(c) 555 to the nearest ten   _____

(d) 65.549 to one decimal place   _____

(e) 2.518 to two decimal places   _____

(f) 10.752 to one decimal place   _____

(g) 8.2384 to three decimal places   _____

5. Complete the following subtractions. (Do not round off.)

(a) 13.57 - 4.23   = _____

(b) 84.027 - 5.009   = _____

(c) 37.008 - 17.215   = _____

(d) 38.251 - 15.3162   = _____

(e) 618.25 - 52.819   = _____

(f) 315.537 - 106.658   = _____

6. Bonnie Oswalt owed $189.15 on her doctor's bill. She paid $13.89. How much remains to be paid?

   $ _____

7. Complete each of the following multiplications.

   (a) 3.5 x 1.2   = _____

   (b) 62.87 x 0.5   = _____

   (c) 20.88 x 5.25   = _____

   (d) 152.3 x 3.125   = _____

   (e) 618 x 0.005   = _____

   (f) 0.02 x 0.17   = _____

8. Complete each of the following divisions. Round each answer to the proper place.

   (a) 75.45 ÷ 15   = _____
   (b) 52.56 ÷ 0.8   = _____
   (c) 64.48 ÷ 1.6   = _____
   (d) 32.20 ÷ 9.2   = _____
   (e) 0.128 ÷ 0.75   = _____
   (f) 79 ÷ 4.6   = _____
   (g) 181.86 ÷ 3.5   = _____
   (h) 204.736 ÷ 5.6   = _____
   (i) 16.28 ÷ 0.005   = _____
   (j) 9.96 ÷ 0.75   = _____

UNIT 3

Percentage Amounts in Business

When making a large purchase, have you ever tried to figure out how much it will cost you to finance (pay over time) as opposed to paying cash for the purchase? Open up your wallet or purse and look at the credit cards you have acquired. Attached to each of these cards are related costs. Most credit cards are not provided free of charge to the user. Do you know what percentage you are paying in finance charges for purchases you make using one of these cards? Have you taken time to calculate the annual fees you may be paying in addition to finance charges (particularly if you have several cards)? These applications involve using percentages in business mathematics.

Included in this unit are activities relating to basic percentage computations using amount, base, and rate. Real-life applications using these fundamentals are included relating to discounts on purchases and finance charges.

CONVERSION OF PERCENTAGES

Performance Objectives

1. Convert decimals to percents.
2. Convert percents to decimals.
3. Convert fractions to percents.
4. Define and apply the percentage formula to business applications.

Percentages are commonly used in both business and personal activities. A discount on an airline ticket purchase, interest on a home mortgage, sales taxes, and discounts on clothing purchases are only a few examples of applications that require percentage computations.

CONVERSIONS

The terms *percent* and *percentage* are often confused. Percent is the *rate* and has a percent sign after the number, such as 14%. Percentage is the *number represented by the percent.* For example, a professional basketball team won 80%, or 40, of the 50 games it played during the season. In this example, 80% is the percent and 40 is the percentage. Because percentage refers to an amount, the term *amount* will be used in chapter discussions and illustrations in place of the term *percentage.*

Rate is another way of expressing numbers as a *fractional part of 100.* A rate, such as 80%, means 80 parts out of 100 possible parts. This rate may also be written as 80/100. When converting a rate to a fraction, the numerator of the fraction is the specific rate, and the denominator is always 100. The fraction is normally reduced to its lowest terms. In this example, 80/100 reduces to 4/5.

A rate can be converted to a fraction as shown above. Other conversions include converting decimals to rates, rates to decimals, and fractions to rates.

Figure 9.1 illustrates the relationship between 80%, 20%, and 100%. The entire circle represents 100%. The games won represent 80 parts out of 100, or 80%. The games lost represent 20 parts out of 100, or 20%. The entire circle represents the total games played, or 100%. This chart was completed using graphic software and a microcomputer.

Percent is expressed as a rate, such as 25%.

Percentage is expressed as an amount, such as $14.25.

The percent or rate is a part of the value 100.

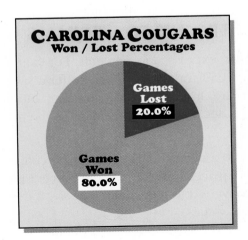

Figure 9.1 Percentage Relationships

CONVERTING DECIMALS TO PERCENTS

Change the decimal value to a percent by moving the decimal point two places to the right.

As shown in Model 9.1, a decimal is converted to a percent by (1) moving the decimal point two places to the right and (2) adding a percent sign at the end of the value.

MODEL 9.1

Conversion effectively multiplies the decimal value by the value 100. For example, .75 times 100 = 75.

Converting decimals to percents

Problem: Convert the following decimal values to rates expressed as a percent: .75, .253, .5, 3, 2.25, and .007.

Solution:

.75	=	75%
.253	=	25.3 %
.5	=	50%
3.	=	300%
2.25	=	225%
.007	=	.7 %

Apply Your Skills

Howard Steinberg divided his insurance deduction ($21.60) by his weekly earnings ($480) to compute the following decimal value: 0.045. What percent of insurance is represented by this value? _____4.5%_____

Notice that each conversion required the decimal point to be moved two places to the right. Some conversions require caution. For example, .007 converts to .7%, which is read seven-tenths percent, which is less than one percent. Notice that when .5 was converted to 50%, a zero was added in order to move the decimal point two places to the right.

CONVERTING PERCENTS TO DECIMALS

Convert a percent to a decimal value by moving the decimal point two places to the left.

Computations are often expressed as percents. For example, the cost of a dress may be reduced 25%, or an airline may offer a special fare that is 20% less than the regular fare. In order to make a computation, the percent should first be converted to a decimal. This conversion is the reverse of the one illustrated above.

To convert a percent to a decimal, (1) drop the percent symbol and (2) move the decimal point two places to the *left*. If the percent includes a fraction, the fraction should be converted to a decimal. Model 9.2 demonstrates conversion of percents to decimal values.

Converting percents to decimal values

Problem: Convert the following percents to decimal values: 24%, 15.8%, 125%, 75.3%, .8%, and 7 3/4%.

Solution:

24%	=	.24
15.8%	=	.158
125%	=	1.25
75.3 %	=	.753
.8%	=	.008
7 3/4%	=	.0775

MODEL 9.2

Conversion to a decimal effectively divides the percent by the value 100. For example, 24% ÷ 100 = .24

Apply Your Skills

Top Rank Financial Group estimates that 28.5% of their employees will be eligible for retirement within 6 years. What is the decimal equivalent for this percent?

0.285

CONVERTING FRACTIONS TO PERCENTS

A fraction can be converted to a rate expressed as a percent by (1) dividing the numerator by the denominator, (2) moving the decimal point two places to the right, and (3) adding the percent sign, as shown in Model 10.3.

Divide the numerator by the denominator and then convert the decimal value to a percent.

Converting fractions to percents

Problem: Convert the following fractions to percents: 3/4, 1/2, and 1/25.

Solution:

3/4	=	.75	=	75%
1/2	=	.5	=	50%
1/25	=	.04	=	4%

MODEL 9.3

Apply Your Skills

City College normally pays 7/10 of the moving expenses for each new faculty member. What is the percent equivalent for this fraction? *7/10 = 0.7 = 70%*

BUSINESS APPLICATIONS OF PERCENTAGE

All percentage problems use the following basic formula: *Amount = Base times Rate* or abbreviated A = B × R *or* B × R = A (if using a calculator). In this formula, *A* is amount, *B* is base, and *R* is rate. The relationship of these three components is shown in Figure 9.2.

Many business problems require percentage computation.

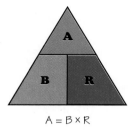

$$A = B \times R$$

Figure 9.2 Percentage formula

In this diagram, the horizontal line represents a fraction bar, and the vertical line represents a multiplication sign.

If you know the amount and the base and you want to find the rate, cover the R section. This gives the formula for the rate:

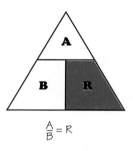

$$\frac{A}{B} = R$$

Figure 9.3 Rate Formula

If you know the amount and the rate and you want to find the base, cover the B section to get the formula for the base:

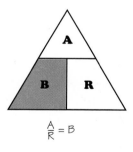

$$\frac{A}{R} = B$$

Figure 9.4 Base Formula

If you are trying to find the amount, cover the A section to get the formula for the amount:

B × R = A

Figure 9.5 Amount Formula

Notice that the percent is converted to a decimal value prior to making the calculation, as shown in Model 9.4

Computing amount when base and rate are known

Problem: The Seaside Fruit Stand estimates that 25% of the fruit will sell during the day. If the fruit is valued at $1,500, what amount of the fruit will sell today?

Solution: Base   x   Rate   =   Amount

$1,500   x   .25   = $375

Apply Your Skills

City College found that 45 percent of its 780 faculty members are female. How many female faculty members are employed at the college?   *351*

MODEL 9.4

Base and rate are known.

The amount may be larger than the base because the rate can be larger than 100%. However, the same basic computation is required. See Model 9.5.

Computing amount when rate is greater than 100%

Problem: Betty Weaver, a salesperson, had a $2,500 sales goal for the week. Her sales were 110 percent of her goal. How much were her sales?

Solution: Base   x   Rate   =   Amount

$2,500   x   1.10   = $2,750

Apply Your Skills

Brad Martin estimates that his sales quota will be 115 percent of this year's $240,000 quota. What will his new quota amount be? $ *276,000*

MODEL 9.5

The rate may also be expressed in fractions instead of percents, as shown in Model 9.6.

MODEL 9.6

Expressing rate as a fraction

Problem: The Ace Furniture Store had 80 recliners in the warehouse. During a rainstorm, 1/4 of the recliners were damaged. How many were damaged? How many were not damaged?

Solution:

Base	x	Rate	=	Amount
80	x	1/4	=	20 Damaged
80	x	3/4	=	60 Not damaged

Apply Your Skills

A review of attendance records indicated that 1/5 of the 800 employees were absent for one or more days last week. How many did **not** miss work last week?

160 - 800 = 640

PERFORMANCE APPLICATION 9.1

1. Convert each of the following percents to a decimal and a fraction. The first problem is completed as an example.

No.	Percent	Decimal Equivalent	Fractional Equivalent
	20%	.20 (or .2)	20/100, reduced to 1/5
1	30%	.30 (or .3)	30/100, reduced to
2	5%	.05 (or .05)	
3	8%	.08 (or .08)	
4	7%	.07 (or .07)	
5	15%	.15 (or	

2. Compute the amount for each of the following problems. Round answers to two decimal places.

(a) 52% of $520   = $ _2,70.4_

(b) 3% of $1,640   = $ _49.20_

(c) 20% of $1,840   = $ _368_

(d) 1/2% of $3,640   = $ _1,820_

(e) 4 1/2% of $764   = $ _34.38_

(f) 8% of $514.85   = $ _41,188_

(g) 7% of $316.38   = $ _22.15_

(h) 17 3/4% of $42   = $ _7.45_

3. Last year a musical production was attended by 15,500 persons. This year's attendance was 92% of last year's attendance. How many attended this year?

_____14,260_____   15,500 92%
                    X .92
                    14.260

4. The Monroe City Council voted to place a 2% tax on personal incomes. If the average employee in Monroe had income of $14,514, how much average tax was levied on each employee?

$ _____290.28_____

5. Binford Peeples made $820 per week. If he received a raise of 8%, find the amount of his (a) raise and (b) new salary.

(a) $ _____65.60_____ + 820 = 885.60
(b) $ _____885.60_____

6. Bert Brown and Clara Johnson were partners in a business with an annual profit of $64,500. Mr. Brown received 47% of the net profit, and Ms. Johnson received 53% of the net profit. How much did (a) Mr. Brown and (b) Ms. Johnson receive?

(a) $ _____30,315_____ 64,500 X .47
(b) $ _____34,185_____ 64,500 X .53

7. Randy Schwartz purchased a condominium for $85,500. The depreciation allowance for tax purposes was 5% per year. How much was the annual depreciation allowance for the condominium?

$ _____4,2750_____   85,500   5 %
                      X   .05   = .05
                      42750   = 50%

8. Roxanne Adams owned a bond worth $2,000 that paid interest at 8 1/2% per year. How much interest did she earn each year on the bond?

$ _____170_____   2,000   8.50%
                   X .085   =. 085%
                   170

PERFORMANCE APPLICATION 9.2

1. The salaries and merit raise indexes for six employees are shown below. Multiply the salary amount by the raise index rate to compute the new salary amount.

(a) Salary $1,500.00
Raise Index 108%
New Salary $ 1,620

(b) Salary $1,450.00
Raise Index 109%
New Salary $ 1,580.50

(c) Salary $1,670.00
Raise Index 110 1/2% = 1.105
New Salary $ 1,845.35

(d) Salary $1,548.00
Raise Index 112 1/2%
New Salary $

(e) Salary $1,476.00
Raise Index 104 3/4%
New Salary $

(f) Salary $1,950.00
Raise Index 111%
New Salary $

2. Use the formula, Rate x Base = Amount, to find the following:

    Rate X Base = Amount

    (a) 9/10 of 650 = _585_

    (b) 4/5 of 785 = _____

    (c) 3/8 of 248 = _____

    (d) 5/6 of 66 = _____

    (e) 3/4 of 76 = _____

    (f) 5/7 of 56 = _____

    (g) 2/3 of 780 = _____

    (h) 1/12 of 144 = _____

    (i) 1/9 of 162 = _____

3. Dr. Ernest Bishop had a gross earned income of $120,000. Of this amount, 42% represented income from patients who paid cash for their medical services, and 58% represented income from patients who charged their medical services. How much of the gross earned income was from (a) cash patients and (b) charge patients?

    (a) $ _____

    (b) $ _____

4. The building owned by Brodnex Jewelry Store had an assessed value of $220,000 for property tax purposes. Tax rates were as follows: city, 3.6%; county, 5.3%; and special business, 2.5%. How much tax was owed on the building for (a) city, (b) county, and (c) special business taxes?

    (a) $ _____

    (b) $ _____

    (c) $ _____

5. Bill White owned a house valued at $120,000 and furniture valued at $25,000. The house was insured at 80% of its value, and the furniture was insured at 65% of its value. For how much was (a) the house insured and (b) the furniture insured? Assuming that the above amounts represented realistic values, (c) How much would Mr. White lose if the house and furniture were completely destroyed by fire?

(a) $ _____

(b) $ _____

(c) $ _____

6. Canty Importers had annual sales of $250,000 during the first year of operation. Second-year sales were projected to be 125% of first-year sales. Third-year sales were projected to be 130% of second-year sales. What are the projected sales for the (a) second year and (b) third year?

(a) $ _____

(b) $ _____

7. The Wilson Florist Shop used 2,600 liters of gasoline last year in its delivery truck. By purchasing a more fuel-efficient truck, the company would realize an estimated 7% savings in gasoline next year. If this were true, (a) how much gasoline would be saved next year, and (b) how much gasoline would be used next year?

(a) _____

(b) _____

8. Connie Gaines had a monthly salary of $2,400. Deductions were made as follows: payroll taxes, 28%; credit union, 8%; and savings account, 12 1/2%. How much was deducted from her check for (a) payroll taxes, (b) credit union, and (c) savings account?

(a) $ _____

(b) $ _____

(c) $ _____

PRACTICE TEST FOR CHAPTER 9
CONVERSION OF PERCENTAGES

Complete each of the following problems and then compare your answers with the ones on page 647.

1. Holly Satterfield earned $42,500 last year. She received notice that an 8.5% raise will be provided. What were the (a) raise amount and (b) salary after the raise?

    (a) $ _3612.50_

    (b) $ _46,112.50_

2. City Finance sold an $8,000 bond at the beginning of the year. The bond paid 7.5% interest during the year. How much did the bond earn last year?
    $ _____

3. Dr. Bernard DeCarlo had $140,500 income and $80,200 expenses last year. He estimates that his income will increase by 8% and that his expenses will increase by 6.5%. What amount will the (a) income and (b) expenses increase next year?

    (a) $ _____

    (b) $ _____

4. Capital Jewelry Store offered a $6,500 engagement ring for a 45% discount during a special sale. What were the (a) discount and (b) discounted sales price amounts?

    (a) $ _____

    (b) $ _____

5. Cruz Novelty Store had $180,000 gross sales during their first year of operation. Projections were made that second year sales would be 120% of first year sales and that third year sales would be 120% of second year sales. What were the (a) second-year and (b) third-year projections?

    (a) $ _____

    (b) $ _____

9.1 The chart shown below indicates the percent of women who skip annual exams with gynecologists for various reasons. Assume that there are 46,000 women in a city located in a nearby state and that the women are representative of the survey results shown in the chart. How many women will skip the exam for (a) cost/no insurance, (b) too busy, and (c) other (fear, procrastination) reasons?

(a) _____

(b) _____

(c) _____

CONNECTIONS

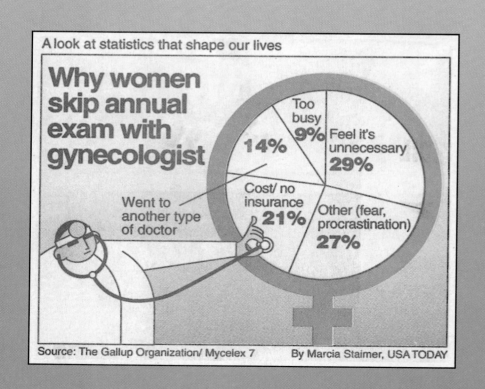

A look at statistics that shape our lives

Why women skip annual exam with gynecologist

Too busy 9%

Feel it's unnecessary 29%

14%

Went to another type of doctor

Cost/ no insurance 21%

Other (fear, procrastination) 27%

Source: The Gallup Organization/ Mycelex 7   By Marcia Staimer, USA TODAY

9.2 The advertisement shown below was used to promote a special furniture store warehouse clearance sale. Lane recliners have a $299 price. A count indicated that there were 70 recliners available for the sale. The recliners will be reduced by 40 percent of the price. What are (a) the total amount of reduction for the 70 recliners and (b) the sale price for each recliner?

(a) $ _____

(b) $ _____

9.1 Mendez and Diaz, Attorneys, had $80,000 gross income from 240 clients last month. Records indicate that 1/4 of the clients were late making account payments last month. Diaz decides to leave the partnership and form a separate law office. Ninety-six of the clients, which provided $44,400 of the gross income, are represented by Diaz. Based on the above figures, what (a) percent of the clients and (b) percent of the gross earnings remain with Mendez?

(a) _____

(b) _____

9.2 Review the current edition of the daily newspaper in your area. Based on advertisements, articles, or other information in the newspaper, develop three problems relating to use of percentage in business. State the problem and then provide a solution to the problem. Compare your problems with the ones developed by other members of your class.

DECISIONS

CONVERSION OF PERCENTAGES
Chapter Review and Quick Reference

Topic	Main Point	Typical Example	Text Page
Percent	Percent is expressed as a rate.	An 8% raise was provided.	157
Percentage	Percentage refers to an amount.	A $700 raise was provided.	157
Converting decimals to percents	A decimal value can be converted to a percent by moving the decimal point two places to the right.	0.735 = 73.5% 0.008 = 0.8% 1.15 = 115%	158
Converting percents to decimals	A percent can be converted to a decimal value by moving the decimal point two places to the left.	73% = 0.73 15.5% = 0.155 112% = 1.12	158
Converting fractions to percents	The numerator is first divided by the denominator. Then the decimal is converted to a percent.	1/4 = 0.25 0.25 = 25%	159
Amount	The base is multiplied by the rate to compute the amount.	A $42,000 salary was raised by 8%. What is the raise amount? Base: $ 42,000 x Rate: 0.08 = Amount $ 3,360	161

Base and Rate Applications

Performance Objectives

1. Determine the relationship of percents to numbers.
2. Determine the relationships between amount, base, and rate.
3. Convert decimals to percents.
4. Determine exact computations using aliquot parts.

Percentage amounts in business were introduced in Chapter 10. This chapter expands the discussion of percentage amounts to include computations for base and rate.

OVERVIEW OF BASE AND RATE

The *amount* (A) is obtained by multiplying the base by the rate. The *rate* (R) is a percent, fraction, or decimal that indicates which part of the base is to be used in the calculation. The *base* (B) represents the entire amount and always has a value of 100%. Examples in this chapter show the relationships between the amount, base, and rate and how each is computed.

The chart shown in Figure 10.1 can be used to illustrate relationships that exist between the amount, base, and rate. Notice that computations relate directly to the location of factors in the chart and that two known factors can be used to compute the third unknown factor. (1) The amount over base equals rate **or** (2) the amount over rate equals base **or** (3) the base times the rate equals the amount. Refer to this chart often while making computations in this chapter and later chapters. This same principle applies to many business mathematical computations, such as determining interest on loan amounts or determining commissions for marketing representatives, which are included in later chapters. Part of the problem-solving activity is to appropriately identify the amount, base, and rate. Then, the mechanics require that the correct formula be used.

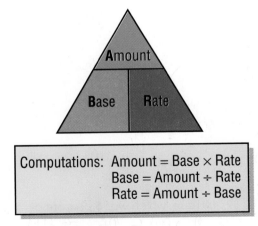

Figure 10.1 Amount/Base/Rate Relationships

If two factors are known, the other factor can be easily computed.

REVIEW OF PERCENTAGE

The formula *Base x Rate = Amount* was introduced in Chapter 9 and is always used to compute the percentage (amount). See Model 10.1.

**MODEL
10.1**

*Amount =
Base x Rate*

Computing the percentage

Problem: The Novelty Shoppe estimates that 5% of its daily charge sales will be uncollectible. If the shop's daily charge sales today were $3,500, how much will be uncollectible?

Solution: Base   x   Rate   =   Amount

        $3,500   x   .05   = $175

- -

Apply Your Skills

Dietz Manufacturing estimated that 3 percent of its 900 employees will be absent next week. How many employees were estimated to be absent?

$900 \times .03 = 27$

COMPUTING THE BASE

The same three elements needed to compute the amount are needed to compute the base. The following formula is used to compute the base: *Amount ÷ Rate = Base*. See Model 10.2.

**MODEL
10.2**

*Base =
Amount ÷ Rate*

Computing the base

Problem: Emily Gomez earned $80 in commissions on her job. If the commission rate was 20%, how much in sales were required to provide the commission?

Solution: Amount   ÷   Rate   =   Base

        $80   ÷   .20   = $400

- -

Apply Your Skills

Frank Fraum received a $2,200 raise, which was 5 percent of his annual salary. What was his annual salary? $ $2,200 ÷ .05 = $44,000$

You may now complete Performance Application 10.1.

COMPUTING THE RATE

If the amount and base are known, the rate can be computed by using the following formula: *Amount ÷ Base = Rate*. See Model 10.3.

Computing the rate

Problem: Emily Gomez received $80 in sales commission. If her daily sales were $400, what was her rate of commission?

Solution: Amount ÷ Base = Rate

$80 ÷ $400 = .20 or 20 %

- -

Apply Your Skills

Katz Tire Store paid $80 for a tire and then priced the tire to make a $32 profit. What was their rate of profit based on the cost of the tire? *$32 ÷ 80 = 0.4 = 40%*

MODEL 10.3

The rate will be computed as a decimal and then converted to a percent.

Rate = Amount/Base

$R = \dfrac{A}{B}$

$A = B \times R$

When working with problems involving amount, base, and rate, the missing element can be computed if the other two elements are known. In these instances, analyze the problem carefully to determine which two elements are known so that the appropriate formula will be used to determine the element that is not known.

RATE OF PERCENT INCREASE

The same basic formula can be used to determine the rate of increase, as shown in Model 10.4.

Notice that the basic formula was used to compute the rate. The amount ($1,760) was divided by the base ($22,000) to compute the 8% rate (Amount ÷ Base = Rate).

MODEL
10.4

First compute the amount and then the rate of increase.

Computing rate of increase

Problem: Robert Newport earned $22,000 last year. His salary this year is $23,760. What was his rate of increase?

Solution: **Step 1** Find the *amount* of increase.

Current salary	-	Previous salary	=	Amount of increase
$23,760	-	$22,000	=	$1,760

Step 2 Find the *rate* of increase

Amount of increase	÷	Previous salary	=	Rate of increase
$1,760	÷	$22,000	=	.08 or 8%

Apply Your Skills

Allen and Palvia, Accountants, employed 120 people last year. This year, there are 132 persons employed in the firm. What was the rate of increase?

Handwritten:
Current employ - Prev. E = A of I
132 - 120 = 12

A of I ÷ P. E = Rate of Inc
12 ÷ 120 = 0.10

10 %

RATE OF PERCENT DECREASE

The rate of percent may represent an increase as shown in Model 10.4, or it may represent a decrease. In either case, the computations are similar. Model 10.5 illustrates computation of the rate of percent decrease.

MODEL
10.5

Computing rate of decrease

Problem: The Easy Stop Grocery had 780 customers last week. This week there were only 663 customers—a decrease of 117 customers (780-663=117). What was the rate of decrease from last week?

Solution:

Customer decrease	÷	Customers last week	=	Rate of decrease
117	÷	780	=	.15 or 15%

Handwritten:
B A
E E Decrease
1400 - 1050 = 350
Employees Employee
decrease ÷ Rate of d.
350 ÷ 1400 = 0.25
B

Apply Your Skills

Micro Tech, a national microcomputer distribution center, employed 1,400 employees last year. This year, the firm reduced expenses by cutting the work force to 1,050 employees. What was the rate of decrease?

Handwritten: 25%

ALIQUOT PARTS

Using aliquot parts can make some types of multiplication problems easier to solve and the solutions more accurate. An *aliquot part* of a number is any number (whole or mixed) that can be divided into the number evenly (that is, without leaving a remainder). For example, 2 is an aliquot part of 10, 5 is an aliquot part of 50, 7 1/2 is an aliquot part of 15, and 8 1/3 is an aliquot part of 25.

ALIQUOT PARTS OF $1

Using aliquot parts of $1 may make multiplication easier. For example, the purchase of 220 items at 25 cents each can be computed by mentally determining the cost of the same number of items at $1. Since 25 cents is an aliquot part (1/4) of $1, the final computation can be made by multiplying $220 by 1/4: $220 x 1/4 = $55. Of course, the same result could be obtained by multiplying 220 by $0.25.

The commonly used aliquot parts of $1 are shown in Figure 10.2.

$1/2$ = 50 cents
$1/3$ = $33 1/3$ cents; $2/3$ = $66 2/3$ cents
$1/4$ = 25 cents; $3/4$ = 75 cents
$1/5$ = 20 cents; $2/5$ = 40 cents; $3/5$ = 60 cents; $4/5$ = 80 cents
$1/6$ = $16 2/3$ cents; $5/6$ = $83 1/3$ cents
$1/8$ = $12 1/2$ cents; $3/8$ = $37 1/2$ cents; $5/8$ = $62 1/2$ cents; $7/8$ = $87 1/2$ cents
$1/10$ = 10 cents; $3/10$ = 30 cents; $7/10$ = 70 cents; $9/10$ = 90 cents
$1/12$ = $8 1/3$ cents
$1/15$ = $62/3$ cents
$1/16$ = $6 1/4$ cents
$1/20$ = 5 cents

Figure 10.2 Commonly Used Aliquot Parts of $1

An **aliquot part** is any value (whole number, decimal, or fraction) that divides evenly into another value.

An **aliquot part** must be evenly divisible into the number.

Computations with aliquot parts use fractions.

Use of a table is easier than memorizing commonly used aliquot parts.

Even if a calculator is used, using aliquot parts provides a more accurate answer when the price involves an odd part of $1, such as 8 1/3 cents in Model 10.6.

Notice that 1/12 was shown in the table in Figure 10.2 to be the aliquot part of $1 based on a price of 8 1/3 cents. This answer is easy to compute and more accurate than multiplying 1,800 by $0.0833333, which will yield an answer of $149.99994.

MODEL 10.6

Use of aliquot parts for some values makes computation more accurate.

Aliquot parts are often used to make computations easier.

Computing cost using an aliquot part

Problem: Marshall Office Supply purchased 1,800 tablets for 8 1/3 cents each. What was the cost of the order?

Solution: **Step 1** Find the cost of the order at $1 per item.

No. of items x $1 = Cost at $1
1,800   x $1 = $1,800

Step 2 Find the cost using the aliquot part of $1.

Cost at $1 x Aliquot part of $1 = Cost
$1,800   x 1/12   = $150

Apply Your Skills

Brent Pelz purchased 300 pencils for 6 2/3 cents each. What was the cost of the order? $ _20.00_

You may now complete Performance Application 10.2.

No. of pencils x $1 = Cost at $1
300   x $1 = $300 $1
300
2) Cost at $1 x Aliquot part of $1 = cost
$300   x 1/15 =   = $20.05

PERFORMANCE APPLICATION 10.1

1. Compute the base for each of the following problems. The first problem is completed as an example.

No.	Amount	Rate	Base
	$ 35.63	7%	$509.00
1	96.48	8%	$ 1206.
2	45.11	10%	$ 451.10
3	21.60	6%	$ 360.00
4	180.00	120%	$ 150.00 ✗
5	500.00	125%	$ 400.00 ✗

2. Compute the base *or* amount for each of the following problems. The first problem is completed as an example.

No.	Amount	Rate	Base
	$ 3.93	6%	$ 65.50
1	$360.81	9%	$ 4,009.00
2	$ 25.99	4.6%	$565.00
3	$ 43.20	6%	$720.00
4	$ 37.80	4.5%	$ 840
5	$ 31.36	4%	$ 784

3. Harry Summer earned 8.5% on a savings account. His annual interest was $382.50. How much money did he have in his savings account? $ 32,312.50 ✗

0.085

4. Sales of stereo equipment at Berclair Electronics for one year were $250,000, which was 25% more than sales for the previous year. How much were the company's sales for the previous year?
$ _____

Based on what Bill earned John earned 15% more

5. John Eastridge earned $138 during the week on his part-time job. This was 15% more than Bill Randal earned. How much did Bill earn?
$ ___120___

$\frac{138}{1.15} = 120$

6. The Smithson family spent $31.20 during the week on entertainment. This represented 6.5% of their weekly income. How much was their weekly income?
$ _____

7. The Dayton Furniture Store sold a bedroom suite for $1,500. This was 80% of its regular price. What was the regular price of the bedroom suite?
$ _____

8. The Barker Real Estate Company earned $5,950, which represented a 7% commission based on the selling price of a house. What was the selling price of the house?

$ _____

9. Josephine Higginbottom bought a used car by making a down payment of $1,465, which represented 25% of the price of the car. What was the price of the car?
$ _____

10. Anne Mabry donated $480 to the church building fund. This represented 1.6% of the donations received. How much had been donated so far?
$ _____

PERFORMANCE APPLICATION 10.2

1. Supply the missing information for each of the following problems. The first problem is completed as an example.

No.	Amount	Base	Rate
	$50.00	$200.00	25%
1	$ _43.20_	$360.00	12%
2	$32.00	$ _400.00_	8%
3	$45.00	$500.00	_9%_
4	$ _119.00_	$850.00	14%
5	$25.03	$ _500.60_	5%

2. Wanda Rockford earned $50 on her savings account on a balance of $400. What was her rate of interest?

   _12.5 %_ $\frac{5}{40} = .125 = 12.5\%$

3. The East Auto Shop sold 40 cars this week and sold 32 cars last week. What was the rate of increase in number of cars sold this week over last week?

   _0.8 %_

4. Harry Yong loaned $2,000 to a customer who agreed to pay back $2,250 one year later. What was the rate of interest on the loan?

   X

   _____

5. Henri Lee purchased a car for $400 and sold the car for $520. What percent of profit did Mr. Lee make based on the original price of the car?

   _____

6. Bill Anderson missed 10 days of work last year. He missed 12 days this year. What was the rate of increase this year?

   _____

A R % B   Fortext

R   B   A
20% X 85 = A
     A = 17

7. A furniture store sold a sofa for $800. The sofa was regularly priced at $1,000. What was the rate of discount?

_____20%_____

8. A store had 85 TV sets in inventory last week. During the past week, 20% of the sets were sold. How many were sold during the week? _____17_____

9. A business decided that 4% of its total sales of $84,500 was uncollectible. How much in sales was uncollectible?

$ _____

10. An engineering firm had revenue of $450,000 with profits of $11,250. What percent of its sales were its profits?

_____

11. A firm had 25 non-union members. This represented 4% of its total workers. How many persons were employed by the firm?

_____

12. Reigel Management Services owned 1,725 apartments. An additional 4% were purchased. (a) How many apartments were purchased, and (b) how many did the company then own?

(a) _____

(b) _____

13. The Crowe Manufacturing company produced 27,400 chair frames last year and 28,085 chair frames this year. What was the rate of increase in production this year?

_____

14. Ralph Flannary's weekly salary was $450.00 before deductions and $337.50 after deductions. What percent of his weekly salary was deducted?

_____

Practice Test for Chapter 10
Base and Rate Applications

Complete each of the following problems and then compare your answers with the ones on page 647.

1. Sales personnel working at Ruiz Real Estate Company earn a 6% commission based on sales price. Marco Diaz was the salesperson and listing agent for a $325,500 sale of a new house. What was his commission?

   $ _____

2. Brandy O'Conner, an agent with MicroTech Computer Sales, has an option of earning $2,500 per month or 8.5 % of sales, whichever is higher. Her sales last month were $30,500. How much did she earn for the month?

   $ _____

3. Mandy Cranfield earned $780 on her $12,000 savings account balance last year. What was her rate of interest?

   A   B

   _0.6.5 %_   A (R) B = 780
                     780   12,000   12 000

4. Frolick Management Services owned 1,625 apartments in six states. An additional 8% were recently purchased. (a) How many were recently purchased and (b) how many did the company own after the purchase?

   (a) _____

   (b) _____

5. Kevin Flanagan had a $42,000 annual salary last year. He received a $3,360 raise for next year. What percent of last year's salary was represented by the raise?

   B

   _8 %_

CONNECTIONS

10.1 The chart shown below indicates the surge in law school graduates. What was the rate of increase (a) between 1990 and 1992? Assuming this same rate of increase continued, (b) what was the number of graduates in 1994? Assuming this same rate of increase continued, (c) what was the number of graduates in 1996? (Round the percent to one decimal place and the number of graduates to the nearest whole number.)

(a) _____

(b) _____

(c) _____

A look at statistics that shape the nation

Surge in law school grads

Number of graduates:

42,037

38,800

36,985

1990   1991   1992

Source: American Bar Association   By Cliff Vancura, USA TODAY

10.2 The advertisement shown below appeared to encourage renewal of subscriptions for a popular magazine. What was the rate of discount based on the newsstand price of the magazine? (Round the percent to one decimal place.)

_____

Just 54¢

That's all I'll pay for each issue of *Cycle*Week when I subscribe at the low basic rate of just $28 for 52 weekly issues, a saving of $73 off the newsstand price. Sign me up!

Name _____

Address _____

City _____ State _____ ZIP _____

436X

☐ New subscription   ☐ Renewal

☐ Payment enclosed   ☐ Bill me later

Canada and other foreign countries add an additional **$32** U.S. for surface postage.

☐ I would prefer not to receive information or advertising from companies not affiliated with Crown Communications.

Cycle
Week

10.1 City Landscape Services decided to bid on a job to beautify a local park in the downtown area. An estimated 200 plants costing $31 each, $4,000 total labor cost, and $3,500 total materials will be needed. The estimator is instructed to prepare a bid amount based on a profit of 15 percent of the cost of plants, materials, and labor or $15,500, whichever is higher. (a) How much should the company bid for the job and (b) how much represents profit?

(a) $ _____

(b) $ _____

10.2 Cole and Maxwell, Accountants, normally charge clients an $85 hourly rate. Clients were billed for 88 hours last week. Total expenses for the week were $4,700. Cole receives 60 percent of the profit and Maxwell receives 40 percent of the profit. (Profit represents the difference between total charges and total expenses.) What were the (a) rate of profit (rounded to 1 decimal place) based on total charges, (b) profit amount earned by Cole, and (c) profit amount earned by Maxwell?

(a) _____

(b) $ _____

(c) $ _____

DECISIONS

BASE AND RATE APPLICATIONS
Chapter Review and Quick Reference

Topic	Main Point	Typical Example	Text Page
Relationships	Base, rate, and percentage (amount) have a relationship that permits computation when two are known.	Amount = Base x Rate	175
Computing the amount	Amount equals the rate times the base.	Salary equals $850. Raise equals 10%. What is the raise amount? A = B x R **or** $850 x 0.10 = **$85**.	176
Computing the base	Base equals the amount divided by the rate.	An $1,800 raise amount represents 5% of the salary. What is the salary base? B = A ÷ R **or** $1,800 ÷ 0.05 = **$36,000.00**.	176
Converting decimal to a percent	Move the decimal point two places to the right.	80÷400 = 0.20, which converts to **20%**.	177
Computing the rate	Rate equals the amount divided by the base.	Salary, $40,000; raise, $3,200. What was the rate of raise increase? R = A ÷ B **or** 3,200 ÷ 40,000 = **0.08** or **8%**.	177
Aliquot part	An **aliquot part** of a number is any number that can be divided evenly into the number.	8 1/3 cents is an aliquot part (1/12) of $1. (Note that 8 1/3 times 12 equals 100.)	179

Chapter **11**

FINANCE CHARGES

Performance Objectives

1. Compute finance charges for installment and credit card purchases.
2. Determine amount financed for credit purchases.
3. Determine monthly payments for installment loans.
4. Utilize formula to compute estimated APR.
5. Determine early payoff and canceled interest for installment loans while using the Rule of 78.

Many retail businesses permit customers to purchase merchandise and pay for the purchase over a period of time. This method is called a *credit purchase* or *charge purchase*. On credit purchases, the business charges extra for allowing the customer to pay for the purchase over a period of time. This *finance charge* is the amount the customer pays for this use of credit.

There are several legal methods that businesses may use to compute finance charges. The method used can make a big difference in the amount of finance charge that the customer will eventually pay, so it is important to develop a good understanding of these methods of computing finance charges. Two typical methods are shown in Figure 11.1.

The **cash price** is the purchase price if payment is made at the time of sale.

The **finance charge** is the difference between the cash price and the total price paid in installments.

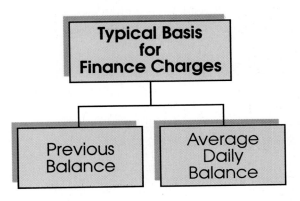

Figure 11.1 Diagram of Typical Basis for Finance Charges

THE TRUTH-IN-LENDING ACT

The Truth-in-Lending Act was passed by Congress in 1969 to protect consumers from companies that try to hide the true rate of finance charges being assessed. This law requires businesses to reveal (a) the exact amount of finance charge and (b) the *annual percentage rate* (APR) of the total finance charge, as shown in Figure 11.2. The act does not specify the maximum amount of interest that can be charged, but it requires that the rate be revealed to the customer. Some states set a maximum finance rate charge. Regardless, the APR must be stated for *all* credit purchases. Therefore, ask the company to indicate the APR prior to making a purchase. Use this rate to compare rates provided by various businesses offering the same product.

Balance Information	Previous Balance	New Purchases and Advances	Payments	Credits, Fees, and Adjustments (net)	FINANCE CHARGE	New Balance
Purchases	2944|35	3725|98	2944|35CR	102|84CR	0|00	3623|14
Cash Advances	0|00	0|00	0|00	0|00	0|00	0|00
Total	2944|35	3725|98	2944|35CR	102|84CR	0|00	3623|14

How Your FINANCE CHARGES Are Calculated	Portion of Average Daily Principal Balance	MONTHLY Periodic Rates		Corresponding ANNUAL PERCENTAGE RATE	
		Purchases	Cash Advances	Purchases	Cash Advances
	$0.01 AND ABOVE	1.3125%	1.3125%	15.7500%	15.7500%

Figure 11.2 Finance Charge Rates

The basis for making computations will be specified in the credit card agreement.

If you were employed by a business that charged more than the maximum APR allowed by law, should you report the employer? This is an ethical issue faced by some employees.

The APR is usually stated as an annual or monthly rate. If the rate is stated as a monthly rate, simply multiply the rate by 12 (12 months in a year) to obtain the annual rate, as shown in Model 11.1.

MODEL 11.1

The APR is included on monthly statements that include credit purchases.

Computing annual percentage rates

Problem: Ted Jones decided to purchase a sofa. Various department stores quoted the following monthly finance rates: 1 1/2%, 1 2/3%, and 1.575%. What is the APR for each of these rates?

Solution:

Monthly rate				Annual percentage rate
1 1/2%	X	12	=	18%
1 2/3%	X	12	=	20%
1.575%	X	12	=	18.9%

Apply Your Skills

Brent Cooper was quoted a 1 3/4% monthly finance rate while purchasing a new range. What yearly or annual rate is equivalent to this rate?

_____

CREDIT CARD FINANCE CHARGES

The Truth-in-Lending Simplification and Reform Act, passed in 1980, included a Regulation Z to further define the Truth-in-Lending Act.

Many department stores and oil companies offer credit cards for use in purchasing their products. General purpose credit cards such as American Express, MasterCard, and VISA cards are also available. Most of these cards are usually offered on a *revolving charge* basis, whereby the finance charge is based on either the *balance from the previous month* or the *average daily balance* during the month. Regardless, the Truth-in-Lending Act requires the credit card company to inform all customers of the annual percentage rate charged. A typical credit card statement is shown in Figure 11.3.

POSTING DATE	DESCRIPTION	TRANSACTION DATE	REFERENCE NUMBER	AMOUNT CR=CREDIT PY=PAYMENT
07-30	PAYMENT RECEIVED - THANK YOU	07-30	74458305211321100015812	8.95PY
08-04	CONSUMERWISE CAR CLUB SAN FRANCISCO CA	08-02	74301343215970267580074 7399	89.00
08-05	COMPUSERVE COLUMBUS OH	08-02	74443005216945660803008 7372	8.95
08-06	BUDGET RENT A CAR / MEMPHIS TN	08-04	74681203217060909276104 3366	252.47
08-13	CONSUMERWISE CAR CLUB SAN FRANCISCO CA		74301343224970267580172 7399	89.00CR

AVERAGE DAILY BALANCE SUBJECT TO FINANCE CHARGE	VARIABLE MONTHLY PERIODIC RATE	ANNUAL PERCENTAGE RATE	FINANCE CHARGE	ACCOUNT NUMBER 45483210978	ACCOUNT SUMMARY

PURCHASES $ .00 .6666% 8.00% $ .00

CASH ADVANCES $ .00 .6666% 8.00% $ .00

SEND INQUIRIES TO:
CREDIT CARD CUSTOMER SERVICE
P.O. BOX 1545
MEMPHIS, TN 38101-1545

CREDIT LINE 10,000 NUMBER OF DAYS IN BILLING CYCLE 30
AVAILABLE CREDIT 9,738 CLOSING DATE AUG 18,19--
MINIMUM PAYMENT DUE $ 10.00
PAYMENT DUE DATE SEP 12,19--

ACCOUNT SUMMARY	
PREVIOUS BALANCE	$ 8.95
PURCHASES & OTHER CHARGES +	350.42
CASH ADVANCES +	.00
CREDITS -	89.00
PAYMENTS -	8.95
LATE PAYMENT CHARGE +	.00
FINANCE CHARGE +	.00
NEW BALANCE =	$ 261.42

CUSTOMER SERVICE TELEPHONE
MEMPHIS (901) 555-5800   OUTSIDE MEMPHIS 1-800-555-2840

SEE REVERSE SIDE FOR IMPORTANT INFORMATION

GRACE PERIOD FOR REPAYMENT OF PURCHASES: TO AVOID ADDITIONAL FINANCE CHARGE ON PURCHASES PAY ENTIRE NEW BALANCE BY PAYMENT DUE DATE. FINANCE CHARGE ACCRUES ON CASH ADVANCES DAILY UNTIL PAID AND WILL BE BILLED IN YOUR NEXT STATEMENT.

VISA

Figure 11.3 Credit Card Statement

An *installment loan* is one that is paid back through a specified number of payments. An *open-end loan* is one that has no specific number of payments. The borrower makes payments until the debt is cleared. Many credit card accounts use the open-end procedure. Many department stores, oil companies, and other providers of credit cards use a revolving charge procedure, which permits the customer to pay a minimum amount each month. The *Fair Credit and Charge Disclosure Act of 1988* was passed by Congress to require solicitations for credit cards to provide specific details about all fees charged, grace period allowed before interest is charged, and other matters important to the customer. A typical credit card is shown in Figure 11.4.

Figure 11.4 Credit Card

FINANCE CHARGES BASED ON PREVIOUS BALANCE

The number of days in the billing cycle depends on the number of days in the month.

The finance rate must be stated on the application for the credit card and on each account statement the customer receives. If the balance is based on the previous month's balance, computation is fairly easy, as shown in Model 11.2.

Results should be carried to four decimal places and rounded to two decimal places (the nearest cent). Customers usually have the option of paying the entire balance at any time without further finance charges.

MODEL 11.2

Computing account balances and finance charges

Problem: Juan Perez purchased $350 worth of clothes on May 1 while using his credit card. Terms are that unpaid balances will be assessed a 1 1/2% monthly finance charge. He made a $50 payment on June 8 and another $50 payment on July 8. What are his account's balances and finance charges?

Solution:

Balance Subject to Finance Charge after June 1	$	350.00
Finance Charge = $350 x .015 (1 1/2%)	+	5.25
Amount Due after Finance Charge		355.25
Less Payment (June 8)	-	50.00
Balance after Payment		305.25
Finance Charge after July 1 ($305.25 x .015)	+	4.58
Amount Due after Finance Charge		309.83
Less Payment (July 8)	-	50.00
Balance after Payment	$	259.83

Apply Your Skills

Marshall Huntziger's previous credit statement for March showed a $4,000 previous month's balance. Monthly finance charges are 1% based on the previous month's balance. He makes a $600 payment on March 5. He makes another $600 payment on April 5. What is his balance after the April 5 payment?

$ _____

Companies that provide credit cards normally permit customers a specified period of time (such as 30 days) to pay the balance with no additional interest charges. Under these terms, additional purchases may not be subjected to a finance charge until 30 days have elapsed. See Model 11.3.

Notice that the finance charge after March 1 is based on the previous balance ($405) and *not* on the current balance ($1,205) because the purchase ($800) is not subject to a finance charge until after 30 days elapse. Some companies base the finance charge on the unpaid balance at the end of the month (rather than the previous month's balance). In this case, the finance charge would have been based on the unpaid balance ($1,205). This points out another reason why the terms of the credit agreement should be read carefully.

Computing account balances and finance charges

MODEL 11.3

Problem: Bill Smothers purchased furniture for the following amounts: $500 on January 1 and $800 on February 10. Finance charges are 1% per month, with a $100 minimum payment each month. Bill made $100 payments on February 8, March 8, and April 8. No finance charges are assessed if payments are received within 30 days of purchase. What were his balances and finance charges for the three months?

Solution:

Balance Subject to Finance Charge on February 1	$ 500.00
Finance Charge ($500 x .01)	+ 5.00
Amount Due after Finance Charge	$ 505.00
Less Payment (February 8)	- 100.00
Balance after Payment	405.00
Additional Purchase on February 10	+ 800.00
Balance after Additional Purchase	1,205.00
Finance Charge after March 1 ($405 x .01)	+ 4.05
Balance after Finance Charge	1,209.05
Less Payment (March 8)	- 100.00
Balance after Payment	1,109.05
Finance Charge after April 1 ($1,109.05 x .01)	+ 11.09
Balance after Finance Charge	$ 1,120.14

Apply Your Skills

Mohammad Amini has an installment agreement that includes a 1% monthly finance charge, but allows a 30-day grace period for each purchase without finance charges. His balance subject to finance charge on October 1 was $900. He made a $200 payment on October 6 and a $500 purchase on October 8. He made an additional $300 payment on November 3. What will the finance charges be for his (a) October 1, (b) November 1, and (c) December 1 statements if no additional purchases or payments are made for the account?

(a) October 1 $ _____

(b) November 1 $ _____

(c) December 1 $ _____

You may now complete Performance Application 11.1.

FINANCE CHARGES BASED ON AVERAGE DAILY BALANCE

Many department stores, as well as other credit card finance companies, compute the finance charge based on the actual number of days that an amount was owed during the month. For example, a purchase made 10 days prior to the end of the month will draw finance charges for 10 days. Although this computation is fairly simple, the number of computations is large. Therefore, a computer is used for this type of computation, using the steps shown in Model 11.4.

$$\text{Average daily balance} = \frac{\text{Sum of daily balances}}{\text{Number of days in the billing cycle}}$$

MODEL 11.4

Computing average daily balance and finance charges

Problem: Ted Swanson made a $400 purchase on February 8 and a $500 purchase on February 18. Using the average daily balance method, what are the average daily balance and finance charges? The finance rate is 1%.

Solution: **Step 1** Determine the number of equivalent dollar days that the credit was used for each amount by multiplying each amount by the number of days the amount was used.

$400 x 20 = $8,000 (equivalent dollar days for first purchase, February 8 to February 28)

$500 x 10 = $5,000 (equivalent dollar days for second purchase, February 18 to February 28)

Step 2 Determine the total dollar days by adding the amounts obtained in Step 1.

$8,000 + $5,000 = $13,000 (total equivalent dollar days)

Step 3 Determine the average daily balance by dividing the total dollar days obtained in Step 2 by the number of days in the month (28 for February).

$13,000/28 = $464.29 (average daily balance, 28 days in February)

Step 4 Multiply the average daily balance by the monthly finance rate to determine monthly finance charge.

$464.29 x .01 = $4.64 (monthly finance charge)

Apply Your Skills

Jeffrey Elston made a $600 purchase on June 4 and an $800 purchase on June 15. A 1 1/2% monthly finance charge was assessed, based on the average daily balance. What were his (a) average daily balance and (b) monthly finance charge?

(a) $ _____

(b) $ _____

MINIMUM PAYMENTS

Companies usually base minimum payments on the account balance. The larger the balance, the larger the minimum payment required will be. A schedule used by one financial institution is shown in Figure 11.5 and utilized in Model 11.5.

MINIMUM MONTHLY PAYMENT SCHEDULE. Your minimum monthly payment will change only at the time of a later advance.

BALANCE: (immediately after latest advance)	REGULAR MINIMUM MONTHLY PAYMENT	BALANCE: (immediately after latest advance)	REGULAR MINIMUM MONTHLY PAYMENT
$ .01 - 1,500.00	$ 50	$5,400.01 - 5,700.00	$140
1,500.01 - 1,800.00	55	5,700.01 - 6,000.00	145
1,800.01 - 2,000.00	60	6,000.01 - 6,300.00	150
2,000.01 - 2,150.00	65	6,300.01 - 6,500.00	155
2,150.01 - 2,300.00	70	6,500.01 - 6,700.00	160
2,300.01 - 2,450.00	75	6,700.01 - 6,900.00	165
2,450.01 - 2,600.00	80	6,900.01 - 7,200.00	170
2,600.01 - 2,750.00	85	7,200.01 - 7,400.00	175
2,750.01 - 2,900.00	90	7,400.01 - 7,700.00	180
2,900.01 - 3,300.00	95	7,700.01 - 8,000.00	185
3,300.01 - 3,600.00	100	8,000.01 - 8,300.00	190
3,600.01 - 3,900.00	105	8,300.01 - 8,600.00	195
3,900.01 - 4,200.00	110	8,600.01 - 8,900.00	200
4,200.01 - 4,440.00	115	8,900.01 - 9,100.00	205
4,440.01 - 4,600.00	120	9,100.01 - 9,400.00	210
4,600.01 - 4,800.00	125	9,400.01 - 9,800.00	215
4,800.01 - 5,100.00	130	9,800.01 - 10,200.00	220
5,100.01 - 5,400.00	135	10,200.01 - 11,000.00	225

% OF BALANCE ROUNDED
TO NEXT HIGHER $5.00

$11,000.01 - and over	2.05%

Figure 11.5 Minimum Monthly Payment Schedule

MODEL 11.5

Computing minimum monthly payment

Problem: Don Fogelman received a credit card statement showing a $2,798 balance. What is the minimum monthly payment due?

Solution: **Step 1** Find the range containing the balance (in this example, $2,750.01 - $2,900.00).

Step 2 Find the corresponding regular minimum monthly payment due (in this example, $90).

- -

Apply Your Skills

Emin Babbas received a credit card statement showing a $4,561.89 balance. Use the minimum monthly payment schedule to determine the minimum monthly payment due. What is the amount?

$ _____

INSTALLMENT PURCHASES AND APR

Many companies add finance charges to the purchase price to determine the amount due, as illustrated in Figure 11.6. The amount due is then spread evenly over the number of months for paying for the purchase.

$99⁹⁹ PER MONTH*

PLUS: FREE RUST PROOFING, CHROME & PAINT SEALER ✪ *FREE GIFT WHEN YOU BUY* ✪ ASK FOR DETAILS.

*60 mos w/$633 dn. 9.85% APR, plus tax, title, fee & freight with approved credit. Total of payments $5999.40

Figure 11.6 Advertisement of Installment Purchase Plan

MODEL 11.6

Payment equals the finance charge plus the amount financed divided by the number of payments.

*The APR is often called the **effective rate** and is usually higher than the stated rate.*

Calculating finance charges

Problem: Joe Wright purchased an automobile for $15,000. A finance charge of 6% per year was added to the purchase price. What are the finance charges and monthly payments if payments are made over 48 months (4 years)?

Solution: **Step 1** Find the finance charge amount.

Purchase price		Interest rate		Number of years		Finance charge
$15,000	x	.06	x	4	=	$3,600

Step 2 Find the total amount due.

Purchase price		Finance charge		Total due
$15,000	+	$3,600	=	$18,600

Step 3 Find the monthly payment amount.

Total due		Number of payments		Monthly payment
$18,600	÷	48 (4 x 12)	=	$387.50

Apply Your Skills

Howard Tuckman purchased a new cherry bedroom suite for $6,000. A 10% annual finance charge was added to the purchase price. Howard plans to pay for the furniture over a 3-year period. What were his (a) finance charge, (b) total due, and (c) monthly payment?

(a) $ _____   (c) $ _____

(b) $ _____

Notice that the interest rate stated in Model 11.6 is 6%. However, 6% is not the APR or true interest rate because the interest rate was applied to the full amount ($15,000) of the purchase. This could be misleading because the full amount was not owed for the full term. Actually, $15,000 was owed only until the time of the first payment. During the last month, only $387.50 was owed. As a general rule, the APR will be approximately double the interest rate stated for this type of finance plan.

The following formula can be used to compute the actual APR:

$$APR = \frac{2 \times \text{Number of payments per year} \times \text{Interest charge}}{\text{Amount financed} \times (\text{Total number of payments} + 1)}$$

Computing annual percentage rate

Problem: In the previous example, Joe Wright purchased an automobile for $15,000. While paying for the automobile on an installment basis, his finance charges will be $3,600. His monthly payments will be $387.50 for 48 months. What is the APR?

Solution: Note: Amounts from the example are substituted for parts in the above formula to compute the APR.

$$APR = \frac{2 \times 12 \times \$3,600}{\$15,000 \times 49 \ (48 + 1)}$$

$$APR = \frac{\$86,400}{\$735,000} = 0.117551 \text{ or } 11.76\%$$

$$APR = \frac{2 \times M \times I}{P \times (N + 1)}$$

Apply Your Skills

Howard Tuckman wanted to know the APR for his purchase made in the Apply Your Skills 11.6 example. What is the APR for the purchase? (Round the answer to two decimal places, if needed.)

RULE OF 78

Purchase agreements on installment credit usually offer the buyer the option of paying off the loan early. For example, if the purchaser of an automobile under a 48-month agreement decides to pay the remaining balance in less than 48 months, the lender must decide on the amount of interest that is canceled, or which will not be paid. A common method to compute this amount is the *Rule of 78*. Under this method, the amount of finance charge assessed is greatest during the early months and decreases each subsequent month. Under this method, paying off the loan halfway through the finance period will not result in having half of the interest amount canceled.

The following formula is used to compute the amount of finance charge that is considered unearned:

$$\text{Canceled finance charge} = \frac{\text{Sum of digits of remaining months}}{\text{Sum of digits in life of contract}} \times \text{Total finance charges}$$

The sum of digits method is shown in Model 11.8.

MODEL 11.8

Computing canceled finance charges

Problem: The Burkhart Furniture Company sold a sofa with payments to be made for 12 months. Computed total finance charges were $312. After making 8 payments, the customer decided to pay the balance. What finance charge should be canceled?

Solution: **Step 1** Find the sum of digits of remaining months.

$1 + 2 + 3 + 4 = 10$ (four months remaining)

Step 2 Find the sum of the digits in life of contract.

$1 + 2 + 3 + 4 + 5 + 6 + 7 + 8 + 9 + 10 + 11 + 12 = 78$ (twelve months in contract)

Step 3 Compute the amount of canceled finance charge.

$\frac{10}{78} \times \$312 = \$40$

Apply Your Skills

City Finance Center sold an appliance for $1,200. Installment payments were to be made over a 12-month period. Finance charges ($234) were added to the purchase price. After 9 monthly payments, the customer decided to pay the balance with the tenth payment. Using the Rule of 78, find the amount of finance charge canceled.

$ _____

Therefore, $40 of the original $312 finance charge will be canceled because of early payment in Model 11.8.

A shortcut method to determine the numbers to use in Steps 1 and 2 is to use the formula $N \times (N + 1) \div 2$, where N equals the number of periods. For example, 12 periods using this formula will be $(12 \times 13) \div 2$, or 78. The formula used for 4 periods will be $(4 \times 5) \div 2$, or 10. Notice that these are the same values as were computed in the example, but the shortcut method saves time.

Computing canceled finance charges

Problem: Joe Roth purchased a lawnmower under a 6-month installment plan with $12.60 total finance charges. After 4 months, he decided to pay the balance. Using the Rule of 78 and the shortcut method, how much finance charge should be canceled?

Solution:
$$\frac{[2(2 + 1)] \div 2 = 3}{[6(6 + 1)] \div 2 = 21}$$

$$\frac{3}{21} \times \$12.60 = \$1.80$$

Formula to compute cancellation fraction:

$$\frac{[n(n + 1)] \div 2}{[N(N + 1)] \div 2}$$

*where **n** is the number of months remaining and **N** is the total number of months.*

- -

Apply Your Skills

David Poole purchased a new fishing boat under a 6-month installment plan with $63 finance charges. After 3 payments, he decided to pay the balance with the fourth payment. Using the shortcut method and the Rule of 78, how much finance charge should be canceled?

$ _____

You may now complete Performance Application 11.2.

PERFORMANCE APPLICATION 11.1

1. Jin Cheng purchased a stereo using a credit card with a 1.75% monthly finance charge. What is the annual percentage rate?

   _____

2. Bill Barksdale purchased a television set for $900 with monthly finance charges of 1 1/2% based on the previous balance. He decided to pay $50 after the first month. How much of the payment would apply to the (a) balance and (b) finance charge?

   (a) $ _____

   (b) $ _____

3. Sarah Brown purchased a new office safe for $1,240 with monthly finance charges of 1% based on the previous balance. She decided to pay $63 after the first month. How much of the payment will apply to the (a) balance and (b) finance charge? (c) What will the balance be after the payment?

   (a) $ _____

   (b) $ _____

   (c) $ _____

4. Jerry Sellers purchased a new watch for a $180 cash price. The amount can be financed for 12 monthly payments of $15 plus a down payment of $50. If he decided to buy the watch on credit, (a) how much will the total finance charge equal? (b) How much will the credit price of the watch equal? (c) How much can be saved by paying cash for the watch?

   (a) $ _____

   (b) $ _____

   (c) $ _____

5. James Fung can purchase a used car for a base price of $6,000 plus sales taxes of $360. A down payment of $1,200 will be required to purchase the car at this price. Finance charges equal 2% of the previous balance. (a) What is the total cost of the car, excluding finance charges? (b) How much will Mr. Fung borrow to finance the car? (c) How much will the finance charge be for the first month?

    (a) $ _____

    (b) $ _____

    (c) $ _____

6. Pearline Bronger purchased merchandise from the Bestway Specialty Shop totaling $400. Finance charges are 1% per month based on the previous balance. She decided to pay $30 per month. Compute the finance charge for (a) the first month and (b) the second month.

    (a) $ _____

    (b) $ _____

7. Jim Munice purchased merchandise totaling $300 on February 10 and merchandise totaling $520 on March 10. Terms are 1% per month based on the balance from the previous month with no finance charge assessed for 30 days after purchase. Statements are issued on the first day of each month. Payments were made on April 1 ($100) and on May 1 ($100). Compute the balance due on (a) April 1 and (b) May 1 and the finance charges on (c) April 1 and (d) May 1.

    (a) $ _____

    (b) $ _____

    (c) $ _____

    (d) $ _____

PERFORMANCE APPLICATION 11.2

1. The Discount Furniture Store makes finance charges of 1% per month based on the average daily balance during the month. Ysing Inertz bought a chair on June 10 costing $420 and an end table for $210 on June 15. Compute the following amounts:

   (a) Equivalent dollar days, first purchase

   $ _____

   (b) Equivalent dollar days, second purchase

   $ _____

   (c) Equivalent dollar days, combined purchases

   $ _____

   (d) Average daily balance

   $ _____

   (e) Monthly finance charge

   $ _____

2. Botter Distributors sold automotive parts to John Collier. There was no beginning balance as of September 1. A sale for $170 was made on September 5, and a sale for $60 was made on September 20. Finance charges are based on 1 1/2% of the average daily balance. Compute the following amounts:

   (a) Equivalent dollar days, first purchase

   $ _____

   (b) Equivalent dollar days, second purchase

   $ _____

   (c) Equivalent dollar days, combined purchases

   $ _____

   (d) Average daily balance

   $ _____

   (e) Monthly finance charge

   $ _____

3. Using the Rule of 78, compute the amount of finance charge that will be canceled under each of the following conditions.

Total Finance Charge	Total in Contract Months	Early Payoff	Finance Charge Canceled
$ 420.00	6	End of Month 3	$_____
1,260.00	6	End of Month 4	$_____
2,379.00	12	End of Month 8	$_____
427.50	18	End of Month 15	$_____
3,727.50	20	End of Month 10	$_____

4. John White's credit card balance was $4,725. Under the Minimum Monthly Payment Schedule in Figure 11.5, what is the amount of his minimum monthly payment?

   $ _____

5. Florence Robertson's credit card balance was $2,424.89. Under the Minimum Monthly Payment Schedule in Figure 11.5, what is the amount of her minimum monthly payment?

   $ _____

6. A customer purchased a used car for a $5,600 cash price or 12 monthly payments of $550. (a) What is the amount of the finance charge? (b) How much of the finance charge will be canceled if the balance is paid after the seventh month using the Rule of 78? (Round your answer to two decimal places.)

   (a) $ _____   (b) $ _____

7. A dinette set was sold for an $800 cash price. The customer can pay a 20% finance charge added to the cash price and make 12 equal monthly payments. (a) What is the amount of the finance charge? (b) How much of the finance charge will be canceled if the balance is paid after the tenth month using the Rule of 78?

   (a) $ _____   (b) $ _____

8. Ginny Runyan purchased a television for $800. She agreed to make 24 payments of $38 each over a 2-year period. What were her (a) interest charge and (b) annual percentage rate (APR) for the finance charges?

   (a) $ _____   (b) _____

PRACTICE TEST FOR CHAPTER 11
FINANCE CHARGES

Complete each of the following problems and then compare your answers with the ones on page 647.

1. Fung Jewelry Store sold a $6,500 diamond ring to a customer last month on credit. Monthly finance charges (1 1/2% of the previous balance) applied during the second month. The customer made a $200 payment at the end of the second month. How much applied to the (a) finance charge and (b) balance?

   (a) $ _____

   (b) $ _____

2. Fung Jewelry Store sold a $900 dress watch to be financed over 12 months. A 12% finance charge was added to the price of the watch. What were the (a) total amount due and (b) monthly payments?

   (a) $ _____

   (b) $ _____

3. Kurt Flexner opened an account and made the following purchases during June, a 30-day billing cycle: June 4, $500, and June 10, $400. Finance charges (1 1/2%) were based on average daily balance during the cycle with no grace period. What was the finance charge? $ _____

4. Binzwagner Audio sold a CD player for $150 plus $14 finance charges for a 6-month period. The customer paid the full amount with the fourth payment. Using the Rule of 78, how much of the finance charge will be canceled?

   $ _____

5. Andrea Sniezak purchased a used automobile for $3,800 and agreed to make 24 payments at $200 each over a 2-year period. What were her (a) interest charge and (b) annual percentage rate (APR) for the finance charges? (Round the rate, if needed, to two decimal places.)

   (a) $ _____

   (b) _____

11.1 The credit card shown in the ad below is an option for persons over 50 years old. Assume that a local department store offered a camcorder for an $800 cash price or 12 equal payments of $80. A decision must be made about whether to use the credit card or the installment credit option. Which one offered the lowest APR?

_____

12.9%
Annual
Percentage
Rate

$**10**
Annual
Fee

CONNECTIONS

11.2 The laser printer shown in the ad below was offered for a $600 cash price or for $660 if paid in 12 monthly installments. What were the (a) monthly payment and (b) annual percentage rate (APR)?

(a) $ _____

(b) _____

$599⁹⁹

OfficeMart Everyday Low Price

CONNECTIONS

11.1 Visit the credit department in a local department store in your area. Inquire about credit plans and/or credit card plans that are available at the store. Determine answers to questions such as the following: What APR is charged for credit purchases? What is the basis for finance charges (average daily balance, unpaid balance, and so forth)? What grace period is allowed? What percentage of business is done on credit? What standards are used for allowing credit purchases? What types of forms are required for credit applications? Finally, write a one-page report describing credit practices at the department store. Compare your experience with the experiences of other students in the class.

11.2 Assume that you are considering the purchase of a home entertainment center to be paid for in 12 equal installments. McNeil Store offered the center for $2,400 with an 18% finance charge based on the purchase price. MagicLand offered the center for $2,400 with a $360 finance charge. Lu Chuho Store normally prices the center for $2,400 and will sell it for 12 monthly payments of $220 each. (a) Which store offered the lowest annual percentage rate (APR)? (b) Which store offered the lowest monthly payment?

(a) _____

(b) _____

DECISIONS

FINANCE CHARGES
Chapter Review and Quick Reference

Topic	Main Point	Typical Example	Text Page
Annual interest rate	Interest rates are often stated in monthly terms, which can be converted to an annual rate.	Monthly rate: 1½% Annual rate: 1½% x 12 = 18%	191
Charges based on previous balance	The interest rate is based on amount carried from previous month.	Previous balance: $600 Finance rate: 1 1/2% Interest: $600 x 0.015 = **$9**	194
Charges based on average daily balance	The interest rate is based on the average daily balance for the period.	Purchase on 1/11: $400 Purchase on 1/21: $300 $400 x 20 = $8,000 $300 x 10 = $3,000 $11,000 ÷ 31 = **$354.84**	196
Finding minimum payment using a table	Most credit card and installment loans require a minimum payment to be paid each month.	Balance: $4,000 Using the table, the minimum payment = **$110**	197
Monthly payment	The monthly payment is the payment required to pay the amount due within the desired time.	Amount due: $960 Time period: 12 months Monthly payment $960 ÷ 12 = **$80**	197
Amount due	The finance charge is added to the purchase price.	Price: $800 Finance charge: $80 Amount due: **$880**	198
Annual percentage rate (APR)	The APR, required by law to be disclosed, is the effective interest rate being charged. $$APR = \frac{2 \times N \times I}{A \times (TN + 1)}$$	No. payments/year: 12 Interest charge: $3,600 Amount financed: $15,000 Total No. payments: 48 $$APR = \frac{2 \times 12 \times \$3,600}{\$15,000 \times (48 + 1)}$$ APR = **0.117551 (11.76%)**	199
Rule of 78	The Rule of 78 is a method for computing canceled finance charges when loans are paid early. It favors the lender.	Finance charge: $84 Term: 6 months Payoff: 0 with fourth payment 1 + 2 = **3** 1 + 2 + 3 + 4 + 5 + 6 = **21** 3 ÷ 21 x $84 = **$12** (canceled interest after early payoff)	199

Chapter 12

Discounts on Purchases

Performance Objectives

1. Understand relationship between normal or list price and discounted price of merchandise items.
2. Determine quantity discounts.
3. Determine penalty and bonus amounts based on time.
4. Compute discounted sales price.

Businesses take advantage of discounts on purchases for many reasons. The major reason is to save money on the purchase by taking advantage of a discount to reduce the purchase price. Several additional ways that businesses take advantage of discounts on merchandise purchases will be discussed in Chapter 13.

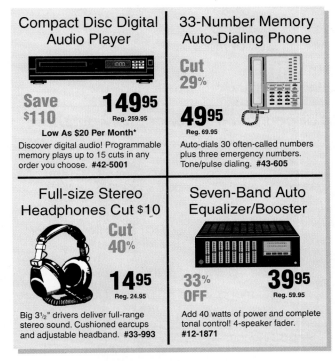

Figure 12.1 Sales Discounts

Figure 12.2 Discounted Price

QUANTITY DISCOUNTS

Businesses may be encouraged to make larger purchases if quantity discounts are offered. To determine the best alternative, however, the cost of warehouse space to store the purchases must be compared to the savings in purchase price. One wholesaler offers goods according to the following schedule:

Discount is a reduction in the normal price of a product.

Discounts are often based on quantity of purchases to encourage larger purchases.

213

DISCOUNT SCHEDULE

Items Purchased	Discount
0-20	0%
21-40	1%
41-60	2%
61-80	3%
81-100	4%
100 or more	5%

Use this schedule to solve the problem in Model 12.1.

MODEL 12.1

Discounts are also offered to sell slow moving or seasonal items.

1) 50 × 26.50 = 1,325

2) 1325 × 0.02 = 26.5

3) 1325 − 26.5 = 1298.5

Computing discounted cost for quantity purchase

Problem: Novelties of Distinction purchased 87 items consisting of calendars for sale during the Christmas season. The normal cost of these items is $1.25. What is the total discounted cost of the order if the quantity discount schedule is used?

Solution: **Step 1** Find the cost of the order at the regular price.

Number of items	x	Cost per item	=	Normal cost
87	x	$1.25	=	$108.75

Step 2 Find the amount of the discount.

Normal cost	x	Discount rate	=	Discount
$108.75	x	0.04	=	$4.35

Step 3 Find the discounted cost.

Normal cost	-	Discount	=	Discounted cost
$108.75	-	$4.35	=	$104.40

Apply Your Skills

Dietz Card shop purchased items from a supplier that allowed quantity discounts based on the above schedule. The shop purchased 50 figurines with a $26.50 normal cost. What is the discounted cost of the order? $ 1,298.50

The discount is often stated as a percent, which is converted to a decimal value for computation.

COST BASED ON TIME

Many construction bids are based on project completion time. For example, a company may offer a construction company a bonus to the bid price if a building is completed by a certain date that is earlier than the bid date. This bonus may permit the construction company to hire additional personnel or to pay employees overtime to finish the project early.

Computing bonus amount

MODEL
12.2

Problem: The Acme Construction Company bid on a project to pave two miles of city streets for a total price of $2,225,000. The bid contract stipulated that a 17% bonus would be awarded if the project was completed by August 31. The project was completed on August 15. What is the amount of the bonus?

*275.000 X 0.09
= 24,750.00*

Solution: Project amount x Bonus rate = Bonus amount
$2,225,000   x 0.17   = $378,250

Apply Your Skills

Haaz Ready Mix completed a $275,000 job on April 12. The contract stipulated a 9% bonus if the job was completed by April 21. What was the bonus amount?

$ *24,750.00*

Some contracts may also include a penalty if the job is not completed on time.

The bid contract may also include penalties if the project is delayed beyond a specified date, as shown in Model 12.3.

Computing discount with a penalty

MODEL
12.3

Problem: Benson and Associates, a construction company, offered a $12,540,000 bid on an office building. The bid contract stipulated that a penalty of 1.5% would be assessed if the project was not completed by March 31. The project was completed on April 20. What is the amount of the penalty? How much will the company receive for the project?

A second approach is to subtract the penalty percent from 100 to determine the percent left after the penalty (1.00 - 0.015 = 0.985.) Then multiply the amount by this percent ($12,540,000 x 0.985 = $12,351,900).

Solution: **Step 1** Find the amount of the penalty.

Original amount x Penalty percent = Penalty
$12,540,000   x 0.015   = $188,100

Step 2 Find the amount received for the project.

Original amount - Penalty   = Amount received
$12,540,000   - $188,100   = $12,351,900

Apply Your Skills

Don Kapan, Certified Public Accountant, completed an $18,000 auditing job that contained a stipulation that a 2.5% penalty would be assessed if the project was not completed within 30 days. Forty-five days were required for the job. How much did Don receive for the job?

$ *17,550*

1) 18.000 X 2.5 = $450
2) 18.000 − 450 = $17.550

SPECIAL SALES DISCOUNTS

Sales are often offered to lure customers to the store.

Many retail stores offer special sales discounts to attract customers during certain holiday periods or to reduce their inventory of specific merchandise items. Advertising notices similar to the one in Figure 12.3 are published in newspapers to promote special sales.

Figure 12.3 Advertisement of Sales Discount

MODEL 12.4

Computing discounted cost

Problem: The Brookview Sports Center offered a special 35% discount on a discontinued line of sportswear. How much will a $125 jogging suit cost after the discount?

Solution: **Step 1** Find the discount.

Original price	x	Discount rate	=	Discount
$125	x	0.35	=	$43.75

Step 2 Find the discounted price.

Original price	-	Discount	=	Discounted price
$125	-	$43.75	=	$81.25

Apply Your Skills

Brookmeade Book Store offered a 25% discount on books that were removed from the best seller list. A local library purchased 100 books. The original price was $13.95 each. How much was the book purchase after the discount? $ ___1,046.25___

1,395 × 0.25 = 348.75 discount
2) 1,395 - 348.75 = $1,046.25
normal - discount (sales price)

PERFORMANCE APPLICATION 12.1

1. The Franklin Book Store offers a 17.5% discount on all purchases over $30. Norman Marichial made a purchase totaling $46.25. How much is his discount?

   $ _____

   [handwritten: D46.25 x 1.75]
   [handwritten: D46.25 x 0.02=0.925]
   [handwritten: D46.25 = 0.925 = 45.325]

2. The Benton House of Fashion offers a 15% discount on purchases of $100-$200, a 20% discount on purchases of $201-$300, and a 25% discount on purchases of $301-$400. On a $275 sale, how much is the discount?

   $ _____

3. The City Card Center offers a 5% discount on the purchase of 5-10 items, a 9% discount on the purchase of 11-15 items, and a 12% discount on all purchases of more than 15 items. Harry Jacobs purchased 12 cards at $2.50 each. How much is his total discount?

   $ _____

4. Distinctive Fashions offered a special sale on shoes by offering the second pair of shoes at one-half price if the first pair was purchased at the regular price. What is the cost of 2 pairs of shoes if each pair normally sells for $49.80?

   $ _____

5. The Best Construction Co. won a $345,500 construction contract with a stipulation that a 1% bonus would be awarded for each day that the job was finished ahead of schedule. The job was finished 13 days ahead of schedule. How much were the (a) bonus and (b) total amount received?

   (a) $ _____

   (b) $ _____

6. The Best Construction Co. won a $298,700 construction contract with a stipulation that a 1.75% per day penalty would be assessed if the job was not finished on time. The job was finished 12 days late. How much were the (a) penalty and (b) total amount received?

   (a) $ _____

   (b) $ _____

7. The Roane Ready Mix Concrete Co. won a highway paving contract amounting to $3,498,500. If they finish by the deadline, they will receive a 2.5% bonus. If they finish later than the deadline, they will be assessed a 2.5% penalty. How much is the (a) most and (b) least that they can receive from the contract?

(a) $ _____

(b) $ _____

8. The Roane Ready Mix Concrete Co. won a highway paving contract amounting to $2,546,800. There will be a $975-per-day penalty for each day the contract is not finished after April 3. If they finish the job on May 8, how much will the (a) penalty and (b) final amount received be?

(a) $ _____

(b) $ _____

9. The Oslow Book Store offered a special sale on selected books by providing a 28% discount. On a $187.50 order, how much was the (a) discount and (b) amount due for the order?

(a) $ _____

(b) $ _____

10. The Video Scene offered a 15% discount if total sales are above $57. Harold Robbins purchased 5 video tapes for a total cost of $122.40. How much was the (a) discount and (b) amount due?

(a) $ _____

(b) $ _____

11. Kiddie Korner offered a promotional sale by selling the second pair of shoes at one-half price if the first pair was purchased at the regular price. Sarah Hughes purchased two pairs of shoes with a price of $39.50 each. What was the total price of the shoes?

$ _____

12. Joan Diaz decided to purchase several toys costing $12.37 each. She has $287. How many toys could she purchase if a 20% discount was offered on each toy?

_____

PRACTICE TEST FOR CHAPTER 12
DISCOUNT ON PURCHASES

Complete each of the following problems and then compare your answers with the ones on page 647.

1. City Travel Agency offered a special travel package to Bermuda. A 15% discount was offered to the first passenger. A 50% discount was offered to the second passenger staying in the same room. The normal package price was $599. What was the package price for two persons?

   $ _____

2. Brea Builders accepted a $345,000 contract to build a house. A stipulation was included that provided a 1.5% penalty if the house was not completed within 9 months and a 3.5% bonus if the house was completed within 9 months. What total amount was due if the house was completed in (a) 8 months and (b) 10 months?

   (a) $ _____

   (b) $ _____

3. Dinstul Ready Mix won a highway paving contract amounting to $1,250,000. There would be an $825 per day penalty for each day the job was not completed after August 1. The job was completed on August 14. How much were the (a) penalty and (b) final amount received?

   (a) $ _____

   (b) $ _____

4. Mardi Breon decided to purchase Smiling Kathy dolls costing $37.25 each for donation to a local charity. A 20% discount was offered for each doll. How many can Mardi purchase for $835.00?

   _____

5. The rings shown in Figure 12.3 on page 216 were offered by City Jewelry Store. What were the discount amounts from original price for the (a) 2-carat diamond and (b) blue topaz rings?

   (a) $ _____

   (b) $ _____

12.1 The auto rental advertisement shown below provides an additional 5% discount to members of an auto club. Assume that you have membership in the club. What is the discounted rate for (a) midweek daily, (b) freedom daily, and (c) Florida/So. California weekly?

(a) $ _____

(b) $ _____

(c) $ _____

CONNECTIONS

Midweek Rate	Freedom Rates	Florida/ So. California
Minivan	Economy	Economy
$39 per day	$19⁹⁹ per day	$119 per week
	Ask for Rate HRTZ.	
	When kept over a Sat. Night.	
Valid thru 6/30/--.	Valid thru 6/30/--.	Valid thru 6/30/--.

12.2 The Exercise Store offered the following items during a special sales promotion. What was the discount rate, based on original or list price, for the (a) dual action bikes and (b) recumbent bikes?

(a) _____

(b) _____

Dual Action Bike

Includes heart rate monitor and calorie burn.
List $600.

$489

Recumbent Bikes

Tunturi. Burns 50% more calories.
Trims hips, thighs, Buttocks.
List $473.

$389

CONNECTIONS

12.1 The Novelty Center sells small and unusual toys to the general public. The store normally purchases 70,000 items, costing $750,000, each year. Supplier A agreed to provide a 5% purchase discount. An additional 3% discount will be provided if 50,000 or more items are purchased during the year. Supplier B agreed to provide a 7.5% purchase discount, with no additional quantity discount. Which supplier offered the best price?

_____

_____

_____

12.2 Visit a local furniture or other retail store in your city. Make a listing that includes five items that are provided with discounts from the normal price. List the item, normal price, discount rate, and discount price for each item. Compare your listing with the listings developed by other members of your class. Then answer the following questions.

1. Why do companies provide discounts?

_____

2. How can the company discount from the normal price and still make a profit?

_____

3. How does the company decide which products will be offered at a discount?

_____

DECISIONS

DISCOUNTS ON PURCHASES
Chapter Review and Quick Reference

Topic	Main Point	Typical Example	Text Page
Quantity discounts	Discounts based on size of purchase encourage larger purchases.	1-10 items, 2% discount; 11-20 items, 3% discount. Fifteen items were purchased for $10 each. $10 x 0.03 = $3.00 discount per item	213
Time discounts	Rewards may be offered to encourage early completion of services.	A $30,000 job included a 2% bonus if completed by April 1. $30,000 x 0.02 = $600 bonus	214
Time penalty	Penalties may be incurred for late completion of services.	A $30,000 job included a 3% penalty if not completed by May 15. $30,000 x 0.03 = $900 penalty	215
Sales discounts	A discount may be offered to increase sales or to sell slow moving items.	A pen normally selling for $80 was discounted 20%. $80 x 0.20 = $16 discount	216
Discounted price	Discounted price is the sales price after discount reduction.	A pen normally selling for $80 was discounted $16. $80 - $16 = $64 discounted sales price	216

COMMUNICATIONS

Read the press release at the right and answer the questions below.

Zap, Inc. Zaps Competitors with Real Innovation

The new star on the computer gaming software horizon is the Seattle-based Zap, Inc. The company's success has been spurred by enthusiastic consumer response to two Zap, Inc. titles, Intergalactica and Zoom Land. Investors are jumping up and down too, since returns on Zap, Inc.'s stock have been consistently impressive.

Why has Zap, Inc. made such an impression with buyers? Innovation, creativity and interactivity appear to be the answers according to industry analysts. "With sticker prices starting at $40 a pop, you better believe the consumer expects something like Zoom Land. Users want wholly interactive game experiences. Zap, Inc. is definitely the current darling of the game-buying market," declares Yolanda Fishbein, a software analyst with Andrew, Worthy, & Smythe, a New York investment house.

Zap, Inc.'s rise has outpaced the performance of its much bigger gaming competitors, such as Game King, unchanged for the year; Champion, up 17% and Entertain Co, up 29%. Analysts say the reason for Zap, Inc.'s galloping stock price--up to $35 from $15 a year ago--is obvious. Sales are booming.

Zap, Inc.'s sales more than doubled to $5.8 million from $2.6 million a year earlier. Sales like these are nothing to sniff at, considering that the four-year old company has just six software products in the marketplace.

The company announced a new children's title, Caperville, will be released early April, along with the much anticipated Zoom Land II. Analysts speculate that these releases will fuel additional interest and growth in the highly successful Zap, Inc.

1. Here are the actual sales figures for the four gaming manufacturers mentioned in the article. Does the writer of the article correctly state each company's performance?

Company	Sales (in Millions)	
	This Year	Last Year
Zap, Inc.	$ 5.8	$ 2.6
Game King	46.4	46.5
Champion	36.6	31.3
Entertain Co.	22.0	19.5

2. How many percent has Zap, Inc. stock risen in the past year?

3. By how many percent did Game King sales exceed Zap, Inc. sales this year?

4. Which company must attain sales of $73.2 next year to double its sales?

5. Use the language of business to describe the financial picture of Zap, Inc. after Caperville and Zoom Land II yield a 46% increase in sales for the company in the first three months following their release.

UNIT 3 SPREADSHEET APPLICATION 1:
DISCOUNT LISTING

The following spreadsheet is used to compute the discount amount and final price for each item. It also computes the total cost for the number of units purchased for each item. Totals are computed for the number purchased and total cost columns. The original price is multiplied by the discount rate to compute the discount amount. The discount amount is then deducted from the original price to compute the final price of each item. The final price is multiplied by the number purchased to compute the total cost for each item. Amounts for Product Number B-217 are computed as an example for checking the logic of your computations. Do not round discount amount and final price when computing total cost.

	A	B	C	D	E	F	G
1	John's Shoppe		DISCOUNT LISTING				
2	--						
3	Product	Original	Discount	Discount	Final	Number	Total
4	Number	Price	Rate	Amount	Price	Purchased	Cost
5	--						
6	B-217	2.33	.25	.58	1.75	20	34.95
7	B-218	4.59	.25			15	
8	C-243	3.67	.20			12	
9	C-316	14.75	.20			25	
10	R-345	3.80	.18			27	
11	R-349	4.52	.18			25	
12	R-364	3.74	.23			8	
13	T-008	10.25	.15			35	
14	T-111	2.17	.25			12	
15	T-113	2.43	.25			50	
16	T-426	8.43	.15			27	
17	T-457	6.30	.35			25	
18	--						
19	Totals	************************************					

Refer to the spreadsheet on the previous page to answer the following questions.

1. What is the discount amount for Product Number C- 243?

   $ _____

2. What is the final price for Product Number R-349?

   $ _____

3. What is the final price for Product Number T-111?

   $ _____

4. What is the total cost for Product Number T-426?

   $ _____

5. What is the total number purchased?

   _____

6. Which product number had the highest total cost?

   _____

7. Which product number had the lowest final price?

   _____

8. How many product numbers had a discount amount greater than $1.00?

   _____

9. How many product numbers had a total cost greater than $100.00?

   _____

10. What is the average total cost for all items (the sum of the total cost column divided by the sum of the number purchased column)?

    $ _____

UNIT 3 SPREADSHEET APPLICATION 2:
FINANCE CHARGES

The following spreadsheet is used to determine the finance charge, total due, monthly payment, and annual percentage rate (APR) for a series of purchases. Sums of the finance charge and total due columns are also computed. The finance charge is computed by multiplying the purchase price times the interest rate times the years financed. The total due is computed by adding the purchase price to the finance charge. The monthly payment is computed by dividing the total due by the number of payments. The APR is computed by using the following formula:

$$APR = \frac{2 \ \times \ \text{Number of payments per year} \ \times \ \text{Interest charge}}{\text{Amount financed} \ \times \ (\text{Total number of payments} + 1)}$$

The computed amounts for the first purchase are shown in the spreadsheet to permit you to determine whether or not your logic is correct.

	A	B	C	D	E	F	G	H
1	City Savings Bank			FINANCE CHARGES				
2	-------	-------	-------	-------	-------	-------	-------	-------
3	Purchase	Interest	Years	Finance	Total	Number of	Monthly	APR
4	Price	Rate	Financed	Charge	Due	Payments	Payment	
5	-------	-------	-------	-------	-------	-------	-------	-------
6	15,000	.06	4	3,600	18,600	48	387.50	11.76%
7	17,000	.08	5			60		
8	12,000	.05	4			48		
9	10,000	.09	3			36		
10	9,000	.06	4			48		
11	600	.10	5			60		
12	2,000	.08	4			48		
13	3,000	.12	3			36		
14	4,000	.08	4			48		
15	5,000	.06	3			36		
16	400	.09	5			60		
17	3,000	.07	5			60		
18	-------	-------	-------	-------	-------	-------	-------	-------
19	Totals	**************************************						

Refer to the spreadsheet on the previous page to answer the following questions.

1. What is the finance charge for the $12,000 purchase price?

   $ _____

2. What is the finance charge for the $3,000 purchase price on line 17?

   $ _____

3. What is the total due for the $600 purchase price?

   $ _____

4. What is the total due for the $400 purchase price?

   $ _____

5. What is the monthly payment for the $17,000 purchase price?

   $ _____

6. What is the monthly payment for the $4,000 purchase price?

   $ _____

7. What is the APR for the $10,000 purchase price?

   _____

8. What is the APR for the $4,000 purchase price?

   _____

9. How much are the total finance charges?

   $ _____

10. How many purchases had monthly payments greater than $225.00?

    _____

UNIT 3 SELF-TEST
PERCENTAGE AMOUNTS IN BUSINESS

1. Compute each of the following amounts (Rate X Base = Amount):

    (a) 15% of $720 = $ _____

    (b) 8% of $120.30 = $ _____

    (c) 16 1/2% of $320 = $ _____

    (d) 12 3/4% of $1,200 = $ _____

    (e) 8% of $675 = $ _____

    (f) 25% of $680.48 = $ _____

2. Carl Swift contributed 12% of his salary to foundations. If his salary was $18,360, how much did he contribute?

    $ _____

3. Joy Carlisle spent $191.21 on a new radio for her car. If this amount represented 8.5% of her savings account, how much savings did she have? $ _____

4. The Crocker Auto Service offered to repair a car for $276. This was 15% more than the repair estimate by The Auto Shoppe. How much was the estimate by The Auto Shoppe?

    $ _____

5. The Dolly Furniture Store ran a special sale with items selling at 60% of their regular price. If the sale price of an item is $750, what was the regular price for the item?

    $ _____

6. Bill Brock had sales of $2,800 this month. This was 12% more than his sales last month. How much were his sales last month?

    $ _____

7. Turner Auto Sales bought a car for $800 and sold it for $1,000. What was the percent of profit based on the original price of the car? _____

8. Carl Johnson missed 10 days of work last year. He missed 14 days of work this year. What was the rate of increase this year?

    _____

229

9. Carla Brower answered 80 questions correctly on an exam. On a second exam, she answered 100 questions correctly. What was the percent of increase in her performance?

   _____

10. Brad Simpson had a monthly salary of $1,200. He spent $300 during the first week. What percent of his salary did he spend during the first week of the month?

    _____

11. Use an aliquot part of $1.00 to compute the following:

    (a) 78 items @ 16 2/3 cents = $ _____

    (b) 45 items @ 6 2/3 cents   = $ _____

    (c) 150 items @ 33 1/3 cents = $ _____

    (d) 48 items @ 12 1/2 cents = $ _____

12. Inez Anderson bought a new car for $12,000 and made a down payment of 12 1/2%. How much was her down payment?

    $ _____

13. A grain bin holds 624 tons. It appears to be 33 1/3% full. How much grain is in the bin?

    _____

14. Jennie Sue Runyan makes $12 per hour. If she received an 8 1/3% raise, how much would her raise be?

    $ _____

15. Juan Ramos bought a new watch for $650. If the first monthly finance charge was 1 1/2% of the purchase price, how much was the first month's finance charge?

    $ _____

16. Meryl Studebaker bought a new television for $900 with monthly finance charges of 1 1/2%. If a payment of $60 was made at the end of one month, how much of the payment applied to the (a) balance and (b) finance charge?

    (a) $ _____

    (b) $ _____

UNIT 4

Marketing Mathematics

Have you ever thought about what stores pay for the merchandise they are selling to the public? Do they determine how much to charge for merchandise without considering what their competitors are able to do? Have you wondered why the same CD may cost anywhere form $9.95 to $15.95 or why clothing stores can afford to sell merchandise at 30 to 40% off and still make a profit? Would a store actually sell something for less than they had to pay for it? These are all questions relating to marketing mathematics. We are all included in a world of marketing whether we choose to be or not. On a daily basis, we must buy, buy, and buy some more in order to exist in today's commercial world, and many of us in turn must sell, sell, and sell.

Stop and think about what you must buy today in order to maintain your lifestyle. Did you drive a car or take a bus? Will you buy your lunch in a restaurant or did you buy food in a grocery store to bring it with you? Are you paying someone each time you turn on a light in a room? You may even be paying someone to live in that room. In this unit, you will learn how prices and salespersons' commissions are computed; how cash and trade discounts affect the pricing structure; and what discounts are commonly offered by manufacturers and wholesalers to retailers. These are marketing concepts you will be able to use in real-life situations.

CASH DISCOUNTS

Performance Objectives

1. Use cash discount terms correctly.
2. Determine discount schedule and compute cash discounts.
3. Use a table to determine exact days.
4. Determine net cash prices.
5. Calculate cash discounts that include freight charges and purchase returns.

Companies selling merchandise like to receive payment for the merchandise as soon as possible after delivery to keep cash flowing back to the business. To encourage buyers to pay by a specified date, the seller often offers a *cash discount*, or reduction from the net price of the invoice. This chapter will show you how cash discounts and specified dates are determined.

OVERVIEW OF CASH DISCOUNTS

Many companies offer cash discounts for prompt payment of accounts for merchandise sold. This can benefit both the buyer and the seller because the seller receives early payment and the buyer does not have to pay the full amount for the purchase. Costs and quantities of items purchased are listed on an *invoice*. The customary procedure is to allow a cash discount only if payment is received by a specified date, as indicated by the seller on the invoice. After the specified date, the buyer must pay the full price for items listed on the invoice.

Cash discount: A reduction in the amount of an invoice to encourage early payment of the bill.

Merchandise purchases are sometimes accompanied by a check to cover the cost of the merchandise and possible shipping charges and taxes. However, many purchase agreements include an understanding that the merchandise will be shipped with payment on a later date. It is to the seller's advantage to receive payment as soon as possible. To encourage earlier payment, the seller will often provide a **cash discount**, or reduction from the price of the invoice, if payment is received within a specified period of time, such as 10 days from the date of the invoice. Explanations in this chapter will illustrate how cash discounts are determined. Figure 13.1 shows a typical transaction.

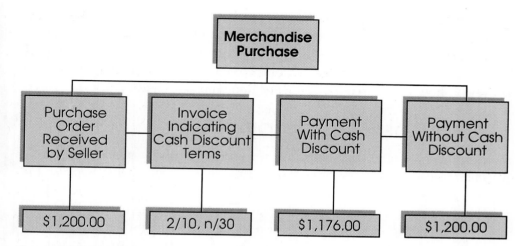

Figure 13.1 Merchandise Purchase

TYPICAL CASH DISCOUNT TERMS

Both buyer and seller must abide by the terms of the cash discount, as indicated on the invoice. However, payment must be made by the specified due date to qualify for the cash discount, if any. For example, terms such as 2/10, n/30 (read *two ten, net thirty*) mean that a 2% discount will be allowed if payment is made within 10 days from the date of the invoice, and the full amount must be paid within 30 days. No cash discount will be allowed from Day 11 to Day 30. Other typical discount terms are expressed as follows:

5/15, n/45. This means that the full amount is due within 45 days from the date of the invoice. However, a 5% discount will be given if the bill is paid within 15 days from the date of the invoice. (Read *five fifteen, net forty-five.*)

3/10 EOM, n/30 EOM. The full amount is due within 30 days after the end of the month (EOM). However, a 3% discount will be given if the bill is paid within 10 days after the end of the month. (Read *three ten end of month, net thirty end of month.*)

n/30. The full amount is due within 30 days from the date of the invoice. No discount is given for early payment (Read *net thirty.*)

3/20, 1/45, n/90. The full amount is due within 90 days from the date of the invoice. However, a 3% discount will be given if the bill is paid within 20 days, or a 1% discount will be given if payment is received later than 20 days but within 45 days after the date of the invoice. (Read *three twenty, one forty-five, net ninety.*) A sample invoice form is shown in Figure 13.2.

INVOICE	GD Electronics					INVOICE No. 241628

GD Electronics
3987 Park Heights Avenue
Baltimore, MD 21215

SOLD TO
City Record Store
Attn: Mr. Clyde Androtti
389 Pasadena Avenue
St. Petersburg, FL 33707

SHIP TO
Same

Customer's Order No. 42003	Purchase Order 1027	Salesperson R. Perez	Terms 3/15, n/60	Ship Via FedEx	Our Order No. 37890-1	Date 4/5/--

No.	Product	DESCRIPTION	QTY.	UNIT PRICE	TOTAL
1	XY27	Hill City Blues (CD)	30	11.95	358.50
2	YR29	Dusty Roads (CD)	20	10.50	210.00
3	TE48	Highway Sixteen (Tape)	15	9.75	146.25
4					
5					
6				Shipping	28.75
7				Subtotal	743.50
8				Tax	44.59
9				Total	788.09

ORIGINAL   THANK YOU

Figure 13.2 Sample Invoice Form

DETERMINING THE CASH DISCOUNT AND DUE DATES

The exact date that is the last date for taking the cash discount must be determined to ensure that both the buyer and seller will know about this date. For this reason, exact calendar days are used based on the number of days that elapse from the date of the invoice.

The spreadsheet table in Figure 13.3 can be used to compute the last date for taking the cash discount and/or the due date. The values in the table represent the number of days that elapse after January 1 each year. The steps for using this table are shown in Model 13.1.

Exact calendar days: Calendar days are used to determine discount period.

235

	A	B	C	D	E	F	G	H	I	J	K	L	M
1	Spreadsheet Table to Compute Exact Days-in-a-Year (excluding leap year)												
2	---												
3	Day of	Jan.	Feb.	Mar.	Apr.	May	June	July	Aug.	Sept.	Oct.	Nov.	Dec.
4	Month	31	28	31	30	31	30	31	31	30	31	30	31
5	---												
6	1	1	32	60	91	121	152	182	213	244	274	305	335
7	2	2	33	61	92	122	153	183	214	245	275	306	336
8	3	3	34	62	93	123	154	184	215	246	276	307	337
9	4	4	35	63	94	124	155	185	216	247	277	308	338
10	5	5	36	64	95	125	156	186	217	248	278	309	339
11	6	6	37	65	96	126	157	187	218	249	279	310	340
12	7	7	38	66	97	127	158	188	219	250	280	311	341
13	8	8	39	67	98	128	159	189	220	251	281	312	342
14	9	9	40	68	99	129	160	190	221	252	282	313	343
15	10	10	41	69	100	130	161	191	222	253	283	314	344
16	11	11	42	70	101	131	162	192	223	254	284	315	345
17	12	12	43	71	102	132	163	193	224	255	285	316	346
18	13	13	44	72	103	133	164	194	225	256	286	317	347
19	14	14	45	73	104	134	165	195	226	257	287	318	348
20	15	15	46	74	105	135	166	196	227	258	288	319	349
21	16	16	47	75	106	136	167	197	228	259	289	320	350
22	17	17	48	76	107	137	168	198	229	260	290	321	351
23	18	18	49	77	108	138	169	199	230	261	291	322	352
24	19	19	50	78	109	139	170	200	231	262	292	323	353
25	20	20	51	79	110	140	171	201	232	263	293	324	354
26	21	21	52	80	111	141	172	202	233	264	294	325	355
27	22	22	53	81	112	142	173	203	234	265	295	326	356
28	23	23	54	82	113	143	174	204	235	266	296	327	357
29	24	24	55	83	114	144	175	205	236	267	297	328	358
30	25	25	56	84	115	145	176	206	237	268	298	329	359
31	26	26	57	85	116	146	177	207	238	269	299	330	360
32	27	27	58	86	117	147	178	208	239	270	300	331	361
33	28	28	59	87	118	148	179	209	240	271	301	332	362
34	29	29	****	88	119	149	180	210	241	272	302	333	363
35	30	30	****	89	120	150	181	211	242	273	303	334	364
36	31	31	****	90	****	151	****	212	243	****	304	****	365

Figure 13.3 Exact Days-in-a-Year Calendar Spreadsheet

A table, similar to the one shown above, is often used to determine exact days.

As an introduction to using the table, assume that the current date is July 14. How many days remain until Christmas (December 25)? Subtract the value in the table for July 14 (195) from the value in the table for December 25 (359); the result is 164 days. You may want to practice with other dates, such as the number of days until your birthday or the number of days until your next college break from classes.

Model 13.1 shows how to use the table to solve cash discount problems and find due dates.

Using the spreadsheet table to determine a due date

Problem: The date of an invoice is February 26 with terms of 2/10, n/45. What are the (a) last day to take the cash discount and (b) due date?

Solution: **Step 1** Move down Column A until you locate the day of the month representing the date of the invoice: in this example, 26 on Row 31.

Step 2 Move across the row to the column representing the month for the invoice date: in this example, February in Column C (Row 31). The value 57 is in this location.

Step 3 Find the last date for the cash discount by adding 10 to this value (57 + 10) = 67. Find the month above this value (located in Column D, Row 13: March). Find the day in Column A that is to the left of this value: 8. Therefore, the date is March 8.

Step 4 Find the due date in the table by adding 45 to the value located in Step 2 (57 + 45) = 102. Find the month above this value (located in Column E, Row 17: April). Find the day in Column A that is to the left of this value: 12. Therefore, the due date is April 12.

Apply Your Skills

Reitz Sports Center purchased exercise equipment from a wholesaler. Reitz received an invoice dated April 28 with terms of 3/15, n/60. What are the (a) last date to take the cash discount and (b) due date?

(a) _____

(b) _____

With practice, you will find this table easy to use. The cash discount and due dates are given for Models 13.2 and 13.3. For practice, use the table to determine the dates and see if you arrive at the same dates as the ones provided.

145

MODEL 13.2

End-of-Month (EOM): *Last day to receive cash discount is a specified period after the first day of the following invoice month date.*

Finding cash discount dates and due dates

Problem: Find the cash discount and due dates for invoices dated August 10 with the following terms: (a) 3/10, n/30, (b) 3/10 EOM, n/30 EOM, (c) n/30, (d) n/EOM, and ((e) 3/15, 2/30, n/45.

Solution:

Terms	Last Cash Discount Date	Due Date
3/10, n/30	August 20	September 9
3/10 EOM, n/30 EOM	September 10	September 30
n/30	None	September 9
n/EOM	None	August 31
3/15, 2/30, n/45	August 25 or September 9	September 24

Apply Your Skills

City Beauty Salon purchased makeup and hair care supplies from a distributor in Dallas, Texas. An invoice, dated August 20 with terms of 3/10 EOM, n/60, is received with delivery of the supplies. What are the (a) last date to take the cash discount and (b) due date?

(a) *Sept. 10*

(b) *Oct. 19*

COMPUTING THE CASH DISCOUNT

You must determine whether the *date of payment* is on or before the cash discount date in order to qualify for the cash discount. If the date of payment qualifies the buyer for a cash discount, compute the cash discount using the steps shown in Model 13.3. Computation of cash discount for an invoice with no freight charges or returns bases the discount rate on the net invoice price. Returns represent merchandise that comes back to the seller due to damage or other reasons. Amounts should be rounded to the nearest cent for each computation.

Computing cash discount and cash price

Problem: The Bullhart Equipment Center purchased merchandise totaling $656.50 with terms of 2/10, n/30. The invoice, dated January 28, was paid on February 3. What are the cash discount and cash price?

Solution: **Step 1** Find the cash discount.

Net price x   Cash discount rate = Cash discount
$656.50   x   .02 (2%)   = $13.13

Step 2 Find the cash price.

Net price - Cash discount = Cash price
$656.50   - $13.13   = $643.37

Apply Your Skills

7% ↾ n/60

Martin Office Supply Store received an invoice for merchandise purchased totaling $1,929.50. The invoice is dated January 22 with terms of 4/15, n/60. If the invoice is paid on February 1, what are the (a) cash discount and (b) cash price?

(a) $ _77.18_

(b) $ _1852.32_

FREIGHT TERMS

Freight charges are necessary when merchandise is shipped to the buyer. These charges may be paid by the seller or the buyer depending on the terms of the sales invoice. *FOB* (Free on Board) *shipping point* means that the buyer pays the shipping costs. *FOB destination* means that the seller pays the shipping costs. Regardless of who pays the shipping costs, any cash discount does not apply to the portion of the invoice relating to shipping costs. Freight charges and returns, if any, should be deducted from the net invoice amount prior to computing the cash discount, as shown in Model 13.4.

FOB shipping point: *Stands for free on board and requires the buyer to pay shipping charges.*

FOB destination: *This indication requires the seller to pay shipping charges.*

2580.76
2580.78

239

MODEL 13.4

Cash discounts are not given for freight and returned merchandise purchases.

Computing net price subject to the cash discount

Problem: The City Sports Center purchased goods with a net invoice amount of $324.52, including $16.37 freight charges and $14.00 in returns. What is the net price subject to the cash discount?

Solution:

Net invoice amount	-	Freight charges	-	Purchase returns	=	Net price
$324.52	-	$16.37	-	$14.00	=	$294.15

Apply Your Skills

Roger Ball Construction Company purchased building supplies with a net invoice amount of $1,274.78, including $37.98 freight charges and $79.27 purchase returns. Terms are 3/10, n/45. What is the net price subject to the cash discount?

$ _____

MODEL 13.5

Deduct freight charges, if any.

Compute the cash discount.

Add freight charges to compute cash price.

Computing net price subject to freight charges

Problem: The Culver Shoppe purchased goods with a net invoice amount of $750.56, including $12.38 for freight charges and $26.00 in returns. The invoice, dated August 18 with terms of 3/15, n/45, was paid on September 1. What are the net price subject to discount, cash discount, and final cash price for the invoice?

Solution:

Step 1
Net invoice amount =		$ 750.56
Less prepaid freight charges	$ 12.38	
and returns	+ 26.00	- 38.38
Net price subject to discount =		712.18

Step 2 Cash discount = $712.18 X .03 = 21.3654 — - 21.37

Step 3
Net price =	690.81
Plus freight charges	+ 12.38
Cash price =	$ 703.19

Apply Your Skills

Refer to Apply Your Skills 13.4. Assuming that the invoice is paid within 15 days of the invoice date, what are the (a) cash discount and (b) cash price?

(a) $ _____

(b) $ _____

PERFORMANCE APPLICATION 13.1

1. Determine the cash discount date and due date for each of the following invoices. The first entry is completed as an example.

Invoice No.	Invoice Date	Terms	Cash Discount Date(s)	Due Date
	May 25	2/10, n/30	June 4	June 24
1	January 18	2/10, n/30	_January 28_	_February 17_
2	April 17	3/15, n/45		
3	July 19	3/20, n/40		
4	August 10	2/15 EOM, n/30 EOM		
5	September 9	n/EOM		
6	October 10	2/10, 1/20, n/30		
7	March 23	5/10, n/30		
8	December 8	3/10, n/10 EOM		
9	February 28	2/15, n/60		
10	June 30	1/10, n/20		

2. Assume that the following invoices are paid within the cash discount periods. Compute the cash discount and the cash price for each invoice. The first entry is completed as an example.

Invoice No.	Net Price	Discount Terms	Cash Discount	Cash Price
	$ 354.17	2/10, n/30	$7.08	$347.09
1	750.50	2/10, n/30	$	$
2	296.18	3/15, n/30	$	$
3	641.76	3/20, n/45	$	$
4	711.80	4/15, n/40	$	$
5	2,716.58	5/10, n/30	$	$

3. The following invoice is for merchandise from Lanko Wholesalers. Complete the extensions for each item, total the extensions to compute the net price, compute the cash discount, and compute the cash price if the invoice is paid on October 5.

Sold to:			Invoice No. 1820
Harrah's Shop		Date:	9/15/--
2800 Kirby Parkway		Terms:	4/10 EOM, n/60
Memphis, TN 38119		Account No.:	28-9732
		Via:	Truck

Catalog No.	Quantity	Unit Price	Amount
A-341	18	$19.85	$
A-362	12	16.34	$
B-681	9	32.14	$
F-111	18	14.18	$
Z-819	7	21.36	$
		NET PRICE	$
		CASH DISCOUNT	$
		CASH PRICE	$

4. An invoice for merchandise from Fay's Fashions is shown below. Complete the extensions for each item, total the extensions to compute the net price, compute the cash discount, and compute the cash price if the invoice is paid on April 4.

Sold to:			Invoice No. 2945
Distinctive Shop		Date:	3/27/--
1 Office Park Circle		Terms:	2/15, n/30
Birmingham, AL 15223		Account No.:	34-2845
		Freight:	FOB Destination

Catalog No.	Quantity	Unit Price	Amount
C-423	17	$ 89.45	$
B-679	13	115.75	$
GG-98	14	78.35	$
H-562	8	35.98	$
		NET PRICE	$
		CASH DISCOUNT	$
		CASH PRICE	$

Performance Application 13.2

1. Roberts Electronics sold merchandise to Simon's Shop on March 4 with a net price of $384.76. Cash discount terms were 3/10, n/30. If the invoice is paid on March 9, how much will Roberts Electronics receive as the cash price for the invoice?

   $ _____

2. Rembrook and Associates received an invoice dated August 8 with a net price of $312.80 and cash discount terms of 2/10 EOM, n/90. (a) What was the last day that the invoice could have been paid and still have been subject to the cash discount? (b) What was the due date for the invoice? (c) If the invoice was paid on September 3, what was the cash price? (d) If the invoice was paid on September 15, what was the cash price?

   (a) _____   (c) $ _____

   (b) _____   (d) $ _____

3. Maple Products purchased merchandise with a net price of $478.24 (including freight charges of $36.00). The invoice date was October 29 with terms of 3/10, 2/30, n/45 EOM. What was the cash price to be paid if the invoice was paid on each of the following dates? (a) November 3, (b) November 7, and (c) November 20.

   (a) $ _____   (c) $ _____

   (b) $ _____

4. Fulmer Enterprises ships merchandise to customers in the United States and several foreign countries. A discount of 7 1/2% is offered to customers who pay within 30 days from the date of the invoice. A recent invoice dated February 11 was received by the Ramrod Corporation with a net price of $1,760.80, including freight charges of $30.00. Assume that the invoice was paid on March 1. (a) How much was the cash discount? (b) How much was the cash price including freight charges?

(c) What was the last date that the invoice could be paid and still be subject to the cash discount?

(a) $ _____   (c) _____

(b) $ _____

5. Beacon Unlimited has cash discount terms of 3/10, 2/20, n/45. On an invoice to Abel Co. dated June 16 for $2,340.20, how much will be due if the invoice is paid on (a) June 22, (b) June 30, and (c) July 31?

(a) $ _____   (c) $ _____

(b) $ _____

6. Ramsey's Chair Factory sent merchandise to the Freemore Furniture Store with an invoice date of April 15, cash discount terms of 3/10, n/30, and a net price of $2,986.40. Freight charges of $50 were included in the net price. They returned merchandise costing $175 to Ramsey's on April 20. Compute the (a) cash discount on April 23 and (b) amount of the check that should have been written on April 23.

(a) $ _____   (b) $ _____

7. Bardow's Department Store sent an invoice with an October 13 date and a total net price of $12,713.48 to Wade Bargers. Terms were 11/10 EOM, 7/30 EOM. The bill was paid on November 23. Compute the (a) last date to receive the 11% discount, (b) last date to receive the 7% discount, (c) amount of the cash discount on November 23, and (d) cash price on November 23.

(a) _____   (c) $ _____

(b) _____   (d) $ _____

8. The House of Dave sent an invoice dated January 23 for $85.20 with terms of 3/10, n/30. (a) What would the cash discount price be if the bill was paid on February 1? (b) What amount will be due if the invoice is paid on February 5?

(a) $ _____

(b) $ _____

PERFORMANCE APPLICATION 13.3

Assume that the following invoice was paid on January 15. The cash discount should be based on the total price of the merchandise **only**. Shipping charges will remain the same. The amount charged for taxes should equal 6% of the cash price.

(a)   What is the cash discount amount? $ _____

(b)   What is the tax amount? $ _____

(c)   What is the total amount due? $ _____

INVOICE	**City Computer Shoppe**				**INVOICE No.**	
	2536 Frost Street				241628	
	San Diego, CA 92120				Packing Slip 27152	

SOLD TO
Computer Retail Outlet
2795 S. Alameda
Corpus Cristi, TX 78411

SHIP TO
Same

Customer's Order No. 378218	Purchase Order 37218	Salesperson Perez, J.	Terms 2/10, n/30	Ship Via UPS	Our Order No. 27421	Date 1/8/--
No.	Product	DESCRIPTION		QTY.	UNIT PRICE	TOTAL
1	R-78Y	CD-ROM		20	219.35	4,387.00
2	T-83H	Tape Backup		36	225.50	8,118.00
3	U-78N	Sound Blaster		10	220.75	2,207.50
4						
5						
6					Shipping	75.25
7					Subtotal	14,787.75
8					Tax	882.75
9					Total	15,670.50

ORIGINAL

THANK YOU

PRACTICE TEST FOR CHAPTER 13
CASH DISCOUNTS

Complete each of the following problems and then compare your answers with the ones on page 648.

1. An invoice is dated December 18 with terms of 2/15, n/60. What is the last date that the invoice can be paid and still earn a cash discount?

    _____

2. An invoice is dated November 12 with terms of 2/10 EOM, n/60. What is the last date the invoice can be paid and still earn a cash discount?

    _____

3. An invoice was dated September 21 with cash discount terms of 2/20, n/50. What are the (a) last day that the invoice can be paid and still receive a cash discount and (b) last day that the invoice can be paid and not be overdue?

    (a) _____

    (b) _____

4. Ramirez Furniture Center purchased merchandise from the manufacturer in North Carolina. The $24,500 invoice was dated March 23 with cash discount terms of 2/15, n/45. The invoice was paid on April 2. What were the (a) cash discount and (b) cash price?

    (a) $ _____

    (b) $ _____

5. Hardaway Enterprises purchased furniture for their new office. The invoice, dated July 14, totaled $7,385, which included $37.85 shipping charges. One office chair, costing $74.50, was damaged and returned. What is the amount that is subject to a cash discount?

    $ _____

CONNECTIONS

13.1 The chart shown below indicates the percent of people who are on unemployment. Review the chart and then answer the questions shown below. Assume that you live in a city with a working population of 120,000 people.

(a) How many people were unemployed in your city during the beginning of the first term of President George Bush?

_____

(b) How many people were unemployed in your city during the beginning of the first term of President Bill Clinton?

_____

(c) In your city, how many people were unemployed during the first month of Jimmy Carter's first term? (Assume that unemployment figures are similar to the ones shown in the chart.)

_____

CONFRONTING UNEMPLOYMENT

Rates when presidents took office

Richard Nixon (Jan. 1969)	3.2%
Jimmy Carter (Jan. 1977)	8%
Ronald Reagan (Jan. 1981)	8%
George Bush (Jan. 1989)	5.4%
Bill Clinton (Jan. 1993)	7.1%

13.2 The chart shown below indicates the wages of workers with earnings in various income level categories. Review the chart and answer the questions shown below. Assume that you live in a city with 109,000 persons employed and that the chart is typical of workers in your city.

(a) How many workers earn between $24,000 and $35,000?

_____

(b) How many workers earn less than $14,000?

_____

(c) In the actual city where you live, how many workers earn more than $50,000? (Assume that your city is typical of the chart distribution of wages.)

_____

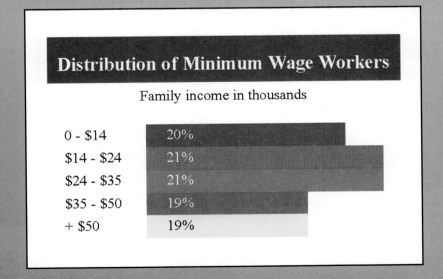

Distribution of Minimum Wage Workers

Family income in thousands

0 - $14	20%
$14 - $24	21%
$24 - $35	21%
$35 - $50	19%
+ $50	19%

CONNECTIONS

13.1 Perez and Smith, Attorneys, opened a law practice three years ago. They decided to purchase 6 new microcomputers for the office. City Computer Center will sell the computers for $1,785 each. A cash discount is provided if the invoice is paid within 30 days. Otherwise, the full amount is due within 90 days. The attorneys presently have low bank funds and may need to borrow funds from a local bank in order to take advantage of the cash discount. What factors or questions should be considered while making a decision about whether or not to borrow funds to take the cash discount?

_____

_____

_____

13.2 Some manufacturers and wholesale/distributors provide cash discounts to encourage early payment of invoices. Use the local telephone directory to locate phone numbers for several retail stores in your city. Call them to determine whether or not they are awarded cash discounts from their suppliers. For the ones that do not receive cash discounts, determine whether or not they would like to have this incentive from their suppliers. Prepare a one-page report to indicate the results of your survey.

DECISIONS

CASH DISCOUNTS
Chapter Review and Quick Reference

Topic	Main Point	Typical Example	Text Page
Invoice	An invoice is a form listing merchandise costs, items purchased, and other information.	4 microcomputers purchased for $1,250 4 x $1,250 = $5,000	235
Discount term	A period is provided for early payment of bill.	2/10, n/30 read "two ten; net 30"	235
Cash discount date	The last date to pay invoice and still receive cash discount is the cash discount date.	2/15, n/60. Invoice dated June 10. Cash discount date is **June 25**.	238
Due date	The last date to pay invoice without its being past due is the due date.	2/15, n/60. Invoice dated June 17. Due date is **August 16**.	238
Cash discount	The cash discount is the deduction for payment by the cash discount date.	Invoice amount $750.35 with terms of 2/10, n/30 and paid by cash discount date: $750.35 x 0.02 = **$15.01** (rounded)	239
Net price	The amount subject to a cash discount is the net price.	Invoice amount, $835.28; freight, $37.18; and purchase returns, $35.00. $835.28 - $37.18 - $35.00 = **$763.10**.	240

TRADE DISCOUNTS

Performance Objectives

1. Determine trade discount amounts using the formula method.
2. Determine trade discount amounts using the complement method.
3. Determine the net price and trade discount amounts using single percentages and trade discount series.
4. Utilize shortcut methods to determine trade discount rates.

Many manufacturers and suppliers of merchandise provide a catalog that includes a description and list or catalog price for each item. This price is often the suggested retail or selling price. Stores buying the merchandise for resale are provided a separate discount sheet showing a *trade discount* from the list price. In this chapter, you will learn how to compute the trade discount and how to determine the price that retailers are charged for merchandise purchased from manufacturers and suppliers.

The illustration in Figure 14.1 indicates the supply channel from the manufacturer to the consumer. Trade discounts may be applied during any of the positions in the channel.

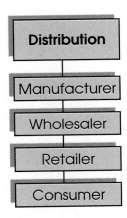

Figure 14.1 Supply Channel

OVERVIEW OF TRADE DISCOUNTS

Manufacturers, wholesalers, and other suppliers provide a catalog that lists information about the various products they have available for sale. The *trade discount* is a reduction in list price allowed to dealers in the same line of business or trade. The amount to be paid after the trade discount is deducted is the *net price*. A *cash discount* may be provided in addition to the trade discount to encourage prompt payment.

Owners and managers should be aware of suppliers that offer large trade discounts. The trade discount decreases the amount actually required to purchase the merchandise. Trade discounts may be stated as single discount rates or as a chain or series of two or more discount rates. Trade discounts are based on the list price of merchandise. Freight charges, if any, should be deducted from the invoice before computing the trade discount.

The catalog price is also called the list price.

Trade discount: *The amount deducted from the list price.*

Single discount rate: *Indicates that only one discount rate is applied to the list price.*

COMPUTING A SINGLE TRADE DISCOUNT

The trade discount may be quoted as a single rate. The base list price is then reduced by the amount of the discount to compute the final net price. The basic formula (*Base* x *Rate*) = *Amount* can be used here, as shown in Model 14.1.

MODEL 14.1

Basic Formula

(B)		List Price
(R)	x	Discount Rate
(A)	=	Discount Amount

Computing trade discount and net price

Problem: Merkle Wholesale Distributors sells merchandise with a $1,200 list price and a single trade discount of 40%. What will be the trade discount and net price for this order?

Solution: **Step 1** Find the trade discount.

(Base)	x	(Rate)	=	(Amount)
List price	x	Trade discount rate	=	Trade discount
$1,200.00	x	0.40 (40%)	=	$480.00

Step 2 Find the net price.

List price	-	Trade discount	=	Net price
$1,200.00	-	$480.00	=	$720.00

Apply Your Skills

A review of the catalog from North Furniture Wholesale Co. indicates that a dining room was priced at $2,400 with a single trade discount rate of 35 percent. What was the (a) trade discount and (b) net price?

(a) $ _____

(b) $ _____

Net price: *The result after subtracting the discount rate from the list price.*

COMPUTING NET PRICE: COMPLEMENT METHOD

Complement or net price rate: *The result after subtracting the trade discount rate from 100%.*

The *complement method* provides an alternative computation for finding the net price. In percentage terms, list price represents the whole or base (100%), and the net price represents the amount left after the trade discount rate has been subtracted. In other words, after deducting a trade discount of 40%, the net price (60%) equals the rate charged. To illustrate this method, merchandise with a list price of $1,200.00 and a trade discount of 40% will leave a net price of $720.00 as computed by the steps shown in Model 14.2.

Notice that the same net price amount ($720.00) was obtained using either the regular method in the previous example or the complement method used in this example.

Computing complement trade discount rate

Problem: Merkle Wholesale Distributors sells merchandise with a $1,200 list price and a single trade discount of 40%. What will be the complement trade discount rate and net price for this order?

Solution: **Step 1** Find the complement trade discount rate.

1.00	-	Trade discount rate	=	Net price rate	
1.00	-	0.40	=	0.60 (60%)	

Step 2 Find the net price.

List price	x	Net price rate	=	Net price
$1,200	x	0.60	=	$720.00

Complement Method

*1.00 -
discount rate =
net price rate*

*list price x
net price rate =
net price*

Apply Your Skills

Donovan Sports Center lists a particular brand of tennis racket for $57.50 with a single trade discount of 20%. If 60 of the rackets were ordered, what were the (a) net price rate and (b) net price for the order?

(a) _____

(b) $ _____

COMPUTING NET PRICE USING A SERIES OF TRADE DISCOUNTS

Trade discount series: Two or more discounts that are deducted successively from the list price.

Suppliers may decide to offer two or more trade discounts to encourage companies to purchase slow-moving items, to promote their products, or to sell larger orders. Trade discounts are often written as a series, such as 25/20/5, or 25% less 20% less 5%. The first discount is deducted from the list price to compute the first net price. The second discount is deducted from the first net price to obtain the second net price. The third discount is deducted from the second net price to obtain the third or final net price in this example. Assume a list price of $180 and 25/20/5 as the trade discount series being offered. The final net price should be rounded to the nearest cent. However, calculations made before the final net price should be rounded to four places. See Model 14.3.

In Model 14.3, $102.60 is the amount due after the series of three trade discounts has been given. Suppliers often offer both trade and cash discounts. Cash discounts, if any, are based on the final net price ($102.60 in this example) and provide an additional deduction for prompt payment.

To illustrate, the trade discounts of 25/20/5, plus a cash discount of 5% will result in an additional discount of $5.13 ($102.60 X 0.05).

MODEL 14.3

Caution: Apply the rates in the order listed. Do not just add the rates together to determine the equivalent rate.

Computation if a calculator is used:
180 x 0.75 x 0.80 x 0.95 = 102.60

Chain discount: *This term is sometimes used instead of series discount.*

Net price equivalent percentage: *A single discount rate that is equivalent to a series of discount rates.*

Computing net price after a series of discounts

Problem: An invoice shows a $180.00 list price with 25/20/5 as the trade discount series being offered. What is the final net price, rounded to the nearest cent?

Solution:

List Price	$180.00
First Trade Discount ($180 x 0.25 (25%))	- 45.00
First Net Price	135.00
Second Trade Discount ($135 x 0.20 (20%))	- 27.00
Second Net Price	108.00
Third Trade Discount ($108 x 0.05 (5%))	- 5.40
Third and Final Net Price	$102.60

Apply Your Skills

The Fulmer Garden Center offers products with a trade discount series of 15/20/10. Items with a $2,000 catalog list price were ordered. What was the final net price of the order?

$ _____

You may now complete Performance Application 14.1

COMPUTING AN EQUIVALENT SINGLE DISCOUNT

In the preceding model, three trade discounts were applied, one at a time, to determine the final net price. Several methods can be used to compute a single discount rate that is equivalent to the series of discounts. Three of these methods are discussed in this section. A procedure similar to the one used above can be used, except the value 1.00 always replaces the list price in the computation. The final percent computed represents the final *net price*. To obtain the equivalent single discount rate, the final percent must be subtracted from 1.00.

Computing a single equivalent discount

Problem: An invoice offers 25/20/5 as the series of trade discounts. What is the single equivalent discount for this series?

Solution: **Step 1** Find the net price equivalent percentage.

List Price (always use 1.00)	1.00
First Discount (1.00 x 0.25)	- 0.25
First Reduced Percentage (1.00 - 0.25)	0.75
Second Discount (0.75 x 0.20)	- 0.15
Second Reduced Percentage (0.75 - 0.15)	0.60
Third Discount (0.60 x 0.05)	- 0.03
Net Price Equivalent Percentage (0.60 - 0.03)	0.57

Step 2 Find the single equivalent discount of the series, 25/20/5.

$$1.00 - \frac{\text{Net price equivalent}}{\text{percentage}} = \frac{\text{Single equivalent}}{\text{discount}}$$

$$1.00 - \qquad 0.57 \qquad = \qquad 0.43 \ (43\%)$$

Computation if a calculator is being used:

1.0 x 0.75 x 0.80 x 0.95 = 0.57

Notice that the complement percentage is used each time.

1.00 - Net price equiv. = Single equivalent discount rate

Apply Your Skills

A mail order company in California offers trade discount terms of 10/10/20 to its best customers. What is the single equivalent discount percent for this series?

_____

After the single equivalent discount rate has been determined, computations for the trade discount and final net price are fairly easy, as shown in Model 14.5.

Computing net price

Problem: Assume that the above trade discount series (25/20/5) is offered for a $180.00 list price. What are the trade discount and net price?

Solution: **Step 1** Find the single equivalent discount. Note: Use the steps shown in Model 14.4. Based on that example, 0.43 was computed as the single equivalent discount.

Step 2 Find the trade discount.

		Single equivalent discount rate		
List price	x	discount rate	=	Trade discount
$180	x	0.43	=	$77.40

Step 3 Find the final net price.

List price	-	Trade discount	=	Net price
$180	-	$77.40	=	$102.60

If a calculator is being used, multiply by the complement as follows: 1 x .75 x .8 x. 95 = 0.57 to compute net price equivalent.

List price x Single rate = Trade discount

List price - Trade discount = Net price

Apply Your Skills

Assume that items are ordered with a $7,500 total list price and trade discount terms of 20/5. What are the (a) single equivalent discount rate, (b) trade discount amount, and net price of the order?

(a) _____

(b) _____

(c) _____

The following example in Model 14.6 provides extra practice for computing a single equivalent discount rate. Although this series contains only two rates, the same procedures shown earlier are used.

MODEL 14.6

Computing equivalent trade price and net price

Problem: The Usterholf Company offers a 30/15 trade discount series for an invoice with a $1,200 list price. What are the single equivalent discount percent, trade discount, and final net price?

Solution:

List Price Equivalent (always use 1.00)	1.00
First Discount (1.00 x 0.30)	- 0.30
First Reduced Equivalent Rate (1.00 - 0.30)	0.70
Second Discount (0.70 x 0.15)	- 0.105
Net Price Equivalent Rate (0.70 - 0.105)	0.595 (59.5%)
Equivalent Trade Discount Rate (1.00 - 0.595)	0.405 (40.5%)
Final Net Price Amount ($1,200 x 0.595)	$714.00
Trade Discount Amount ($1,200 x 0.405)	$486.00

Note: The equivalent single discount for 30% and 15% is 40.5%.

Trade discount rates are applied to successively lower amounts — reduced by the previous discount rate.

Apply Your Skills

Ravi Krovi Exporters offers a 15/10/20 discount series. In addition, a 10% cash discount is offered. Using the shortcut method for computing the single equivalent discount rate, what are the (a) single equivalent discount rate, (b) trade discount, (c) net price, and (d) cash price for an order with an $8,000 list price?

(a) _____

(b) $ _____

(c) $ _____

(d) $ _____

SHORTCUT METHODS FOR COMPUTING AN EQUIVALENT SINGLE DISCOUNT

Two basic shortcut methods for computing an equivalent single discount rate are discussed below. The first is for trade discount series with only two rates, and the second is for trade discount series with two, three, or more rates.

SHORTCUT METHOD 1

This shortcut method can be used to find the equivalent single discount when the series of discounts contains *only two* rates of discount.

MODEL 14.7

Computing a single equivalent trade discount rate

Problem: Robertson Suppliers offers a 25/15 trade discount series. Using the shortcut method, what is the single equivalent trade discount rate?

Solution: **Step 1** Find the sum of the two rates.

.25 + .15 = .40

Step 2 Find the product of the two rates.

.25 x .15 = .0375

Step 3 Subtract the product in Step 2 from the sum in Step 1 to compute the single equivalent trade discount rate.

.40 - .0375 = .3625 (36.25%)

*This shortcut method can be used when there are **only** two discount rates in the series.*

Apply Your Skills

Grant and Associates make a purchase with trade discount terms of 20/10. What is the single equivalent trade discount rate? _____

SHORTCUT METHOD 2

A fairly simple shortcut method to obtain the single equivalent discount rate is outlined in Model 14.8. This method can be used with a series of two, three, or more discount rates.

Shortcut methods are designed to save time and reduce errors. The longer methods introduced in the first part of this chapter give the same results. The shortcut methods are much easier when working with computers, however, because a single formula can be designed to make desired computations.

MODEL 14.8

Use this shortcut method to determine the equivalent rate when there are two or more rates in the series.

Deduct the trade discount from the list price prior to computing the cash discount.

The electronic calculator is a handy tool for making computations.

Computing a single equivalent trade discount rate

Problem: Pyum Exporters offers a 25/15/10 trade discount series. Using the shortcut method, what is the single equivalent trade discount rate and the trade discount amount for an invoice with a $600 list price?

Solution: **Step 1** Subtract each rate in the series from 1.00.

1.00 - 0.25 = 0.75
1.00 - 0.15 = 0.85
1.00 - 0.10 = 0.90

Step 2 Find the rate representing the net price by multiplying the values obtained in Step 1.

0.75 x 0.85 x 0.90 = 0.57375 or 57.375%

Step 3 Find the single equivalent discount rate.

1.00 - Rate from Step 2 = Single equivalent rate
1.00 - 0.57375 = 0.42625 or 42.63%

Step 4 Find the trade discount amount.

(Base) x (Rate) = (Amount)
List price x Equivalent rate = Trade discount
$600 x 0.42625 = $255.75

Apply Your Skills

One of your customers is granted a 20/10/5 trade discount series. What is the single equivalent trade discount rate?

_____

PERFORMANCE APPLICATION 14.1

1. Compute the trade discount and the net price amounts for each of the following invoices. The first item is completed as an example.

Invoice No.	List Price	Trade Discount Rate	Trade Discount Amount	Net Price Amount
	$ 850.00	0.09	$76.50	$773.50
1	650.00	0.08	$ _____	$ _____
2	1,600.00	0.125	$ _____	$ _____
3	960.00	0.30	$ _____	$ _____
4	545.00	0.20	$ _____	$ _____
5	675.00	0.35	$ _____	$ _____

2. Use the complement method to compute the net price for each of the following invoices. The first item is completed as an example.

Invoice No.	List Price	Trade Discount Rate	Net Price Complement Percent	Net Price Amount
	$ 850.00	0.09	91%	$773.50
1	860.00	0.20	_____	$ _____
2	1,640.00	0.35	_____	$ _____
3	4,875.00	0.40	_____	$ _____
4	1,583.00	0.25	_____	$ _____
5	855.00	0.30	_____	$ _____

3. Compute the net price for the following invoice for which a series of discounts was provided. Use the method discussed in Model 15.3. The Baker Company allows trade discounts of 25/20/5 on all purchases above $1,000. Complete the following schedule for a purchase with a list price of $1,600 to determine the net price.

List Price $ _____

First Trade Discount $ _____

First Net Price	$ _____
Second Trade Discount	$ _____
Second Net Price	$ _____
Third Trade Discount	$ _____
Final Net Price	$ _____

4. A new discount sheet from Unique Product Unlimited shows that the company's new policy is to offer trade discounts of 40/20/10. How much will the net price be for an anticipated purchase of $6,000?

    $ _____

5. Assume that you determine that another supplier, Paradise Importers, offers the same merchandise as Unique Products Unlimited in the above problem. The merchandise also has a list price of $6,000, but a trade discount series of 20/40/10 is offered by Paradise Importers. (a) How much will the net price be if the merchandise is purchased from Paradise Importers? (b) How much can be saved by purchasing the merchandise from Unique Products Unlimited instead of Paradise Importers?

    (a) $ _____

    (b) $ _____

6. Marshall Wholesalers offers merchandise with trade discounts of 20/10. In addition, customers with list price amounts over $1,000 receive an additional 10% discount on the amount exceeding $1,000. An invoice has a list price of $1,600. (a) Compute the amount of the trade discount based only on the 20/10 trade discount series. (b) Compute the amount of the extra cash discount provided for the amount over $1,000. (c) Compute the amount of the total discount. (d) Compute the net price.

    (a) $ _____

    (b) $ _____

    (c) $ _____

    (d) $ _____

PERFORMANCE APPLICATION 14.2

1. Compute the net price equivalent discount rate and single equivalent discount rate for each of the following series of trade discounts. Use the method that is explained in Model 15.4. The first item is completed as an example.

Invoice No.	Trade Discount Series	Net Price Equivalent Rate	Single Equivalent Discount Rate
	30/10/10	56.7	43.3
1	40/20/10	_____	_____
2	40/30/5	_____	_____
3	40/15/10	_____	_____
4	20/20/10	_____	_____
5	30/10	_____	_____

2. The Brossnax Jewelry Supply Company offered merchandise with a trade discount of 30/20/10. An invoice had a list price of $6,300. (a) Compute the single equivalent trade discount rate. (b) Compute the amount of the net price. (c) Compute the amount of the trade discount.

   (a) _____

   (b) $ _____

   (c) $ _____

3. Use one of the shortcut methods to compute the single equivalent discount rate in Problem 2 above. If your rates are not the same, make computations for both methods again to determine which one is correct.

4. The Austin Automotive Parts Store offers merchandise with trade discount terms of 20/10 and cash discount terms of 2/10, n/30. The list price for Invoice No. 2688, dated October 11, showed merchandise purchases of $648 plus $16.22 for freight charges. Payment was made on October 20. Compute the (a) amount of the trade discount, (b) amount of the cash discount, and (c) amount needed to pay the bill.

   (a) $ _____

   (b) $ _____

   (c) $ _____

263

5. The spreadsheet format shown below can be used to compute the single discount equivalent rate for a trade discount series, trade discount amount, and final net price. Totals for trade discount amount and final net price (Columns E and F) should also be computed. As with other spreadsheet problems, you can use manual methods, an electronic calculator, or microcomputer spreadsheet software depending on resources available and directions from your instructor. Regardless, compute the needed values and enter the answers in the appropriate cell addresses on the spreadsheet. The first set of answers (Row 7) has been computed for you.

	A	B	C	D	E	F	G
1	Aschew and Associates			TRADE DISCOUNT COMPUTATIONS			
2	--						
3			Trade	Single	Trade	Final	*******
4	Invoice	List	Discount	Discount	Discount	Net	*******
5	No.	Price	Terms	Equivalent	Amount	Price	*******
6	--						
7	1021	850.00	10/20	.28	238.00	612.00	*******
8	1022	1,000.00	10/10				*******
9	1023	600.00	5/10				*******
10	1024	350.00	30				Spreadsheet
11	1025	400.00	25				Analysis
12	1026	1,200.00	10/25				*******
13	1027	600.00	5/10/10				*******
14	1028	800.00	5/10/10				*******
15	1029	900.00	10/5				*******
16	1030	740.00	35				*******
17	--						
18	Total	7,440.00	********************				

PERFORMANCE APPLICATION 14.3

1. Rogue Wholesale Suppliers offers merchandise for resale in retail
   outlets. Complete the following invoice to show payment of the
   bill on April 11. (Round all amounts to two decimal places.)

Invoice No. 87

Sold to: Winston Department Store
5993 Elmore Avenue
Paducah, KY 42001

Date: April 5, 19--
Terms: 2/10, n/30

Qty.	Description	Unit Price	Amount	Net Amount
18	Delta Air Pumps	$17.28	$_____	
15	Misong Automatic Air Pumps	34.16	$_____	
10	Beta Air Jackets	15.28	$_____	
	TOTAL		$_____	
	LESS 20/10 TRADE DISCOUNTS		$_____	
	NET PRICE			$_____
16	Gloss-More Reading Lamps	41.48	$_____	
18	Teak Floor Lamps	92.46	$_____	
15	Brass Table Lamps	78.60	$_____	
	TOTAL		$_____	
	LESS 30/20 TRADE DISCOUNTS		$_____	
	NET PRICE			$_____
	INVOICE NET PRICE TOTAL			$_____
	LESS CASH DISCOUNT			$_____
	CASH PRICE			$_____

2. The accountant at Computer Retail Outlet reviewed the following invoice and discovered several errors. First of all, the company should have been entitled to a trade discount series of 10/10/20. Since the invoice amount was paid on January 15, a cash discount should have been granted on the net price amount. Shipping charges remain the same. The amount charged for taxes should equal 6 percent of the cash price.

(a) What is the trade cash discount amount?
$ _____

(b) What is the cash discount amount? $ _____

(c) What is the tax amount? $ _____

(d) What is the total amount due? $ _____

INVOICE **City Computer Shoppe**					INVOICE No.
2536 Frost Street					241628
San Diego, CA 92120					Packing Slip 27152

SOLD TO	SHIP TO
Computer Retail Outlet	Same
2795 S. Alameda	
Corpus Cristi, TX 78411	

Customer's Order No. 378218	Purchase Order 37218	Salesperson Perez, J.	Terms 2/10, n/30	Ship Via UPS	Our Order No. 27421	Date 1/8/--

No.	Product	DESCRIPTION	QTY.	UNIT PRICE	TOTAL
1	R-78Y	CD-ROM	20	219.35	4,387.00
2	T-83H	Tape Backup	36	225.50	8,118.00
3	U-78N	Sound Blaster	10	220.75	2,207.50
4					
5					
6				Shipping	75.25
7				Subtotal	14,787.75
8				Tax	882.75
9				Total	15,670.50

ORIGINAL

THANK YOU

PRACTICE TEST FOR CHAPTER 14

TRADE DISCOUNTS

Complete each of the following problems and then compare your answers with the ones on page xxx. If needed, round final answers to two decimal places.

1. City Sports Center offers merchandise to distributors without a trade discount. Based on an order for a wide variety of sporting equipment, the price was $37,173. Metro Sports Center offers merchandise to distributors with a trade discount of 30%. A similar order to the above has a list price of $52,500. Which company offered the best price?

   _____

2. A catalog lists ceiling fans with a $52.80 price and trade discount terms of 10/20. What are the (a) trade discount and (b) net price of 50 fans?

   (a) $ _____

   (b) $ _____

3. What is the single equivalent discount percent for a trade discount series of 10/20/5?

   _____

4. Gifts International, Inc., offers trade terms of 5/40. An order was received for items with a $12,500 total list price. What were the (a) single equivalent discount percent, (b) discount amount, and (c) net price?

   (a) _____

   (b) $ _____

   (c) $ _____

5. Future Unlimited, a supplier of products for hair care salons, offers trade discount terms of 10/15/10. In addition, a 6% cash discount is offered for invoices paid within 20 days. An order for items with a $15,000 list price was received. The customer paid for the invoice within 10 days. What were the (a) net price and (b) cash price for the order?

   (a) $ _____

   (b) $ _____

14.1 The chart shown below indicates the types of books that people are reading based on a survey of Opinion Research Corporation as reported in *USA Today*. Assume that you decide to open a small bookstore and have space for 15,000 books. A decision is made to carry books in the categories shown in the chart. (a) Assuming that the survey was representative of people in a city with a population of 120,000, how many were likely to read romance novels? (b) A decision was made to order 3,000 mystery/thriller books with an average $24 list price. If the supplier offers trade discounts of 20/5/5, what is the net price of books ordered in the mystery/thriller category?

(a) _____

(b) $ _____

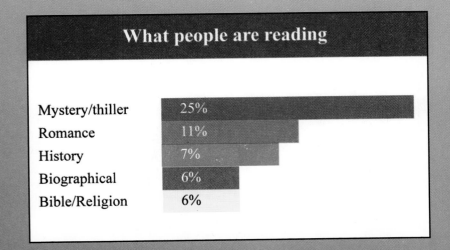

What people are reading

Mystery/thiller	25%
Romance	11%
History	7%
Biographical	6%
Bible/Religion	6%

CONNECTIONS

14.2 The chart shown below indicates the percentage of executives who were likely to be using microcomputers (PCs) in the years 1989 and 1993. Management at Cloverdale House of Fashion employs 200 executive level personnel in its home office. A decision was made to purchase PCs in direct proportion to the percentage of executives in the 1993 survey who were using PCs regularly at work. (a) How many PCs should be ordered? (b) Assuming an $1,800 per microcomputer price and trade discount terms of 10/20/5, what was the net price of the order? (c) Assuming that 200 executives were also employed in 1989, how many additional executives were using microcomputers in 1993 than in 1989?

(a) _____

(b) $ _____

(c) _____

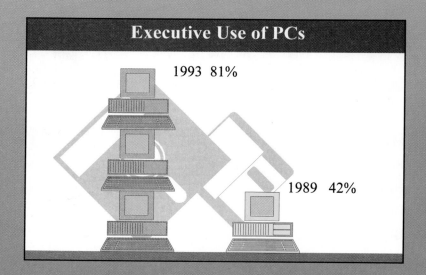

Executive Use of PCs

1993 81%

1989 42%

CONNECTIONS

14.1 Toys-R-Fun in New Orleans decided to order a series of games in preparation for the tourist season. Based on the catalog from Games of Distinction in Chicago, the entire order has a list price equal to $80,000 with a trade discount series of 20/40/10. Another wholesaler, Games Unlimited, located in New York, offered the same merchandise for a list price equal to $80,000 with a trade discount series of 10/25/35. Which wholesaler offered the lowest price?

_____

14.2 Assume that you work in the purchasing department at International Insurance Company and that an order for $100,000 in paper products is being placed. Your supervisor asks you to make a recommendation about which of two suppliers should be chosen for the order. Based on a review of catalogs you find that Modern Stationery Supply offers a trade discount series of 20/15 with cash discounts of 5/10, n/30. A competitor, Dintstul Paper Products, offers a trade discount series of 20/17 with cash discount terms of n/60. List prices are the same for both companies. Which company should be recommended if payment is to be made as follows: (a) 5 days after receipt of invoice, (b) 20 days after receipt of invoice, and (c) 30 days after receipt of invoice? (d) Assuming that cash reserves are short at your company, which supplier should be recommended?

(a) _____

(b) _____

(c) _____

(d) _____

DECISIONS

TRADE DISCOUNTS
Chapter Review and Quick Reference

Topic	Main Point	Typical Example	Text Page
Single trade discount	A single trade discount is a reduction in the list price using a single discount rate.	List price: $2,500 Discount rate: 35% Trade Discount: $2,500 x 0.35 = **$875**	254
Net price	The net price is the amount after deducting the trade discount.	List price: $2,500 Trade discount: $875 Net price: $2,500 - $875 = **$1,625**	254
Complement	The discount rate is subtracted from 1.00.	Discount rate: 0.25. The complement: 1.00 - 0.25 = **0.75 (75%)**	254
Net price using the complement method	Use the complement to more easily compute the net price.	List price: $2,800 Discount rate: 25% Complement: 1.00 - 0.25 = **0.75**. Net price: $2,800 x 0.75 = **$2,100**.	255
Using a series of trade discounts to compute the net price	Rates are applied to successively lower amounts reduced by the previous rate.	List price: $600 Rates: 20/10/30 Net price: $600 x 0.20 = $120 $600 - $120 + $480 $480 x 0.10 = $48 $480 - $48 = $432 $432 x 0.30 = $129.60 $432 - $129.60 = **$302.40**	256
Converting a series discount rate to a single rate	Using a single rate net price equivalent percentage makes computation of the net price easier.	Discount series: 10/20 Single rate equivalent: 1 - 0.9 (1 x 0.1) - 0.9 0.9 - 0.18 (.9 x .2) = **0.72** 1.00 - 0.72 = **0.28**	257

Topic	Main Point	Typical Example	Text Page
Determine net price using single rate equivalent	The net price can be easily computed by using the net price equivalent percentage rate.	List price: $800 Discount series: 10/20 Single rate equivalent from above: 0.72 Net price: $800 x 0.72 = **$576**	257
Shortcut method to determine a discount rate	A series of two rates can be converted to a single trade discount rate.	Series: 15/20 Discount rate: .15 + .20 = .35 .15 x .20 = .03 .35 - .03 = **.32**	259
Shortcut method to determine a single discount rate	A discount series of two or more rates can be converted to a single trade discount rate.	Series: 20/15/10 Discount rate: 1.00 - 0.20 = 0.80 1.00 - 0.15 = 0.85 1.00 - 0.10 = 0.90 .8 x .85 x .9 = 0.612 1.00 - 0.612 = **0.388**	259
Trade discount using shortcut method	The trade discount can be computed while using a single trade discount rate.	List Price: $4,500 Series: 20/15/10 Single rate: 0.388 Trade discount: $4,500 x 0.388 = **$1,746**	260

Chapter *15*

MARKUP ON PURCHASES

Performance Objectives

1. Understand the relationship between selling price, cost, and markup.
2. Determine the amount of markup based on a percentage of product cost.
3. Determine the amount of markup based on a percentage of product selling price.
4. Determine the markup rate based on product selling price and cost.
5. Compare the markup based on cost with the markup based on selling price.

Many companies are engaged in a business that buys merchandise at one price and sells the merchandise for a higher price. The difference between the selling price and the cost price is the *markup*. Computation of markup is important because markup must be sufficient to pay expenses such as salaries, rent, and utilities while making a profit and yet remain low enough to be competitive with similar businesses offering the same type of merchandise. Material in this chapter shows you how markup is computed.

OVERVIEW OF MARKUP

Each step required to get a product to the consumer results in a markup. For example, the manufacturer must purchase raw materials and then place a final price on the product that covers production cost and provides a profit. Retail stores normally purchase merchandise from wholesalers or wholesale distributors and then set a price that is high enough to cover operating expenses and provide a reasonable profit. Some types of stores, such as a jewelry store, may have a fairly high markup rate due to the limited number of items sold each day. Other types of stores, such as a supermarket, may have a very low markup rate and depend on selling a high volume. Some stores may relate the markup rate to product cost while other stores may relate the rate to the selling price. Regardless, each retail store must make a decision about guidelines for establishing an appropriate markup pricing structure in order to be competitive with other stores offering similar products and still cover the cost of the product, cover operating expenses, and provide a reasonable profit. See Figure 15.1.

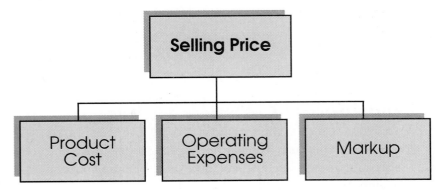

Figure 15.1 Factors in Determining Selling Price

$$\frac{A}{B \times R}$$

Figure 15.3
provides
examples utilizing
these 3
equations:

Selling price
- Cost
= Markup

Cost
+ Markup
= Selling price

Selling price
- Markup amount
= Cost

Calculating
markup and
selling price when
markup rate is
based on cost.

Alternate
computation if a
calculator is used:

Selling price =
(1 + Markup%) x Cost

Selling price =
(1 + 0.20) x 8.50 or
1.20 x 8.50 = 10.20

Whether the business concern is a *retail store* selling merchandise to the general public or a *wholesale business* selling merchandise to other businesses for resale, the goal is to maintain markup sufficient to cover cost of the product, related expenses, and desired profit. *Markup*, the difference between the cost of purchasing or manufacturing the product and the sales price of the product, is also called *gross profit* or *markon*. The relationship between selling price, cost, and markup is expressed in the equations in Figure 15.2.

> Selling price - Cost = Markup (Gross profit)
> Cost + Markup = Selling price
> Selling price - Markup = Cost

Figure 15.2 Selling Price, Cost, Markup Relationship

1. Assume that a product costing $30 sells for $45. Markup is computed as follows:

   $45 - $30 = $15

2. Assume that a company desired a markup of $15 on a product costing $30. Selling price is computed as follows:

   $30 + $15 = $45

3. Assume a selling price of $45 and a markup of $15. Cost is computed as follows:

   $45 - $15 = $30

Figure 15.3 Computation of Markup, Selling Price, and Cost

For computational purposes, markup is usually stated as a decimal or percent rate. Businesses may base the markup rate on the *cost price* or the *selling price*. Both types of computations are illustrated in the following section.

COMPUTING MARKUP BASED ON COST

Computing markup based on the cost price is fairly easy because the seller knows the cost of the product. The markup rate must be sufficient to cover the cost plus related expenses (salaries, rent, and similar items), make a profit, and still be competitive with prices offered by similar businesses.

When using cost price as a basis for markup computation, cost is the base (100%). Markup is added to the cost to determine the selling price. Stated in percentage terms with a markup of 20%, cost equals 100%, markup equals 20%, and selling price equals 120% (100% + 20%). Model 15.1 shows computations of markup amount and selling price for an item costing $8.50 (base) with a markup rate of 20%.

Computing markup and selling price

MODEL 15.1

Problem: The Novelty Shoppe purchased a new toy for $8.50. The store plans a 20% markup prior to selling the product. What are the markup and selling price of each product?

Solution: **Step 1** Find the markup amount.

Cost x Markup rate = Markup
$8.50 x 0.20 = $1.70

Step 2 Find the selling price.

Cost + Markup = Selling price
$8.50 + $1.70 = $10.20

- -

Apply Your Skills

The Record Shop purchased several CDs for resale. The store paid $8.75 and plans a 40% markup prior to selling the product. What are the (a) markup and (b) selling price for each CD?

(a) $ _3.50_

(b) $ _12.25_

If the cost and selling price are known, the markup rate can be computed by dividing the markup by the cost of the product, as shown in Model 15.2.

Computing markup rate

MODEL 15.2

Problem: A product cost $4.80. The selling price is $6.12. The markup is $1.32 ($6.12 - $4.80). What is the markup rate? (Amount÷Base=Rate)

Solution: Markup÷Cost = Markup rate
$1.32÷$4.80 = 0.275 (27.5%)

Amount ÷ Base = Rate

Markup ÷ Cost = Rate

- -

Apply Your Skills

The Toy Center sells a toy, Space Invaders, for $18.90. This toy costs the store $14. What are the (a) markup and (b) markup rate for this product?

(a) $ _4.9_

(b) _35 %_

$4.9 \div 14 = 35\%$

You may now complete Performance Application 15.1.

COMPUTING MARKUP BASED ON SELLING PRICE

Markup may be based on the cost or selling price amounts.

Most retail stores base the markup rate on the selling price. In this method, the selling price is the base representing 100%. The markup rate represents the portion of the sales price that is markup. As in previous illustrations, the selling price minus the markup equals cost. Stated in percentage terms, with a markup rate of 25% based on a base selling price, selling price amount equals 100%, markup equals 25%, and cost equals 75% (100% - 25%). This is further illustrated in Model 15.3.

MODEL 15.3

Calculating markup and cost when markup is based on selling price.

Computing markup amount and cost price

Problem: The Sports Center sells binoculars for $42.00 with a markup rate of 30% based on selling price. What are the markup amount and cost price?

Solution: **Step 1** Find the markup amount.

(Base)	x	(Rate)	= (Amount)
Selling price	x	Markup rate	= Markup
$42.00	x	0.30	= $12.60

Step 2 Find the cost price.

Selling price - Markup = Cost
$42.00   - $12.60 = $29.40

Apply Your Skills

Landscape Creations bases its markups on the prices quoted for jobs. On a job for Juan Perez, a $3,200 price was quoted for a landscape job. A 25% markup of sales price is desired. What are the landscaper's (a) markup and (b) cost for the job?

(a) $ _____800_____

(b) $ _____2400_____

The rate of markup based on selling price can be computed when both the cost and selling price are known. Markup rate equals the amount of the markup divided by the selling price, as shown in Model 15.4.

Computing markup and markup rate

MODEL 15.4

Problem: A product costing $45.00 sells for $60.00. What are the markup and markup rate (based on selling price)?

Solution: **Step 1** Find the markup amount.

Selling price - Cost = Markup
$60.00 - $45.00 = $15.00

Step 2 Find the markup rate (based on selling price).

(Amount) ÷ (Base) = (Rate)
Markup ÷ Selling price = Markup rate
$15.00 ÷ $60.00 = 0.25 (25%)

Selling price - Cost = Markup amount

Markup amount ÷ Selling price = Markup rate

Apply Your Skills

Ace Fence Company bids $1,000 on a proposal to build a fence at City College. Cost for the job will be $800. What are the (a) markup and (b) markup rate (based on selling price) for the job?

(a) $ _200_

(b) _20%_

When the cost and markup rate based on selling price are known, the selling price can be computed by dividing the cost by the rate representing cost, as shown in Model 15.5.

Computing cost rate and selling price

MODEL 15.5

Problem: The Urban Department Store purchased a new line of wrist watches costing $120.00 each, and the store desires a markup of 60% based on selling price. What is the rate representing cost and what is the selling price of the watches?

Solution: **Step 1** Find the rate representing cost.

100% - Markup rate = Cost rate
100% - 60% = 40% (0.40)

Step 2 Find the selling price.

Cost ÷ Cost rate = Selling price
$120.00 ÷ 0.40 (40%) = $300.00

100% - Markup rate = Cost rate

Cost ÷ Cost rate = Selling price

Apply Your Skills

House of Hair Design sells hair care products to customers: Smooth as Silk, a hair spray, costs the store $12. The store desires a 25% markup rate, based on the selling price. What selling price should be set for the product?

$ _16.00_

In Model 15.5, notice that 40% of the selling price represents cost and that 60% of the selling price represents markup. In this example, the selling price represents 100%.

PERFORMANCE APPLICATION 15.1

1. Find the markup for each of the following items. The first item is completed as an example.

Item	Selling Price	Cost	Markup
	$180.00	$160.00	$20.00
1	18.00	12.00	$_____
2	5.35	4.18	$_____
3	125.00	97.25	$_____
4	79.15	42.79	$_____
5	84.16	76.40	$_____

2. Compute the selling price for each of the following items. The first item is completed as an example.

Item	Cost	Markup	Selling Price
	$10.00	$ 2.40	$12.40
1	8.60	1.20	$_____
2	14.28	3.79	$_____
3	87.30	15.20	$_____
4	1.88	0.27	$_____
5	5.48	1.22	$_____

3. Compute the cost of each of the following items. The first item is completed as an example.

Item	Selling Price	Markup	Cost
	$14.20	$ 2.00	$12.20
1	5.60	1.20	$_____
2	81.65	16.85	$_____
3	3.80	0.76	$_____
4	1.69	0.32	$_____
5	14.65	3.15	$_____

4. A sweater costs $35.50 and sells for $48.50. What is the markup on the sweater?

    $ _____ 13.00 _____

5. A radio costing $28.75 was marked to sell for $37.99. What was the markup on the radio?

    $ _____ 9.24 _____

6. A baseball glove costing $32 had a markup of $12.80. What was the selling price of the glove?

    $ _____ 44.80 _____

7. A clothes dryer cost the retail store $250.00. A 30% markup rate was desired. (a) What was the markup? (b) What was the selling price?

    (a) $ _____ 75.00 _____ $250 X .30 = 75.

    (b) $ _____ 325.00 _____   75 + 250 = 325

    C↑M=S. *325 130 = S*

    A / B / R.   325· 40%

    A· 325· 40%

8. A color television cost $325.00 when purchased from the wholesaler. The retail store desired a markup rate of 40%. (a) What was the markup? (b) What was the selling price?

    (a) $ _____ 130 √ _____ = 325 X 0.40 =

    (b) $ _____ 455 √ _____ 325 + 130 = 455   A/B

9. Best Breakfast Foods, Inc. is able to manufacture Good Morning Breakfast Cereal for $5.60 per case. The cereal is sold to retail food stores for $8.12 per case. (a) How much is the markup? (b) What is the markup rate?

    (a) $ _____ 2.52 _____

    (b) _____ 45% _____

PERFORMANCE APPLICATION 15.2

1. Compute the cost for each of the following items when markup rate is based on selling price. The first item is completed as an example.

Item	Markup Rate	Selling Price	Cost
	0.40	$ 20.00	$12.00
1	0.25	425.80	$_____
2	0.20	36.50	$_____
3	0.35	14.80	$_____
4	0.45	17.80	$_____
5	0.60	4.50	$_____

2. Compute the markup percent based on selling price for each of the following items. The first item is completed as an example.

Item	Cost	Selling Price	Markup Rate
	$ 25.00	$ 40.00	37.5
1	180.00	240.00	_____
2	4.20	5.00	_____
3	6.12	8.00	_____
4	10.22	14.00	_____
5	6.00	8.00	_____

3. Compute the selling price for each of the following items. The markup rate is based on selling price. The first item is completed as an example.

Item	Cost	Markup Rate	Selling Price
	$ 70.00	65%	$200.00
1	45.00	25%	$_____
2	180.00	40%	$_____
3	6.30	30%	$_____
4	20.30	27.5%	$_____
5	4.00	20%	$_____

4. The Animal House of Fun sold dog beds for $32.50. This amount included a 20% markup based on selling price. (a) How much was the markup? (b) What was the cost price?

   (a) $ _____

   (b) $ _____

5. The Ace Hardware Store sold hammers for $18.00 that cost $13.50. (a) How much was the markup? (b) What was the markup rate based on sales price?

   (a) $ _____

   (b) _____

6. The Allbright Jewelry Store sold bracelets for $16 that cost $9.04. (a) How much was the markup? (b) What was the markup rate based on sales price?

   (a) $ _____

   (b) _____

7. Cooper Importers bought decorative pictures for $18.00. A 40% markup rate based on selling price is desired. What should the sales price be to provide the desired markup?

   $ _____

8. The Sports Center received a new supply of sports warmup jackets costing $37.80 each. A 30% markup rate based on selling price is desired for this product. (a) What should the sales price be to provide the desired markup? (b) How much should the markup be?

   (a) $ _____

   (b) $ _____

PERFORMANCE APPLICATION 15.3

1. The Old South Shop manufactures fine candies. Chocolate Delight Bars cost $8.00 per box to manufacture. The company desires a markup of $4.00 per box. (a) If markup is based on cost, what will be the markup rate? (b) If markup is based on selling price, what will be the markup rate? (c) Which method results in the higher stated rate?

    (a) _____

    (b) _____

    (c) _____

2. Novelties of Distinction decided that salaries, rent, and other related expenses equaled 20% of sales ($120,000) for last year. This year's sales are also expected to be $120,000, with markup based on 35% of the sales price. Assume the above forecast is accurate. (a) How much of the $120,000 in sales represents markup? (b) How much will the net profit (markup minus expenses) be for this year? (c) What is the cost price of the merchandise?

    (a) $ _____

    (b) $ _____

    (c) $ _____

3. The Bono Card Shop desires a markup of $80,000 for this year's sales. If sales are $200,000 for the year, (a) what markup rate based on cost is needed to obtain the desired markup? (b) What markup rate based on selling price is needed to obtain the desired markup?

    (a) _____

    (b) _____

4. Queen Appliances needs a markup of $100,000 to break even for the year. Sales for the year were $400,000. (a) What markup rate based on sales price is needed to break even? (b) What markup rate based on sales price is needed to make a profit of $50,000 in addition to expenses of $100,000?

    (a) _____

    (b) _____

5. The Fuller Furniture Center uses a markup of 40% based on cost for all furniture items. Compute the sales price for each of the following items.

   (a) Sofa costing $825 $ _____

   (b) Chair costing $375 $ _____

   (c) Love seat costing $750 $ _____

6. Carie's Office Supply Company is considering adding a new line of desk pads to its inventory. The cost prices and suggested retail prices for three products are shown below.

   Product A: Cost = $25.00 and Sales Price = $37.50
   Product B: Cost = $28.00 and Sales Price = $41.58
   Product C: Cost = $20.00 and Sales Price = $32.00

   (a) Which product will result in the highest dollar markup? (b) Which product will result in the highest markup rate based on cost? (c) Which product will result in the lowest markup rate based on cost? (d) Which product will result in the lowest dollar markup?

   (a) _____

   (b) _____

   (c) _____

   (d) _____

7. The Bush Bedding Supply Company marks up items to sell for 175% of the cost price. Bath towels cost $8 each. (a) What must the selling price be to produce the desired markup rate? (b) How much will the markup be? (c) What is the markup rate based on selling price?

   (a) $ __14_____

   (b) $ __6_____

   (c) __42.9 %_____

8. A retail store outlet is considering a markup rate of 40% based on cost or a markup rate of 50% based on selling price. The store purchases an item for $48. (a) Which markup method will result in the higher selling price? (b) What will the selling price be using the method that results in the higher selling price?

   (a) _____

   (b) $ _____

PERFORMANCE APPLICATION 15.4

The quotation shown on the following form was provided for a proposed job for City College. Design Custom Draperies normally makes a 60% markup on materials and a 40% markup on labor (installation). Both markups are based on cost. If this job is accepted, how much profit can the company expect? (Round to the nearest cent.)

$ _____

QUOTATION

TO:

City College
325 Americana Court
Des Moines, IA 50314

QUOTE DATE: 1/15/19--

REQUEST No: R3426

FROM:

Design Custom Draperies
4532 Haverty Circle
Des Moines IA 50317

OUR QUOTE No: T23713

THIS QUOTATION IS VALID ONLY
FROM 1/15/19-- TO 1/31/19--

Delivery Date Promised	Delivery VIA	FOB		Terms
4/10/19--	Truck	Des Moines		2/10, n/30 EOM

Item	Qty. Ordered	DESCRIPTION	Unit Count	Unit Price	Total Amount
1	30	Draperies per Specs	30	96.00	$2,880.00
2		Installation of Draperies			$ 600.00
		Total			$3,480.00

COMMENTS:
Satisfaction Guaranteed!

Thank you for requesting a quotation from us. We are pleased to provide this quotation. If you have any questions, please feel free to call me.

Quotation Approval

PRACTICE TEST FOR CHAPTER 15

MARKUP ON PURCHASES

Complete each of the following problems and then compare your answers with the ones on page 648.

1. A home entertainment center cost the Norris Department Store $1,275. A 40% markup (based on cost) was then desired. What were the (a) markup and (b) selling price?

   (a) $ _____

   (b) $ _____

2. Home Decor paid $56 for a tool set. The tool set was then marked to sell for $75.60. What were the (a) markup and (b) markup rate (based on cost price) for the set?

   (a) $ _____

   (b) _____

3. City Furniture Center purchased a new line of sofas costing $400 each. The furniture store desired a 60% profit, based on the sales price. What selling price must be set for the sofas to provide the desired markup rate?

   $ _____

4. The Glass Shoppe, a novelty store, had $450,000 in product sales last year. The markup policy was to use a 40% markup rate (based on sales) for all products. Operating expenses were $105,000. What were the (a) cost price for the products sold and (b) net profit for the year?

   (a) $ _____

   (b) $ _____

5. City College paid $24 for a textbook, *Keyboarding Made Easy*. The book was then priced to sell for $30. What were the (a) markup rate based on cost and (b) markup rate based on selling price?

   (a) _____

   (b) _____

CONNECTIONS

15.1 Review the insurance rates shown below. Assume that the typical auto insurance policy has a markup of 15% based on the premium charged. What is the markup for (a) a premium in the state with the highest premium, (b) a premium in the state with the lowest premium, and (c) the USA average premium?

(a) $ _____

(b) $ _____

(c) $ _____

A look at statistics that shape the nation

What's spent on car insurance

(Annual average)

USA $595.54

HIGHEST

New Jersey $983.89
Hawaii $874.25
Connecticut $841.22

LOWEST

Pay to the order of Insurance Company

South Dakota $308.90
North Dakota $328.99
Wyoming $330.44

Source: National Association of Insurance Commissioners (1991)

By Julie Stacey, USA TODAY

15.2 The chart shown below indicates the amount spent by consumers to purchase children's books during selected years. Bookstores typically add a 25% markup to their cost (cost to the bookstores). This markup must cover operating expenses and profit needed to run the business. Based on money spent on children's books, how much was the total markup for the following: (a) 1987, (b) 1988, (c) 1989, (d) 1991, and (e) total markup for the 6 years?

(a) $ _____

(b) $ _____

(c) $ _____

(d) $ _____

(e) $ _____

A look at statistics that shape our lives

How much people spend on children's books

(billions)

$1.0 · $1.3 · $1.5 · $1.7 · $1.9 · $2.0

'87 '88 '89 '90 '91 '92

Source: Book Industry Study Group, Inc. By Bob Laird, USA TODAY

CONNECTIONS

15.1 Novelties of Distinction used a 25% markup rate, based on sales price, for glass figurines. House of Glass, a store located in the same city, used a 35% markup rate, based on cost price for glass figurines. Lady on a Horse, a popular figurine, had a $960 wholesale price. What selling price must be set by each retailer in order to provide the desired markup?

Novelties of Distinction: $ _____

House of Glass: $ _____

15.2 Call or visit three retail stores in your city. Determine whether or not each of them uses a markup rate based on cost or one based on selling price for products sold by the store. Ask about markup rates for typical products carried by the store. (Note: Some stores may not provide this information).

Develop one word problem based on a markup application for each of the three stores, similar to problems in this chapter. Ask another student in your class to complete the problems. Revise the problems, if needed. Then submit a copy of the problems to your instructor.

DECISIONS

MARKUP ON PURCHASES
Chapter Review and Quick Reference

Topic	Main Point	Typical Example	Text Page
Markup	Markup is the difference between the cost and the selling price.	A suit costing a store $180 was sold for $235. Markup: $235 - $180 = $55	275
Markup based on cost	**Base x Rate = Amount**	An auto tire costing $88 had a 25% markup rate. Markup: $88 x 0.25 = $22	276
Selling price	Cost + Markup = Selling price	An auto tire costing $88 had a $22 markup. Selling price: $88 + $22 = $110	277
Markup rate (based on cost price)	Markup ÷ Cost = Markup rate	An auto tire costing $88 had a $22 markup. Markup rate: 22 ÷ 88 = 0.25 or 25%	277
Markup based on selling price	**Base x Rate = Amount**	A toy selling for $48 had a 25% markup based on selling price. Markup: $48 x 0.25 = $12	278
Cost price	Selling price - Markup = Cost	A toy selling for $48 had a $12 markup. Cost: $48 - $12 = $36	279
Markup rate (based on selling price)	Markup ÷ Selling price = Markup rate	A computer had a $2,000 sales price with a $300 markup. Markup rate: 300 ÷ 2,000 = 0.15 or 15%	279
Selling price when cost and markup rate based on selling price are known	Cost ÷ Cost rate = Selling price **Note: Selling price - Markup = Cost**	A drill costing the store $72 is sold with a 25% desired markup based on selling price. Selling price: $72 ÷ 0.75 = $96 **Note: 100% - 25% = 75%**	279

Chapter **16**

MARKDOWN ON SALE PRICE

Performance Objectives

1. Understand the relationship between listed sale price and reduced sale price.
2. Determine the amount of markdown based on sale price.
3. Determine the markdown rate.
4. Compare and distinguish between percent of markdown and markdown stated in dollars.

Businesses may reduce the selling price of merchandise to create special sales promotions or to encourage sales of slow-moving items. This chapter illustrates computations used by businesses to mark down, discount, or reduce the selling price of merchandise.

OVERVIEW OF MARKDOWN

A *markdown* is a reduction in the listed selling price of merchandise. Markdown is stated as a percent of the selling price, such as a markdown rate of 20%. Businesses mark up the price of merchandise to determine the selling price, then mark down the selling price to indicate that a discount or special price is being offered. When markup and markdown are computed in the same problem, markup is always computed first. While many businesses offer special discounts, other businesses sometimes inflate the selling price prior to the markdown so that buyers will think they are receiving a special price. In fact, the marked-down price may not be lower than the regular price offered by other suppliers for the same merchandise; in some cases it may even be higher. Buyers should be aware that the original sales price used in some sales promotions may be a suggested list price or other inflated price and not the regular price charged for the product.

The previous chapter illustrated that the markup rate can be based on one of several figures, such as the cost and list prices of merchandise items. However, the markdown rate is almost always based on the list price. Companies normally purchase merchandise for resale, mark up the price, and then provide a markdown as a way to discount the price of the item and encourage customers to make purchases. The customer then feels like a bargain is being offered. The diagrams shown in Figure 16.1 illustrate this procedure.

> **Markdown:**
> A discount on the sale price to encourage sales of the item.
>
> Markdowns are often used to move perishable items or slow-selling items.
>
> Determine markup, if any, prior to determining markdown.

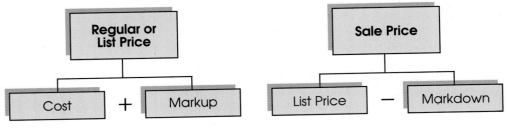

Figure 16.1 Markdown Procedure

COMPUTING THE AMOUNT OF MARKDOWN

Businesses often provide sales promotional material that shows the price before and after the markdown (usually called discount in sales promotion literature). The amount of the markdown, the difference between the two amounts, is computed as shown in Model 16.1.

**MODEL
16.1**

*Regular price
- Discount price
= Markdown*

Computing markdown amount

Problem: The Vestal Clothing Store normally sells a shirt for $14.30. The shirt is placed on sale for $11.10. What is the markdown amount?

Solution: Regular price - Discount price = Markdown
$14.30   - $11.10   = $3.20

Apply Your Skills

City Office Supply normally sells a fountain pen for $39.95. During a special sale, it was priced for $28.45. What was the markdown amount? $ __11.50__

COMPUTING MARKDOWN STATED AS A PERCENT

Markdown is usually stated as a percent of sale price.

The markdown is often stated in percent terms as a reduction in the selling price as shown in Model 16.2. For example, a product may be promoted as being offered at a 15% discount. The following equations should be used when the markdown is stated as a percent. Once again, the basic formula (Base X Rate = Amount) applies to many examples in this chapter.

**MODEL
16.2**

$$\frac{Markdown\ Amount}{Base \times Rate}$$

Sale price: *Cost after deducting markdown.*

Computing sale price based on markdown percent

Problem: The Dinstul Variety Store normally sells a calculator for $15.95. During a special sale, the price is marked down 30%. What is the sale price?

Solution: **Step 1** Find the markdown amount.

(Base)   X (Rate)   = (Amount)
Regular price X Markdown rate = Markdown
$15.95   X 0.30   = $4.79 (rounded)

Step 2 Find the sale price.

Regular price - Markdown = Sale price
$15.95   - $4.79   = $11.16

Apply Your Skills

Merry Candy Store normally sells chocolate pretzels for $7.95 per pound. During a special sale, the price was marked down 20%. What were the (a) markdown and (b) sale price?

(a) $ _1.59_

(b) $ _6.36_

You may now complete Performance Application 16.1.

COMPUTING MARKDOWN RATE

When the regular selling price and the marked-down price are known, the markdown rate can easily be determined. Assume a regular selling price of $15 and a marked-down price of $9. The procedures shown in Model 16.3 can be used to compute the markdown rate given these two factors using the formula (Amount ÷ Base = Rate).

Regular price
- Sale price
= Markdown

Computing markdown rate

Problem: A particular item normally selling for $15 is offered for a marked down price of $9. What is the markdown rate?

Solution: Markdown ÷ Regular price = Markdown rate
$6 ($15 - $9) ÷ $15 = .40 (40%)

MODEL 16.3

Markdown
÷ Regular price
= Markdown rate

Apply Your Skills

City Auto offered the following truck at a reduced price during a recent sales promotion. What was the markdown rate from the list price (rounded to two decimal places)? _13.49%_

RED TAG SALE
NEW IMPORT TRUCK

V6 Engine, Air Cond., Power Steering, Power Brakes, Sport Package, 4-Wheel Drive, Driver-side Airbag

0% DOWN

LIST $15,591

NO HAGGLE PRICE $13,488 OR $289/mo.

COMPUTING MARKUP AND MARKDOWN

Markup must be computed before computing markdown. The markup rate may be based on either the cost price or the selling price, but the markdown rate is *always* based on the selling price, as shown in Model 16.4.

MODEL 16.4

Cost price +
Markup amount =
Regular price

Regular price -
Markdown amount =
Sale price

Computing sale price

Problem: Apex wrist watches cost the Baland Discount Store $150. The store has a practice of pricing the watches by adding 40% to the cost price. During a July 4 special sale, the watches are marked down 20% off the regular selling price. What are the regular selling price and sale price of the watches?

Solution: **Step 1** Find the regular selling price.

Cost price	+	Markup amount	=	Regular price
$150	+	$60 ($150 x 0.40)	=	$210

Step 2 Find the sale price.

Regular price	-	Markdown amount	=	Sale price
$210	-	$42 ($210 x 0.20)	=	$168

To further illustrate, assume that a special group of table lamps is purchased at a cost of $65 with a markup of $48 per lamp. The lamps are promoted as being offered at a 30% markdown. The sale price is calculated as follows:

Step 1 $65.00 + $48.00 = $113.00 (regular selling price)

Step 2 $113.00 - $33.90 ($113 x .30) = $79.10 (sale price)

Note: The business still makes a gross profit of $14.10 ($79.10 - $65.00) with a gross profit rate of 21.69% ($14.10 ÷ $65.00).

Cost price +
Markup amount =
Regular price

Regular price -
Markdown amount =
Sale price

- - - - - - - - - -

Apply Your Skills

Outdoors Sporting Goods purchased a particular baseball glove from the manufacturer for $60. A 30% markup is then added to the cost price. Three Rivers Junior College was provided with a 15% markdown. What were the (a) regular price and (b) sale price?

(a) $ _78.00_

(b) $ _66.30_

PERFORMANCE APPLICATION 16.1

1. The Goonce Department Store decided to reduce each of five glassware items. Since these items had not been selling well, this discount was intended to improve sales of these items and to reduce the inventory level. Compute the sale price for each item. The first item is completed as an example.

Item	Regular Selling Price	Markdown	Sale Price
	$37.80	$ 6.15	$31.65
1	42.75	7.30	$ _35.45_
2	40.29	7.30	$ _32.99_
3	38.40	8.35	$ _30.05_
4	38.55	10.60	$ _27.95_
5	41.99	10.50	$ _31.49_

2. The Realprice Specialty Shop has overstocked several items of merchandise. In an effort to reduce the inventory level, the sale prices of these items were reduced. Compute the markdown and sale price for each item. (When computing discounts, round answers to the nearest cent.) The first item is completed as an example.

Item	Regular Selling Price	Markdown Rate	Markdown	Sale Price
	$ 35.60	.20	$7.12	$28.48
1	48.50	.10	$ _4.85_	$ _43.65_
2	165.75	.40	$ _66.30_	$ _99.45_
3	87.95	.35	$ _30.78_	$ _57.17_
4	156.78	.38	$ _59.58_	$ _97.20_
5	55.75	.25	$ _13.94_	$ _41.81_

3. The All Occasion Gift Shop discounts Christmas cards by 60% during January each year. Style A normally sells for $5.40 per box, and Style B normally sells for $5.75 per box. How much will the sale price be for (a) Style A and (b) Style B?

    (a) $ _2.16_   5.40

    (b) $ _2.30_   5.75

4. The Brea TV Shop offered its 24-inch color television set at a 30% discount during the Easter Sale Days. The set normally sells for $599.60. How much were the (a) markdown and (b) sale price?

(a) $ _____

(b) $ _____

5. East Auto Sales marked down midsize cars by 12% during the month of October to make space available for newer models. For a car with a list price of $8,875.95, what would be the (a) markdown and (b) sale price?

(a) $ _____

(b) $ _____

6. The Hartford Department Store purchased a special order of men's suits for their annual Spring Sale. The suits cost the store $80 each and were marked to sell for $150. During the sale, the suits were reduced 20%. (a) How much was the markdown? (b) How much was the sale price? (c) How much gross profit did the store make on each suit?

(a) $ _____

(b) $ _____

(c) $ _____

7. The Midtown Record Shop discounted top ten records by 10% during a sales promotion campaign. A customer purchased three records with the following regular selling prices: Record 1, $8.50; Record 2, $8.00; and Record 3, $8.80. (a) What was the total discount for the three records? (b) What was the total sale price for the three records?

(a) $ _____

(b) $ _____

8. Rick Brunson decided to buy a new AM/FM radio. Store A offered a radio for $85.50 with a 20% markdown. Store B offered the same quality radio for $92.40 with a 25% markdown. (a) Which store offered the lower price? (b) How much did Rick pay for the lower-priced radio?

(a) _____

(b) $ _____

PERFORMANCE APPLICATION 16.2

1. Compute the markdown percent for each of the following items. (Round percents to two decimal places.) The first item is completed as an example.

Item	Regular Selling Price	Sale Price	Markdown Rate
	$ 16.00	$ 12.00	25%
1	20.00	13.00	_____
2	160.50	128.64	_____
3	30.50	28.75	_____
4	65.00	59.80	_____
5	75.00	37.50	_____

2. Compute the regular selling price and sale price for each of the following items. (Round amounts to two decimal places.) The first item is completed as an example.

Item	Cost	Markup	Regular Price	Markdown	Sale Price
	$40.00	25%	$50.00	5%	$47.50
1	50.75	40%	$_____	20%	$_____
2	4.25	20%	$_____	10%	$_____
3	1.26	50%	$_____	15%	$_____
4	18.30	30%	$_____	18%	$_____
5	2.48	25%	$_____	7%	$_____

3. The United Beauty Supply Company provides supplies for hair care centers. The Holly Hills Beauty Salon purchased 10 cases of a new hair spray designed for active persons. The salon purchased the hair spray for $72 per case, which was $6 per can. The suggested retail price was $10 per can. If each can of hair spray was marked down from the list price to show a $2 gross profit, what was the markdown rate?

_____

4. The Grisham Corporation manufactures tennis rackets and other sports equipment. Perfect Touch tennis rackets cost $24 to manufacture, with a regular selling price to retail stores of $36. During a special sale, the tennis rackets were offered by Grisham Corporation for 1/6 off the regular selling price. (a) What was the price offered to retail stores? (b) What was the profit rate based on cost after the discount?

   (a) $ _____

   (b) _____

5. The Dan Crocker Garden Center purchased rose bushes from a local nursery for $6 per plant. The plants were marked up 100% based on the cost price. During the summer, the plants were offered for sale at a 25% discount. What were the (a) regular selling price, (b) sale price, and (c) gross profit percent based on cost after the markdown?

   (a) $ _____

   (b) $ _____

   (c) _____

6. Randy Rent-A-Car offered cars at a 20% discount from the regular rental price during the July 4 weekend. A compact car normally rents for $38 per day with unlimited mileage. During the holiday weekend, (a) how much discount will be provided, and (b) how much will be saved over the regular rental rate for the three-day weekend?

   (a) $ _____

   (b) $ _____

7. The Village Travel Agency offers a special vacation package for $780 per person. If two persons purchase the package, a 20% discount is given to each person. How much will each person save?

   $ _____

8. T-Shirts Unlimited and T-Shirts Now stores each purchased a particular brand of shirt for $8. T-Shirts Unlimited marked up the shirts 25% based on cost, and T-Shirts Now marked up the shirts 50% based on cost. Each store advertised the brand at a 10% markdown. How much was saved by purchasing the shirt from T-Shirts Unlimited?

   $ _____

PERFORMANCE APPLICATION 16.3

Automobile agencies often discount prices to stimulate sales of the autos. The newspaper ad shown below is typical of these types of promotions. What was the (a) markdown and (b) markdown rate for the Dodge Shadow? What was the (c) markdown and (d) markdown rate for the Dodge Caravan?

(a) $ _____

(b) _____

(c) $ _____

(d) _____

RED TAG SALE
NEW MODEL SEDAN
Automatic, Air Cond., Power Steering, Power Brakes, Stk. #12155
0% DOWN
LIST $12,842
NO HAGGLE PRICE $9988   OR $199/mo.

RED TAG SALE
NEW MODEL VAN
Automatic, Power Steering, Power Brakes, 7 Passenger. Stk. #17428
0% DOWN
LIST $16,505
NO HAGGLE PRICE $13,988   OR $299/mo.

PRACTICE TEST FOR CHAPTER 16
MARKDOWN ON SALE PRICE

Complete each of the following problems and then compare your answers with the ones on page 648.

1. Mendez Hair Care Center normally offers Beauty Shampoo for $7.95 per bottle. During a special sale, the product is offered for a $1.09 discount. What is the sale price?

   $_____

2. An automobile agency had an auto with a $17,500 list price. A 15% markdown was offered at the end of the year. What was the (a) markdown and (b) sale price?

   (a) $ _____

   (b) $ _____

3. Product A had an $18 list price and a 15% markdown. Product B had a $19 list price and a 17% markdown. Which product had the lowest sale price?

   _____

4. Ace Hardware normally sells a lawn mower for $180. During a special sale, the price was reduced to $153. What was the markdown rate?

   _____

5. Tower Rent-A-Car offered a $36 per day rental rate. The weekend rate was $29.88. What markdown rate was offered for the weekend?

   _____

16.1 The chart shown below represents the value of the dollar compared to the Japanese yen in 1985 and 1993. How much was (a) the decrease amount and (b) the percentage of decrease (rounded to two decimal places) in the price of the dollar compared to the yen since 1985?

(a) $ _____

(b) _____

A look at statistics that shape your finances

Yen flexes muscles

The dollar has been hitting record lows against the yen.

Yen per dollar

Dollar's record low
116.36
Feb. 22, 1993

Dollar's record high
263.50
Feb. 25, 1985

Source: USA TODAY research

By Marty Baumann, USA TODAY

CONNECTIONS

16.2 Popularity of the convertible auto has had many ups and downs during the past 10 years. The chart below indicates the leading makes of convertibles during 1992. What was the (a) number and (b) percentage of increase (rounded to two decimal places) in sales of the Chrysler LeBaron compared to the Mazda Miata during 1992?

(a) _____

(b) _____

A look at statistics that shape your finances

Cruisin' with the top down

Lee Iacocca brought the ragtop back at Chrysler in 1982. Top-selling convertibles in 1992:[1]

Make	Sales
Chrysler LeBaron	36,400
Mazda Miata	24,800
Ford Mustang	23,600
Mercury Capri	17,000
Geo Metro	14,000

1– based on model year registrations

Source: Autodata

By Cliff Vancura, USA TODAY

CONNECTIONS

16.1 The local newspaper in your town should list many items that are marked down from the regular or list price. Review your local newspaper and prepare a chart showing list price, markdown, and markdown rate for five products that are listed in the newspaper.

16.2 Your supervisor requested that you make a recommendation for the purchase of a new microcomputer for the office and indicated that $1,650 was budgeted for the microcomputer. Company A offered a microcomputer for $1,675 with no additional discounts. The microcomputer cost Company B $1,400, and a 17% markup was then added to determine the sale price. Company C normally sells the microcomputer for $1,820, but offered a 12% markdown. Which company offered the lowest sale price? Which companies are within the budgeted amount?

_____

_____

_____

_____

DECISIONS

Markdown on Sale Price
Chapter Review and Quick Reference

Topic	Main Point	Typical Example	Text Page
Markdown amount	Regular or listed price - Discount price = Markdown	An item with a $42 regular price is sold for $38. Markdown amount = $42 - $38 = **$4**	296
Sale price	(1) Regular price x Markdown rate = Markdown (2) Regular price - Markdown = Sale price	An item normally selling for $60 is marked down 20%. Markdown = $60 x 0.2 = $12 Sale price = $60 - $12 = **$48**	296
Markdown rate	Markdown ÷ Regular price = Markdown rate	An item normally selling for $80 is marked down to $60. Markdown rate = 20÷80 = **0.25 or 25%**	297
Markup followed by markdown	(1) Cost + Markup = Regular price (2) Regular price - Markdown = Sale price	An item costing $40 is marked up 50% and then marked down 25%. Regular price = $40 + $20 = $60 Sale price = $60 - $15 = **$45**	298

Chapter *17*

COMMISSION ON SALES

Performance Objectives

1. Determine the relationship between sales and commissions for marketing personnel.
2. Determine straight commission amounts.
3. Determine graduated commission amounts.
4. Determine commission on consignment sales.

People in sales and marketing areas often receive a *commission*, which is a specified amount of money for making each sale, or a *commission rate*, which is based on the sales amount, for selling the product or service. In this chapter, you will learn ways to compute the commission for selling products or services.

OVERVIEW OF COMMISSION

Many salespersons receive a commission as payment for selling products or services. These persons may also receive a basic salary in addition to the commission (called *salary plus commission*), or they may receive only a commission (called *straight commission*) with no additional salary compensation. Real estate and advertising are examples of businesses where compensation is usually based on salary plus commission or straight commission. Many retail clerks also receive a commission on sales. Commission rate is usually stated as a percent of the sales amount.

Persons or businesses may also accept merchandise for resale from another person or business, which is called *consignment*. Persons or businesses, called *principals* or *consignors*, engage another business or person, called *commission merchant* or *consignee*, to act as an agent for selling items such as farm produce, auto parts, cotton, and dairy products. In return for selling the product, the agent earns a commission.

A unique feature of the principal/commission merchant arrangement is that title to the goods remains with the principal until sold. Any loss due to spoilage or breakage must be the responsibility of the principal. After selling the product, the commission merchant charges a commission. This commission is based on the total sales price or the *gross proceeds*. The amount, after deducting for advertising, storage, insurance, and similar items necessary to sell the product, is called the *net proceeds*. An *account sales invoice*, a detailed statement of sales and related charges, must be provided to the principal to account for the commission and the sale. The account sales invoice is prepared by the commission merchant and sent to the principal along with a check for the net proceeds.

Many personnel work in an environment where all or part of their earnings are based on the amount of merchandise sold during a specific time period, such as a month or year. This procedure provides a way to measure productivity, compare personnel in similar positions, and reward for good performance. This chapter presents a discussion about business mathematics relating to the marketing area. Other employee compensation plans are presented in greater detail in the unit relating to payroll beginning on page 334. Although various procedures can be used for computing commission on sales, each plan includes a procedure to relate commissions earned to marketing productivity, as shown in Figure 17.1.

Commission:
Amount paid for selling a product or service.

Commissions serve as an incentive to sell more items.

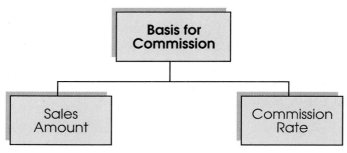

Figure 17.1 Basis for Commission

COMPUTING SALESPERSONS' COMMISSION

Many career opportunities are available for marketing personnel.

Salespersons may receive a commission. Returns are deducted from the amount of sales when computing the commission. The amount of commission is computed by multiplying the sales amount by the commission rate, as illustrated in Model 17.1.

MODEL 17.1

Sales amount x Commission rate = Commission

Computing commission on sales

Problem: Walter Plough is a salesperson for a company that pays a 6% commission rate. His sales last week were $7,200. What was his commission earned?

Solution: Sales   x   Commission rate   =   Commission earned
$7,200   x   0.06 (6%)   = $432

Apply Your Skills

Juan Perez works at City Furniture, a company that pays a 5% commission rate. What was his commission for selling a $695 sofa? $ _34.75_

Commissions are usually stated as percents.

Marketing representatives for products such as computers, life insurance, office equipment, household furniture, and pharmaceutical supplies often receive a *graduated commission rate*, whereby the rate is increased as the sales amount is increased. For example, the commission may be 2% for the first $10,000 in sales and 3% for all sales in excess of $10,000. This serves as an incentive and increases the reward for greater effort by salespersons.

Frances Cortez receives a 4% commission rate for the first $2,000 in sales, a 5% commission rate for sales from $2,001 to $4,000, and a 6% commission rate for sales above $4,000. During the most recent period, Ms. Cortez had sales of $5,000. Computation of her commission is shown in Model 17.2. Notice that sales times the commission rate equals the commission (Base × Rate = Amount).

Computing commission on sales

Problem: Frances Cortez receives a 4% commission rate for the first $2,000 in sales, a 5% commission rate for sales from $2,001 to $4,000, and a 6% commission rate for sales above $4,000. What will her commission be if sales are $5,000?

Solution: **Step 1** Find the amount of commission on the first $2,000 in sales at a 4% commission rate.

Sales	×	Commission rate	=	Commission
$2,000	×	0.04	=	$80

Step 2 Find the commission on sales from $2,001 to $4,000 at 5%.

Sales	×	Commission rate	=	Commission
$2,000	×	0.05	=	$100

Step 3 Find the commission on sales above $4,000 at 6%.

Sales	×	Commission rate	=	Commission
$1,000 ($5,000 - $4,000)	×	0.06	=	$60

Step 4 Find the sum of commissions from graduated levels to determine total commission earned.

Step 1	+	Step 2	+	Step 3	=	Total commission
$80	+	$100	+	$60	=	$240

MODEL 17.2

Many calculators have a percent key that makes computation of amounts involving percents easier to determine.

This is a **graduated** *or* **sliding scale** *since the commission increases as the sales amount increases.*

Apply Your Skills

Partee Medical Supplies provides a 7% commission on the first $10,000 in sales, a 10% commission on sales from $10,001 to $15,000, and a 12% commission on sales above $15,000. What commission will be paid to a marketing representative with $30,000 in sales during the month? $ 3,500

You may now complete Performance Application 17.1.

1) 10,000 × 0.07 = 700

2) 10.000 × 0.10 = 1000

3) 1500 (30,000 - 15.000) × 0.12 = 1800

4) 700 + 1000 + 1800 = 3500

COMPUTING COMMISSION ON CONSIGNMENT SALES

The commission merchant normally receives a shipment of merchandise (on consignment) for sale. Remember that title to the merchandise remains with the principal until the merchandise is sold or returned by the commission merchant. The customary procedure, at first, sounds complicated, but it is really fairly simple. Simply stated, the commission merchant making the sale receives full payment (gross proceeds) when the goods are sold. The commission merchant deducts a commission based on gross proceeds, deducts amounts for related charges, and sends the remainder (net proceeds) to the principal. These computations are shown in Model 17.3. An account sales invoice is sent with a check for the net proceeds to show proof of the gross proceeds and related charges.

MODEL 17.3

$$\frac{Amount}{Base \times Rate}$$

Computing net proceeds

Problem: Donnelson and Brubaker, commission merchants, receive goods on consignment that are sold for $3,400. Freight ($30) and storage ($65) charges are incurred for the goods. The commission rate is 20%. What is the amount of net proceeds for this transaction?

Solution: **Step 1** Find the commission amount.

Gross proceeds x Commission rate = Commission
$3,400 x 0.20 = $680

Step 2 Find the total of related charges.

Freight + Storage = Related charges
$30 + $65 = $95

Step 3 Find the net proceeds amount.

Gross proceeds	-	Commission	-	Related charges	=	Net proceeds
$3,400	-	$680	-	$95	=	$2,625

Apply Your Skills

The Pro Shop received goods on consignment that were sold for $760. Freight charges were $35. The commission rate was 15%. What is the net proceeds amount?

$ _611.00_

Step 1 = Find the commission amount
Gross proceeds X Commission rate = Commission
$760 × 0.15 = $114

Step 2 = Find the net proceeds amount.
Gross — Commission — related charges = Net Proceeds
760 — 114 — 35 = $611.00

PERFORMANCE APPLICATION 17.1

1. Compute the commission for each of the following salespersons.

Salesperson	Sales	Commission Rate	Commission
John Glaze	$2,800.00	6%	$168.00
Esther Highgate	3,100.00	7%	$ _217_
Naomi Jones	2,875.00	4%	$ _115_
David Maybry	2,850.00	6 ½%	$ _185.25_
John Pitts	3,238.00	5 ½%	$ _178.09_
Charles Rolf	2,637.00	8%	$ _210.96_

$\frac{1}{2} = 0.5$

$= .065$

$= \frac{1}{2} = .05$

$.055$

Identify the base, rate, and amount before solving each of the following problems.

2. James Davis is an agent for the Carver Real Estate Company and works on his listings for a 2.75% straight commission. Last week he sold a house for $113,500. What was his sales commission? $ _3,121.25_

113,500 × .275 =

3. Edna Ivey works on a salary plus commission plan. Last week her salary was $250.00 plus a 4 1/2% commission on sales of $7,920. What was her gross pay? $ _606.40_

7,920 × .045 = 356.40

7,920 + 356.40 + 250 = 8526.40

7920 − 8526.40

= 606.40

4. Arthur Reed sold 13 sets of encyclopedias during the past week. If his commission was $48.50 per set, what was his gross pay? $ _630.50_

5. Novvel Rector works for a company that pays a commission of 7% on all sales up to $6,000 and 9% on all sales above $6,000. If his sales are $9,500, what is his commission?

$ _735.00_

6. Milton Guthrie worked for Gurley's Furniture Showroom, Inc., with a sales quota of $1,800 per week. He was paid $335 per week plus a commission of 8% on all sales and an additional 2% on sales exceeding the quota. What was his gross pay if his sales for the week were $2,675? $ _566.50_

7. David Monger works for Dixie Carpet Sales, Inc. They pay a weekly salary of $485 plus a commission of 8% for all sales exceeding the quota. His territory carries a sales quota of $2,500 per week. What would his gross pay be on sales of $4,875? $ _675.00_

8. Diggons Auto Sales pays its employees $150 for each car sold. During the week, Sarah Dabbs sold 5 cars with total sales of $53,500. (a) What was her commission? (b) What was her commission rate?

   (a) $ _750_

   (b) _1.4 %_

   $150 \times 5 = ?=750$

   $53,500$

   commission amount

   $A = 750 / 57,500 = 1.4\%$

9. A salesperson for the Greenwich Department Store received a commission of $822.50 for selling items that totalled $23,500. What was the commission rate? _35%_

   total sales

   $R = A/B$

   $\dfrac{822.50}{23500} = 0.035 = 35\%$

PERFORMANCE APPLICATION 17.2

1. A commission merchant sold goods held on consignment for
    $3,250 with the following related charges: freight, $50.00;
    storage, $60.00; and handling, $35.00. A commission of 7% was
    charged. What were the (a) commission and (b) net
    proceeds?

    (a) $ _227.50_

    (b) $ _2,877.50_

2. A principal sent goods to Lakefront Auto Parts with a total retail
    value of $3,875.00. The contract called for a commission of
    4.4%. Lakefront charged $61.54 for freight and $11.60 for
    handling. (a) How much was the commission? (b) What were
    the net proceeds?

    (a) $ _170.50_

    (b) $ _3,631.36_

3. Fruit Basket, Inc. received 380 bags of apples with a retail sales
    price of $6.50 per bag. Related charges were freight, $75.00;
    spoilage, $53.00; and handling, $53.00. A commission of 8 1/2%
    was charged. (a) How much was the commission? (b) What
    amount should Fruit Basket, Inc. send to the principal?

    (a) $ _209.95_

    (b) $ _2,079.05_

4. Demarco and Associates received 10 microcomputers on
    consignment with an average retail price of $4,995 each.
    Charges were as follows: freight, $120.00; storage, $130.00; and
    guarantee, 1% of gross proceeds. The commission rate was
    15%. Assuming that the microcomputers sold for an average
    retail price of $4,995, what were the (a) total charges, (b)
    commission, and (c) net proceeds?

    (a) $ _8,242.00_

    (b) $ _7,942.50_

    (c) $ _41,708.00_

5. Complete the following account sales invoice.

ACCOUNT SALES INVOICE				No. 56382-LM
				Date: September 23,19--

Sold for the Account of: Bates Battery Manufacturers
5100 Poplar Avenue
Memphis, TN 38117
Commission: 15%

Model No.	Quantity	Cost Per Unit	Extension	Total
12V-28A	18	$47.20	$849.60	
12V-26A	24	56.44	$1,354.56	
8V-30A	8	52.75	$422.00	
8V-30B	12	50.48	$605.76	
			GROSS PROCEEDS	$3,231.92
		CHARGES: Commission	$484.79	
		Freight	$88.50	
		Storage	$150.00	
		Handling	$124.00	
		TOTAL CHARGES	$847.29	
		NET PROCEEDS	$2,384.63	

5) 849.60
1,354.56
422.00
605.76
3,231.92
484.79

PERFORMANCE APPLICATION 17.3
COMMISSION APPLICATION

Rhonda Fogelman graduated from City Community College with an associate degree in sales marketing. She applied for and was hired for the job described in the classified ad shown below. She was guaranteed $350 per week or 6.25% of sales, whichever is greater, during the first year. Rhonda had sales totaling $475,500 during her first year. (a) Was her commission greater than the guaranteed salary? (b) Did she reach the annual range shown in the ad?

(a) _____

(b) _____

Practice Test for Chapter 17

Commission on Sales

Complete each of the following problems and then compare your answers with the ones on page 649.

1. Prashant Palvia is a marketing representative for Tower Motor Company and is paid a 1.25% commission. Yesterday, he sold a new automobile for $13,676. What was his commission?

   $ _____

2. Salespersons at Duncan Furniture had the following daily sales yesterday: $4,565.84, $3,581.75, and $3,890.16. The store pays a 2.4% commission. How much commission did the sales force earn?

   $ _____

3. Maria Retzlaff is a sales agent for Tungston Real Estate Agency and earns a 7% commission. Yesterday, she sold a $240,980 house. What was her commission?

   $ _____

4. Francis Bsat has a commission plan that pays a 3% commission rate on the first $3,000 in sales, a 4% commission rate for sales from $3,001 to $5,000, and a 6% commission rate for sales above $5,000. What was her commission for $7,500 in sales?

   $ _____

5. City Exchange received goods on consignment that were sold for $8,500. Freight ($37.50) and storage ($55) were incurred for the goods. The commission rate was 40%. What were the (a) commission and (b) net proceeds for the sale?

   (a) $ _____

   (b) $ _____

17.1 National Discount Office Supply pays a 2% commission to sales personnel. Juan Hernandez, who calls on businesses within the city, sold 4 Canon fax machines and 2 Smith Corona word processors to a law office. These items were listed in the catalog as shown below. (Round all answers to two decimal places.)

(a) How much commission was paid to Juan Hernandez for the sale? $ _____

(b) What was the discount rate from list price for the word processor?

_____

(c) Assuming that the above sales represented average sales per hour for the week, how much was earned during a 40-hour week?

$ _____

Save 55%

16 Fax Machine

- 98' paper roll
- 10, one-touch speed dial
- Auto fax/tel switch
- 16-level grey scale
- 25-location coded dialing
- 20-second transmission

Catalog List Price $795.00
030275027426

$349⁹⁰
OfficeMart Everyday Low Price

Save $210⁰⁰

- 8-line x 80-character display
- 3.5" built-in disk drive
- 720K disk capacity
- Spell-Right 75,000-word electronic dictionary
- Personal dictionary
- Thesarurus

Catalog List Price $459.99
036652864707

$249⁹⁹
OfficeMart Everyday Low Price

CONNECTIONS

CONNECTIONS

17.2 The world population continues to grow, with a projected 10 billion population by the year 2050. This growth in population will result in a greater need for goods and services.

(a) What was the projected percentage increase from 1987 to 1998?

_____

(b) What was the projected percentage increase from 1987 to 2019?

_____

(c) What was the projected percentage increase from 2019 to 2050?

_____

(d) Assuming that the percentage increase in "c." continues at the same rate, what will the population be in the year 2081?

_____

A look at statistics that shape the nation

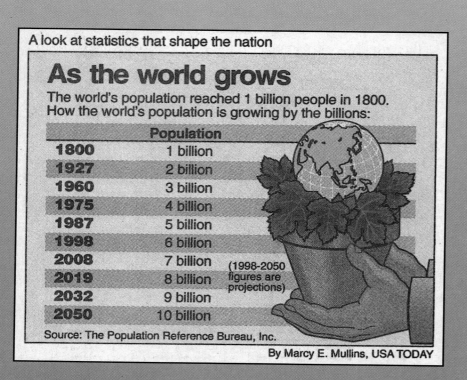

As the world grows

The world's population reached 1 billion people in 1800. How the world's population is growing by the billions:

	Population
1800	1 billion
1927	2 billion
1960	3 billion
1975	4 billion
1987	5 billion
1998	6 billion
2008	7 billion
2019	8 billion
2032	9 billion
2050	10 billion

(1998-2050 figures are projections)

Source: The Population Reference Bureau, Inc.

By Marcy E. Mullins, USA TODAY

17.1 Frank McKenzie is offered a position with an organization in Dallas, Texas. He is permitted to choose from the following plans to apply during the first year of employment. Plan A: $3,950 monthly salary. Plan B: $2,000 monthly salary plus a 4.5% commission on sales. Plan C: No salary, but a 6.75% commission rate for the first $200,000 in sales and a 9.5% commission rate for sales in excess of $200,000 during the year. Frank estimates that annual sales will be $585,000. Which plan will result in the highest earnings?

_____

What are major factors that Frank should consider while making a decision about the best pay plan to accept?

_____

_____

17.2 Many companies provide commissions to marketing representatives. Some may provide a salary plus a commission, while others may have graduated commission plans. Develop a questionnaire that can be used in surveying a company in your city that sells a product or service to determine their policy for paying marketing representatives. Prepare a one-page report to indicate the results of your survey. Compare your survey results with other students' results.

DECISIONS

COMMISSION ON SALES
Chapter Review and Quick Reference

Topic	Main Point	Typical Example	Text Page
Commission	Marketing personnel are typically compensated in whole or in part by commission.	Harry Feinstein is employed by AARCO Medical. He is compensated with a commission based on an annual sales quota.	311
Commission amount	Sales amount x Commission rate = Commission	A 5.5% commission rate is paid for a $900 sale. Commission amount = $900 x 0.055 = **$49.50**	312
Graduated commission rate	(1) Find commission on first range. (2) Find commission on next range. (3) Add commissions from each range.	A 4% commission is paid for the first $2,000 in sales. A 6% commission is paid on sales above $2,000. The commission for a $5,000 sale is computed as follows: (1) $2,000 x 0.04 = $80 (2) $3,000 x 0.06 = $180 (3) $80 + $180 = **$260**	313
Net proceeds on consigned sales	(1) Gross proceeds x Commission rate = Commission (2) Total related charges. (3) Gross proceeds - Commission - Related charges = Net proceeds	Consigned goods with a 10% commission are sold for $1,800. Freight is $45 and storage is $100. Net proceeds = (1) $1,800 x 0.10 = $180 (2) $45 + $100 = $145 (3) $1,800 - $180 - $145 = **$1,475**	314

Read the following scenario and answer the questions.

As a media assistant in an advertising agency, Dirk Jordan reviews copy before it goes on the air. This morning he must proof this ad for a music store.

"With spring here and summer just around the corner, it's time for World Beat Music's annual Global Warming Sale. And our prices are hot! Check it out--

Regularly priced $16.99 compact discs now just under $13.00!

Regularly priced $14.99 compact discs now barely over $11.00!

Regularly priced $10.99 compact discs now barely over $8.00!

Every artist and title are on sale at 25% off for one week only! So don't wait for the glaciers to melt--hurry down to World Beat Music and stock up on your favorite music. Mention this ad and receive an additional 5% off!

1. Dirk thinks the ad will be more effective if the actual sale prices are given. Rewrite the ad to state the exact sale prices. _____

2. Are the markdowns calculated based on cost price or selling price? _____

3. The manager from World Beat called Dirk and asked him to mention shirts on sale in the ad. Use the following information to weave a pitch for shirts into the radio spot: tie-dyed tank tops 30% off $13.99; short-sleeve t-shirts 35% off $17.99; long-sleeve t-shirts 40% off $18.99.

    _____

4. Calculate the cost of purchasing three $16.99 compact discs on sale. Note that the buyer is eligible for the additional discount because she mentioned the radio ad. The purchase is subject to a 6% tax.

    _____

COMMUNICATIONS

UNIT 4 SPREADSHEET APPLICATION 1:

MARKUP AND MARKUP RATES

The following spreadsheet is used to compute the markup, markup rate based on selling price, and markup rate based on cost price. Totals for markup, selling price, and cost price amounts are also computed. The markup is computed by subtracting the cost price from the selling price. The markup rate based on selling price is computed by dividing the amount of markup by the base selling price. The markup rate based on cost price is computed by dividing the markup by the cost price. Enter your answers in the spaces provided on the spreadsheet. **Neither a computer or spreadsheet software is required for completing this application.**

	A	B	C	D	E	F
1	Beacon Stores		MARKUP AND MARKUP RATES			
2	-------	-------	-------	-------	-------	-------
3					Markup Rate	Markup Rate
4	Item	Selling	Cost	Markup	Based on	Based on
5	Code	Price	Price	Amount	Selling Price	Cost Price
6	-------	-------	-------	-------	-------	-------
7		200.00	150.00	50.00	25.00%	33.33%
8	A1	180.00	140.00			
9	A2	275.00	220.00			
10	A3	420.00	320.00			
11	A4	320.00	175.00			
12	A5	140.00	90.00			
13	A6	280.00	230.00			
14	A7	185.00	110.00			
15	A8	240.00	190.00			
16	A9	420.00	345.00			
17	A10	450.00	280.00			
18	-------	-------	-------	-------	-------	-------
19	Total			*************************************		

Refer to the completed spreadsheet above to answer the following questions:

1. What is the markup amount for Item A3? $ _____

2. What is the markup amount for Item A8? $ _____

3. What is the markup rate based on selling price for Item A5?

   _____

4. What is the markup rate based on cost price for Item A6?

   _____

5. What is the markup rate based on cost price for Item A10?

    _____

6. Which item had the highest markup rate based on selling price?

    _____

7. Which item had the lowest markup rate based on cost price?

    _____

8. What was the total of the markup amount column?

    $ _____

9. How many items had markup rates higher than 26.00% based on selling price? _____

10. How many items had markup rates lower than 50.00% based on cost price? _____

UNIT 4 SELF-TEST MARKETING MATHEMATICS

Note: Identify base, rate, and amount before solving each of the following problems.

1. Annette Collins bought merchandise on August 14 with an invoice price of $425.86. Cash discount terms were 2/10, n/30. The invoice was paid on August 20. How much was the (a) cash discount and (b) net amount?

   (a) $ _____

   (b) $ _____

2. Crossnoe Printing Services has cash discount terms of 4/10, 2/20, n/45. On an invoice to Security Alarm Systems dated January 18 for $1,200, how much will be due if the invoice is paid (a) January 23, (b) January 31, and (c) February 18?

   (a) $ _____

   (b) $ _____

   (c) $ _____

3. Analytical Laboratories sells products with cash terms of 4/5, 2/10, n/20 EOM. The invoice amount was $680, and the date was February 5. What was the cash price to be received if the invoice was paid on each of the following dates:
   (a) February 8, (b) February 14, and (c) February 26?

   (a) $ _____

   (b) $ _____

   (c) $ _____

4. Lorentz Appliances bought merchandise with terms of 3/10, 2/15, n/30. An invoice for $760 was dated March 28. Compute the following items: (a) the last date of payment to receive the 3% discount, (b) the last date to receive the 2% discount, and (c) the last date to pay the full amount due.

   (a) _____

   (b) _____

   (c) _____

5. Compute the net price for an invoice showing a list price of $1,500 and trade discount terms of 5/20/10. Complete the schedule shown below to provide the solutions.

List Price	$ _____
First Trade Discount	$ _____
First Net Price	$ _____
Second Trade Discount	$ _____
Second Net Price	$ _____
Third Trade Discount	$ _____
Third and Final Net Price	$ _____

6. Quick Business Services offers trade discount terms of 40/20. How much is the net price for a list price of $5,000?

$ _____

7. Future Brides Unlimited offers merchandise with trade discount terms of 20/10 and cash discount terms of 1/10, n/30. The list price for Invoice No. 1821, dated August 15, shows merchandise purchases of $500 plus $20 delivery charges. Payment was made on August 21. Compute the (a) amount of the trade discount, (b) amount of the cash discount, and (c) amount needed to pay the bill.

(a) $ _____

(b) $ _____

(c) $ _____

8. A refrigerator cost $720.00 when purchased from the wholesaler. The retailer received a 30% markup based on cost. What were the (a) markup and (b) selling price?

(a) $ _____

(b) $ _____

9. An electric toaster costing $36.25 was marked to sell for $52.20. What were the (a) markup and (b) markup rate based on cost price?

(a) $ _____

(b) _____

10. The Book Depot sold a particular book for $20.80 that cost $16.00. (a) How much was the markup and (b) what was the markup rate based on cost price?

    (a) $ _____

    (b) _____

11. The Ritz Jewelry Store sells anklets for $32 that cost $18.08. (a) How much is the markup, and (b) what is the markup rate based on sales price?

    (a) $ _____

    (b) _____

12. The House of Lights sells a "touch-on" table lamp for $120 that cost $90. (a) How much is the markup, and (b) what is the markup rate based on sales price?

    (a) $ _____

    (b) _____

13. Clothes of Distinction paid $16.96 for a new line of sweaters. A markup rate of 75% based on cost is desired. What will the sales price of the sweaters be with this markup?

    $ _____

14. A new sports car sold for $20,000, which provided a profit of $8,000. What was the markup rate based on (a) sales price and (b) cost price?

    (a) _____

    (b) _____

15. The Novelty Shoppe discounts Christmas cards by 75% during January each year. If cards normally sell for $6.80 per box, how much will the (a) discount and (b) sales price be?

    (a) $ _____

    (b) $ _____

16. The Turner Tire Store bought a line of nylon tires for $48 and then added a 50% markup based on cost. If the tires are then reduced 20%, what will the sales price be?

    $ _____

17. Nadine Kidd worked for $150 per week plus a commission equal to 8% of sales. If her sales for the week were $2,500, what was her total pay?

    $ _____

18. Leon Milligan receives a 6% commission rate on sales up to $3,500 and a 9% rate for sales in excess of $3,500. On sales of $5,200, how much commission would he earn?

    $ _____

19. William Miner earns $353 per week or a commission rate of 3 1/2% of sales, whichever is greater. On sales of $12,500, how much would he earn for the week?

    $ 437.50   more than

20. Allison Dickerson earns a 5% commission rate on sales up to $2,500 and a 7% rate for sales in excess of $3,600. On sales of $3,600, how much commission would she earn?

    $ 202

UNIT 5

Accounting and Financial Mathematics

When we are young and begin to work for an allowance or a privilege, we begin to understand the concept of employment and accounting. Can you remember the first work you did where you received a wage? Were you paid by the hour or by the amount of work you completed? In the world of business, maintaining accounts and accurate financial statements are crucial aspects of the daily business operations. Of course, the government is also involved in assuring the accuracy of these records. A business has great accountability and responsibility to demonstrate the accuracy of all financial records.

Think about the ramifications and the people who will be affected if a business misrepresents the amount of money it is spending and receiving. Government regulations are designed to prohibit illegal activity and provide a free enterprise system that is fair to all. In this unit, several of the fundamental accounting operations involved in a typical business are presented, including payroll computation, property taxes, merchandise inventory, and depreciation. These are real-life accounting and financial operations you will encounter.

Chapter *18*

PAYROLL
COMPUTATIONS

Performance Objectives

1. Define and compare basic pay plans: annual, monthly, biweekly, weekly, hourly, piece-rate, and commission.
2. Find the gross pay for salaried employees.
3. Find the gross pay for employees paid hourly wages.
4. Find the gross pay for employees paid piece-rate wages.
5. Determine commission amount.
6. Complete a payroll worksheet.

Every business, large or small, must compute the payroll and payroll employees. Some computations are required simply to keep records ⟨ and salaries paid to employees, while other computations are necessa reports to state and federal governmental agencies. This chapter prese⟩ procedures for computing the payroll and methods for computing payr taxes. Since many companies have pay periods as often as once each w accurate payroll computations are essential.

PAYROLL TERMINOLOGY OVERVIEW

A single company may use several procedures for computing the payroll, as shown in Figure 18.1. For example, some employees may be paid weekly, while others are paid biweekly (once every two weeks) or monthly. Some employees are paid on an *hourly basis plan*, while others are paid on a *piece-rate plan* according to the amount of work produced. Still others are paid on a *straight salary plan*, which is a fixed amount each pay period (see Figure 18.2). Amounts earned on an hourly basis or a piece-rate basis are generally called *wages*, and amounts earned on a straight salary plan are generally called *salaries*. For example, factory workers usually earn wages, and supervisors and office personnel usually earn salaries.

Regardless of the procedure, the first task in computing payroll is to compute *gross wages* (pay before deductions) for individual employees. Computations are then made to determine the various deductions required for social security and state and/or federal income taxes, as well as optional deductions requested by employees for items such as savings bonds, retirement fund, credit union, and insurance. Gross pay minus amounts for required and optional deductions equals *net pay*.

Net pay: The amount remaining after subtracting deductions from gross pay.

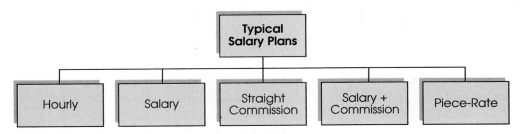

Figure 18.1 Typical Salary Plans

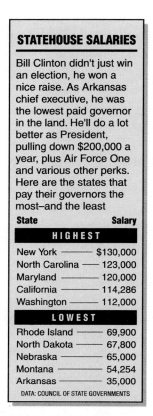

Figure 18.2 Straight Salary Plan

COMPUTING GROSS PAY FOR SALARIED EMPLOYEES

Salary: *A fixed amount of money earned on a regular basis, such as $3,000 per month or $36,000 per year.*

Office, executive, supervisory, and similar employees are often paid an annual or monthly salary. These classes of employees are paid a specified salary and may not be eligible for overtime pay. For example, a person may be employed at an annual salary of $18,000, which represents a monthly salary of $1,500 ($18,000 ÷ 12), a weekly salary of $346.15 ($18,000 ÷ 52), or a biweekly salary of $692.31 ($18,000 ÷ 26).

Salaries are usually quoted at monthly or annual amounts and can be converted to accommodate various payroll periods mentioned above for preparing periodic payrolls, as shown in Figure 18.3. For a second example, assume that an employee is hired for a monthly salary of $1,600. This equals an annual salary of $19,200 ($1,600 x 12), a weekly salary of $369.23 ($19,200 ÷ 52), or a biweekly salary of $738.46 ($19,200 ÷ 26).

Sample Earnings Table for a $60,000 Salary		
Time Basis	**Payments per Year**	**Earnings per Payment**
Weekly	52 (once a week)	$1,153.85
Biweekly	26 (every other week)	$2,307.69
Semimonthly	24 (twice a month)	$2,500.00
Monthly	12 (once a month)	$5,000.00

Figure 18.3 Sample Earnings Table

COMPUTING GROSS PAY FOR HOURLY EMPLOYEES

Employees may receive an hourly wage amount based on factors such as experience, type of work performed, and quality of work produced. The normal work week is usually considered to be 40 hours or less. Workers are usually paid a specified hourly rate for the first 40 hours worked and overtime pay for hours worked in excess of 40. Computation of gross pay for an hourly employee is illustrated in Model 18.1.

Gross earnings:
The amount earned before deductions.

Computing gross pay for hours worked

MODEL 18.1

Problem: Hector Cruz earned $9.50 per hour while working 35 hours last week. What was his gross pay?

Solution: Hours worked x Pay rate = Gross pay
35 x $9.50 = $332.50

- -

Apply Your Skills

Mario Lopez earned $15.75 per hour while working 37 hours at City Garage last week. What was his gross pay? $ *582.75*

The **Fair Labor Standards Act of 1938** set a minimum hourly wage for employees covered by federal law. The minimum hourly rate, currently $4.25 per hour, has been raised periodically over the years. This law also set a standard 40-hour work week, with covered employees earning at least 1.5 times the regular rate for overtime hours. That is, persons working in excess of 40 hours each week receive the regular rate for the first 40 hours worked, and a rate that is at least 1 1/2 (1.5) times the regular pay rate for hours worked in excess of 40. For example, an employee who works 45 hours during the week will have worked 40 regular hours plus 5 (45 - 40) overtime hours.

Overtime: Hours worked each week in excess of 40 hours.

Hourly rate: *Rate of pay for each hour worked.*

Overtime rate: *Rate of pay for hours worked in excess of 40. It must be at least 1.5 times the regular rate.*

Employees such as managers and supervisors are paid on a salary basis, such as $3,000 per month. The act requiring overtime pay does not apply to employees in this category.

Many companies pay employees in excess of the required 1.5 times the regular pay overtime rate for special holidays such as Christmas and Thanksgiving. In addition, some companies pay on an overtime basis for all hours worked in excess of 8 on any particular day even if the total of hours worked during the week is not in excess of 40. Unless instructed otherwise, assume that the overtime rate is 1.5 times the regular rate for problems in this chapter.

To compute the hours worked, time is normally computed to the nearest quarter of an hour. For example, an employee who punches in at 8:07 has time computed from 8:00, and an employee who punches in at 8:08 has time computed from 8:15. Time cards and a time clock are often used to record times when employees begin and end their work days. Computation of gross pay for an hourly employee with overtime hours is shown in Model 18.2.

MODEL 18.2

Computing gross pay for hours worked

Problem: William Speros worked 43 hours last week. His regular pay rate is $10.00 per hour. What were his regular pay, overtime pay, and total gross pay?

Solution: **Step 1** Compute regular pay.

$$40 \ \times \ \text{Pay rate} \ = \ \text{Regular pay}$$
$$40 \ \times \ \$10.00 \ = \ \$400.00$$

Step 2 Compute overtime pay.

$$\text{Overtime hours} \ \times \ \text{Pay rate} \ \times \ 1.5 \ = \ \text{Overtime pay}$$
$$3 \ (43 - 40) \ \times \ \$10.00 \ \times \ 1.5 \ = \ \$45.00$$

Step 3 Compute total gross pay.

$$\text{Regular pay} \ + \ \text{Overtime pay} \ = \ \text{Gross pay}$$
$$\$400.00 \ + \ \$45.00 \ = \ \$445.00$$

Apply Your Skills

Anfernee Hardaway worked 46 hours last week. His regular pay is $14.00 per hour. What were his (a) regular pay, (b) overtime pay, and (c) total gross pay?

(a) $ _560.00_

(b) $ _126.00_

(c) $ _686.00_

You may now complete Performance Application 18.1.

COMPUTING GROSS PAY FOR PIECE-RATE EMPLOYEES

Some workers, particularly production employees, are paid according to the number of units they make or produce in a period of time. Under the *straight piece-rate plan*, the employee is paid a specific amount for each unit produced to compute gross pay. This plan permits employers to reward employees based on their amount of production. For example, one worker produces 2,320 units during the week at a specific rate of 20¢ per unit. Gross pay is computed as shown in Model 18.3.

Piece rate: Pay based on number of units produced.

Computing gross pay at piece rate

MODEL 18.3

Problem: Nicole Spencer works in a manufacturing plant. She produced 2,320 units last week. The company paid her $0.20 for each unit. What was her gross pay?

Solution: Units produced x Rate per unit = Gross pay

2,320   x $0.20   = $464.00

Apply Your Skills

Juyum Song works on a production line at City Manufacturing. He produced 3,485 units last week. The company paid him $0.21 per unit. What was his gross pay?

$ _____

Under a differential piece-rate plan, employees are paid a higher rate per item produced as their production increases. Some employees may earn a specific salary or wage plus extra compensation based on production, as shown in Model 18.4.

Differential piece rate: A plan that increases the pay rate as productivity increases.

MODEL 18.4

Units produced in excess of 2,000:
*2,800 - 2,000 = **800***

Differential piece rate

Problem: Jane Canty earns an hourly wage of $6.50 plus $0.15 for each unit produced *in excess* of 2,000 units during the 40-hour week. She produced 2,800 units during the week. What was her total gross pay?

Solution:

Step 1 Find the hourly pay.

Hours worked	x	Pay rate	=	Hourly pay
40	x	$6.50	=	$260.00

Step 2 Find the piece-rate pay.

Units produced
(in excess of 2,000) x Pay rate = Piece-rate pay
800 x $0.15 = $120.00

Step 3 Find the total gross pay.

Regular pay + Piece-rate pay = Gross pay
$260.00 + $120.00 = $380.00

Apply Your Skills

Sarah Fung works in a manufacturing plant that pays a $9.75 hourly wage plus $0.20 for each unit produced. She worked 40 hours and produced 1,800 units last week. What was her gross pay?

$ _____

COMPUTING GROSS PAY FOR COMMISSIONED EMPLOYEES

Amount (Commission) = **Base** (Sales) x **Rate** (Commission rate)

Salary plus commission: Provides for a basic salary plus a certain percent of total sales.

Many personnel who are involved in selling a product or service are paid on a commission basis as determined by total sales. A **salary plus commission** basis provides a salary plus an opportunity to earn a commission above this amount. Personnel may be given a **quota**, which may be a sales dollar amount. They will then earn a commission after achieving the quota. Computation of gross earnings based on salary plus commission is shown in Model 18.5.

Gross earnings: Salary plus commission

Problem: Daryl Evans is marketing representative for Fletcher Medical Supplies. He earns a $37,000 annual salary plus 3% of sales in excess of his $400,000 quota. Last year, his sales were $525,000. What were his gross earnings?

Solution: **Step 1** Determine excess over quota.

Sales	-	Quota	=	Excess
$525,000	-	$400,000	=	$125,000

Step 2 Determine commission.

Excess	x	Rate of commission	=	Commission
$125,000	x	.03 (3%)		= $3,750

Step 3 Determine gross earnings.

Salary	+	Commission	=	Gross earnings
$37,000	+	$3,750		= $40,750

Straight commission: Pay is based entirely on a percent of total sales. A *graduated commission* offers a different rate for each sales level.

Apply Your Skills

Susie Wang is a marketing representative for a popular computer manufacturer. She is paid a $45,000 annual salary plus 3.5% commission for sales in excess of her $2,000,000 quota. Her sales last year were $2,750,000. What was her gross pay for the year?

$ _____

PREPARING A PAYROLL WORKSHEET

The government requires businesses to keep accurate records and to make periodic reports to provide the government with information about each employee's income and deductions.

A record is normally made to show earnings and deductions for employees for each payroll period, which may be weekly, biweekly, semimonthly, or monthly depending on company policy. The record for computing income is called various names, such as *payroll sheet* or *payroll worksheet*. If the record is expanded to include income and deductions, it is usually called a *payroll register*. The typical payroll worksheet shown in Figure 18.4 includes daily hours worked and weekly earnings.

Payroll worksheet: A form that maintains a record of hours worked and gross earnings. A *payroll register* shows earnings and deductions.

Emp. No.	Status	Hours Worked M T W T F	Total Hours	O.T. Hours	Reg. Hours	Pay Rate	Regular Pay	Overtime Pay	Gross Pay
1	M-3	8 8 8 8 8	40		40	10.50	$ 420.00		$ 420.00
2	M-2	7 8 6 8 8	37	4	37	9.75	$ 360.75	$72.00	$ 360.75
3	M-3	10 8 8 8 10	44		40	12.00	$ 480.00		$ 552.00
Total			121	4	117		$1260.75	$72.00	$1332.75

Figure 18.4 Weekly Payroll Worksheet

PERFORMANCE APPLICATION 18.1

1. Richard Slayer is paid an annual salary of $19,800. What are his
    (a) monthly, (b) biweekly, and (c) weekly salary amounts?
    (a) $ _1650_
    (b) $ _761.54_
    (c) $ _380.77_

2. Constance Summers is paid a monthly salary of $1,575. What
    are her (a) annual, (b) biweekly, and (c) weekly salary
    amounts?
    (a) $ _18,900_
    (b) $ _726.92_
    (c) $ _363.46_

3. Max Shiff works the following numbers of hours from Monday to
    Friday during the week: 8, 8, 7, 7, and 6. What are his gross
    earnings if his hourly pay rate is $7.30?
    $ _262.80_

4. Clifford Vincent worked 46 hours during the week at an hourly
    rate of $7.80. How much were his (a) regular earnings, (b)
    overtime earnings, and (c) gross earnings? (Assume the
    overtime rate is 1.5 times the regular rate for all hours worked in
    excess of 40.)
    (a) $ _312.00_
    (b) $ _70.20_
    (c) $ _382.20_

5. Eve Wagner worked the following numbers of hours from Monday to Friday during the week: 8, 10, 9, 8, and 4. Assuming a regular rate of $8.20 per hour and an overtime rate for all hours worked in excess of 8 hours each day, what were her (a) regular earnings, (b) overtime earnings, and (c) gross earnings for the week?

(a) $ _295.20_

(b) $ _36.90_

(c) $ _332.10_

6. Charles Kistler worked the following numbers of hours from Monday to Saturday during the week: 8, 10, 8, 8, 10, and 4. Assume an overtime rate of 1.5 times the regular rate for hours worked in excess of 8 hours each day and an overtime rate of 2 times the regular rate for hours worked on Saturday. His regular pay rate is $8 per hour. What were his (a) regular earnings, (b) overtime earnings, and (c) gross earnings for the week?

(a) $ _320.00_

(b) $ _112.00_

(c) $ _432.00_

7. Angela Waller is a marketing representative for Koontz Microcomputer Services. She is paid a $34,500 annual salary plus a 3.5% commission on sales in excess of $200,000. Her sales were $375,000 last year. What were her total gross earnings for the year?

$ _40,625_

PERFORMANCE APPLICATION 18.2

1. Paul Lape produced 825 units during a week. Andrea Lotta produced 837 units during the week. If the piecework rate was 26¢, what were the gross earnings for (a) Lape and (b) Lotta?

    (a) $ _214.30_

    (b) $ _277.62_

2. David Lax produced 918 units during the week, and Larry Kreamer produced 892 units. Company policy is to pay 18¢ for each unit produced up to 750 and 22¢ for units produced in excess of 750. What were the gross earnings for (a) Lax and (b) Kreamer if minimum earnings of $150 are guaranteed?

    (a) $ _171.96_

    (b) $ _166.24_

3. Irene LeBlanc had a weekly output of 429 units, while Kevin Kirshbaum had a weekly output of 385 units. Both worked 40 hours during the week. Company policy is to pay an hourly rate of $6.28 plus 64¢ for each unit produced in excess of 400. What were the gross earnings for (a) LeBlanc and (b) Kirshbaum?

    (a) $ _____

    (b) $ _____

4. Gordon Krag produced 823 units during the week, and Lyn Hamilton produced 761 units. Both worked 40 hours. Company policy is to pay 18¢ for the first 700 units produced and 21¢ for units produced in excess of 700, or $5.38 per hour, whichever is greater. What were the gross earnings for (a) Krag and (b) Hamilton?

    (a) $ _215.20_

    (b) $ _215.20_

5. Complete the following payroll worksheet for the week ending March 7, 19--.

Payroll Worksheet							for Week Ending March 7, 19–		
No.	Employee Name	M	T	W	T	F	Total Hours Worked	Hourly Rate	Gross Earnings
1	Jim Crowley	8	7	8	8	5	_____	$7.28	$_____
2	Sam Dean	8	8	5	4	7	_____	7.35	$_____
3	Cory Fry	7	6	8	7	8	_____	7.25	$_____
4	Sue Gore	8	8	8	8	8	_____	8.25	$_____
5	Teri Green	5	8	8	6	6	_____	7.46	$_____
6	Art King	8	8	8	7	7	_____	7.52	$_____
7	June Lee	8	8	7	6	6	_____	7.65	$_____
8	Berdi Nethers	7	7	7	7	7	_____	7.25	$_____
9	Clon Reid	4	4	4	5	7	_____	7.25	$_____
10	Ron Scranton	4	4	4	5	5	_____	7.37	$_____
	TOTAL EARNINGS								$_____

PERFORMANCE APPLICATION 18.3

1. Complete the following payroll register. Hours worked in excess of 40 each week earn an overtime rate of 1.5 times the regular rate.

Emp. No.	Status	Hours Worked						Total Hours	O.T. Hours	Reg. Hours	Pay Rate	Regular Pay	Overtime Pay	Gross Pay
		M	T	W	T	F	S							
1	M-3	8	8	8	8	8	-	40		40	8.50	$340.00	$_____	$340.00
2	S-1	8	8	8	8	8	4	44	4	40	7.80	$312.00	$46.80	$358.80
3	M-4	6	8	8	8	6	6	42	2	40	8.22	$328.80	$24.66	$353.46
4	S-2	8	10	8	8	10	-	44	4	40	7.96	$318.40	$47.76	$366.16
5	M-3	8	8	8	8	8	8	48	8	40	8.36	$334.40	$_____	$_____
6	M-5	10	10	10	10	8	-	48	8	40	7.90	$316.00	$_____	$_____
7	M-6	8	8	0	8	8	4	36		36	8.18	$294.48	$_____	$_____
8	M-3	7	7	7	7	8	-	36		36	8.20	$295.20	$_____	$_____
9	S-1	4	6	8	8	8	8	42	2	40	8.62	$344.80	$_____	$_____
10	M-4	6	6	0	6	6	4	28		28	8.10	$226.80	$_____	$_____
TOTALS								170	10	160		$1,299.20	$119.22	$1,418.42

2. Complete the following payroll register. Hours worked in excess of 8 each day (Monday through Friday) earn 1.5 times the regular rate. All hours worked on Saturday earn 2 times the regular rate. The first item has been completed as an example. Do not include the example in your totals.

PAYROLL REGISTER											FOR WEEK ENDING APRIL 16, 19–
Emp. No.	Status	Hours Worked M T W T F S						Total Hours	O.T. Hours	Reg. Hours	Pay Rate	Regular Pay	Overtime Pay	Gross Pay
	S-1	8 10 8 8 8 4						46	2/4	40	6.00	$240.00	$ 66.00	$306.00
1	M-2	8 10 8 8 8 4						___	___	___	6.50	$___	$___	$___
2	M-3	8 8 8 8 8 4						___	___	___	6.00	$___	$___	$___
3	M-5	6 6 8 8 6 2						___	___	___	6.50	$___	$___	$___
4	S-1	6 8 0 6 8 0						___	___	___	6.00	$___	$___	$___
5	M-4	8 8 8 8 6 4						___	___	___	6.30	$___	$___	$___
6	M-2	8 6 6 6 6 0						___	___	___	6.35	$___	$___	$___
7	S-2	8 8 10 10 8 3						___	___	___	6.20	$___	$___	$___
8	M-6	8 10 7 8 8 0						___	___	___	6.18	$___	$___	$___
9	S-1	8 8 8 8 8 0						___	___	___	6.23	$___	$___	$___
10	M-3	8 8 8 8 4 0						___	___	___	6.27	$___	$___	$___
TOTALS								___	___	___		$___	$___	$___

3. Donald Spence has an opportunity to be promoted to supervisor at a weekly salary of $380. During the past year he has worked an average of 50 hours per week at a regular hourly rate of $5.80 plus hours worked in excess of 40 at 1.5 times the regular rate. How much will his total weekly pay increase in his new position?

$ _____

PRACTICE TEST FOR CHAPTER 18

PAYROLL COMPUTATIONS

Complete each of the following problems and then compare your answers with the ones on page 649.

1. Rachel Bernardi is paid a $2,575 monthly salary. What are her (a) annual, (b) biweekly, and (c) weekly salary amounts?

    (a) $ _____

    (b) $ _____

    (c) $ _____

2. Max Carrington worked the following number of hours from Monday to Friday during the week: 8, 7, 6, 8, and 8. What were his gross earnings if his hourly rate is $12.35?

    $ _____

3. Bernetta Carlson worked the following number of hours from Monday to Friday during the week: 8, 10, 12, 8, and 9. She is paid at an overtime rate that is 1.5 times the $14.20 hourly rate. What were her (a) regular and (b) overtime earnings?

    (a) $ _____

    (b) $ _____

4. Tammy Li works on a piece-rate basis as follows: $0.72 per unit for first 225 units, $0.89 for units 226 to 500, and $0.95 for units produced in excess of 500. How much did Ms. Li earn last week if she produced 900 units?

    $ _____

5. Fred Pancost currently earns $12.60 per hour with 1.5 times the regular rate for hours worked in excess of 40 each week. He normally works 50 hours per week. A competing firm offered him a supervisor's position and a $39,500 annual salary. Which position will result in the higher annual salary?

    (a) Current position _____

    (b) Supervisory position _____

18.1 The chart shown below indicates the number of vacation days mandated by government in selected countries. Assume that an employee earns $10.80 per hour and works 8 hours daily. How much will be earned during vacations for employees working in (a) Sweden, (b) Japan, and (c) Germany? (d) Indicate what you believe to be the single most important reason that companies provide vacation days to employees.

(a) $ _____

(b) $ _____

(c) $ _____

(d) _____

CONNECTIONS

A look at statistics that shape our lives

Where vacations are required

30

No federal law mandates vacation time for employees in the USA. Where governments require the most vacation days:

25

22

19

18

Sweden   France   Brazil   Japan   Germany

Source: William M. Mercer, Inc.   By Patti Stang and Suzy Parker, USA TODAY

18.2 The chart shown below indicates the average income for medical doctors and for the U.S. work force in general during the 1985–91 period. (a) List two reasons you think that the discrepancy has developed. If the rate of income increase continues unchanged, what will the income be for (b) doctors and (c) the general U.S. work force in 1997?

(a) _____

_____

(b) $ _____

(c) $ _____

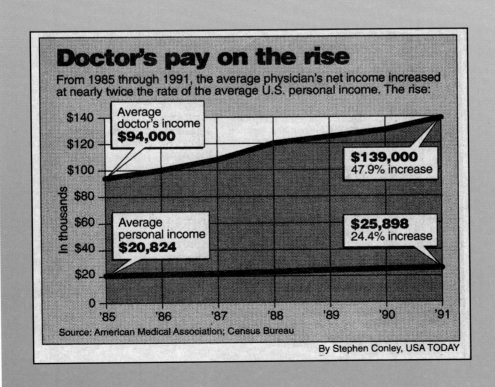

Doctor's pay on the rise

From 1985 through 1991, the average physician's net income increased at nearly twice the rate of the average U.S. personal income. The rise:

Average doctor's income **$94,000**

$139,000 47.9% increase

Average personal income **$20,824**

$25,898 24.4% increase

Source: American Medical Association; Census Bureau

By Stephen Conley, USA TODAY

CONNECTIONS

DECISIONS

18.1 Frank Snellenbarger works as an accountant for B & P Enterprises. He is currently paid $2,830 per month. A competing firm, Dunn and Associates, offered him a $30,000 annual salary and a profit sharing program that equals 5% of his first $20,000 of annual salary and 7% of annual salary in excess of $20,000. Which company offered a job that will result in a higher annual income?

_____

18.2 Donald Carson is a foreman at Menendez Manufacturing and earns $15.40 per hour, with overtime at 1.5 regular earnings. He normally works 50 hours weekly. He was offered an opportunity to move from an hourly basis to a piece-rate basis, based on productivity of his shift, as follows: $0.19 per unit for the first 2,000 units produced and $0.23 for each unit produced in excess of 2,000 units each week. Donald estimated that his area can produce 4,300 units. Should Donald (a) accept the piece rate or (b) keep the hourly pay rate basis?

(a) Piece rate _____

(b) Hourly pay rate _____

PAYROLL COMPUTATIONS
Chapter Review and Quick Reference

Topic	Main Point	Typical Example	Text Page
Salary vs. wages	Supervisors are often paid a salary. Other employees are often paid wages.	Don Li, president, earns an $85,000 annual salary. Carl Jones, a welder, is paid $16.80 per hour wages.	336
Pay basis for salaried employees	Salaried employees are often quoted an annual salary, which can be converted to other pay periods.	Annual: $84,000 Monthly: $7,000 (÷**12**) Biweekly: $3,230.77 (÷**26**) Weekly: $1,615.38 (÷**52**)	337
Gross pay for hourly employees	Employees are often paid according to the number of hours worked.	John earned $14.60 per hour while working 40 hours. Gross pay: **$14.60 x 40 = $584**	337
Overtime pay	Employers must pay hourly employees at least 1.5 times the regular hourly rate for hours over 40.	Karen earned $18 per hour while working 48 hours last week. Overtime: **8 x $18 x 1.5 = $216**	338
Piece-rate pay	Some employees, particularly factory workers, are paid according to productivity.	Gary earned $1.28 per unit while producing 500 units last week. Gross pay: **500 x $1.28 = $640**	339
Differential piece rate	Rate of pay may increase as productivity increases.	Martin earned $1 for the first 200 units and $2 for units produced in excess of 200. He produced 250 units. Gross pay: **200 x $1 = $200 + 50 x $2 = $100 = $300**	340
Payroll worksheet	A worksheet is prepared to maintain a record of hours worked, pay rate, and other information needed to determine gross earnings.	Leo worked the following hours last week: 8, 7, 8, 6, and 8. Pay rate: $12.50 / hour. Total hours: 37. Gross pay: $462.50	341

Chapter 19

PAYROLL
WITHHOLDINGS

Performance Objectives

1. Calculate income tax liability using brackets.
2. Calculate income tax withholding using table wage brackets and percentage method.
3. Calculate the amount for exemption allowance.
4. Determine whether to use itemized deductions or standard deduction.
5. Calculate FICA tax liability using the formula method.
6. Compute state and federal unemployment tax liability.
7. Explain the purpose of the W-2 and W-4 forms.

Many people beginning employment assume that gross pay is the amount of money they will have available for spending. Several item amounts, however, are withheld from the employee's paycheck. The two most common ones are income tax (state and/or federal) and social security tax deductions.

OVERVIEW OF PAYROLL WITHHOLDINGS

Earnings are generated in several ways. Typical ways include hourly wage, commission, salary, bonus, and interest income. There are several deductions for items such as income taxes, FICA taxes, insurance, and savings. Examples in this chapter concentrate on tax withholdings. Finally, the paycheck includes an amount equal to the earnings less deductions as illustrated in Figure 19.1. This diagram illustrates the relationship between gross earnings, deductions, and net pay.

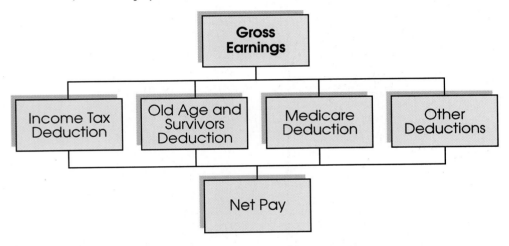

Figure 19.1 Gross Earnings, Deductions, and Net Pay Diagram

TAX REFORM ACTS OF 1986 AND 1993

The Tax Reform Act of 1986 overhauled the tax system to make it easier for people to compute the amount of income tax they owe. A dramatic effect of this law was the eventual reduction of the number of tax brackets from 15 to 3 with a series of surtaxes. The new system went into full effect in 1988, with a gradual "blending" during 1987.

The next major income tax reform came in 1993 with passage of the Omnibus Budget Reconciliation Act of 1993 (OBRA 1993). An effort was made to reduce or eliminate certain deductions in order to increase the taxes paid by high-income taxpayers and reduce the income taxes paid by lower-income taxpayers.

Congress has the power to levy, raise, or lower taxes.

*The **Omnibus Budget Reconciliation Act of 1993** was passed to shift more taxes to wealthy tax-payers.*

355

This tax package was effective with the 1993 calendar tax year for persons filing in 1994. Congress has the power to raise or lower taxes when deemed appropriate or needed.

TAX BRACKETS

Tax brackets are based on taxable income.

The tax package passed by Congress in 1993 established five tax brackets: 15%, 28%, 31%, 36%, and 39.6%. The tables shown in Figure 19.2 provide the tax brackets in effect with the 1994 tax year. The rates apply to **taxable income**, which is income after adjustments, exemptions, and deductions. These brackets can be adjusted by Congress at any time. Provisions were made to adjust income levels for future years based on inflation indexes.

Income categories within brackets will adjust for inflation each year.

Income Tax Rates (1994)

SINGLE

Taxable Income	Tax Rate
Up to $22,750	15%
$22,751 to $55,100	28
$55,101 to $115,000	31
$115,001 to $250,000	36
$250,001 or over	39.6

MARRIED FILING JOINTLY

Taxable Income	Tax Rate
Up to $38,000	15%
$38,001 to $91,850	28
$91,851 to $140,000	31
$140,001 to $250,000	36
$250,001 or over	39.6

HEAD OF HOUSEHOLD

Taxable Income	Tax Rate
Up to $30,500	15%
$30,501 to $78,700	28
$78,701 to $127,500	31
$127,501 to $250,000	36
$250,001 or over	39.6

MARRIED FILING SEPARATELY

Taxable Income	Tax Rate
Up to $19,000	15%
$19,001 to $45,925	28
$45,926 to $70,000	31
$70,001 to $125,000	36
$125,001 or over	39.6

Figure 19.2 Income Tax Rate Chart

Amounts in the tax brackets shown in Figure 19.2 are based on **taxable income** for the entire year. Model 19.1 provides an illustration using these tax brackets.

MODEL 19.1

Taxable income:
Income after adjustments, exemptions, and deductions.

Computing income tax liability

Problem: JoAnn Sorknes is single with a $64,000 taxable income for the entire year. What was her tax liability for the year?

Solution: **Step 1** Find the tax for the first bracket.

Income x Rate = Amount
$22,750 x 0.15 = $3,412.50

Step 2 Find the tax for the second bracket.

Income x Rate = Amount
$32,350 x 0.28 = $9,058.00

Step 3 Find the tax for the third bracket.

Income x Rate = Amount
$8,900 x 0.31 = $2,759.00

Step 4 Find the total taxes due.

Bracket 1 + Bracket 2 + Bracket 3 = Taxes
$3,412.50 + $9,058 + $2,759 = $15,229.50

Note that the amount multiplied by the tax rate for *each* bracket includes *only* the earned income that is included in that bracket. The sum of the taxes due from the combined brackets then becomes the annual tax amount due.

Apply Your Skills

Brenda Tieg is a head of household. Her taxable income for last year was $54,000. What was her tax liability for the year?

$ _____

EXEMPTIONS FROM INCOME

Taxpayers are not required to pay taxes on the entire amount of gross pay or income earned during the year. Each taxpayer is allowed personal exemptions of income for him/herself, spouse, dependent children, and other dependents. This amount is currently $2,450 per dependent. In addition, mortgage interest, real estate taxes, and a few other items are exempt from income when determining taxable income.

MODEL 19.2

Multiply the number of exemptions by the amount allowed per exemption.

Computing personal exemptions

Problem: William M. and Kathy A. Whitten claimed themselves, two dependent children, and an elderly aunt as personal exemptions while filing their tax return. What is their personal exemption amount?

Solution: Number of exemptions x $2,450 = Personal exemption
5   x $2,450 = $12,250

- -

Apply Your Skills

Ron Gruenfield is a head of household with 2 dependent children. What amount will be allowed for his personal exemptions?

$ _____

Taxpayers have the right to subtract itemized deductions (such as mortgage interest and real estate taxes) from gross income (Schedule A, Form 1040) in computing taxable income. They also have the alternative of taking a standard deduction if this amount is greater than itemized deductions. Amounts for the 1994 taxable year (returns filed in 1995) are shown in Figure 19.3. The amounts will probably be increased for future years to allow for inflation, but the computation methods will be similar.

Standard Deduction Amounts for 1994

Category	Amount Allowed
Single person	$3,800
Married filing jointly	6,350
Married filing separately	3,175
Head of household	5,600

Note: Additional allowances are provided for persons over 65 years old and/or disabled (blind).

Figure 19.3 Standard Deductions

Determining itemized or standard deduction

Problem: Dan Bartow completed Schedule A and determined that he had itemized deductions totaling $4,789. He will file a joint return with his wife Barbara. What is the amount of his deductions?

Solution: Dan should compare total itemized deductions with the amount in Figure 19.3. Since the standard deduction ($6,350) is higher than the itemized deductions ($4,789), Dan will choose to use the standard deduction.

Apply Your Skills

Brad Barcardi, a single taxpayer, had $4,250 in itemized deductions. Should he (a) itemize deductions or (b) take the standard deduction?

_____

MODEL 19.3

Taxpayers must choose one of the alternatives. Choosing both options is not permitted.

Exemptions for dependents are allowed regardless of whether standard or itemized deductions are used.

The actual tax rates are based on taxable income, which is the amount that remains after amounts for personal exemptions and itemized or standard deductions are subtracted from gross income. Model 19.4 illustrates computation of taxable income.

Computing taxable income

MODEL 19.4

Problem: Jae and Jin Lu had combined gross income from salaries amounting to $70,000 plus $2,000 interest income. They have 2 dependent children. They have $5,200 itemized deductions. What is their taxable income?

Solution: **Step 1** Determine exempted income amount.

Personal exemptions	+	Standard deduction	=	Exempted income
$9,800	+	$6,350	=	$16,150

Step 2 Determine taxable income amount.

Gross income	-	Exempted income	=	Taxable income
$72,000	-	$16,150	=	$55,850

Apply Your Skills

Carl and Judy Shoaf had combined $85,500 gross income and $8,400 itemized deductions. They have 1 dependent child. What was their taxable income?

$ _____

Data in Model 19.5 can then be used to determine the amount of tax liability for the year.

**MODEL
19.5**

$38,000
+ 18,600
$56,600

Computing income tax liability

Problem: Jae and Jin Lu, filing jointly, had $72,000 gross income and $56,600 taxable income last year. Based on the table in Figure 19.2, what was their income tax liability for the year?

Solution: Taxable income x Tax rate = Tax liability

$38,000	x 0.15	= $5,700
18,600	x 0.28	= 5,208
	Total liability =	$10,908

- - - - - - -

Apply Your Skills

David Munger, filing as head of household with 1 dependent child, had $70,000 gross income and $58,500 taxable income last year. What was his income tax liability for the year? (Note: Use Figure 19.2.)

$ _____

INCOME TAX WITHHOLDING

Tax tables or computer software are often used to compute taxes.

The IRS may assess a penalty if the amount due is too large.

The previous discussion shows how the final taxes due for the year are computed. Most individuals prepare income tax returns once each year. If the calendar year is used as the basis for the return, the return must be filed by April 15 each year. Employers withhold a tax amount from every paycheck. The tax return is then used to balance the amount withheld during the year with the amount of taxes due that year. If the amount withheld is greater than the amount due, the taxpayer applies for a refund. Otherwise, the taxpayer pays the government the amount of the difference when the tax return is filed with the Internal Revenue Service at the end of the year.

**MODEL
19.6**

The refund or amount due is normally computed at the end of the tax year.

Computing amount of income tax refund

Problem: John Richardson's employer withheld $4,278 from his gross pay during the year for income taxes. Taxes due for the year totaled $3,725. What is the amount of refund due?

Solution: Amount withheld - Amount due = Refund

$4,278 - $3,725 = $553

Apply Your Skills

Uttam Shah's employer withheld $7,582 from his gross salary last year for income tax purposes. Taxes due for the year were $7,938. (a) Will this result in a refund or taxes due? and (b) What is the amount?

(a) _____

(b) $ _____

WITHHOLDING TAX TABLES

Most employers use tax tables or computer software programs to compute the amount that should be withheld from employee pay for income tax purposes. The amounts included in Figure 19.4a represent a partial table to show withholding amounts for married persons paid on a weekly basis. The amount of allowances (exemptions) claimed varies with the number of dependents and factors such as itemized deductions. To use the table, first locate the income level in the two columns on the left. Then move horizontally across the table until reaching the column containing the appropriate number of exemptions at the top.

If the wages are—		And the number of withholding allowances claimed is—										
At least	But less than	0	1	2	3	4	5	6	7	8	9	10
		The amount of income tax to be withheld is—										
800	810	106	96	89	83	76	69	62	55	49	42	35
810	820	108	98	91	84	77	70	64	57	50	43	37
820	830	111	99	92	86	79	72	65	58	52	45	38
830	840	114	101	94	87	80	73	67	60	53	46	40
840	850	117	104	95	89	82	75	68	61	55	48	41
850	860	120	107	97	90	83	76	70	63	56	49	43
860	870	122	110	98	92	85	78	71	64	58	51	44
870	880	125	113	100	93	86	79	73	66	59	52	46
880	890	128	115	103	95	88	81	74	67	61	54	47
890	900	131	118	106	96	89	82	76	69	62	55	49
900	910	134	121	108	98	91	84	77	70	64	57	50
910	920	136	124	111	99	92	85	79	72	65	58	52
920	930	139	127	114	101	94	87	80	73	67	60	53
930	940	142	129	117	104	95	88	82	75	68	61	55
940	950	145	132	120	107	97	90	83	76	70	63	56
950	960	148	135	122	110	98	91	85	78	71	64	58
960	970	150	138	125	112	100	93	86	79	73	66	59
970	980	153	141	128	115	103	94	88	81	74	67	61
980	990	156	143	131	118	105	96	89	82	76	69	62
990	1,000	159	146	134	121	108	97	91	84	77	70	64
1,000	1,010	162	149	136	124	111	99	92	85	79	72	65
1,010	1,020	164	152	139	126	114	101	94	87	80	73	67
1,020	1,030	167	155	142	129	117	104	95	88	82	75	68
1,030	1,040	170	157	145	132	119	107	97	90	83	76	70
1,040	1,050	173	160	148	135	122	110	98	91	85	78	71
1,050	1,060	176	163	150	138	125	112	100	93	86	79	73
1,060	1,070	178	166	153	140	128	115	103	94	88	81	74
1,070	1,080	181	169	156	143	131	118	105	96	89	82	76
1,080	1,090	184	171	159	146	133	121	108	97	91	84	77
1,090	1,100	187	174	162	149	136	124	111	99	92	85	79
1,100	1,110	190	177	164	152	139	126	114	101	94	87	80
1,110	1,120	192	180	167	154	142	129	117	104	95	88	82
1,120	1,130	195	183	170	157	145	132	119	107	97	90	83
1,130	1,140	198	185	173	160	147	135	122	109	98	91	85
1,140	1,150	201	188	176	163	150	138	125	112	100	93	86
1,150	1,160	204	191	178	166	153	140	128	115	102	94	88
1,160	1,170	206	194	181	168	156	143	131	118	105	96	89
1,170	1,180	209	197	184	171	159	146	133	121	108	97	91
1,180	1,190	212	199	187	174	161	149	136	123	111	99	92
1,190	1,200	215	202	190	177	164	152	139	126	114	101	94
1,200	1,210	218	205	192	180	167	154	142	129	116	104	95

Figure 19.4a Married Persons Income Tax Withholding Tax Table

If the wages are—		And the number of withholding allowances claimed is—										
At least	But less than	0	1	2	3	4	5	6	7	8	9	10
		The amount of income tax to be withheld is—										
600	610	103	91	78	66	56	50	43	36	29	22	16
610	620	106	94	81	68	58	51	44	38	31	24	17
620	630	109	96	84	71	59	53	46	39	32	25	19
630	640	112	99	87	74	61	54	47	41	34	27	20
640	650	115	102	89	77	64	56	49	42	35	28	22
650	660	117	105	92	80	67	57	50	44	37	30	23
660	670	120	108	95	82	70	59	52	45	38	31	25
670	680	123	110	98	85	72	60	53	47	40	33	26
680	690	126	113	101	88	75	63	55	48	41	34	28
690	700	129	116	103	91	78	65	56	50	43	36	29
700	710	131	119	106	94	81	68	58	51	44	37	31
710	720	134	122	109	96	84	71	59	53	46	39	32
720	730	137	124	112	99	86	74	61	54	47	40	34
730	740	140	127	115	102	89	77	64	56	49	42	35
740	750	143	130	117	105	92	79	67	57	50	43	37
750	760	145	133	120	108	95	82	70	59	52	45	38
760	770	148	136	123	110	98	85	72	60	53	46	40
770	780	151	138	126	113	100	88	75	63	55	48	41
780	790	154	141	129	116	103	91	78	65	56	49	43
790	800	157	144	131	119	106	93	81	68	58	51	44
800	810	159	147	134	122	109	96	84	71	59	52	46
810	820	162	150	137	124	112	99	86	74	61	54	47
820	830	165	152	140	127	114	102	89	77	64	55	49
830	840	168	155	143	130	117	105	92	79	67	57	50
840	850	171	158	145	133	120	107	95	82	69	58	52
850	860	173	161	148	136	123	110	98	85	72	60	53
860	870	176	164	151	138	126	113	100	88	75	62	55
870	880	179	166	154	141	128	116	103	91	78	65	56
880	890	182	169	157	144	131	119	106	93	81	68	58
890	900	185	172	159	147	134	121	109	96	83	71	59
900	910	187	175	162	150	137	124	112	99	86	74	61
910	920	190	178	165	152	140	127	114	102	89	76	64
920	930	193	180	168	155	142	130	117	105	92	79	67
930	940	196	183	171	158	145	133	120	107	95	82	69
940	950	199	186	173	161	148	135	123	110	97	85	72
950	960	202	189	176	164	151	138	126	113	100	88	75
960	970	205	192	179	166	154	141	128	116	103	90	78
970	980	208	194	182	169	156	144	131	119	106	93	81
980	990	211	197	185	172	159	147	134	121	109	96	83
990	1,000	214	200	187	175	162	149	137	124	111	99	86
1,000	1,010	217	203	190	178	165	152	140	127	114	102	89
1,010	1,020	220	206	193	180	168	155	142	130	117	104	92
1,020	1,030	224	210	196	183	170	158	145	133	120	107	95
1,030	1,040	227	213	199	186	173	161	148	135	123	110	97
1,040	1,050	230	216	202	189	176	163	151	138	125	113	100
1,050	1,060	233	219	205	192	179	166	154	141	128	116	103
1,060	1,070	236	222	208	194	182	169	156	144	131	118	106
1,070	1,080	239	225	211	197	184	172	159	147	134	121	109
1,080	1,090	242	228	214	200	187	175	162	149	137	124	111
1,090	1,100	245	231	217	203	190	177	165	152	139	127	114
1,100	1,110	248	234	220	206	193	180	168	155	142	130	117

Figure 19.4b Single Persons Income Tax Withholding Tax Table

MODEL 19.7

Using a table to determine income tax withholding

Problem: Jae Lu had $60,000 salary, paid on a weekly basis, last year. His weekly earnings were $1,153.85. He is married and had 4 exemptions. Using the amounts in Figure 19.4a as a basis, what was his weekly withholding amount for income tax purposes?

Solution: **Step 1** Find the income interval in the two columns on the left (**$1,150** to **$1,160** in this example).

Step 2 Move horizontally across the table until reaching the column containing the number of exemptions at the top ($153 in this example).

Therefore, Jae's employer should withhold $153 each week for submission to the Internal Revenue Service.

- - - - - - - - - -

Apply Your Skills

Carla Beach is married with a $53,976 annual salary, paid on a weekly basis. She has 3 total exemptions. (a) What should the weekly withholding amount be for income tax purposes? (Note: Use Figure 19.4a.) Next year, Carla will earn a $57,200 annual salary. She decides to reduce her exemptions to 2 to increase her deduction. (b) Based on rates in Figure 19.4a, what will her weekly income tax withholding be?

(a) $ _____

(b) $ _____

WITHHOLDING FOR FICA TAXES

With only a few exceptions, employees working in the United States must pay FICA (Federal Insurance Contributions Act) tax, which is more commonly called the social security tax. This program was enacted in 1937 and was first designed to assist workers who become unable to work, to provide a retirement pension, and to assist family members when a worker dies. Protection against illness was added through the medicare program in 1966.

Tables similar to the ones used to determine income tax withholding are available to determine FICA tax withholding. However, the computational method is illustrated in Model 19.8.

The amount of tax to be withheld is determined by multiplying the tax rate by the gross wages (base) up to a specified amount. The original FICA rate was 1% of gross earnings on the first $3,000 earned each year. Congress has increased both the rate and the amount gradually over the years to its 1995 rate of 7.65% based on the first $61,200 of earnings. Beginning in 1991, Congress separated old age and survivors coverage from medicare coverage since the maximum cap changed for the two areas. This percent represents 6.2% for old age and survivors coverage and 1.45% for medicare. The medicare portion (1.45%) does not have a maximum income base.

Tax rates and gross earnings used to compute taxes change periodically by acts of Congress. The method used to compute the tax, however, does not change. For low-income earners, the amount of FICA tax withheld may be greater than the amount withheld for income taxes.

Old age and survivors, based on up to $61,200 earnings: 6.2%

Employers also pay an equal amount of social security taxes. Self-employed persons must pay both shares.

Computing FICA tax withholding

MODEL 19.8

Problem: Jae Lu earned $60,000 last year. How much should be withheld from his paycheck during the year for FICA?

Solution: **Step 1** Determine the amount of old age and survivors withholding.

Income x Rate = Withholding
$60,000 x 0.062 = $3,720.00

Step 2 Determine the amount of medicare withholding.

Income x Rate = Withholding
$60,000 x 0.0145 = $870.00

Step 3 Combine the amounts obtained above.

Old age and survivors + Medicare = FICA total
$3,720 + $870 = $4,590

Note that the maximum earnings subject to old age and survivors insurance withholding was the first $61,200 earned during the year. However, total earnings were subject to medicare withholding.

Apply Your Skills

Cecil Cranfield earned $37,450 last year. How much should be withheld from his paycheck for FICA during the year?

$ _____

Remember that the FICA tax is based on a maximum of $61,200 earnings, with no maximum cap for the medicare portion.

COMPUTING NET PAY

Net pay: *Gross pay minus deductions*

Net pay represents the amount of the paycheck. Deductions from gross earnings are made for income tax and FICA tax amounts. In addition, deductions for items such as insurance contributions, credit union contributions, and union dues may also be deducted from gross earnings to compute the net pay amount as shown in Model 19.9.

MODEL 19.9

Computing net pay

Problem: Jae Lu is married with four dependents and a $60,000 annual salary or $1,153.85 weekly salary. His weekly deductions were as follows: income taxes, $153.00; FICA, $71.54; and insurance premium, $16.73. What was his weekly net pay amount?

Solution: **Step 1** Find the total deductions.

Income tax + FICA tax + Insurance premium = Deductions
$153.00 + $71.54 + $16.73 = $241.27

Step 2 Find the net pay.

Gross pay - Deductions = Net pay
$1,153.85 - $241.27 = $912.58

Apply Your Skills

Rhonda Solomito has a $50,180 annual salary, paid on a weekly basis. Her weekly deductions were as follows: income taxes, $175; FICA, $73.82; and union dues, $8.25. What was her weekly net pay amount?

$ _____

The accounting and personnel departments must cooperate to prepare payroll records.

Payroll applications require accuracy and attention to details. Many bookkeeping, financial, and accounting functions relate directly to this area.

PERCENTAGE METHOD WITHHOLDING

Another popular method for determining income tax withholding amounts is to use a table for percentage method of withholding similar to the one shown in Figure 19.5. The table showing withholding allowances in Figure 19.6 is used to determine exemptions.

Tables for Percentage Method of Withholding
(For Wages Paid in 1993)

TABLE 1—WEEKLY Payroll Period

(a) SINGLE person (including head of household)—

If the amount of wages (after subtracting withholding allowances) is:	The amount of income tax to withhold is:
Not over $49.	$0

Over—	But not over—		of excess over—
$49	—$451	15%	—$49
$451	—$942	$60.30 plus 28%	—$451
$942		$197.78 plus 31%	—$942

(b) MARRIED person—

If the amount of wages (after subtracting withholding allowances) is:	The amount of income tax to withhold is:
Not over $119	$0

Over—	But not over—		of excess over—
$119	—$784	15%	—$119
$784	—$1,563	$99.75 plus 28%	—$784
$1,563		$317.87 plus 31%	—$1,563

TABLE 2—BIWEEKLY Payroll Period

(a) SINGLE person (including head of household)—

If the amount of wages (after subtracting withholding allowances) is:	The amount of income tax to withhold is:
Not over $97.	$0

Over—	But not over—		of excess over—
$97	—$902	15%	—$97
$902	—$1,884	$120.75 plus 28%	—$902
$1,884		$395.71 plus 31%	—$1,884

(b) MARRIED person—

If the amount of wages (after subtracting withholding allowances) is:	The amount of income tax to withhold is:
Not over $238	$0

Over—	But not over—		of excess over—
$238	—$1,567	15%	—$238
$1,567	—$3,125	$199.35 plus 28%	—$1,567
$3,125		$635.59 plus 31%	—$3,125

TABLE 3—SEMIMONTHLY Payroll Period

(a) SINGLE person (including head of household)—

If the amount of wages (after subtracting withholding allowances) is:	The amount of income tax to withhold is:
Not over $105	$0

Over—	But not over—		of excess over—
$105	—$977	15%	—$105
$977	—$2,041	$130.80 plus 28%	—$977
$2,041		$428.72 plus 31%	—$2,041

(b) MARRIED person—

If the amount of wages (after subtracting withholding allowances) is:	The amount of income tax to withhold is:
Not over $258	$0

Over—	But not over—		of excess over—
$258	—$1,698	15%	—$258
$1,698	—$3,385	$216.00 plus 28%	—$1,698
$3,385		$688.36 plus 31%	—$3,385

TABLE 4—MONTHLY Payroll Period

(a) SINGLE person (including head of household)—

If the amount of wages (after subtracting withholding allowances) is:	The amount of income tax to withhold is:
Not over $210	$0

Over—	But not over—		of excess over—
$210	—$1,954	15%	—$210
$1,954	—$4,081	$261.60 plus 28%	—$1,954
$4,081		$857.16 plus 31%	—$4,081

(b) MARRIED person—

If the amount of wages (after subtracting withholding allowances) is:	The amount of income tax to withhold is:
Not over $517	$0

Over—	But not over—		of excess over—
$517	—$3,396	15%	—$517
$3,396	—$6,771	$431.85 plus 28%	—$3,396
$6,771		$1,376.85 plus 31%	—$6,771

Figure 19.5 Tables for Percentage Method of Withholding

Percentage Method–Amount for One Withholding Allowance

Payroll Period	One withholding allowance
Weekly	$45.19
Biweekly	90.38
Semimonthly	97.92
Monthly	195.83
Quarterly	587.50
Semiannually	1,175.00
Annually	2,350.00
Daily or miscellaneous (each day of the payroll period)	9.04

Figure 19.6 Percentage Method Withholding Allowance

MODEL 19.10

Computing withholding using the percentage method

Problem: Frank Latimer is married with 1 dependent child. His monthly earnings are $2,500. What is his monthly income tax withholding amount?

Solution: **Step 1** Use Figure 19.6 to determine his withholding allowance.

Allowance for monthly	x	No. of allowances	=	Withholding allowance
$195.83	x	3	=	$587.49

Step 2 Determine taxable income.

Gross income	-	Withholding allowance	=	Taxable income
$2,500	-	$587.49	=	$1,912.51

Step 3 Use Figure 19.5, Table 4, to determine his withholding amount.

Taxable income over $517	x	Tax rate	=	Withholding amount
$1,395.51	x	0.15	=	$209.33 (rounded)

$1,912.51
- 517.00
$1,395.51

Apply Your Skills

Robert Berl, a single taxpayer, earns $52,000 annually, paid on a biweekly basis. What is his biweekly withholding amount for income tax purposes? (Note: Use the percentage method.)

$ _____

EMPLOYER'S TAXES

Employers are also assessed payroll taxes. In addition to FICA taxes equal to the employee's assessment, the employer pays a Federal Unemployment Tax Act (FUTA) assessment of 6.2% of the first $7,000 earned by each employee less taxes paid under State Unemployment Tax Act (SUTA) assessment, which is currently 5.4% of the first $7,000 earned by each employee. SUTA is not the same for each state and is based on the firm's employment record. To compute these taxes, first compute the SUTA amount. Compute the FUTA amount and then subtract the amount of SUTA assessed as shown in Model 19.11. Regardless, employer taxes do not affect the amount assessed to employees.

SUTA is subtracted from FUTA to determine the final FUTA amount.

FUTA and SUTA tax computation

MODEL 19.11

Problem: Harry Jablinski earned $34,000 last year. His company has a good employment record and is assessed 4.2% under SUTA. What is the amount of SUTA and FUTA that his employer must pay?

Solution: **Step 1** Determine the SUTA assessment.

Income	x SUTA percent	= SUTA tax
$7,000	x 0.042	= $294.00

Step 2 Determine the maximum FUTA amount.

Income	x FUTA percent	= Maximum FUTA
$7,000	x 0.062	= $434.00

Step 3 Determine the FUTA assessment.

Maximum FUTA	- SUTA tax	= FUTA tax
$434	- $294	= $140.00

- -

Apply Your Skills

Martin Keller earned $43,800 last year. His company is assessed a 2.5% rate under SUTA. What is the amount of (a) SUTA and (b) FUTA that his employer must pay?

(a) $ _____

(b) $ _____

TAX FORMS

The Fair Labor Standards Act requires that accurate records be maintained showing individual earnings records for each employee. This record must include a quarterly summary of earnings and deductions.

Numerous tax forms must be completed by the employer. Tax Form 8109 is used to make deposits of taxes due. This deposit can be made to a Federal Reserve Bank or authorized financial institution. Employers must complete Form 941 quarterly, which summarizes deposits needed for the employee's FICA tax, the employer's FICA tax, and the employee's federal income tax. These forms are normally completed by personnel in the accounting department.

Employees normally see a couple of forms on an annual basis. Employees must maintain a current copy of Form W-4, Figure 19.7, to indicate the number of exemptions claimed for income tax withholding from gross earnings. Employers must supply Form W-2, Figure 19.8, within one month after the end of the tax year to indicate annual earnings and income tax and FICA withholding amounts.

Form **W-4** Department of the Treasury Internal Revenue Service

Employee's Withholding Allowance Certificate

▶ **For Privacy Act and Paperwork Reduction Act Notice, see reverse.**

OMB No. 1545-0010 **19**

1 Type or print your first name and middle initial | Last name | 2 Your social security number

Home address (number and street or rural route) | 3 ☐ Single ☐ Married ☐ Married, but withhold at higher Single rate. **Note:** *If married, but legally separated, or spouse is a nonresident alien, check the Single box.*

City or town, state, and ZIP code | 4 If your last name differs from that on your social security card, check here and call 1-800-772-1213 for more information . . . . ▶ ☐

5 Total number of allowances you are claiming (from line G above or from the worksheets on page 2 if they apply) . 5

6 Additional amount, if any, you want withheld from each paycheck . . . . 6 $

7 I claim exemption from withholding for 1993 and I certify that I meet **ALL** of the following conditions for exemption:

- Last year I had a right to a refund of **ALL** Federal income tax withheld because I had **NO** tax liability; **AND**
- This year I expect a refund of **ALL** Federal income tax withheld because I expect to have **NO** tax liability; **AND**
- This year if my income exceeds $600 and includes nonwage income, another person cannot claim me as a dependent.

If you meet all of the above conditions, enter "EXEMPT" here . . . . ▶ 7

Under penalties of perjury, I certify that I am entitled to the number of withholding allowances claimed on this certificate or entitled to claim exempt status.

Employee's signature ▶ **Date** ▶ , 19

8 Employer's name and address (Employer: Complete 8 and 10 only if sending to the IRS) | 9 Office code (optional) | 10 Employer identification number

Cat. No. 10220Q

Figure 19.7 Form W-4

1 Control number | OMB No. 1545-0008

2 Employer's name, address, and ZIP code | 6 Statutory employee ☐ Deceased ☐ Pension plan ☐ Legal rep. ☐ 942 emp. ☐ Subtotal ☐ Deferred compensation ☐ Void ☐

7 Allocated tips | 8 Advance EIC payment

9 Federal income tax withheld | 10 Wages, tips, other compensation

3 Employer's identification number | 4 Employer's state I.D. number | 11 Social security tax withheld | 12 Social security wages

5 Employee's social security number | 13 Social security tips | 14 Medicare wages and tips

19 Employee's name, address, and ZIP code | 15 Medicare tax withheld | 16 Nonqualified plans

17 | 18 Other

20 | 21 | 22 Dependent care benefits | 23 Benefits included in Box 10

24 State income tax | 25 State wages, tips, etc. | 26 Name of state | 27 Local income tax | 28 Local wages, tips, etc. | 29 Name of locality

Copy 1 For State, City, or Local Tax Department Department of the Treasury—Internal Revenue Service

Form **W-2 Wage and Tax Statement**

Employee's and employer's copy compared ☐

Figure 19.8 Form W-2

PERFORMANCE APPLICATION 19.1

You will use tax tables in the text for several problems in this assignment.

1. John and Rachel Moore are married with 3 children. How many exemptions can they claim on their income tax?

   _____

2. Howard Tucker is divorced. He has custody of his son, who is 13 years old. How many exemptions can he claim on his income tax?

   _____

3. Torrey Dodson is single with a taxable annual income of $46,750. What is his income tax liability for the year?

   $ _____

4. Beverly Ronsiek is single with a taxable annual income of $52,700. What is her income tax liability for the year?

   $ _____

5. Alicia Rosenfield is married. However, she and her husband are filing separate tax returns. Her annual income is $42,780. What is her income tax liability for the year?

   $ _____

6. Emmett and Maxine Greganti are a married couple filing a joint return. Their combined taxable income is $78,980. What is their income tax liability for the year?

   $ _____

7. Michael Polk is single with a taxable annual income of $52,750. What is his income tax liability?

   $ _____

8. Patsy and Carl Latimer are a married couple with a combined taxable income of $83,985. If they file a joint return, what is their income tax liability?

   $ _____

9. Sue Dempsey has 3 personal tax exemptions. If each exemption equals $2,450, what is the amount of her personal exemptions?

    $ _____

10. Scott and Ethel Petrowski are married and filing a joint tax return. Their itemized deductions total $4,387. They decide to take the larger of the itemized deductions or their standard deduction. What amount will they be able to deduct?

    $ _____

11. Terry and Thomas Rogers earned income last year amounting to $43,570. Assume 3 personal exemptions and the standard deduction for a joint return. What is the amount of their taxable income?

    $ _____

12. Delores Grantham is single. Her only personal exemption is herself. Her income last year was $37,800. Assuming that she takes the standard deduction, what is the amount of her taxable income?

    $ _____

13. Kent Halzup is single with 1 allowance. His weekly earnings are $850. What amount should be withheld from his paycheck for income taxes each week?

    $ _____

14. Alga Kingsford is a married taxpayer. Her weekly earnings are $950. What amount should be withheld from her weekly paycheck for income taxes?

    $ _____

15. Debra Finley's gross earnings are $876 per week. Based on a FICA rate of 7.65%, what amount should be withheld for FICA taxes from her weekly paycheck?

    $ _____

16. John and Betty Dilworth have combined salaries of $5,600 each month. Based on a FICA rate of 7.65%, what amount should be withheld for FICA taxes each month?

    $ _____

PERFORMANCE APPLICATION 19.2

1. Compute the portion of the payroll register shown below using the appropriate withholding tax table shown in the text. Round all amounts to the nearest cent. The first item has been completed as an example. Do not include amounts in the example in your totals.

   Note: The Status column is coded. For example S-1 means single with 1 allowance or M-2 means married with 2 allowances. Assume a 7.65% FICA rate. Use Figures 19.4 and 19.6 for Federal Income Tax deduction and withholding allowance.

No.	Employee Name	Status	Gross Pay	Federal	FICA	Other	Total Deductions	Net Pay
		S-1	$ 800	$147.00	$61.20	(insur.) 35.00	$243.20	$556.80
1	Craig, Carmie D.	M-8	900	$	$	-0-	$	$
2	Dees, Lucy A.	S-0	950	$	$	-0-	$	$
3	Hodgin, Allen C.	S-1	790	$	$	-0- (cr. un.)	$	$
4	Huff, Millie R.	M-2	975	$	$	30.00	$	$
5	Kelsey, Donald A.	M-1	1,205	$	$	-0-	$	$
6	Larson, Felix T.	M-2	1,050	$	$	-0-	$	$
7	Maddox, Tony B.	M-2	920	$	$	-0- (insur.)	$	$
8	Monroe, Linda K.	M-8	1,200	$	$	35.00	$	$
9	Parr, Willie J.	S-0	850	$	$	-0-	$	$
10	Piretti, Bernice	S-1	980	$	$	-0-	$	$
11	Poynor, Ted P.	M-0	800	$	$	-0-	$	$
12	Ryndes, Eddie E.	S-2	1,100	$	$	-0- (cr. un.)	$	$
13	Shaul, Percy O.	S-1	950	$	$	18.00	$	$
14	Wade, Roland A.	M-4	1,000	$	$	-0-	$	$
15	Young, Adam T.	S-1	900	$	$	-0-	$	$
TOTALS			$	$	$	$	$	$

PAYROLL REGISTER — FOR WEEK ENDING JULY 8, 19--

2. Janet Ross, a single person with 2 personal allowances, had prior earnings for the year of $36,000. During the current week, she earned $600. Using information in the text, compute the (a) federal income taxes and (b) FICA taxes that should be withheld from her current earnings.

   (a) $ _____

   (b) $ _____

3. Thomas Curtis, a married person with 4 allowances, had prior earnings for the year of $8,628. During the current week, he earned $900. Using information in the text, compute the (a) federal income taxes and (b) FICA taxes that should be withheld from his current earnings.

   (a) $ _____

   (b) $ _____

4. Lillian Watkins' earnings for the year totaled $18,675.40 prior to her current month's earnings of $1,418. Assume that the income tax withholding rate is 15% of gross pay with a 7.65% FICA rate. What are her monthly (a) deduction for federal income taxes, (b) deduction for FICA taxes, and (c) net pay?

   (a) $ _____

   (b) $ _____

   (c) $ _____

5. Sandra Swenson's earnings for the year totaled $12,785.83 prior to her current week's earnings of $700. She is single and claims 1 allowance on her W-4 form. Use the tax withholding table and a 7.65% FICA rate to compute withholdings. What are her weekly (a) deduction for federal income taxes, (b) deduction for FICA taxes, and (c) net pay?

   (a) $ _____

   (b) $ _____

   (c) $ _____

6. Daryl Evans earned $42,000 last year. His employer was assessed 2.1% under SUTA. What were his employer's (a) SUTA and (b) FUTA tax liabilities?

   (a) $ _____

   (b) $ _____

PRACTICE TEST FOR CHAPTER 19

PAYROLL WITHHOLDING

Complete each of the following problems and then compare your answers with the ones on page 649. Use the appropriate charts in the chapter to supply needed information.

1. Martin and Trudy Muir are married with 3 dependent children. What is the total personal exemption that can be claimed for tax purposes? $ _____

2. The Johnson family (husband, wife, and 2 dependent children) have $54,000 gross annual income and $15,000 itemized deductions. What was their tax liability for the year for a joint return? $ _____

3. Nanalee Roark is a single mother with 1 child. She qualifies to file as head of household. Her annual income was $48,500. She has no itemized deductions, so she will take the standard deduction. What was her tax liability for the year?

   $ _____

4. Roberta Dacus earned $52,000 last year. What was her **total** FICA tax liability for the year? $ _____

5. Jacob Ashley, single with a total of 3 dependents, accepted a position earning $49,920 per year. What is the amount of his weekly income tax withholding? $ _____

19.1 The chart shown below indicates total individual income taxes collected during selected years from 1970 to 1990. Assuming that the same increase from 1985 to 1990 will be experienced during the 1990 to 1995 period, (a) what will the collections be for 1995? Assuming the same increase during the next five years, (b) what will the collections be for 2000? Survey five persons not in your class to determine their estimates about the income tax collections estimated for the year 2000. (c) What was their average estimate? (d) Was their estimate reasonably close to your estimate?

(a) $ _____

(b) $ _____

(c) $ _____

(d) _____

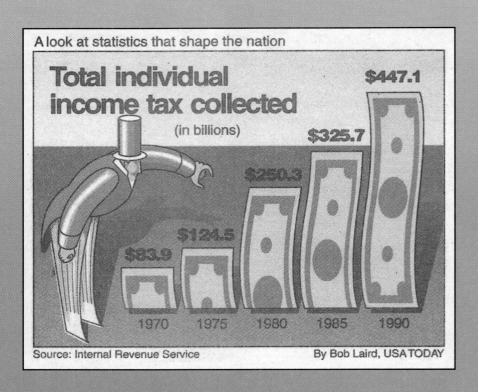

A look at statistics that shape the nation

Total individual income tax collected

(in billions)

$447.1

$325.7

$250.3

$124.5

$83.9

1970   1975   1980   1985   1990

Source: Internal Revenue Service   By Bob Laird, USA TODAY

CONNECTIONS

19.2 The chart shown below indicates the biggest employment gain and smallest employment loss on a monthly basis in history. Review articles in your local newspaper or other financial publication to determine national trends in employment. (a) Is employment increasing or decreasing for the month? (b) List factors that will result in an employment increase. Compare your responses with responses from three other persons in your class.

(a) _____

(b) _____

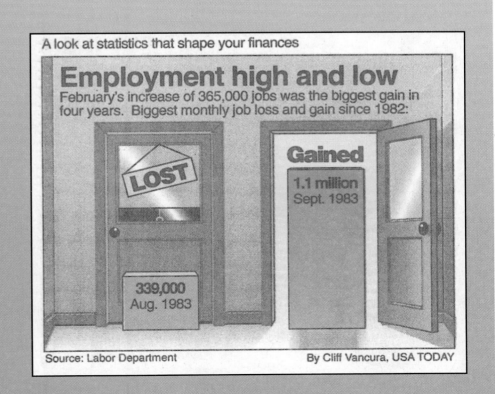

A look at statistics that shape your finances

Employment high and low
February's increase of 365,000 jobs was the biggest gain in four years. Biggest monthly job loss and gain since 1982:

LOST

Gained

339,000
Aug. 1983

1.1 million
Sept. 1983

Source: Labor Department

By Cliff Vancura, USA TODAY

CONNECTIONS

375

19.1 The table shown below indicates major league baseball salaries for 1993 with committed salaries through the 1998 year. Review the table and answer the following questions. (a) Which team had the highest salary in 1993? (b) Assume that a person desires to purchase a team for $120 million. Based on 1993 salary figures, how much total funds do you *estimate* will be required during the first year, including purchase price, salaries, and estimated operating expenses? Base your estimate on a salary that is in the middle of the salary range. (c) Harvey Feinstein has gathered an ownership group that is capable of contributing $150 million. Will this be sufficient to purchase and operate the Cincinnati team? Give one reason for your response.

(a) $ _____

(b) $ _____

(c) _____
_____

Team-by-team player salary costs

Major league baseball payrolls committed to active players (in millions, includes signing bonus, option years):

Team	No. of Players	1993 Total salary	1994 salary	1995 salary	1996 salary	1997 salary	1998 salary	Total beyond '93
Atlanta	40	$39,849,000	19,075,000	15,000,000	17,250,000	11,500,000	0	62,825,000
Baltimore	36	26,607,500	5,400,000	6,600,000	6,600,000	6,800,000	0	25,400,000
Boston	32	40,059,250	25,013,584	5,655,250	5,500,000	0	0	36,168,834
California	40	25,681,834	12,575,000	4,875,000	0	0	0	17,450,000
Chicago (NL)	39	38,547,666	27,391,667	28,283,334	9,650,000	5,900,000	0	71,225,001
Chicago (AL)	40	34,148,165	24,325,002	10,833,334	5,250,000	3,250,000	0	43,658,336
Cincinnati	40	44,324,167	19,908,333	17,908,334	10,575,000	0	0	48,391,667
Cleveland	39	15,213,000	18,125,001	16,500,000	6,975,000	4,250,000	0	45,850,001
Colorado	40	9,141,500	1,340,000	0	0	0	0	1,340,000
Detroit	38	32,915,832	20,516,668	20,683,334	9,200,000	9,200,000	0	59,600,002
Florida	40	17,474,545	11,175,000	4,875,000	0	0	0	16,050,000
Houston	40	26,695,000	18,100,000	23,050,000	9,500,000	9,550,000	0	60,200,000
Kansas City	40	40,548,666	18,650,001	24,933,334	9,000,000	0	0	52,583,335
Los Angeles	40	37,326,500	24,862,501	19,116,667	0	0	0	43,979,168
Milwaukee	40	24,245,834	16,200,000	2,700,000	0	0	0	18,900,000
Minnesota	40	23,150,000	18,685,000	10,500,000	10,200,000	7,200,000	0	46,585,000
Montreal	41	13,458,334	0	0	0	0	0	0
New York (NL)	36	39,478,167	19,479,167	5,300,000	5,100,000	0	0	29,879,167
New York (AL)	40	41,272,000	34,940,834	29,030,516	11,700,000	0	0	75,671,350
Oakland	37	35,055,834	24,725,000	24,300,000	17,400,000	13,800,000	0	80,225,000
Philadelphia	40	26,611,834	16,800,000	2,400,000	0	0	0	19,200,000
Pittsburgh	40	25,327,467	9,425,000	0	0	0	0	9,425,000
San Diego	40	26,430,333	10,333,333	8,833,334	0	0	0	19,166,667
San Francisco	39	34,905,000	20,112,500	8,166,667	8,416,667	8,666,667	8,916,667	54,279,168
Seattle	40	33,269,833	17,501,667	19,216,667	15,250,000	4,750,000	0	56,718,334
St. Louis	40	24,000,001	6,171,667	4,925,000	2,675,000	0	0	13,771,667
Texas	39	36,015,959	15,602,625	11,700,000	0	0	0	27,302,625
Toronto	39	41,919,666	34,316,668	26,250,000	10,500,000	0	0	71,066,668
Totals	**1,101**	**953,672,887**	**490,751,318**	**351,635,771**	**170,741,667**	**84,866,667**	**8,916,667**	**1,106,911,990**

19.2 Joseph Rodriquez is married with 1 dependent child (total of 3 dependents). He has a $52,000 annual salary. He requested that his employer withhold $230 a week from his salary. Based on data in the withholding chart in the text, (a) will this amount be sufficient for his earnings level? (b) Give one reason why Joseph may want his employer to withhold an amount greater than indicated in the table.

(a) _____

(b) _____

DECISIONS

PAYROLL WITHHOLDINGS
Chapter Review and Quick Reference

Topic	Main Point	Typical Example	Text Page
Tax liability	Assessed income taxes are based on taxable income.	Taxable income: $51,000 Single Tax liability: Up to $22,750: $ 3,412.50 $22,751-$55,100: 7910 Total: **$11,322.50** Note: Use Figure 19.2.	357
Exemptions	Each tax return currently is permitted to subtract $2,450 per dependent from gross earnings.	No. of exemptions: 3 Exemption amount: $2,450 x 3 = **$7,350**	358
Itemized deductions	Taxpayers may consider certain expenses as a deduction to determine taxable income.	Mortgage int.: $3,000 Real est. taxes: 1,100 Total itemized deductions: **$4,100**	359
Standard deduction	A standard deduction amount, depending on filing status, can be subtracted prior to computing taxable income if the standard amount is greater than itemized deductions.	Itemized deductions for a head of household: $3,700. Standard deduction: **$5,600**. The greater amount will be allowed. Use Figure 19.3.	359
Taxable income	Exemptions and deductions can be subtracted from gross earnings to determine taxable income base.	Married person with 1 dependent child, $60,000 gross earnings, and $6,700 itemized deductions. Personal exemptions: 3 x $2,450 = $7,350 Taxable income: $60,000 - $7,350 - $6,700 = **$45,950**	359

Topic	Main Point	Typical Example	Text Page
Tax refund or due	A tax refund or tax due computation is made depending on whether or not tax withholdings are more than tax liability.	Taxes liability: $13,400 Taxes withheld: 12,100 Taxes due: **$ 1,300** This amount must be submitted with tax return. If a tax refund is in order, IRS will send it later.	360
Tax withholding	Employers will with-hold an appropriate amount from each paycheck for submission to the IRS.	Single person with $1,105 weekly earnings and 2 dependents. Withholding: **$206.00** Use Figure 19.4b. Find the income interval and then move across to the exemption column.	362
FICA taxes	Employees and employer each must pay FICA taxes equal to 7.65% of gross pay, old age and survivors (6.2%), plus medicare (1.45%).	Person with $1,105 weekly earnings. FICA tax withholding: $1,105 x 6.2%: $68.51 $1,105 x 1.45%: 16.02 Total FICA: **$84.53** Employer must pay this same amount.	363
Net pay	Net pay or pay-check amount equals gross pay minus deductions.	Gross pay: $1,105.00 Income taxes: - 206.00 FICA taxes - 68.51 Insurance: - 16.02 Net pay **$ 814.47**	364

Topic	Main Point	Typical Example	Text Page
Percentage method withholding	Tables are provided by IRS to determine amounts for exemptions and income tax withholding.	Married person with 1 dependent child and $3,600 monthly income. Withholding allowance from Figure 19.6: $195. 83 x 3 = $587.49. Taxable income: $3,600 - $587.49 = $3,012.51. Withholding amount using Figure 19.5: ($3,012.51 - $517) x 0.15 = **$374.33.**	366
FUTA and SUTA	In addition to matching FICA tax liability, employers pay federal and state unemployment taxes. FUTA = 6.2% and SUTA = up to 5.4% of the first $7,000 earnings per employee. Credit is provided against FUTA for SUTA.	An employee earned $1,200 during January. SUTA is 3%. FUTA: $1,200 x 0.062 = $74.40. SUTA: $1,200 x 0.03 = **$36.** FUTA: $74.40 - $36 = **$38.40** SUTA: **$36.** Notice that credit was given to FUTA for SUTA.	367
Tax forms	Employers must maintain accurate payroll records for each employee and submit completed forms to the government.	Form 8109: Used to make deposits of taxes due. Form 941: Used to summarize deposits of payroll taxes. W-4: Used to record number of exemptions. W-2: Used to report summary of earnings and deductions to employees.	368

Chapter *20*

PROPERTY AND
PROPERTY TAXES

Performance Objectives

1. Determine procedure for setting property tax rate.
2. Determine property tax due based on assessed valuation.
3. Distinguish between market and assessed valuation.
4. Determine property taxes due when expressed property tax rates are in multiple media such as percent, dollars, and mills.
5. Convert decimal tax rate to percent, per unit of assessed valuation ($100 and $1,000), and in mills.

Property taxes are assessed on real property (such as homes, land, and buildings) by counties, cities, states, and school districts as a way to raise money for schools, roads, parks, police and fire protection, and other public services. Property taxes are assessed against individuals and businesses owning real property. Material in this chapter shows you how to compute individual and business property tax assessments.

DETERMINING PROPERTY TAX RATE AND ASSESSMENT

Governmental units that use property taxes as one source of income generally develop a budget to match anticipated operational expenses against anticipated income. This budget is usually completed on an annual basis. Figure 20.1 shows typical property tax uses.

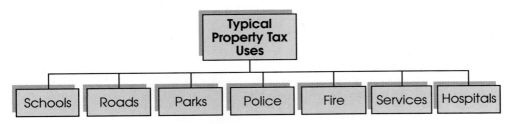

Figure 20.1 Typical Property Tax Uses

The governmental unit sets the property tax rate and assessment based on the worth of the assessed property in the area. Although rates and bases vary widely, the method for computation is fairly uniform (Amount ÷ Base = Rate), as illustrated in Model 20.1.

Property taxes:
State and/or local taxes on property owned by businesses and individuals.

Property tax rate:
The rate that must be paid on assessed value of property. The rate is set by the city and/or county government.

The assessor may recommend a tax rate to the governing body which sets the final tax rate.

Computing property tax rate

MODEL 20.1

Problem: The assessed valuation of property in Fentress County is $3,500,000,000. In order to collect funds for a $140,000,000 budget, what tax rate will be needed?

Solution: Revenue amount needed ÷ Base of assessed valuation = Tax rate

$140,000,000 ÷ $3,500,000,000 = 0.04 (4%)

Using this same procedure, determine the needed tax rate to raise $150,000,000 (amount) if property has an assessed valuation of $5,000,000,000 (base) by using the following steps:

Step 1 Amount needed equals $150,000,000

Step 2 (Amount) ÷ (Base) = (Rate)

$150,000,000 ÷ $5,000,000,000 = 0.03 = 3% tax rate

The large amounts used in these examples are realistic. Property tax valuations may amount to billions of dollars.

Budget needed ÷ Assessed value = Tax rate

Remember that the tax rate is based on assessed valuation.

CHAPTER 20

Amount ÷ Base =
Rate

Assessed value:
The value of
property set by the
assessor. This value
is normally less than
the market value.

Assessed valuation
= Assessment rate
X Market value.

Apply Your Skills

The assessed valuation of property in Cereal County is $5,500,000,000. The city council decided that a $158,500,000 budget is needed from property tax collections. What tax rate will be needed? (Round to one decimal place.)

$ _____

You may now complete Performance Application 20.1.

DETERMINING PROPERTY TAX AMOUNT

To determine the tax assessment for property owners the assessed valuation of each piece of property must be known. Computation of property tax is shown in Model 20.2.

**MODEL
20.2**

Assessed
valuation ÷
Expressed unit =
No. of units

No. of units x
Tax per unit =
Property tax

Computing property tax

Problem: Joseph Burger owns property with an assessed valuation of $54,000. The property tax rate is listed as $2.50 per $100. What is the property tax amount?

Solution: **Step 1** Find the number of units of $100.

Assessed valuation ÷ Expressed unit = No. of units
$54,000 ÷ $100 = 540

Step 2 Find the property tax amount.

No. of units x Tax per unit = Property tax
540 x $2.50 = $1,350

Apply Your Skills

Bill and Brenda Younger purchased a new house with a $300,000 assessed valuation. The property tax rate is $9.75 per $1,000. What is the property tax amount?

$ _____

Property tax bills are usually paid quarterly or semiannually, with the entire amount due within a certain period of time (such as 30 days) after the end of the year. A penalty is usually assessed for late payment of taxes.

Some businesses and individuals receive special tax rates. For example, a business may be given a special tax rate to encourage the business to build a plant in an area where employment is low or to encourage a new business to locate in the area. Schools, churches, and nonprofit organizations often receive special tax rates or may be exempted from property taxes.

EXPRESSING THE TAX RATE IN VARIOUS WAYS

The tax rates in the preceding examples were expressed as decimals (such as 0.04 and 0.03) and as percents (such as 4% and 3%). However, the tax rate can be expressed in other ways. A comparison of how the 0.04 tax rate can be expressed is given in Figure 20.2.

Mill: One-thousandth of a dollar.

Decimal –0.04 times assessed value
Percent –4% of assessed value
Mills –40 mills per dollar (10 mills equal 1 cent) of assessed value
Cents –4 cents per dollar of assessed value
Dollars –$4 per hundred dollars of assessed value

Figure 20.2 Expressing Tax Rates

If the tax rate is expressed in mills per dollar of assessed valuation, the computation can be made by moving the decimal place three places to the left. For example, 35 mills equals $0.035 (35 divided by $1,000). This is further demonstrated in Model 20.3.

Computing property tax

MODEL 20.3

Problem: Venessa Greenway owns a house with an assessed valuation of $92,500. The property tax rate is 32 mills per dollar of assessed valuation. What is the property tax amount?

Solution:

(Base)		(Rate)		(Amount)
Assessed valuation	x	(mills ÷ $1,000)	=	Property tax
$92,500	x	$0.032	=	$2,960

Note: (32 ÷ $1,000 = $0.032)

Base x Rate = Amount

Assessed valuation x Tax rate = Property tax

Apply Your Skills

Village Hardware Store has a $200,000 assessed valuation. The property tax rate is 40 mills per dollar of assessed valuation. What is the property tax amount?

$ _____

Rates are often expressed as $2.50 per $100 or $25 per $1,000 so that smaller numbers can be used to make computations easier. The computer can be used to compute property tax amounts as shown by the spreadsheet in Figure 20.3.

	A	B	C	D
1	PROPERTY TAX COMPUTATIONS			
2	---			
3	Property	Assessed	Tax	Tax
4	Number	Valuation	Rate	Amount
5	---			
6	X-919	74,000	4.5%	3,330
7	X-920	112,000	4.5%	5,040
8	X-921	87,000	4.5%	3,915
9	X-922	76,000	4.5%	3,420
10	X-923	89,000	4.5%	4,005
11	X-924	124,000	4.5%	5,580
12	X-925	56,000	4.5%	2,520

Figure 20.3 Property Tax Spreadsheet

SALES TAXES

Property taxes are normally levied once each year on owned property. Sales taxes are normally levied by state and local governments based on the sale of merchandise. Merchandise can include items from a birthday card to an automobile. Sales tax collections must then be submitted to the appropriate governmental agency.

Sales tax amounts are normally rounded to the nearest cent. A table is often used to compute the tax amount. Also, many cash registers are equipped to compute the sales tax amount and automatically add the amount to the cost of the merchandise to compute amount due. A tax table like the one shown in Figure 20.4, based on a 5% sales tax rate, may be used.

5% SALES TAX

Sales Amount	Tax	Sales Amount	Tax
$0.01 to $0.09	no tax	$3.70 to $3.89	$0.19
$0.10 to $0.29	$0.01	$3.90 to $4.09	$0.20
$0.30 to $0.49	$0.02	$4.10 to $4.29	$0.21
$0.50 to $0.69	$0.03	$4.30 to $4.49	$0.22
$0.70 to $0.89	$0.04	$4.50 to $4.69	$0.23
$0.90 to $1.09	$0.05	$4.70 to $4.89	$0.24
$1.10 to $1.29	$0.06	$4.90 to $5.09	$0.25
$1.30 to $1.49	$0.07	$5.10 to $5.29	$0.26
$1.50 to $1.69	$0.08	$5.30 to $5.49	$0.27
$1.70 to $1.89	$0.09	$5.50 to $5.69	$0.28
$1.90 to $2.09	$0.10	$5.70 to $5.89	$0.29
$2.10 to $2.29	$0.11	$5.90 to $6.09	$0.30
$2.30 to $2.49	$0.12	$6.10 to $6.29	$0.31
$2.50 to $2.69	$0.13	$6.30 to $6.49	$0.32
$2.70 to $2.89	$0.14	$6.50 to $6.69	$0.33
$2.90 to $3.09	$0.15	$6.70 to $6.89	$0.34
$3.10 to $3.29	$0.16	$6.90 to $7.09	$0.35
$3.30 to $3.49	$0.17	$7.10 to $7.29	$0.36
$3.50 to $3.69	$0.18	$7.30 to $7.49	$0.37

Figure 20.4 Sample Sales Tax Table

To practice using the table, first determine the category of the sales amount and then select the corresponding tax amount. For example, a sales amount equal to $2.17 will have a $0.11 tax amount added $2.28 will be due. The formula method can also be used to compute the sales tax amount by multiplying the sales amount by the tax amount: $2.17 times 5% equals $0.11. This computation is further illustrated in Model 20.4.

The amount due can also be computed by multiplying the sales amount by 1.0 plus the tax rate:

67.48 x 1.045 = 70.5166 or **70.52**

MODEL 20.4

Computing sales taxes using a formula

Problem: A customer at City Hardware purchased gardening supplies totaling $67.48. The sales tax rate is 4.5% (state 3% plus local 1.5%). What is the amount that should be paid by the customer?

Solution: **Step 1** Compute the sales tax.

Sales amount	x	Tax rate	=	Tax amount
$67.48	x	0.045	=	$3.04 (rounded)

Step 2 Compute the amount due.

Sales amount	+	Tax amount	=	Amount due
$67.48	+	$3.04	=	$70.52

Apply Your Skills

City Department Store had $125,600 total sales during the day. The sales tax rate is 5.5%. How much sales taxes should have been collected during the day?

$ _____

You may now complete Performance Application 20.2.

PERFORMANCE APPLICATION 20.1

1. Henderson County assessed property at 40% of its true value.
   Compute the assessed valuation of each of the properties in
   Column A and enter the answers in Column C of the following
   spreadsheet.

	A	B	C
1			
2	------------------------------------		
3	Property	True	Assessed
4		Value	Valuation
5	------------------------------------		
6	Metts Construction Company	280,000	_____
7	Malley Beauty Supply	85,500	_____
8	Murphy's Grocery	230,800	_____
9	Murtta Insurance Agency	88,700	_____
10	Nash Salon of Beauty	57,500	_____
11	Dave Rogers Interiors	99,200	_____
12	Pet Grooming Shoppe	62,500	_____
13	Professional Cleaners	119,000	_____
14	Praffer Metals Company	375,000	_____
15	Pyum Deli Shoppe	136,800	_____
	Assessed valuation rate:	40%	

2. Palican City has taxable real property with an assessed
   valuation of $120,682,000. The city's budget for next year is
   $8,280,000, with $3,017,050 to be raised from collection of
   property taxes. In order to collect the needed taxes, what tax
   rate will be needed?

   _____

3. Whiteville Unified School District has taxable real property of $680,500,000. Under Budget Plan A, $23,817,500 will be needed from property taxes. Under Budget Plan B, $26,539,500 will be needed from property taxes. What tax rate will be needed for adoption of (a) Budget Plan A and (b) Budget Plan B?

   (a) _____

   (b) _____

4. Taxable real property in Apple Valley County is $790,500,000. Under the budget adopted by the city and county governments, $23,715,000 will be needed by the city and $17,391,000 will be needed by the county from property taxes. City residents must pay the county rate *plus* the city rate, while county residents pay only the county rate. What is the rate to be paid by (a) city residents and (b) county residents?

   (a) _____

   (b) _____

5. Real property in Brownsville is assessed at 40% of true value for residences and at 25% of true value for businesses. Assuming that a house and a business in Brownsville each have a true value of $127,500, what is the assessed valuation of (a) the residential property and (b) the business property?

   (a) $ _____

   (b) $ _____

6. Cane County assesses business property at 35% of its true value, and Bruner County assesses business property at 50% of its true value. A study shows that the Jones Chair Company can locate in either county with a true value of real property of $350,500. What will be the assessed valuation of property if the company locates in (a) Cane County and (b) Bruner County?

   (a) $ _____

   (b) $ _____

7. Property in Howard County has a true value of $88,798,528,000. If property is assessed at 35% of its true value, what is the assessed valuation of property in Howard County?

   $ _____

PERFORMANCE APPLICATION 20.2

1. Compute the assessed valuation and annual property tax for each of the following pieces of property. The first property is given as an example.

Property	True Value	Valuation Percent	Assessed Valuation	Tax Rate	Annual Tax
	$ 80,000	40	$32,000	0.03	$960.00
A	60,000	40	$_____	0.03	$_____
B	128,500	35	$_____	0.035	$_____
C	98,750	24	$_____	0.042	$_____
D	176,800	66	$_____	0.05	$_____
E	350,000	37	$_____	0.0317	$_____

2. Compute the annual tax for each of the following pieces of property.

Property	Assessed Valuation	Tax Rate	Annual Tax
A	$ 60,000	3.5 percent	$_____
B	86,900	$4.50 per hundred	$_____
C	98,000	$3.17 per hundred	$_____
D	94,000	46 mills	$_____
E	120,000	38.8 mills	$_____
F	135,000	4.4 percent	$_____

3. The tax assessor uses a 40% assessment. The true value of property is $125,000 with a tax rate of 3.5%. What is the (a) assessed value and (b) annual tax for the property?

   (a) $ _____

   (b) $ _____

4. Business property with an assessed value of $350,000 is located in a city with a tax rate of 3.289%. The business is granted a special tax rate of 2.5%. How much is saved by receiving the special tax rate?

   $ _____

5. Toone County has property with an assessed value of $89,580,700,000 and a tax rate of 0.04. How much will the county receive in property taxes during the year?

   $ _____

6. The tax rate for Carter City is $3.50 per $100. For Carter County it is $2.40 per $100. A resident owning a house with an assessed value of $140,000 must pay property taxes to both city and county units. How much will his tax bill be for the (a) city, (b) county, and (c) city and county combined?

   (a) $ _____

   (b) $ _____

   (c) $ _____

7. Wanda Tharpe paid a property tax bill of $1,125 for the year. The tax rate was $2.50 per $100 of assessed value. What is the assessed value of her property?

   $ _____

8. Franklin Haney has a house with an assessed value of $91,800. The property is assessed at 34% of its true value. What is the true value of the property?

   $ _____

9. Lin Lu took clients to a dinner costing $204.80. The sales tax rate is 4.65%. What is the total amount due?

   $ _____

PRACTICE TEST FOR CHAPTER 20

PROPERTY TAXES

Complete each of the following problems and then compare your answers with the ones on page 649.

1. Marshall County has taxable real property with an assessed valuation of $140,000,000. The budget for next year is $9,728,485. The portion to be contributed from collection of property taxes is $4,900,000. What tax rate will be needed in order to collect the needed taxes?

   _____

2. Real property in Haywood county is assessed at 35% of market value for residences and 25% of market value for businesses. Assume that a house and a business each have a $380,000 market value. What is the assessed valuation for (a) the residence and (b) the business?

   (a) $ _____

   (b) $ _____

3. A home in Dixon County has a $170,000 market value. Property is assessed at 45% of market value with a 3.75% tax rate. What are the (a) assessed value and (b) annual tax on the property?

   (a) $ _____

   (b) $ _____

4. Donald Carter paid a $1,683 property tax bill for the year. The tax rate is $2.75 per $100 of assessed value. What is the assessed value of the property?

   $ _____

5. Veronica Baker owns a house with a $120,000 assessed valuation. The tax rate is 32 mills per dollar of assessed valuation. What is the annual property tax?

   $ _____

CONNECTIONS

20.1 The chart shown below indicates various items that make up the cost of a house. Although many homeowners complain about high property taxes, the chart indicates that a relatively small portion of the total cost of owning a home can be attributed to property taxes. Assume that a home is purchased in an area where expenses fit the model shown in the graph with the following exception: Utilities/telephone represents 23 cents instead of 24 cents. Further assume that $18,000 will be spent on housing during the next year. (a) How much should be allocated to each type of expense? (b) Call a real estate agent in your area and request information about how housing costs in your area relate to the model. Prepare a one-paragraph summary to report your findings.

(a) Mortgage interest $ _____
     Utilities/telephone $ _____
     Furnishings/equipment $ _____
     Property taxes $ _____
     House operations/supplies $ _____
     Maintenance/repairs $ _____

(b) _____
     _____
     _____
     _____

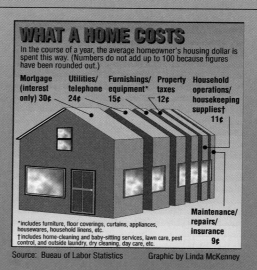

WHAT A HOME COSTS

In the course of a year, the average homeowner's housing dollar is spent this way. (Numbers do not add up to 100 because figures have been rounded out.)

Mortgage (interest only) 30¢   Utilities/ telephone 24¢   Furnishings/ equipment* 15¢   Property taxes 12¢   Household operations/ housekeeping supplies† 11¢

Maintenance/ repairs/ insurance 9¢

*includes furniture, floor coverings, curtains, appliances, housewares, household linens, etc.
†includes home-cleaning and baby-sitting services, lawn care, pest control, and outside laundry, dry cleaning, day care, etc.

Source: Bueau of Labor Statistics   Graphic by Linda McKenney

20.2 The newspaper article shown below discusses a property tax increase and its effect on property tax bills. Assume that you have a house that has a $280,000 market value and an assessed value that is 60% of market value. How much will the city property tax assessment be (a) before the increase and (b) after the increase?

(a) $ _____

(b) $ _____

The City Council's vote Tuesday to increase the city property tax rate by 49 cents will raise the tax bill on a $50,000 home by $62.50 from last year.

For the owner of a $100,000 home, the increase means a $125 increase from last year.

The council voted to increase the tax rate from the certified rate of $2.69 per $100 assessed value to $3.18. It was the second consecutive increase for the city. The council last year approved a 53-cent increase. The certified rate – the rate that must be established after a property reappraisal program – is 1 cent higher than last year's $2.68 rate.

CONNECTIONS

20.1 Wilson County set its budget at $429 million. It is anticipated that $110 million of this amount will be derived from property taxes. Property in the county has an $8 billion market value. Assessed valuation is 50% of market value. The tax rate is $3 per $100 of assessed value. Will property tax collections be sufficient to fund the desired budget portion allocated to property taxes?

(a) Yes. How much in excess funds will be generated?
$ _____

(b) No. How much will the deficit be?
$ _____

20.2 Thomas and Jennifer Mirabelli purchased a new home in Harlow Village, Grover County, for $250,000, which is its market value. Property is assessed at 60% of its market value. The tax rate is 17 mills per dollar of assessed value for the city share plus 10 mills per dollar of assessed value for the county share. The family has budgeted $375 per month for property taxes. Will the property tax amount be (a) above or (b) below their budget?

(a) Above _____

(b) Below _____

DECISIONS

PROPERTY AND PROPERTY TAXES
Chapter Review and Quick Reference

Topic	Main Point	Typical Example	Text Page
Tax rate	Governmental units must set the rate high enough to collect needed taxes. Divide revenue needed by the assessed valuation.	Revenue needed: $120,000,000 Assessed valuation: $4,000,000,000 Tax rate needed: $120,000,000 ÷ $4,000,000,000 = **3%**	381
Tax amount	Tax rates are computed in several ways: 1. Percent of assessed valuation 2. Amount per $100 of assessed valuation 3. Amount per $1,000 of assessed valuation 4. Number of mills per dollar of assessed valuation Notice that the same tax amount is computed since the rate is the same, but expressed in different ways.	Compute the tax rate on a $300,000 building. 1. Tax rate: 3.5% $300,000 × 0.035 = **$10,500** 2. Tax rate: $3.50 per $100 of assessed value. $300,000 ÷ $100 × $3.50 = **$10,500** 3. Tax rate: $35 per $1,000 of assessed value. $300,000 ÷ $1,000 × $35 = **$10,500**. 4. Tax rate: 35 mills per dollar of assessed valuation. $300,000 × 0.035 = **$10,500**.	382
Mill	"Mills" is a common way to express a tax rate in many areas. Divide the number by 1,000 to convert to a decimal.	35 mills converted to a decimal: 35 ÷ 1,000 = **0.035**	383
Sales taxes	Many cities and states assess a tax on sales of merchandise and/or services.	Merchandise sale: $1,500. Sales tax rate: 4.5% Sales taxes: $1,500 × 0.045 = **$67.50**	384

MERCHANDISE INVENTORY VALUATION AND TURNOVER

Performance Objectives

1. Compare inventory valuation methods.
2. Find the inventory valuation and cost of goods sold using the specific identification method.
3. Find the inventory valuation and cost of goods sold using the weighted-average (average cost) method.
4. Find the inventory valuation and cost of goods sold using the FIFO method.
5. Find the inventory valuation and cost of goods sold using the LIFO method.
6. Find the inventory valuation and cost of goods sold using the lower of cost or market method.
7. Determine the merchandise turnover ratio.

Supermarkets, car parts outlets, department stores, and similar companies maintain a supply of goods for sale to other companies or to consumers. The cost value assigned to the supply of goods available for sale is called *merchandise inventory*. In this chapter you will learn about different methods that companies use to determine or estimate the cost value to be assigned to the merchandise inventory.

OVERVIEW OF MERCHANDISE INVENTORY

Companies that sell merchandise or goods periodically determine the value of the supply on hand by counting or computing an estimate of the merchandise inventory available on a given date. The Internal Revenue Service permits companies to select one of several methods to estimate the cost valuation of the merchandise available for sale at the end of the accounting period. Companies with expensive items can actually count the items and determine the cost valuation. However, companies with many small items or with a wide variety of items purchased on various dates may find that a physical count is not possible or practical. This estimate is important because the amount of inventory affects the assets (merchandise available for sale) and the expenses (cost of goods sold) of the company. Four of the most common methods for cost valuation of merchandise inventory are explained in this chapter: (1) specific identification, (2) average cost, (3) first-in, first-out (FIFO), and (4) last-in, first-out (LIFO). Figure 21.1 shows typical inventory valuation methods.

Merchandise:
Items that are obtained for resale.

Taking inventory:
A procedure to list individual items in stock, along with their value.

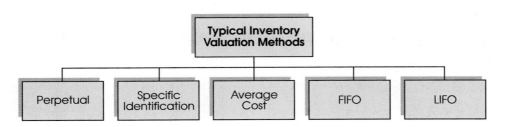

Figure 21.1 Typical Inventory Valuation Methods

Merchandise inventory is normally priced at the cost of the goods or the market price of the goods, whichever is lower. This amount, determined by the *lower of cost or market* method, will usually result in goods being valued at the cost price, especially in a period of rising prices. Companies like to maintain records to determine how often the inventory is sold during a given period of time, such as a quarter or a year. A *merchandise turnover ratio* can be computed to determine the average number of times the inventory is sold during the period. Gross profit on sales can be determined by subtracting the cost of goods sold from the sales to estimate the profit before operating

Inventory valuation methods:
Procedures used to assign a value to items on hand.

expenses are deducted. Although the Internal Revenue Service is liberal about permitting companies to choose an appropriate pricing method for its inventory, the method chosen must be used consistently during each accounting period.

INVENTORY VALUATION METHODS

Perpetual inventory:
A record of merchandise available for sale where inventory is updated after each sale or purchase. A computer is normally used.

Periodic Inventory:
A physical count of merchandise on hand and available for sale.

Companies with computerized equipment may maintain a *perpetual* inventory, which physically tracks each item of merchandise as it enters or leaves inventory. Businesses that carry a relatively low number of high-cost items may find this procedure to be necessary. Typical businesses in this category include automobile dealerships and appliance stores. Some stores such as record and compact disc retail outlets may also maintain inventory in this manner. In these instances, an identification number must be assigned to each piece of merchandise so that it can be readily identified. With the advent of scanners, some retail outlets such as grocery stores can maintain inventory on a perpetual basis. These types of stores with large numbers of items will normally take *periodic inventory* to verify actual inventory on hand. Even with computerized records, merchandise may be lost or stolen, which will not be determined without taking inventory periodically.

The data presented in Figure 21.2 will be used to illustrate four methods for determining the cost valuation of the merchandise inventory. This shows purchases of items during the year. (Assume that a physical count shows that 25 items are on hand at the end of the year.)

Notice that item #A-277 is used in the model solutions and that item #B-288 is used in Apply Your Skills problems for the first four examples.

Transactions relating to purchase of inventory item #A-277			
January 1	Beginning inventory	15 units @ $18	$ 270.00
January 14	Purchased	17 units @ $20	340.00
February 11	Purchased	15 units @ $21	315.00
July 4	Purchased	18 units @ $22	396.00
September 9	Purchased	15 units @ $25	375.00
	Total available	80 units	$1,696.00

Figure 21.2 Typical Inventory Transactions.

The data shown in Figure 21.3, relating to inventory item #B-288, will be used for completing the Apply Your Skills exercises relating to merchandise inventory in this chapter.

Transactions relating to purchase of inventory item #B-288.			
August 1	Beginning inventory	10 units @ $16	$ 160.00
August 8	Purchased	15 units @ $21	315.00
October 1	Purchased	20 units @ $20	400.00
October 9	Purchased	10 units @ $22	220.00
November 1	Purchased	15 units @ $23	345.00
November 9	Purchased	10 units @ $24	240.00
	Total available	80 units	$1,680.00

Figure 21.3 Inventory Transactions

SPECIFIC IDENTIFICATION

Companies that deal in expensive items such as automobiles can use the invoice to determine when an item has been sold. Each car has a specific identification number, and the actual cost of the automobile being sold is indicated. Companies such as department stores and supermarkets use computers to scan identification codes during the checkout process to determine what specific items are being purchased. The increasing use of computers will enable more types of companies to provide accurate and current data about specific items being sold and about items remaining in inventory. Assume that sales invoice codes are used to provide data about the 25 items listed in Model 21.1 that remain in inventory.

Specific identification: *Merchandise is coded so that the cost of the actual item can be determined — such as the VIN number for the automobile.*

MODEL 21.1

Valuation of merchandise inventory: Specific identification method (Item #A-277)

3 items from the January 1 inventory	@ $18 =	$54.00
8 items from the February 11 purchase	@ $21 =	168.00
7 items from the July 4 purchase	@ $22 =	154.00
7 items from the September 9 purchase	@ $25 =	175.00
25 items	TOTAL COST =	$551.00

Apply Your Skills

The company took a physical inventory and found that there were 30 items of #B-288 remaining in inventory. The items were identified as follows: 5 items purchased on November 9, 3 items purchased on November 1, 8 items purchased on October 9, 10 items purchased on October 1, and 4 items remaining from the beginning inventory. What is the value of the ending inventory using the specific identification method?

$ _____

You may now complete Performance Application 21.1.

AVERAGE COST METHOD

Weighted average:
The total cost of merchandise available for sale is divided by the total number of units available for sale to compute the average unit cost.

The *average cost* method, which is also called the *weighted cost* method, for determining the cost valuation of merchandise inventory provides a way to obtain the average cost of units of merchandise on hand during the accounting period. Computation of cost using the average cost method involves the following procedures: (1) Compute the average cost per unit by dividing total cost by the total number of units for each item of merchandise available during the accounting period. (2) Compute the value of merchandise inventory by multiplying the number of units on hand at the end of the period by the average cost.

Using the illustration of item #A-277, the calculations in Model 21.2 are made to compute the value of merchandise inventory using the average cost method.

MODEL 21.2

Total cost ÷ Number available = Average cost

Items on hand x Average cost = Merchandise inventory

Valuation of merchandise inventory: Average cost method (Item #A-277)

Step 1 Total cost ÷ Number of items available = Average cost
$1,696.00 ÷ 80 = $21.20

Step 2 Items on hand x Average cost = Merchandise inventory
25 x $21.20 = $530.00

Apply Your Skills

The company took a physical inventory of item #B-288 and found that there were 30 items remaining in inventory. Using the average cost method, what was the value of the ending inventory?

$ _____

FIRST-IN, FIRST-OUT (FIFO) METHOD

FIFO (first-in, first-out):
Method that considers the oldest items to be sold first, so the most recently purchased items remain in inventory.

The *first-in, first-out* (FIFO) method is used when stores attempt to sell the oldest items in inventory first. For example, a grocery store will normally rotate merchandise to keep the oldest merchandise in front on the shelves so that it will be sold first. This method assumes that the oldest merchandise will be sold first, so the merchandise purchased most recently will be on hand at the end of the accounting period. Follow the procedure used in Model 21.3 to determine the value of the merchandise inventory for Item #A-277. Determine the cost of the last 25 items purchased by multiplying the number of units by the cost per unit.

Valuation of merchandise inventory: FIFO method (Item #A-277)

15 units from September 9 purchase	@ $25	=	$375.00
10 units from July 4 purchase	@ $22	=	220.00
25 units Merchandise inventory value		=	$595.00

- -

Apply Your Skills

The company took a physical inventory of item #B-288 and found that there were 30 items remaining in inventory. Using the first-in, first-out (FIFO) method, what was the value of the ending inventory?

$ _____

LAST-IN, FIRST-OUT (LIFO) METHOD

The *last-in, first-out* (LIFO) method is used when the latest purchases are to be sold first. Therefore, merchandise inventory at the end of an accounting period consists of items available at the beginning of the period plus early purchases. Follow the procedure used in Model 21.4 to determine the value of the inventory for item #A-277. Determine the cost of the first 25 items available or purchased during an accounting period by multiplying the number of units by cost per unit.

LIFO (last-in, first-out): *Method that considers the most recently purchased items to be sold first, so the inventory consists of the oldest items purchased.*

Valuation of merchandise inventory: LIFO method (Item #A- 277)

15 units in the beginning inventory	@ $18	=	$270.00
10 units from January 14 purchase	@ $20	=	200.00
25 units Merchandise inventory value		=	$470.00

- -

Apply Your Skills

The company took a physical inventory of item #B-288 and found that there were 30 items remaining in inventory. Using the last-in, first-out (LIFO) method, what was the value of the ending inventory?

$ _____

LOWER OF COST OR MARKET PRICING

The objective of pricing merchandise inventory is to obtain a logical and practical price for the type of product being evaluated. Previous discussion assumed a *cost* basis for determining the value. Another approach is to value merchandise inventory at original cost per unit or current cost (market price) needed to replace merchandise items. This approach is often practical for items that decrease in value over a period of time. If this method is used, the company records an inventory value of the original cost or market price,

Compare the amount for cost and market. Then choose the lowest amount.

401

whichever is lower, for each type of merchandise on hand. To illustrate this pricing method, assume that 4 items are on hand on the date of the inventory valuation. The item numbers, quantity on hand, original cost price, market price, and cost valuation at the lower of cost or market value are shown in Model 21.5.

MODEL 21.5

Pricing of inventory at the lower of cost or market value

Item No.	Quantity on Hand	Original Unit Cost	Market Unit Cost	Lower of Cost or Market Value
F-38	30	$2.80	$2.85	$ 84.00
F-43	56	2.73	2.65	148.40
G-78	62	4.99	4.90	303.80
H-17	52	6.70	6.75	348.40

Merchandise Inventory Value $884.60

Apply Your Skills

Quantity on hand, cost, and market information about selected products are shown below. Determine the value of the ending inventory, using the lower of cost or market method.

Item No.	Quantity on hand	Original Unit Cost	Market Unit Cost	Lower of Cost or Market Value
R-76	25	$17.60	$15.30	$ _____
R-79	15	20.00	25.00	_____
S-16	30	15.95	19.95	_____
S-19	8	16.78	18.79	_____
S-21	15	17.50	15.00	_____
S-39	12	18.95	19.95	_____

Merchandise Inventory Value: $ _____

MERCHANDISE INVENTORY TURNOVER RATIO

Valuable information can be provided by determining how often the company sells an amount equal to the average supply of goods on hand during the accounting period. A *merchandise inventory turnover ratio* can be computed by dividing the cost of goods sold by the *average merchandise inventory*. This indicates how many times merchandise inventory "turns over" or is sold during a fiscal period. Average merchandise inventory is computed by dividing the sum of the beginning and ending inventories by 2. If an inventory is taken more often than twice a year, the sum of the inventories taken is divided by the number of times the inventory is taken to determine an average inventory amount. A turnover ratio can be computed for the entire merchandise inventory, as well as for individual items, to determine how fast items are selling.

Some retail stores prefer to express the turnover ratio on a cost basis. In this instance, the cost of goods sold is divided by inventory during the same time period computed while using cost amounts.

Assuming a beginning inventory of $125,000, an ending inventory of $119,000, and purchases of $360,000 for the period, the merchandise inventory turnover ratio can be determined using the procedures shown in Models 21.6 and 21.7.

Inventory turnover: *The number of times that the inventory is sold or replaced during a specific period.*

Computing cost of goods available for sale and cost of goods sold

Problem: Determine the inventory turnover ratio.

Solution:

Step 1 Add the purchases to the beginning inventory to compute the cost of goods available for sale.

$125,000 + $360,000 = $485,000 (goods available for sale)

Step 2 Subtract the ending inventory from the cost of goods available obtained in Step 1 to compute the cost of goods sold.

$485,000 - $119,000 = $366,000 (cost of goods sold)

- -

Apply Your Skills

Given a $38,000 beginning inventory, $180,000 purchases, and a $42,000 ending inventory, what were the (a) cost of goods available for sale and (b) cost of goods sold?

(a) $ _____

(b) $ _____

MODEL 21.6

Beginning inventory
+ Purchases
= Mdse. available

Mdse. available
- Ending inventory
= Cost of goods sold

Once the cost of goods sold has been determined, the average merchandise inventory is computed by dividing the sum of the beginning and ending inventories by 2. Then, the average merchandise inventory is divided into the cost of goods sold to compute the merchandise inventory turnover ratio.

MODEL 21.7

Beginning inv. + Ending inv. = Sum of inventories

Sum of inventories ÷ 2 = Average mdse. ratio

Cost of goods sold ÷ Average mdse. inv. = Merchandise turnover ratio

Computing merchandise inventory turnover ratio

Step 1 Beginning + Ending = Sum of ÷ Number of = Average merchandise
inventory   inventory   inventories   inventories   inventory

$125,000 + $119,000 = $244,000 ÷   2   = $122,000

Step 2   Cost of   Average   Merchandise
goods sold ÷ merchandise = turnover ratio
inventory

$366,000   ÷ $122,000   =   3

Apply Your Skills

Given a $38,000 beginning inventory, $180,000 purchases, and a $42,000 ending inventory. What was the merchandise inventory turnover ratio?

In this example, a turnover ratio of 3 was computed. This means that sales equaled 3 times the average merchandise inventory for the accounting period. Companies will strive for different turnover ratios depending on the nature of the product being sold. For example, a supermarket must have a much higher turnover ratio than an automobile dealership to be successful.

COMPARISON OF COST VALUATION METHODS

The method chosen to determine cost valuation for merchandise inventory affects the cost of goods sold amount and, ultimately, the profit to be reported for income tax purposes. Using the merchandise inventory valuations previously obtained by each of the four methods, the results provide a comparison of values as shown in Figure 21.4. For the purpose of this example, assume that for each method, the cost of merchandise available for sale is $1,696. The greater the cost of goods sold, the lower the profit figure for tax purposes. Many companies choose the LIFO method in a period of rising prices for this reason.

The method used will affect net income, but does not necessarily relate directly to movement of merchandise. LIFO, FIFO, and so forth are often used for accounting purposes.

Comparison of valuation methods for costing merchandise inventory		
Method	Merchandise Valuation	Cost of Goods Sold
Specific Identification	$551.00	$1,145.00
Average Cost	530.00	1,226.00
FIFO	595.00	1,101.00
LIFO	470.00	1,226.00

Figure 21.4 Inventory Valuation Comparisons

PERFORMANCE APPLICATION 21.1

1. Carter Farm Supply, Inc., compiled the data shown below relative to Item #C-611. A physical count of the inventory item on December 31 indicates that 23 items are *on hand*. Complete the extensions and determine the cost valuation of the ending inventory using each of the following methods: specific identification, average cost, FIFO, and LIFO.

Date	Transaction	Quantity/Unit Cost	Extension
January 1	Beginning Inventory	12 units @ $12	$_____
March 23	Purchase	4 units @ $20	$_____
May 8	Purchase	15 units @ $14	$_____
September 18	Purchase	9 units @ $16	$_____
December 3	Purchase	10 units @ $18	$_____
Total Merchandise Available for Sale = _____ units			$_____

(a) Cost valuation using the specific identification method. (Records show that 7 units purchased on May 8, 6 units purchased on September 18, and 10 units purchased on December 3 are on hand.)

$ _____

(b) Cost valuation using the average cost method.

$ _____

(c) Cost valuation using the FIFO method.

$ _____

(d) Cost valuation using the LIFO method.

$ _____

2. Inventory records for item #X-784 indicate the beginning inventory and purchases during the month of October as shown below. Computer records indicate that 680 units were *sold* during the month. Complete the extensions and determine the cost valuation of the ending inventory on October 31 using each of the four methods discussed in the text.

October	Transaction	Quantity/Unit Cost	Extension
1	Beginning inventory	110 units @ $2.87	$_____
7	Purchase	140 units @ $2.91	$_____
9	Purchase	145 units @ $2.90	$_____
17	Purchase	145 units @ $2.92	$_____
20	Purchase	130 units @ $2.92	$_____
28	Purchase	130 units @ $2.94	$_____
Total Merchandise Available		_____ units	$_____

(a) Cost valuation using the specific identification method. (Computer records show that all of the merchandise has been sold except for 120 items purchased on October 28.)

$ _____

(b) Cost valuation using the average cost method.

$ _____

(c) Cost valuation using the FIFO method.

$ _____

(d) Cost valuation using the LIFO method.

$ _____

PERFORMANCE APPLICATION 21.2

1. Inventory records for item #P-18 show the beginning inventory and purchases during the month of March as indicated below. Complete the extensions and determine the cost valuation of the ending inventory at the end of the month using the (a) FIFO method and (b) LIFO method. There are 60 units on hand at the end of the month.

March	Transaction	Quantity/Unit Cost	Extension
1	Beginning Balance	50 units @ $25	$_____
10	Purchase	40 units @ $26	$_____
15	Purchase	50 units @ $26	$_____
25	Purchase	40 units @ $27	$_____
Total Merchandise Available		_____ units	$_____

(a) $ _____

(b) $ _____

2. Answer the following questions using the same information that was used in Problem 1 above for item #P-18 and the FIFO and LIFO methods for determining cost valuation of merchandise inventory. (a) How much was the value of the beginning inventory? (b) How much were the purchases for the month? (c) How much merchandise was available for sale during the month? (d) What was the value of the ending inventory? (e) How much was the cost of goods sold for the period?

	(FIFO)	(LIFO)
(a)	$ _____	$ _____
(b)	$ _____	$ _____
(c)	$ _____	$ _____
(d)	$ _____	$ _____
(e)	$ _____	$ _____

3. Determine the merchandise inventory turnover ratio for the Webster Store during each month of the quarter. (Round the turnover ratio to two decimal places.)

Month	Beginning Inventory	Ending Inventory	Cost of Goods Sold	Merchandise Turnover Ratio
First	$50,000	$60,000	$165,000	_____
Second	60,000	64,000	124,000	_____
Third	64,000	58,000	213,500	_____

4. The Lincoln Sporting Goods Store had a beginning merchandise inventory of $56,000, purchases of $300,000, and an ending inventory of $64,000 during the last fiscal year. Indicate the amount of (a) merchandise available for sale and (b) cost of goods sold, and (c) the merchandise turnover ratio. (Round to two decimal places.)

(a) $ _____

(b) $ _____

(c) _____

5. The Bolder Parts Shop completes a physical count of merchandise once each quarter. The balance sheet shows a cost of goods sold of $1,807,416 for the year. During the past year, the following amounts were recorded: January 1, beginning inventory, $328,800; March 31, $352,600; June 30, $345,600; September 30, $350,500; and December 31, $360,400. What were the (a) average inventory during the year and (b) merchandise inventory turnover ratio for the year?

(a) $ _____

(b) _____

PRACTICE TEST FOR CHAPTER 21
MERCHANDISE INVENTORY VALUATION AND TURNOVER

Complete each of the following problems and then compare your answers with the ones on page 650.

Review the following inventory record, when appropriate, prior to working problems on this test.

April	Transaction	Quantity/Unit Cost	Extension
1	Beginning Inventory	90 units @ $5.40	$486.00
6	Purchase	120 units @ $5.20	624.00
10	Purchase	110 units @ $5.50	605.00
20	Purchase	100 units @ $5.52	552.00
28	Purchase	80 units @ $5.60	448.00

Computer records indicated that 350 units were *sold* during the month.

1. What was the value of the ending inventory using the average cost method?

   $ _____

2. What was the value of the ending inventory using the FIFO method?

   $ _____

3. What was the value of the ending inventory using the LIFO method?

   $ _____

4. Assuming that the FIFO method was used, what was the cost of goods sold?

   $ _____

5. Assuming that the FIFO method was used, what was the merchandise turnover ratio (rounded to two decimal places, if needed)?

   _____

21.1 Review the partial income statement (showing cost of products sold) and the partial balance sheet (showing beginning and ending inventories) shown below. Based on this review, what was the merchandise turnover ratio? (Round answer to two decimal places.)

_____

CONNECTIONS

Creative Consolidated Statement of Earnings

(Dollars in thousands except per share data) (Unaudited)	Three months ended March 31	
	1995	**1994**
Net Sales	**$2,045,613**	$1,877,932
Cost of products sold	933,175	844,741
Research and development	202,110	181,508
Selling, general and administrative	464,823	438,538
Total Operating Cost and Expenses	1,600,108	1,464,787

Creative Consolidated Balance Sheet

(Dollars in thousands) (1995 Unaudited)	March 31	December 31
Assets	**1995**	**1994**
Current Assets:		
Cash and cash equivalents	**$51,516**	$116,576
Investment securities, at cost	**202,188**	141,601
Trade receivables, net	**1,345,446**	1,244,396
Inventories	**887,904**	863,808
Prepaid expenses, income taxes, and other receivables	**866,679**	865,357
Total Current Assets	**3,353,733**	3,231,738
Investment Securities Maturing after One Year, at Cost 267,759	270,639	
Net Property and Equipment	**3,162,752**	3,099,238
Deferred Charges and Other Assets	**351,899**	339,621
	$7,136,143	$6,941,236

21.2 Review the weekly chart shown below, which indicates sticker prices for a particular model at a small automobile agency. The agency provides a 9% discount off the sticker price to all customers. The company makes a 6% profit (based on sticker price) on each automobile.

An inventory indicated the following stock numbers remaining in inventory at the end of the week.

Stock No. B8297589, B8297892, and B9777823.

(a) What was the value of the ending inventory, based on sticker price?

$ _____

(b) How much profit was made on the sales?

$ _____

(c) How much was the cost of goods sold?

$ _____

Model Elite for week ending March 12, 19--
Stock No. B4478893, costing $22,789 (beginning inventory)
Stock No. B4892742, costing $23,800 (beginning inventory)
Stock No. B8297589, costing $27,843 (beginning inventory)
Stock No. B8294792, purchased for $28,900
Stock No. B7892792, purchased for $23,893
Stock No. B8297892, purchased for $31,739
Stock No. B9777823, purchased for $23,719
Stock No. B8293422, purchased for $27,891

CONNECTIONS

21.1 Marshall Stores reviewed accounting information about item T-4999 and obtained the following information: beginning balance, 10 items @ $24; March 3 purchase, 10 items @ $23; March 12 purchase, 15 items @ $25; and March 21 purchase, 15 items @ $26. A physical inventory count indicated that there were 20 items remaining in inventory at the end of the month. The owner feels that this item is representative of other products carried by the store. The owner further desires for the cost of goods amount to be as high as possible for income tax purposes. (a) Which of the following methods should be adopted by the store? Weighted average, FIFO, or LIFO? (b) Why?

(a) _____

(b) _____

21.2 Faulkner Small Parts provided records showing a $350,000 beginning merchandise inventory, $800,000 in purchases, and a $300,000 ending merchandise inventory for the third quarter of the fiscal year. Similar businesses consider a merchandise turnover of 2.5 or greater to be acceptable. Was the merchandise turnover ratio for Faulkner Small Parts acceptable?

_____ Yes

_____ No

DECISIONS

MERCHANDISE INVENTORY VALUATION AND TURNOVER
Chapter Review and Quick Reference

Topic	Main Point	Typical Example	Text Page
Inventory	Companies will periodically evaluate the value of merchandise available for resale.	Typical procedures include perpetual; specific identification; average cost; first-in, first-out (FIFO); and last-in, first-out (LIFO).	397
Specific identification method	This procedure identifies exact merchandise items on hand.	**Date Cost per unit Total** May 1, 3 units @ $7 $21 May 8, 5 units @ $5 25 8 $46 Two units from May 1 and 1 unit from May 8 purchases identified as being on hand. $7 x 2 = $14 $5 x 1 = 5 Total $19	399
Average cost method (also called weighted cost method)	Cost per item of ending inventory is based on average cost of items available for sale during the period.	Assume above transactions, with 3 units remaining in inventory. Average cost: $46 ÷ 8 = $5.75 Inventory value: $5.75 x 3 =$17.25	400
First-in, first-out (FIFO)	Cost of items remaining is based on last items to enter inventory.	Assume above transactions, with 3 units remaining in inventory. Inventory value: $5 x 3 = $15	400

413

Topic	Main Point	Typical Example	Text Page
Last-in, first-out (LIFO)	Cost of items remaining is based on first items to enter inventory.	Assume above transactions, with 3 items remaining in inventory. Inventory value: $7 x 3 = $21	401
Lower of cost or market	Cost of items remaining is based on a comparison of the cost and market prices, with the lower price being selected.	Assume above transactions, with 3 items remaining in inventory from the last purchase. All items have an $8 market value. Inventory value: $5 x 3 = $15. (Note: $5 is lower than $8, so cost was chosen.)	402
Cost of goods sold	Indicates the cost of merchandise that has been sold during the period.	Beginning inv.: $8,000 Ending inv.: 6,000 Purchases 10,000 Step 1: Goods available $8,000 + $10,000 = $18,000. Step 2: Cost of goods $18,000 - $6,000 = $12,000.	403
Merchandise turnover ratio	Indicates the number of times the inventory is sold during the period.	Assume same amounts as in previous step. Step 1: Average inventory ($8,000 + $6,000) ÷ 2 = $7,000. Step 2: Mdse. turnover ratio $12,000 ÷ $7,000 = 1.71 (rounded)	404

Chapter 22

DEPRECIATION OF PLANT AND EQUIPMENT

Performance Objectives

1. Understand the concepts of depreciation and book value.
2. Understand the concepts of accumulated depreciation and disposal value.
3. Understand differences in computing depreciation for accounting reports and for IRS tax reporting purposes.
4. Determine depreciation using the following methods: straight-line, sum-of-the-years'-digits, double declining-balance, units-of-production, ACRS, and MACRS.
5. Understand the effects of accelerated depreciation methods.
6. Prepare a depreciation schedule.

Depreciation is the decrease in value of long-term assets. The Internal Revenue Service permits business firms to consider depreciation as an operating expense for tax purposes. In this chapter, you will learn five methods for computing depreciation to extend this expense over the estimated useful life of long-term assets. In addition, you will learn about a system that is based on an allowance for federal income tax purposes instead of the actual useful life of the asset.

OVERVIEW OF DEPRECIATION

Depreciation:
Estimated decrease in value of an asset from its original cost.

Note that a building can be depreciated, but the land under or surrounding the building cannot.

A business firm owns many types of properties called *assets*. Assets are things of value owned by the business and should be put into two broad categories: current assets and long-term assets. Cash and assets that can be converted into cash, sold, or consumed within one year are classified as *current assets*. Examples of current assets are cash, accounts receivable, supplies, and merchandise inventory. *Long-term assets* will not be consumed, sold, or converted into cash within one year. One important group of tangible long-term assets that will be used for a number of years and that are not purchased primarily for resale are known as *plant and equipment* or *fixed assets*. Examples of fixed assets include automobiles, buildings, office equipment, delivery equipment, and land. Typical depreciation methods are shown in Figure 22.1

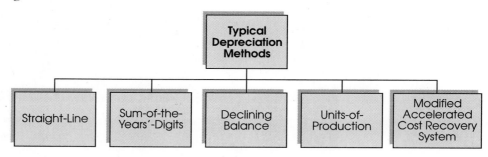

Figure 22.1 Typical Depreciation Methods

Typical assets that can be depreciated: building, equipment, furniture, large tools, and autos.

With the exception of land, all plant and equipment normally decrease in value due to use, obsolescence, and the passage of time. This decrease in value is called *depreciation*. Land is regarded as having an unlimited life and does not depreciate. The Internal Revenue Service permits business firms to charge depreciation as an operating expense for each accounting period in which the asset is used. Using appropriate guidelines, the expense may be deducted as an operating expense from the profits of the firm. If a company does not prepare interim (monthly or quarterly) financial reports, depreciation is calculated on an annual basis.

Remember that depreciation is simply a computed estimate of the decrease in value used by businesses primarily for income tax purposes. Ironically, some assets actually appreciate in value. An antique automobile, a rare stamp, and a painting by a famous artist will probably appreciate in value over the years.

THE STRAIGHT-LINE METHOD

If a business firm decides to depreciate the cost of an asset equally over the asset's estimated useful life, the straight-line method should be used. This method is based on the assumption that the asset will depreciate at the same rate each year. It is the easiest to compute and the most commonly used method for computing depreciation for purposes of financial accounting. The following basic factors should be considered when using the straight-line method:

1. *Total cost* of the property. The total cost includes the purchase price of property plus all expenditures necessary to make an asset ready to use, such as freight, sales taxes, insurance charges, and installation costs.

2. *Estimated life* of the asset. This is the number of years that a firm estimates the asset will remain useful. Although this estimate is normally based on past experience with similar assets, it must be determined for each asset involved. The Internal Revenue Service guidelines should be followed in making estimates.

3. *Disposal value* of the property. This is the estimated value that an asset will have at the end of its useful life. (Disposal value is also called *scrap value, salvage value, resale value, residual value, trade-in value,* or *liquidation value.*)

The straight-line method assumes that disposal value will be deducted to determine the total amount that will be depreciated. To determine annual depreciation, the total depreciation is then spread evenly over the useful life of the property by dividing the total depreciation by the number of years in the estimated life. An alternative method is to divide the useful life into the value 1 and then multiply the total depreciation by that quotient. Both procedures are illustrated in Model 22.1.

Other factors that can cause depreciation include technological advances. For example, computer systems often become obsolete because more advanced computers are being created. Growth is another factor. Buildings and equipment may no longer be adequate as a company increases in size. The formula for basic straight-line depreciation is shown in Figure 22.2.

Straight-line depreciation: *Depreciation is spread evenly over the asset's useful life.*

Estimated useful life: *The number of years or units of production that an asset is expected to be usable.*

Disposal or **salvage** or **trade-in value:** *Estimated value of an asset at the end of its useful life.*

The Internal Revenue Service (IRS) provides guidelines for estimating the useful life of assets for depreciation purposes.

Straight-line Depreciation Computation
Annual depreciation = $\dfrac{\text{Total cost - disposal value}}{\text{Estimated life (in years)}}$

Figure 22.2 Formula for Straight-line Depreciation

MODEL 22.1

Amount depreciated
÷ Useful life
= Annual depreciation

Computing annual depreciation

Problem: The Carter Delivery Service buys a truck for $14,000. It is estimated that the useful life will be 5 years and the disposal value will be $2,000. What is the annual depreciation?

Solution: **Step 1** Find the total amount to be depreciated.

Cost	- Disposal value	= Amount depreciated
$14,000	- $2,000	= $12,000

Step 2 Find the amount of annual depreciation.

Amount depreciated	÷ Years in life	= Annual depreciation
$12,000	÷ 5	= $2,400

Alternative method:

Step 1 Divide 1 by number of years in useful life.

$1 \div 5 = 0.20$

Step 2 Multiply the amount depreciated by the quotient obtained in Step 1.

$12,000 \times 0.20 = $2,400

Apply Your Skills

Ball Ready Mix, Inc., purchased a $56,000 truck for delivering concrete. It was estimated that the useful life will be 8 years with a $6,000 disposal value. The straight-line depreciation method is used. What is the annual depreciation?

$ _____

The *Tax Reform Act of 1986* requires rental property to be depreciated over 27.5 years. Commercial real estate is depreciated over 31.5 years. This act also stipulates that one-half year's depreciation be allowed in the year that personal property is placed into service—regardless of the month—unless over 40% of the property was placed into service during the last quarter. This law also mandates that the straight-line method be used to depreciate real estate.

PARTIAL DEPRECIATION

Depreciation is normally computed on the basis of one fiscal year. However, assets purchased in the middle of a year can be depreciated for the portion of the year that they were in service, as shown in Model 22.2. In this instance, depreciation is based on the number of months the asset was in service during the year. Assets purchased prior to the 15th of a month can be depreciated for the entire month. Depreciation during the month of purchase is not computed for assets purchased after the 15th of the month.

Partial depreciation:
Depreciation computed for less than a full year.

Computing partial year's depreciation

MODEL 22.2

Problem: The Upper Class Beauty Salon purchased a utility vehicle for $16,000 on October 5. The fiscal year runs from January through December. The vehicle will be depreciated over 5 years with a $4,000 disposal value. What are the annual depreciation and the depreciation during the year of purchase?

Solution: **Step 1** Find the total amount to be depreciated.

Cost - Disposal value = Amount depreciated
$16,000 - $4,000   = $12,000

Step 2 Find the amount of annual depreciation.

Amount depreciated ÷ Life = Annual depreciation
$12,000   ÷ 5 = $2,400

Step 3 Find the year of purchase depreciation.

Annual depreciation x (Months ÷ 12) = Partial depreciation
$2,400   x 3 ÷ 12   = $600

Original cost - Disposal value = Amount depreciated

October through December equals 3 months. This is 3/12 of a year.

Apply Your Skills

Yelsin Tool and Dye Company purchased a $74,000 piece of equipment on August 20 with a $2,000 disposal value and a 20-year useful life. The fiscal year ends on December 31. What is the annual depreciation, using the straight-line method, (a) for a full year and (b) for the partial year the asset was placed into service?

(a) $ _____

(b) $ _____

BOOK VALUE

Book value is the estimated worth of an asset at a certain point in time and is computed by subtracting the *accumulated depreciation* from the total cost of the asset, as shown in Model 22.3.

Book value: The original cost of an asset less accumulated depreciation.

MODEL 22.3

Cost
- Accumulated
depreciation
= Book value

Computing book value

Problem: The Upper Class Beauty Salon evaluates the book value of the computer after 3 years. Assuming a cost of $1,200, no disposal value, and annual depreciation of $240, what is the book value after 3 years?

Solution: **Step 1** Find the accumulated depreciation.

Annual depreciation x Years = Accumulated depreciation
$240   x 3   = $720

Step 2 Find the book value.

Cost   - Accumulated depreciation = Book value
$1,200 - $720   = $480

Apply Your Skills

Microcomputer Service Center purchased a $14,000 piece of diagnostic equipment. The equipment has a 7-year useful life with no disposal value. What will the (a) accumulated depreciation and (b) book value be at the end of the fourth year?

(a) $ _____

(b) $ _____

Note that a partial year will be allowed during the last year of the asset's useful life for assets that are purchased at some time during the fiscal year.

The following depreciation schedule shows the book value for the truck purchased in Model 22.1. Businesses normally maintain a depreciation schedule for each asset or class of assets.

End of Year	Amount of Depreciation	Accumulated Depreciation	Book Value
1	$2,400	$ 2,400	$11,600
2	2,400	4,800	9,200
3	2,400	7,200	6,800
4	2,400	9,600	4,400
5	2,400	10,000	2,000
Asset cost: $14,000 Disposal value: $2,000 Life: 5 years			

Figure 22.3 Depreciation Schedule—Straight-line Method

Notice that the book value after the final year of depreciation is the same as the disposal value. Disposal value is also called *salvage value, residual value,* and *scrap value.*

You may now complete Performance Application 22.1.

SUM-OF-THE-YEARS'-DIGITS METHOD

The straight-line method computes an equal amount of depreciation for each year of the asset's useful life. However, the value of many assets decreases more rapidly in the early years of life. For example, a new car depreciates most in the first year, less in the second year, and less in each succeeding year. Depreciation methods that compute a large amount of depreciation in the earlier years in the life of the asset are called *accelerated depreciation* methods. The two most popular accelerated depreciation methods are the sum-of-the-years'-digits and declining-balance methods. The sum-of-the-years'-digits method is discussed in this section.

The value **1** is added to the number of years in the life of the asset. This sum is then divided by the value **2**. This answer is then multiplied by the number of years in the life of the asset. This product then becomes the denominator as shown in Step 2 of Model 22.4.

The denominator can also be computed with the following formula:

$$\frac{n \, (n + 1)}{2}$$

where **n** represents the estimated useful life of the asset. The numerator is represented by the number of years of estimated useful life remaining for each particular year. The denominator for an asset with a 5-year useful life is then computed as follows:

$$\frac{5(n + 1)}{2} = \frac{5(6)}{2} = 15$$

This denominator can be used in Figure 22.4. Notice that 5 years of estimated life remain during the first year, so the depreciation rate fraction becomes 5/15. Four years of estimated life remain during the second year, so the depreciation rate fraction becomes 4/15. This cycle continues until the asset has been depreciated for each year of its estimated life.

Note that the denominator remains constant each year, while the numerator changes each year to represent the years remaining (4 the second year, 3 the third year, and so forth).

Figure 22.4 shows the depreciation amounts for each year.

Year	Remaining Life	Depreciation Computation	Annual Depreciation
1	5	5/15 x $9,600	$3,200
2	4	4/15 x $9,600	2,560
3	3	3/15 x $9,600	1,920
4	2	2/15 x $9,600	1,280
5	1	1/15 x $9,600	640
15	(Sum of the years' digits) TOTAL DEPRECIATION		$9,600

Figure 22.4 Computing Annual Depreciation

MODEL 22.4

Sum-of-the-years'-digits depreciation computation

Step 1 Amount depreciated = Cost - Disposal value

Step 2 Denominator = Sum of digits in asset's life

Step 3 Annual depreciation = Amount depreciated x Years of remaining life ÷ Denominator

Apply Your Skills

Schaefer Dry Cleaners purchased an $18,995 delivery truck with a 5-year useful life and a $5,000 disposal value. The sum-of-the-years'-digits method is used to compute depreciation. What will be the (a) depreciation for the third year and (b) book value at the end of the third year?

(a) $ _____

(b) $ _____

The depreciation schedule for the full 5 years is shown in Figure 22.5. A *depreciation schedule* is usually prepared at the time an asset is acquired to show the cost, depreciation, accumulated depreciation, and book value of the asset over the years of useful life of the asset. Notice that accumulated depreciation amounts from Figure 22.4 are subtracted from asset cost to compute the book value, as shown in Figure 22.5.

End of Year	Amount of Depreciation	Accumulated Depreciation	Book Value
1	$3,200	$3,200	$6,800
2	2,560	5,760	4,240
3	1,920	7,680	2,320
4	1,280	8,960	1,040
5	640	9,600	400

Figure 22.5 Depreciation Schedule—Sum-of-the-Years'-Digits Method

Notice that the book value after 5 years (the estimated life of the asset) is $400, the estimated disposal value.

THE DECLINING-BALANCE METHOD

Declining-balance is an *accelerated depreciation method* because the asset depreciates more in the earlier years than in the later years of the asset's life. This method computes depreciation by applying a constant rate to the book value each year. In addition, disposal value is not considered in this method.

Under the new tax law, personal property, including business automobiles and equipment, is depreciated using the 200-percent-declining-balance method. Remember that real estate has a longer life and is depreciated by the straight-line method discussed earlier.

Notice that the declining-balance method is double the straight-line rate, as shown in Figure 22.6. However, the rate is applied to the total cost of the asset. Disposal value is not subtracted from the total cost as was done with other methods. When this method is used, the book value must be computed after each year since the depreciation rate is based on the book value after the preceding year. Although the rate remains the same each year, the book value decreases, so depreciation will be higher in the earlier years and lower in the later years in the asset's depreciation schedule.

Notice that the depreciation rate is applied to the cost in using the declining-balance method—not cost minus disposal value, as with other methods.

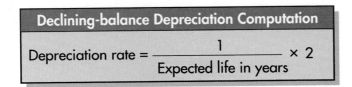

Declining-balance Depreciation Computation

$$\text{Depreciation rate} = \frac{1}{\text{Expected life in years}} \times 2$$

Figure 22.6 Declining-balance Depreciation Computation

The depreciation is then deducted from the book value (cost in the first year) to compute the new book value after depreciation. The depreciation rate is then applied to the new book value for the second year. This process continues for subsequent years until the accelerated depreciation amount is less than the straight-line depreciation amount. Then the straight-line method is used to complete depreciating the asset. This makes the process somewhat complicated and means that both methods must be used to determine when to switch methods.

MODEL 22.5

Depreciation for the second year will be based on a $9,000 book value ($15,000 less $6,000).

$9,000 x 0.40 =
$3,600

Third year book value = $5,400 Depreciation =
$2,160

Fourth year book value = $3,240 Depreciation =
$1,296

Fifth year book value = $1,944 Depreciation =
$777.60

Computing first-year depreciation

Problem: A delivery truck costs $15,000 with a useful life of 5 years. What is the first year's depreciation?

Solution: **Step 1** Find the declining-balance depreciation rate.

1 ÷ Life x 2 = Depreciation rate
1 ÷ 5 x 2 = 0.40 (40%)

Step 2 Find the first year's depreciation.

Book value x Depreciation rate = Depreciation
$15,000 x 0.40 = $6,000

Apply Your Skills

Dillard Manufacturing, Inc., purchased a $125,000 lathe (equipment) with a 10-year useful life. (a) What will the declining-balance depreciation rate be for the asset? What will the depreciation be for (b) the third year? (c) What will the book value be after the end of the third year? The declining-balance method is used by the company.

(a) _____

(b) $ _____

(c) $ _____

COMPARISON OF DEPRECIATION METHODS

A comparison of the declining-balance and straight-line methods for the full 5 years is shown in Figure 22.7.

Notice that the straight-line method produces larger depreciation than the declining-balance method during the third year. Therefore, the tax reform law requires that if depreciation is computed by the declining-balance method for the first 2 years, the straight-line method is used for later years.

	Problem:	A delivery truck is purchased for $15,000 with a useful life of 5 years and no disposal value. What are the annual depreciation amounts for each method (declining-balance and straight-line)?
	Solution:	Year Straight-Line Declining-Balance
		1 $3,000 $6,000.00 (0.40 x $15,000)
		2 3,000 3,600.00 (0.40 x $9,000)
		3 3,000 2,160.00 (0.40 x $5,400)
		4 3,000 1,296.00 (0.40 x $3,240)
		5 3,000 777.60 (0.40 x $1,944)

Figure 22.7 Comparison of Depreciation Methods

Notice that depreciation is greater in the early years in the life of the asset. *Cost recovery* is a term used for depreciation in the tax code.

UNITS-OF-PRODUCTION METHOD

Many machines such as farm equipment, factory machines, and production facilities relating to productivity have a life more closely related to time of use than to other methods. For example, an automobile that is driven 40,000 miles will depreciate more than a similar automobile that is driven 10,000 miles. The *units-of-production depreciation method* uses amount of use as a basis for depreciation. The computation may be based on miles driven, units produced, or hours used, depending on the most predictive measure of depreciation for the asset.

The units-of-production depreciation method is not permitted by IRS without special permission, but is often used for internal accounting purposes. For example, depreciation can be computed with this method for accounting-report purposes, with an IRS-acceptable method (such as MACRS—see next section) used for tax reporting purposes.

This method is based on determining the expected number of units in the useful life of the asset (hours, miles, units, and so forth). The cost, minus disposal value, is then divided by the number of units to compute unit depreciation. Depreciation each year is then determined by multiplying unit depreciation by the number of units used during the year, as shown in Figure 22.8.

Units-of-production method: A method based on depreciation according to productivity, such as miles driven, labels printed, or hours used.

Units-of-Production Depreciation Computation
Step 1 Unit depreciation = $\dfrac{\text{Total cost - disposal value}}{\text{Expected production unit}}$
Step 2 $\dfrac{\text{Annual}}{\text{depreciation}} = \dfrac{\text{Unit}}{\text{depreciation}} \times \dfrac{\text{Units}}{\text{produced}}$

Figure 22.8 Units-of-Production Depreciation Computation

MODEL 22.6

Units-of-production depreciation

Problem: Yeltsin Manufacturing purchased a $60,000 lathe, which is expected to produce 100,000 units and then have a $10,000 disposal value. During the first year, the lathe produced 12,000 units. What was the annual depreciation?

Solution: **Step 1** Determine unit depreciation.

$$\text{Unit depreciation} = \frac{\$60,000 - \$10,000}{100,000} = \$0.50$$

Step 2 Determine annual depreciation.

Depreciation = $0.50 × 12,000 = $6,000.

Apply Your Skills

A $36,000 machine, including shipping and installation, is purchased to place labels on cans. The machine is expected to place 2,000,000 labels on cans during its useful life and then have a $2,000 disposal value. What are the (a) unit depreciation and (b) depreciation amount for placing labels on 125,000 cans?

(a) $ _____

(b) $ _____

ACCELERATED COST RECOVERY SYSTEM

Accelerated cost recovery system (ACRS): A depreciation method that allows faster depreciation during the early years of the asset's life.

The *accelerated cost recovery system (ACRS)* was a tax regulation system that assigned various assets into categories for tax purposes. ACRS applied to assets placed into service after 1980. For example, automobiles were placed into a category that allowed depreciation over a 3-year period. Real estate was placed into a category that allowed for depreciation over 19 years.

The Tax Reform Act of 1986 that took effect in 1987 maintained the ACRS structure. However, the new structure is based on *asset depreciation range (ADR)*, which sets the asset's life more closely to the length of time it is expected to be used in business. For example, under the new law automobiles are to be depreciated over 5 years (as opposed to 3 years under the old law). Typical classes of property are shown in Figure 22.9.

3-year class:	includes small toos used in the manufacutre of certain products
5-year class:	includes light trucks, automobiles, computer equipment, assets used in research and development, oil and gas drilling, construction, and the manufacture of certain products such as chemicals and electronic equipment.
7-year class:	includes office furniture and fixtures and most other machinery and equipment.
10-, 15-, and 20 year class:	includes a limited number of other assests, including land improvements.

Figure 22.9 Typical Classes of Property

The IRS issues guidelines to determine asset classes.

Note that the 150-percent-declining-balance method is used for the 15- and 20-year classes. The 200-percent-declining-balance method is used for all others. The 150-percent basis is 1.5 times the straight-line rate, while the 200-percent method is 2.0 times the straight-line rate. As outlined above, the accelerated method is used until the straight-line rate produces a larger depreciation.

The following table provides rates under the Accelerated Cost-Recovery System (ACRS) Act of 1981 and covers assets placed into service during the 1981 to 1986 period.

Recovery Year	Year Rate Classes			
	3-year	5-year	10-year	15-year
1	25	15	8	5
2	38	22	14	10
3	37	21	12	9
4		21	10	8
5		21	10	7
6			10	7
7			9	6
8			9	6
9			9	6
10			9	6
11				6
12				6
13				6
14				6
15				6

Figure 22.10 ACRS Depreciation Recovery Rates

The IRS provides tables showing depreciation rates.

MODIFIED ACCELERATED COST RECOVERY SYSTEM (MACRS)

The Modified Accelerated Cost Recovery System (MACRS) Act of 1986 and update tax bill of 1989 affect property placed into service after 1986. Assets placed into service during the 1981 to 1986 period will continue to use ACRS. The following information in Figure 22.11 is based on IRS publication 53 and gives typical examples relating to various classes for tax purposes.

The percentages shown in Figure 22.12 can be used to compute depreciation for assets placed into service at midyear while using MACRS guidelines. Notice that 3-, 5-, 7-, and 10-year classes use the 200-percent-declining-balance basis and then switch to a straight-line basis. The declining-balance method is used until the straight-line method produces a higher depreciation. Then the straight-line method is applied for the remaining years. Notice that 15- and 20-year classes use the 150-percent-declining-balance method. The straight-line method is used for 27.5- and 31.5-year classes. If the table is not used, formulas can be used to compute depreciation. The 200-percent basis is double the straight-line rate, while the 150-percent basis is 1.5 times the straight-line rate.

3-year class:	includes race horses over 2 years old when placed in service, any other horse over 12 years old when placed in service, and tractors.
5-year class:	includes automobiles, taxis, trucks, computer equipment, office machines, assets used in research and development, and equipment used to manufacture certain products such as chemicals and electronics equipment.
7-year class:	includes office furniture, fixtures, and single-purpose agricultural and horticultural structures. Property that does not have a class life indicated will normally be placed in this class.
10-year class:	includes water transportation equipment, such as barges, agricultural or horticultural structures, and fruit or nut bearing trees.
15-year class:	includes shrubbery, roads, and wastewater treatment facilities.
20-year class:	includes farm buildings and municipal sewers.
27.5-year class:	includes residential property.
31.5-year class:	includes real property that is not residential.

Figure 22.11 MACRS Classes of Assets (after 1986)

Recovery Year	Year Rate Classes					
	3-year (200%)	5-year (200%)	7-year (200%)	10-year (200%)	15-year (150%)	20-year (150%)
1	33.33	20.00	14.28	10.00	5.00	3.75
2	44.45	32.00	24.49	18.00	9.50	7.22
3	14.81*	19.20	17.49	14.40	8.55	6.68
4	7.41	11.52*	12.49	11.52	7.69	6.18
5		11.52	8.93*	9.22	6.93	5.71
6		5.76	8.93	7.37	6.23	5.29
7			8.93	6.55*	5.90*	4.89
8			4.46	6.55	5.90	4.52
9				6.55	5.90	4.46*
10				6.55	5.90	4.46
11				3.29	5.90	4.46
12					5.90	4.46
13					5.90	4.46
14					5.90	4.46
15					5.90	4.46
16					3.00	4.46
17						4.46
18						4.46
19						4.46
20						4.46
21						2.24

*Indicates the year that the rate changes to straight-line rate.

Figure 22.12 MACRS Depreciation Rates

These rates cover assets placed into operation after 1986.

Notice that ACRS and MACRS methods fully depreciate the asset, leaving no disposal value.

Depreciation during the first year in the life of personal property is computed as if the property were purchased halfway through the year. An exception is made if property is placed into operation during the last three months of the fiscal year. In this instance, a midquarter adjustment is permitted. Publication 534, available from the IRS, provides a complete list of options for computing depreciation under MACRS.

MODEL 22.7

MACRS depreciation

Problem: Boyd Construction Company purchased $40,000 worth of office furniture in 1992. The MACRS method was used to compute depreciation. What was the annual depreciation for the furniture?

Solution:

Step 1 Figure 22.11 indicates the office furniture has a 7-year recovery rate.

Step 2 A review of the table in Figure 22.12 indicates that the depreciation rates are as follows: 14.28%, 24.49%, 17.49%, 12.49%, 8.93%, 8.93%, 8.93% and 4.46%.

Step 3 Complete the depreciation schedule.

Year	Depreciation	
1	$5,712	($40,000 x 0.1428)
2	9,796	($40,000 x 0.2449)
3	6,996	($40,000 x 0.1749)
4	4,996	($40,000 x 0.1249)
5	3,572	($40,000 x 0.0893)
6	3,572	($40,000 x 0.0893)
7	3,572	($40,000 x 0.0893)
8	1,784	($40,000 x 0.0446)

Apply Your Skills

Barton and Rodriquez, Attorneys, purchased a $2,800 microcomputer system in the middle of 1993. (a) To which recovery period does this asset belong (using MACRS)? What were the (b) depreciation for 1995, (c) accumulated depreciation at the end of 1995, and (d) book value at the end of 1995?

(a) _____

(b) $ _____

(c) $ _____

(d) $ _____

PERFORMANCE APPLICATION 22.1

1. Find the total depreciation and the annual depreciation for each of the following assets using the straight-line method.

Asset	Total Cost	Disposal Value	Estimated Useful Life	Total Depreciation	Annual Depreciation
Tools	$ 5,600	$ 600	10 years	$_____	$_____
Automobile	9,700	400	5 years	$_____	$_____
Equipment	7,500	700	8 years	$_____	$_____
Furniture	7,600	300	10 years	$_____	$_____
Machinery	30,200	2,600	30 years	$_____	$_____
Building	152,040	30,000	27 years	$_____	$_____

2. An automobile costing $12,700 with an expected life of 4 years has an estimated disposal value of $1,000. Use the following form to develop a depreciation schedule for the automobile using the straight-line method.

End of Year	Annual Depreciation	Accumulated Depreciation	Book Value
			$12,700
1	$_____	$_____	$_____
2	$_____	$_____	$_____
3	$_____	$_____	$_____
4	$_____	$_____	$_____
AUTOMOBILE: Total cost = $12,700; Disposal value = $1,000; Life = 4 years			

3. Eastmoreland and Associates purchased office equipment for $750 with an estimated life of 5 years and a disposal value of $50. Assuming a straight-line depreciation method, (a) what is the amount of annual depreciation? (b) What will the book value be at the end of the third year? (c) What will the accumulated depreciation be at the end of the third year?

(a) $ _____

(b) $ _____

(c) $ _____

4. Office furniture costing $6,200 was purchased on April 5. The company estimates that the furniture can be used for 12 years with a disposal value of $800. The fiscal year ends on December 31. Assuming a straight-line depreciation method, (a) what will the depreciation be during the first year? (b) What will the depreciation be during the second year? (c) What will the book value be at the end of the eighth year?

(a) $ _____

(b) $ _____

(c) $ _____

5. Modern office equipment cost $18,000 and had an estimated life of 15 years with an estimated disposal value of 20% of its original cost. Assuming a straight-line depreciation method, (a) what is the disposal value? (b) What is the annual depreciation? (c) What will the book value be at the end of the sixth year?

(a) $ _____

(b) $ _____

(c) $ _____

6. Depreciation on an escalator that cost $76,800 was figured at the rate of 12 1/2% a year and has a disposal value of $4,800. What are the (a) estimated life of the asset, (b) amount of the annual depreciation, and (c) book value at the end of the second year?

(a) _____

(b) $ _____

(c) $ _____

PERFORMANCE APPLICATION 22.2

1. Ray's Flower Shop owns a truck costing $14,000 with an estimated life of 5 years and no disposal value. Using the 200-percent-declining-balance method, develop a depreciation schedule using the following form:

End of Year	Rate	Annual Depreciation	Accumulated Depreciation	Book Value
				$14,000
1	_____	$_____	$_____	$_____
2	_____	$_____	$_____	$_____
3	_____	$_____	$_____	$_____
4	_____	$_____	$_____	$_____
5	_____	$_____	$_____	$_____

2. A truck cost $24,000 with an estimated life of 5 years and no disposal value. Use the following form to prepare a depreciation schedule. Use the 200-percent-declining-balance method.

End of Year	Declining-Balance Rate	Annual Depreciation	Accumulated Depreciation	Book Value
				$24,000
1	_____	$_____	$_____	$_____
2	_____	$_____	$_____	$_____
3	_____	$_____	$_____	$_____
4	_____	$_____	$_____	$_____
5	_____	$_____	$_____	$_____

3. Joan's Florist Shoppe purchased a $17,000 truck with a $2,000 disposal value. An estimate was made that the truck can be driven 60,000 miles. The truck was driven 13,420 miles during the first year and 14,780 miles during the second year. Using the units-of-production method, what was the depreciation during the (a) first and (b) second years?

    (a) $ _____

    (b) $ _____

4. The Carson Insurance Agency purchased 7 new office desks. Under MACRS guidelines, how many years will the asset be depreciated?

    _____

5. The Embassy Print Shop purchased a delivery truck in the 5-year class for $18,000. Using the 200-percent-declining-balance method, what are the (a) depreciation and (b) book value after 1 year?

    (a) $ _____

    (b) $ _____

6. The Dreyfus Company purchased small tools that are in the 3-year class for $900. Using the 200-percent-declining-balance method, what are the (a) depreciation and (b) book value after 1 year?

    (a) $ _____

    (b) $ _____

7. The Elliot Sports Center purchased equipment for $38,000. Using MACRS guidelines, what is the depreciation during the (a) first and (b) second years?

    (a) $ _____

    (b) $ _____

8. Aurillian Jordan purchased rental property for $180,125. Based on MACRS guidelines, what is the (a) accumulated depreciation and (b) book value after three years?

    (a) $ _____

    (b) $ _____

PRACTICE TEST FOR CHAPTER 22

DEPRECIATION OF PLANT AND EQUIPMENT

Complete each of the following problems and then compare your answers with the ones on page 650. For each problem, assume that a $14,000 delivery truck was purchased with a $2,000 disposal value. Compute the (a) depreciation during the second year and (b) book value at the end of the second year for each method indicated.

1. Straight-line method. (5-year life)
   (a) $ _____
   (b) $ _____

2. Sum-of-the-years'-digits method. (5-year life)
   (a) $ _____
   (b) $ _____

3. Declining-balance method. (5-year life)
   (a) $ _____
   (b) $ _____

4. Units-of-production method. Assume that the truck has 100,000 miles as an estimated life. It was driven 15,000 miles during the first year and 12,000 miles during the second year.
   (a) $ _____
   (b) $ _____

5. Modified accelerated cost recovery system (MACRS) method.
   (a) $ _____
   (b) $ _____

22.1 The ad shown below indicates the purchase price for an automobile. Assume that the automobile is purchased at midyear for the price indicated to be used for business purposes. Use the MACRS method to compute depreciation and book value for each of the first 3 years.

		Depreciation	Book Value
(a)	Year 1:	$ _____	$ _____
(b)	Year 2:	$ _____	$ _____
(c)	Year 3:	$ _____	$ _____

CONNECTIONS

Automatic
Air Condition
Stereo

$14,941
or Just

$277 mo

Pre-Titled – Stk. #10195

22.2 The chart shown below indicates that construction of rental property is decreasing. Tower Mart, Inc., completed a new apartment complex on January 1, which included two- and three-bedroom units. The cost of the project was $5,500,000. Use the MACRS method to compute depreciation and book value during the first three years. (d) What will the book value be after 20 years? (e) Do you estimate that the market value will be more or less than the book value after 20 years?

		Depreciation	**Book Value**
(a)	Year 1:	$ _____	$ _____
(b)	Year 2:	$ _____	$ _____
(c)	Year 3:	$ _____	$ _____

(d) $ _____

(e) _____ More _____ Less

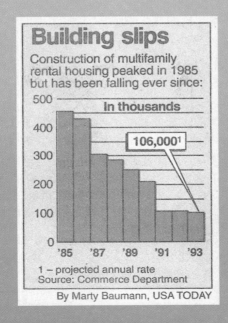

Building slips

Construction of multifamily rental housing peaked in 1985 but has been falling ever since:

In thousands

106,000[1]

'85 '87 '89 '91 '93

1 – projected annual rate
Source: Commerce Department

By Marty Baumann, USA TODAY

22.1 The chart shown here indicates that the number of consumers who are leasing automobiles has increased during recent years. Bramlett Termite and Pest Control Company decided to purchase a truck on July 20 costing

A look at statistics that shape your finances

More new cars leased

Consumers are increasingly leasing – not buying – new cars. The trend is expected to continue the rest of the decade.

1984 — 12%   Percentage leased

1993 — 26%[1]

1998 — 40%[1]

1 – through June 30
2 – projected

Source: CNW Marketing/Research
By Nick Galifianakis, USA TODAY

$18,500. They found that they can lease the same truck for $287 per month. Leased trucks cannot be depreciated. Develop a MACRS depreciation and leasing schedule for the first 3 years. (d) Which option will result in a higher expense for income tax purposes?

		Depreciation	**Leasing**
(a)	Year 1:	$ _____	$ _____
(b)	Year 2:	$ _____	$ _____
(c)	Year 3:	$ _____	$ _____
(d)	_____ Depreciation	_____ Leasing	

22.2 Thomas and Metts, Architectural Design Specialists, decided to purchase equipment needed in their business. The equipment has a $24,000 price, including shipping and installation, and a $3,000 disposal value after 5 years. The company desires to use a depreciation method for reporting purposes that will depreciate as much of the asset as possible during the first three years. (a) Which depreciation method should the company choose? (b) Why did you choose the depreciation method indicated?

(a) _____

(b) _____

_____

_____

DECISIONS

DEPRECIATION OF PLANT AND EQUIPMENT
Chapter Review and Quick Reference

Topic	Main Point	Typical Example	Text Page
Depreciation	Depreciation is computed primarily for income tax purposes. MACRS is used for a majority of assets.	Depreciation methods: Straight-line Sum-of-the-years'-digits Declining-balance Units-of-production ACRS MACRS	416
Straight-line depreciation	Cost - Disposal value ÷ Estimated life Monthly depreciation if purchased prior to the 15th of the month.	$30,000 auto with a $10,000 disposal value and a 4-year life. Annual depreciation: $30,000 - $10,000 ÷ 4 = **$5,000**	417
Partial depreciation	Monthly depreciation for any month if asset is bought prior to the 15th of the month.	Assume the above truck was bought on July 8—6 months of the year. $5,000 ÷ (6/12) = **$2,500**	419
Sum-of-the-years'-digits depreciation	**Step 1** Amount depreciated = Cost - Disposal value. **Step 2** Denominator = Sum-of-the-years'-digits or N(N + 1) / 2 **Step 3** Depreciation = Amount depreciated x Years of remaining life ÷ Denominator	$30,000 auto with a $10,000 disposal value and a 4-year life. **Step 1** $30,000 - $10,000 = **$20,000** **Step 2** 4(4 + 1) ÷ 2 = 20 ÷ 2 = **10** **Step 3:** $20,000 x 4 ÷ 10 = **$8,000**	422

Topic	Main Point	Typical Example	Text Page
Declining-balance depreciation	**Step 1** Rate = 1 ÷ Life x 2 **Step 2** Depreciation = Cost x Rate	$30,000 auto with a $10,000 disposal value and a 4-year life. **Step 1** $1 \div 4 \times 2 = \textbf{0.50}$ **Step 2** $\$30,000 \times 0.50 = \textbf{\$15,000}$	424
Units-of-production depreciation	**Step 1** Unit depreciation = Cost - disposal value ÷ Number of units **Step 2** Depreciation = Unit depreciation x Units produced	$30,000 auto with a $10,000 disposal value and a 50,000 mile useful life. It was driven 15,000 miles. **Step 1** $\$30,000 - \$10,000 \div 50,000 = \textbf{\$0.40}$ **Step 2** $\$0.40 \times 15,000 = \textbf{\$6,000}$	426
MACRS depreciation	IRS requires that most companies use this method for tax reporting purposes. A rate from the table is multiplied by the cost of the asset. This makes an accelerated amount. MACRS applies to assets bought after 1986. The Tax Bill of 1989 updated the guidelines.	A $30,000 auto is purchased for business purposes in 1993. Figure 22.11 indicates that this is a 5-year class. Figure 22.12 indicates a 20% rate for the first year for assets in this class. Depreciation = $\$30,000 \times 0.20 = \textbf{\$6,000}$	430

Chapter 23

FINANCIA
STATEMENT ANALYSI

Performance Objectives

1. Explain terminology relating to financial reports: balance sheet and income statement.
2. Explain key items found on financial reports: balance sheet and income statement.
3. Understand comparative balance sheets and income statements.
4. Explain and complete vertical and horizontal analysis.
5. List, define, explain, and compute financial ratios for financial reports: balance sheets and income statements.

Accountants prepare various reports to provide management and stockholders with knowledge about how well the business is operating financially. The two most popular reports are the balance sheet, which shows the financial condition of the business, and the income statement which shows the income, expenses, and profit (or loss) for a period of time. In this chapter, you will learn basic ways to evaluate information included on these financial reports.

COMPARING BALANCE SHEETS

The balance sheet shows what is owned (assets), what is owed (liabilities), and the net worth (capital or equity) of the business, as shown in Figure 23.1. In other words, the balance sheet shows the financial condition of the business on the day the balance sheet is prepared. Much valuable information can be obtained by comparing data from one period with data from another period to see if items are increasing or decreasing. These changes are usually shown as a percent of increase or decrease of one period over the previous period. The balance sheet shows this comparison.

The comparative balance sheet for XYZ Corporation shown in Figure 23.2 will be used to provide data for many of the examples in this chapter. You should review the balance sheet for each model to determine where the values in the model are located.

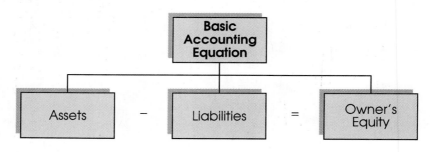

Figure 23.1 Basic Accounting Equation

XYZ CORPORATION

Comparative Balance Sheet
December 31, 19Y1 and 19Y2

	Amounts		Increase or Decrease During 19Y2	
	19Y1	**19Y2**	**Amount**	**Rate**
ASSETS				
Current Assets				
Cash	$ 10,000	$ 12,000	$ 2,000	20.0
Accounts Receivable	12,000	15,000	3,000	25.0
Merchandise Inventory	40,000	35,000	(5,000)	(12.5)
Total Current Assets	62,000	62,000	-0-	-0-
Property-Plant-Equipment				
Land	20,000	20,000	-0-	
Building	80,000	72,000	(8,000)	(10.0)
Equipment	10,000	8,000	(2,000)	(20.0)
Total Property-Plant-Equipment	110,000	100,000	(10,000)	(9.1)
Total Assets	$ 172,000	$162,000	$(10,000)	(5.8)
LIABILITIES AND OWNERS' EQUITY				
Current Liabilities				
Accounts Payable	$ 8,000	$ 10,000	$ 2,000	25.0
Note Payable	4,000	5,000	1,000	25.0
Total Current Liabilities	12,000	15,000	3,000	25.0
Long-term Liabilities				
Mortgage Payable	50,000	60,000	10,000	20.0
Total Liabilities	$ 62,000	$ 75,000	$ 13,000	21.0
Owners' Equity				
Capital Stock	60,000	60,000	-0-	-0-
Retained Earnings	50,000	27,000	(23,000)	(46.0)
Total Owners' Equity	$ 110,000	$ 87,000	$(23,000)	(20.9)
Total Liabilities and Owners' Equity	$ 172,000	$162,000	$(10,000)	(5.8)

Notes: Amounts in parentheses indicate decreases.
Percents have been rounded to one decimal place.

Figure 23.2 Comparative Balance Sheet

ANALYZING THE BALANCE SHEET

There are several ways that the balance sheet for XYZ Corporation can be analyzed to provide useful information to help management personnel make decisions. Some of the more typical ways are presented here. (All computations are rounded to one decimal place.).

The *amount of working capital* tells a business how much its current assets exceed current liabilities. Current assets minus current liabilities equals amount of working capital, as shown in Figure 23.3.

Balance sheet: A statement that shows what is owned, what is owed, and owner's equity. It indicates the financial condition of the business on a given date.

Current assets - Current liabilities = Working capital

Working capital: Indicates how much current assets exceed current debts.

Notice that the balance sheet heading includes the company name, title, and date.

Negative amounts are normally shown in parentheses, with a minus sign, or . with red ink.

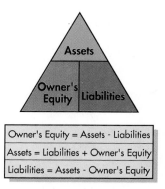

Figure 23.3 Applying the Accounting Equation to the Balance Sheet

READING A BALANCE SHEET

A detailed balance sheet for a large corporation will be lengthy and complicated. Most balance sheets developed for reporting purposes to stockholders will be simplified for ease of understanding. But, the same basic factors exist regardless of complexity. Typical factors that help to read a balance sheet are shown in Figure 23.4. Examples and/or explanations are provided for each one.

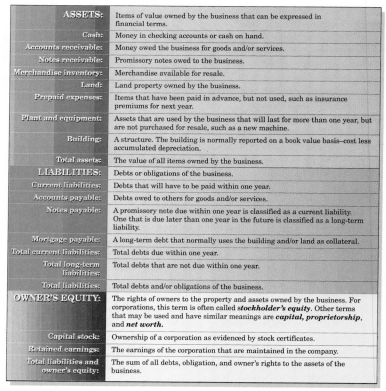

ASSETS:	Items of value owned by the business that can be expressed in financial terms.
Cash:	Money in checking accounts or cash on hand.
Accounts receivable:	Money owed the business for goods and/or services.
Notes receivable:	Promissory notes owed to the business.
Merchandise inventory:	Merchandise available for resale.
Land:	Land property owned by the business.
Prepaid expenses:	Items that have been paid in advance, but not used, such as insurance premiums for next year.
Plant and equipment:	Assets that are used by the business that will last for more than one year, but are not purchased for resale, such as a new machine.
Building:	A structure. The building is normally reported on a book value basis–cost less accumulated depreciation.
Total assets:	The value of all items owned by the business.
LIABILITIES:	Debts or obligations of the business.
Current liabilities:	Debts that will have to be paid within one year.
Accounts payable:	Debts owed to others for goods and/or services.
Notes payable:	A promissory note due within one year is classified as a current liability. One that is due later than one year in the future is classified as a long-term liability.
Mortgage payable:	A long-term debt that normally uses the building and/or land as collateral.
Total current liabilities:	Total debts due within one year.
Total long-term liabilities:	Total debts that are not due within one year.
Total liabilities:	Total debts and/or obligations of the business.
OWNER'S EQUITY:	The rights of owners to the property and assets owned by the business. For corporations, this term is often called *stockholder's equity*. Other terms that may be used and have similar meanings are *capital, proprietorship*, and *net worth*.
Capital stock:	Ownership of a corporation as evidenced by stock certificates.
Retained earnings:	The earnings of the corporation that are maintained in the company.
Total liabilities and owner's equity:	The sum of all debts, obligation, and owner's rights to the assets of the business.

Figure 23.4 Balance Sheet Terminology

READING AN INCOME STATEMENT

Presentation of income statements, like balance sheets, may be fairly simple or fairly complex to interpret and understand. Typical terminology used in income statements is shown in Figure 23.5.

Income:	Revenue received from sales of merchandise or services.
Net sales:	Revenue from merchandise sales less any returns, allowances, or discounts.
Cost of goods sold:	Cost directly related to the making of merchandise that was actually sold or available for sale. Another term that may be used is **cost of merchandise sold.**
Gross profit on sales:	Net sales minus the cost of goods sold.
Operating expenses:	Expenses needed to run the business that are in addition to the cost of goods sold.
General expenses:	Operating expenses that are not directly related to selling the product or service. An example is maintenance of the building.
Selling expenses:	Operating expenses that are directly related to selling the product or service. An example is promotional advertisements.
Total operating expenses:	Total of general and selling expenses.
Net income from	The amount that remains from the gross profit after deducting operating expenses. Other similar terms include **net profit** and **net income.**

Figure 23.5 Income Statement Terminology

Working capital represents the amount left if short-term debts are paid from assets that can quickly be turned into cash.

Interpretation of financial analysis depends on several factors. A ratio that is excellent for one industry may be unacceptable for other industries.

Computing amount of working capital

MODEL 23.1

Problem: The XYZ Corporation's current assets were $62,000, and current liabilities were $15,000 as shown in the comparative balance sheet in Figure 23.2. What was the amount of working capital?

Solution: Current assets - Current liabilities = Working capital
$62,000 - $15,000 = $47,000

Apply Your Skills

Review the figures shown in the comparative balance sheet for XYZ Corporation in Figure 23.2 for the 19Y1 year. What was the amount of working capital?

$ _____

The *current ratio* provides information about how easily creditors can be paid. For example, a bank will be interested in this information when the business applies for a loan because current assets are the primary source of funds for paying current liabilities. Current assets generally consist of cash and other assets that can be quickly converted to cash. Current liabilities generally consist of debts that are short-term (due within one year or less). To compute the current ratio, total current assets is divided by total current liabilities, as shown in Model 23.2. A general rule is that a ratio of 2 to 1 or higher is good.

Current assets ÷ Current liabilities = Current ratio

Current ratio: Indicates how easily creditors can be paid.

MODEL 23.2

Computing current ratio

Problem: The XYZ Corporation's current assets were $62,000, and current liabilities were $15,000. What was the current ratio?

Solution: Current assets ÷ Current liabilities = Current ratio

$62,000 ÷ $15,000 = 4:1

- -

Apply Your Skills

Review the figures shown in the comparative balance sheet for XYZ Corporation in Figure 23.2 for the 19Y1 year. What was the current ratio?

_____

Current assets (with the exception of merchandise inventory) ÷ Current liabilities = Quick ratio

Quick ratio: Indicates how quickly current assets can be used to pay current liabilities. Also called **acid-test ratio**.

The *acid-test ratio*, or *quick ratio*, is similar in purpose to the current ratio. For the quick ratio, however, only current assets or other assets that can be quickly converted to cash (such as accounts receivable) are included. Merchandise inventory usually takes longer to convert and is not included in the acid-test ratio. As a general rule, this ratio should be 1 to 1 or higher. For the XYZ Corporation, total current assets (minus merchandise inventory) is divided by total current liabilities for the year 19Y2, as shown in Model 23.3.

MODEL 23.3

Computing acid-test (quick) ratio

Problem: The XYZ Corporation had $62,000 current assets (including $35,000 in merchandise inventory) and $15,000 current liabilities. What was the acid-test or quick ratio?

Solution: Current assets (less merchandise inventory) ÷ Current liabilities = Quick ratio

$27,000 ÷ $15,000 = 1.8
($62,000 - $35,000 = $27,000)

- -

Apply Your Skills

Review the figures shown in the comparative balance sheets for XYZ Corporation in Figure 23.2 for the 19Y1 year. What was the acid-test (quick) ratio?

_____

Current assets: Cash or other monetary items that will normally be converted to cash within one year.

Current liabilities: Debts that are due within a short time, usually one year.

Owners' equity ÷ Total liabilities = Ratio of owners' equity to total liabilities

The *ratio of owners' equity to total liabilities* provides information about how well the owners' worth in the business can cover the total debts of the business. To compute this ratio, the amount of the owners' equity is divided by total liabilities, as shown in Model 23.4.

Computing ratio of owners' equity to total liabilities

MODEL 23.4

Problem: The XYZ Corporation had $87,000 owners' equity and $75,000 total liabilities. What was the ratio of owners' equity to total liabilities?

Solution: Owners' equity ÷ Total liabilities = Ratio of owners' equity to total liabilities

$87,000 ÷ $75,000 = 1.2

Ratio of owner's equity to total liabilities: Indicates how well the owners' worth can cover the total debts of the business.

Apply Your Skills

Review the figures shown in the comparative balance sheet for XYZ Corporation in Figure 23.2 for the 19Y1 year. What was the ratio of owners' equity to total liabilities?

_____

The *ratio of assets to capital* shows the degree that the owners' equity is covered by total assets of the business. This ratio is computed by dividing total assets by owners' equity. In 19Y2, the ratio is computed as shown in Model 23.5.

Total assets ÷ Owners' equity = Ratio of assets to capital

Computing ratio of assets to capital

MODEL 23.5

Problem: The XYZ Corporation had $162,000 total assets and $87,000 owners' equity. What was the ratio of assets to capital?

Solution: Total assets ÷ Owners' equity = Ratio of assets to capital

$162,000 ÷ $87,000 = 1.9

Ratio of assets to capital: Indicates the degree to which owners' equity is covered by total assets.

Owner's equity: The owner's rights to the assets. Equity is the amount that is left if all liabilities were paid.

Apply Your Skills

Review the figures shown in the comparative balance sheet for XYZ Corporation in Figure 23.2 for the 19Y1 year. What was the ratio of assets to capital?

_____

The *ratio of capital to liabilities* provides information about the total liquidity of the business. It compares the owners' claims on the assets with the claims of outside creditors. Owners' equity is divided by total liabilities for 19Y2's ratio, as shown in Model 23.6.

CHAPTER 23

MODEL 23.6

Owners' equity ÷ Total liabilities = Ratio of capital to liabilities.

Ratio of capital to liabilities: Indicates information about the liquidity of the business.

Ownership may be in the form of a single proprietor, a partnership, or a corporation.

Income statement: A financial report that shows financial operations of the business over a period of time, such as one year.

Most analyses relating to the income statement reflect on net sales in some way.

Comparative income statements: A comparison of two or more income statements, usually for two or more periods.

Notice that the income statement heading includes the company name, title, and period covered.

Computing ratio of capital to liabilities

Problem: The XYZ Corporation had $87,000 owners' equity and $75,000 total liabilities. What was the ratio of capital to liabilities?

Solution: Owners' equity ÷ Total liabilities = Ratio of capital to liabilities
$87,000 ÷ $75,000 = 1.2

Apply Your Skills

Review the figures shown in the comparative balance sheet for XYZ Corporation in Figure 23.2 for the 19Y1 year. What was the ratio of capital to liabilities?

_____

You may now complete Performance Application 23.1.

COMPARING INCOME STATEMENTS

The income statement shows how the operation of a business has been affected over a period of time. The income statement shows costs, expenses, income, and net income (or loss) over a given period of time. A comparison of income statements provides information about how the operation is performing during one period as compared with another period. For example, annual sales of $2 million may sound good if annual sales for last year were only $1 million. However, annual sales of $2 million may be disappointing if last year's sales were $4 million.

The comparison of amounts on the income statement to determine increases and decreases is similar to the method used for comparing balance sheets. In addition, items on the income statement are often compared with net sales because net sales often serve as a basis for decisions. Both types of comparisons for the income statement for the ABC Corporation are shown in Figure 23.6.

ABC CORPORATION
Comparative Income Statement
For the Years Ended December 31, 19Y1 and 19Y2

	Years Ended 19Y1	19Y2	Change Amount	Percent	Percent of Net Sales 19Y1	19Y2
Income:						
Net Sales	$800,000	$880,000	$80,000	10.0	100.0	100.0
Cost of Goods Sold	550,000	594,000	44,000	8.0	68.8	67.5
Gross Profit on Sales	250,000	286,000	36,000	14.4	31.3	32.5
Operating Expenses:						
General Expenses	80,000	72,000	(8,000)	(10.0)	10.0	8.2
Selling Expenses	20,000	15,000	(5,000)	(25.0)	2.5	1.7
Total Operating Expenses	100,000	87,000	(13,000)	(13.0)	12.5	9.9
Net Income from Operations	150,000	199,000	49,000	32.7	18.8	22.6

Figure 23.6 Comparative Income Statement

448

To find the change from the first year (19Y1) to the second year (19Y2), subtract the amount for 19Y1 from the amount for 19Y2. To find the percent of change, divide the change by the amount of the base (19Y1). These computations for the first item on the income statement in Figure 23.6 (net sales) are shown in Model 23.7.

Computing rate of change

Problem: The ABC Corporation had $880,000 net sales this year and $800,000 net sales last year. What was the percent of change from last year to this year?

Solution: **Step 1** Find the amount of change.

This year's net sales	-	Last year's net sales	=	Change
$880,000	-	$800,000	=	$80,000

Step 2 Find the rate of change.

Amount of change	÷	Last year's net sales base	=	Rate of change
$80,000	÷	$800,000	=	0.10 (10%)

Apply Your Skills

Dunn Corp. had $605,340 net sales this year and $560,500 net sales last year. What was the rate of increase or decrease over last year?

_____

MODEL 23.7

Net sales rate of increase:

Step 1 Find the amount of change.

Net sales this year minus net sales last year.

Step 2 Find the rate of change.

Amount of change divided by last year's net sales equals the rate of change.

The *operating ratio* provides information about the ability of net sales to cover the cost of goods sold and operating expenses of the business. Calculation of the operating ratio is illustrated in Model 23.8.

Computing operating ratio

Problem: The ABC Corporation (see Figure 24.6) had $800,000 net sales, $550,000 cost of goods sold, and $100,000 operating expenses for 19Y1. What was the operating ratio?

Solution:

Cost of goods sold	+	Operating expenses	÷	Net sales	=	Operating ratio
$550,000	+	$100,000	÷	$800,000	=	0.8125

Apply Your Skills

Review the figures shown in the comparative income statement for the ABC Corporation in Figure 23.6 for the 19Y2 year. What was the operating ratio?

_____

MODEL 23.8

Cost of goods sold + Operating expenses ÷ Net sales

Operating ratio: Indicates the portion of net sales that are used to pay for operating expenses.

Net sales - Cost of goods sold ÷ Net sales = Gross profit margin ratio

The *gross profit margin ratio* provides information about the average difference between the selling price of merchandise and the cost of goods sold and is computed as shown in Model 23.9. As with other analyses, the computed amount depends on the type of business. A jewelry store may require a high gross profit margin, while a supermarket may be happy with a small gross profit margin because the turnover of merchandise is high.

MODEL 23.9

Gross profit margin ratio: Indicates the average difference between the cost of goods sold and net sales.

Computing gross profit margin ratio

Problem: The ABC Corporation (see Figure 23.6) had $800,000 net sales and $550,000 cost of goods sold for the 19Y1 year. What was the gross profit margin ratio?

Solution:

Net sales	-	Cost of goods sold	÷	Net sales	=	Gross profit margin ratio
$800,000	-	$550,000	÷	$800,000	=	0.3125

Apply Your Skills

Review the figures shown in the comparative income statements for ABC Corporation in Figure 23.6 for the 19Y2 year. What was the gross profit margin ratio?

PERFORMANCE APPLICATION 23.1

1. Make computations to complete the blank spaces in the balance sheet shown below. Round percents to one decimal place.

XYZ CORPORATION
Comparative Balance Sheet
December 31, 19Y1 and 19Y2

	Amounts		Increase or Decrease During 19Y2	
	19Y1	19Y2	Amount	Rate
ASSETS				
Current Assets				
Cash	$ 40,000	$ 44,000	$ 4,000	10.0
Accounts Receivable	18,000	24,000	6,000	33.3
Merchandise Inventory	40,000	42,000	2,000	5%
Total Current Assets	98,000	110,000	12,000	12.%
Property-Plant-Equipment				
Land	75,000	75,000	–0–	–0–
Building	100,000	95,000	(5,000)	5.0%
Equipment	50,000	40,000	(10,000)	20.0%
Total Property-Plant-Equipment	225,000	210,000	(5,000)	6.0%
Total Assets	$ 323,000	$320,000	$ 3,000	0.9.%
LIABILITIES AND OWNERS' EQUITY				
Current Liabilities				
Accounts Payable	$ 24,500	$ 29,400	$ 4900	20%
Long-Term Liabilities				
Mortgage Payable	75,000	73,125	(1875)	(2.5)
Total Liabilities	$ 99,500	$102,525	$	
Owners' Equity				
Capital Stock	175,000	175,000	–0–	
Retained Earnings	48,500	42,475	(6,025)	12.4%
Total Owners' Equity	$ 223,500	$217,475	$ 6,025	2.7%
Total Liabilities and Owners' Equity	$ 323,000	$320,000	$ 3,000	0.9%

2. Compute the following information for each year (19Y1 and 19Y2) using amounts from the comparative balance sheet in Problem 1 above. Round ratios to one decimal place.

Information to be Determined	19Y1	19Y2
Working Capital	$ 73,500	$ 80,600
Current Ratio	4	3.7
Acid-Test Ratio	2.4	2.3
Owners' Equity Total Liability Ratio	2.2	2.1
Assets to Capital Ratio	___	___
Capital to Liabilities Ratio	___	___

3. Current assets for the Byrd Building Supply Company include a counter case ($33,000), accounts receivable ($16,000), and marketable securities ($47,000). Total current liabilities are $38,400. What is the acid-test ratio? $16,000 + $47,000 = $63,000

$63,000 ÷ 38,400 = 1.6

_____1.6_____

4. Enco Services' balance sheet provides the following information: Current Assets, $80,000; Plant-and-Equipment, $280,000; Current Liabilities, $20,000; Long-Term Liabilities, $80,000; and Owners' Equity, $260,000. What are the (a) amount of working capital, (b) current ratio, (c) assets to capital ratio, and (d) capital to liabilities ratio?

(a) $ 60,000 (80,000 − 20,000)

(b) (80,000 ÷ 20,000)

(c) _____

(d) _____

PERFORMANCE APPLICATION 23.2

1. Make computations to complete the blank spaces in the following comparative income statement. Round percents to one decimal place.

ABC CORPORATION
Comparative Income Statement
For the Years Ended December 31, 19Y1 and 19Y2

	Years Ended		Change		Percent of Net Sales	
	19Y1	19Y2	Amount	Rate	19Y1	19Y2
Income:						
Net Sales	$480,000	$528,000	$ ____	____	____	____
Cost of Goods Sold	230,000	253,000	____	____	____	____
Gross Profit on Sales	250,000	275,000	____	____	____	____
Operating Expenses:						
General Expenses	50,000	52,000	____	____	____	____
Selling Expenses	60,000	69,000	____	____	____	____
Total Operating Expenses	110,000	121,000	____	____	____	____
Net Income from Operations	140,000	154,000	____	____	____	____
Other Income:						
Interest Income	8,000	8,000	____	____	____	____
Net Income before Taxes	$148,000	$162,000	____	____	____	____

2. A company owned by Henryk Jablonski had net sales for the past year of $240,000. Selling expenses were $58,800. What percent of the net sales is represented by selling expenses?

_____

3. The Turner Office Supply Company had net sales of $640,000 and selling expenses of $224,000. A study predicts that an increase in selling expenses of 20% will result in an increase in net sales of 10% for the next year if all other amounts remain the same. Compute the percent of net sales represented by selling expenses (a) last year and (b) under the predicted conditions.

(a) _____

(b) _____

4. Collins Industries had net sales of $580,500 last year. Net income before taxes represented 25% of net sales. What was the amount of net income before taxes for the year?

$ _____

5. Operating expenses for the current year for Biggest Burger, Inc. were $281,250, which represented a 25% increase over the previous year. What were the operating expenses for the previous year?

$ _____

6. Hartwell Charities, Inc., received donations last year amounting to $32,500. The company's goal for next year is $44,525. What percent of increase will be needed to meet the goal?

_____

7. A university has an enrollment of 3,500 students. The Dean of Admissions is projecting a 7% increase for next year. What is the projected enrollment for next year?

_____

PRACTICE TEST FOR CHAPTER 23

FINANCIAL STATEMENT ANALYSIS

Complete each of the following problems and then compare your answers with the ones on page 650.

1. Revelation Corporation had $249,000 current assets, which included $47,400 in merchandise inventory, and $96,000 current liabilities. What were the (a) current ratio and (b) acid-test ratio?

   (a) _____

   (b) _____

2. Markus Co. had $360,000 assets, $200,000 liabilities, and $160,000 owners' equity. What were the (a) ratio of owners' equity to total liabilities, (b) ratio of assets to capital, and (c) ratio of capital to liabilities?

   (a) _____

   (b) _____

   (c) _____

3. Markus Co. had $360,000 total assets this year. On the balance sheet last year, there were $346,153 total assets. What were the (a) amount of increase or decrease and (b) rate of increase or decrease (rounded)?

   (a) $ _____

   (b) _____

4. Taft Auto Supply Shop had $240,000 net sales, $120,000 cost of goods sold, and $60,000 operating expenses. What were the (a) operating ratio and (b) gross profit margin ratio?

   (a) _____

   (b) _____

5. Net sales at Belz Sporting Goods were $277,760 this year and $256,000 last year. What were the (a) amount of increase or decrease and (b) rate of increase or decrease?

   (a) $ _____

   (b) _____

23.1 The balance sheet shown below was reviewed to determine information about selected areas. Use amounts for 1993. Notice that amounts are shown in thousands of dollars. What were the (a) amount of working capital, (b) current ratio, (c) acid-test ratio, (d) ratio of owners' equity to total liabilities, and (e) ratio of assets to capital? Round ratios, if needed, to two decimal places.

(a) $ _4,289,671,000_

(b) _1.59_

(c) _0.14_

(d) _0.68_

(e) _____

CONNECTIONS

WAL-MART STORES, INC. AND SUBSIDIARIES
CONDENSED CONSOLIDATED BALANCE SHEETS
(Unaudited - Amounts in thousands)

ASSETS	July 31, 1993	1992
Current assets		
Cash and cash equivalents	$ 14,056	$ 38,524
Receivables	937,072	1,183,457
Inventories	10,509,118	8,516,171
Other current assets	82,482	87,431
Total current assets	11,542,728	9,825,583
Net property, plant and equipment	9,829,435	6,255,454
Net property under capital leases	1,515,277	1,412,847
Other assets	671,280	432,855
Total assets	$ 23,558,720	$ 17,926,739

LIABILITIES AND SHAREHOLDERS' EQUITY	July 31, 1993	1992
Current liabilities		
Commercial paper	$ 1,333,339	$ 1,733,343
Accounts payable	4,363,732	3,895,373
Other	1,555,986	1,081,553
Total current liabilities	7,253,057	6,710,269
Long-term debt	4,807,745	1,718,424
Long-term obligations under capital leases	1,768,809	1,629,918
Deferred income taxes	225,449	191,963
Shareholders' equity	9,503,660	7,676,165
Total liabilities and shareholders' equity	$ 23,558,720	$ 17,926,739

23.2 The income statements shown below indicate income and expenses for two periods. For the period ending July 31, 1993, what were the (a) operating ratio and (b) gross profit margin ratio? For the period from July 31, 1992, to the same period in 1993, what were the (c) amount of increase or decrease in total revenues and (d) rate of increase or decrease in total revenues? Round ratios and percents to two decimal places.

(a) _____

(b) _____

(c) $ _____

(d) _____

WAL-MART STORES, INC. AND SUBSIDIARIES
CONDENSED CONSOLIDATED STATEMENTS OF INCOME

(Unaudited - Amounts in thousands except per share data)

	Three Months Ended July 31,		Six Months Ended July 31,	
	1993	1992	1993	1992
Net sales	$ 16,236,577	$ 13,028,445	$ 30,156,984	$ 24,677,875
Rental and other income	156,196	119,436	300,987	224,347
Total revenues	16,392,773	13,147,881	30,457,971	24,902,222
Cost of sales	12,962,824	10,416,519	23,979,569	19,672,845
Operating, selling and general and administrative expenses	2,519,579	1,995,485	4,765,839	3,803,427
Interest costs:				
Debt	76,696	30,979	131,112	64,245
Capital leases	47,817	37,521	94,159	80,114
Total costs and expenses	15,606,916	12,480,504	28,970,679	23,620,631
Income before income taxes	785,857	667,377	1,487,292	1,281,591
Provision for taxes on income	289,982	246,929	540,767	474,189
Net income	$ 495,875	$ 420,448	$ 946,525	$ 807,402
Net income per share, primary and fully diluted	$ .22	$ .18	$ .41	$ .35
Dividends per share	.0325	.0263	.065	.0525
Beginning of the year shareholders' equity	$ 8,759,180	$ 6,989,710	$ 8,759,180	$ 6,989,710
Return for the period on beginning of the year shareholders' equity	5.66%	6.02%	10.81%	11.55%

CONNECTIONS

23.1 Mario Gifts reviewed their balance sheet on December 31 to determine information about the status of the company. A summary of the balance sheet follows: Current assets, $240,000; Current liabilities, $80,000; Merchandise inventory, $60,000; Total liabilities, $120,000; Owners' equity, $200,000; and Total assets, $320,000. Goals set by the owners are listed below. Indicate whether or not each goal was met.

Analysis	Goal	Evaluation	
Working capital	120,000	_____ Met	_____ Not met
Current ratio	2.8	_____ Met	_____ Not met
Acid-test ratio	2.5	_____ Met	_____ Not met
Assets to capital	1.6	_____ Met	_____ Not met

23.2 Don and Marie Cordeon are considering the purchase of a store that sells compact discs, musical tapes, records, and other music-related items. Mr. Cordeon has been a professional musician, but has limited experience with business-related items. They requested that you suggest the types of analysis of store records that should be completed to help them make a better business decision. What types of financial analysis do you suggest should be conducted to help them make a purchasing decision?

_____

_____

_____

_____

_____

DECISIONS

FINANCIAL STATEMENT ANALYSIS
Chapter Review and Quick Reference

Topic	Main Point	Typical Example	Text Page
Balance Sheet	Shows the financial condition of a business on a given date.	Assets = Liabilities + Owners' equity	442
Horizontal analysis	Is an analysis of comparative amounts from two periods.	Assets in Y2 = $1,000 Assets in Y1 = $800 Increase = **$200** Percent increase = **25%**	442
Vertical analysis	Is an analysis of amounts in a column for the same period.	Assets: $4,000 Liabilities: $1,000 Ratio of assets to liabilities: **4** or **4 to 1**	442
Working capital	Indicates the amount left from current assets if current liabilities are paid.	Current assets $7,000 - Current liab. 2,000 = Working capital **$5,000**	443
Current ratio	Indicates how easily creditors can be paid.	Current assets $7,000 ÷ Current liab. $2,000 = Current ratio **3.5**	445
Acid-test ratio	Similar to current ratio, except merchandise inventory is not considered.	Current assets $7,000 - Mdse. inventory $3,000 = $4,000 ÷ Current liab. 2,000 = Acid-test ratio **2**	446
Ratio of owners' equity to total liabilities	Indicates how well the owners' worth can cover the total debts of the business.	Owners' equity $3,000 ÷ Total liab. 2,000 = Owners' equity ratio **1.5**	447

Topic	Main Point	Typical Example	Text Page
Ratio of assets to capital	Indicates the degree to which the owners' interests are covered by the assets.	Total assets $14,000 ÷ Owner's equity 4,000 = Ratio of assets to capital **3.5**	447
Income statement	An income statement is a report that shows the financial progress of the business over a given period of time.	Revenue $20,000 - Cost of goods 12,000 - Expenses 3,000 = Net income **$5,000**	448
Operating ratio	Indicates the degree to which sales are used to pay for the goods and administrative expenses.	Cost of goods $8,000 + Operating exp. 2,000 = $10,000 ÷ Net sales 4,000 = Operating ratio **2.5**	449
Gross profit margin ratio	Indicates the average difference between cost of goods and selling price.	Net sales $6,000 - Cost of goods 4,000 = $2,000 ÷ Net sales 6,000 = Gross profit margin ratio **0.33**	450

Read the following notice to employees and answer the questions.

Notice to Employees

As of Monday, October 8th, quarterly sales quotas will be reduced from $60,000 to $55,000. The commission rate on sales that exceed the quota will be computed at 3.75%, up from the current rate of 3.5%.

Congratulations to the following employees who joined the Super Achievers Club in the third quarter:

Super Achiever	Third Quarter Sales
Jamaica Rollins	174,000.00
Leeann Gulden	104,500.00
Eric Mueller	125,750.00
David McFarlan	154,350.00
Carlos Degas	137,275.00

In addition to receiving hefty commission checks, Super Achievers will be recognized at the sales banquet on October 19.

1. How much commission did each Super Achiever earn in the third quarter?

2. How much commission would each of the Super Achievers have earned had the new rates been in effect in the third quarter?

3. Eric Mueller has an annual salary of $58,000.00. Calculate his net earnings assuming the following: it represents one week of pay plus his third quarter commissions and it reflects a 7.65% FICA withholding, a 15% federal tax withholding, an 8.2% state withholding, and a $225.00 insurance deduction.

4. Rewrite the notice to reflect a 13% increase in quarterly quotas and an increase in commission rate to 3.65%. Also, revise the Super Achiever list to include only those individuals with sales over $140,000. State this requirement in the notice.

COMMUNICATIONS

UNIT 5 SPREADSHEET APPLICATION 1:

PAYROLL REPORT

The following spreadsheet is used to compute gross wages, income taxes, FICA taxes, and net pay. It is also used to compute totals for the hours worked, gross wages, income taxes, FICA taxes, total taxes, and net pay columns. The number of hours worked is multiplied by the pay rate to compute gross wages. The gross wages amount is multiplied by 0.15 to compute income taxes and by 0.0715 to compute FICA taxes. The sum of the two tax amounts provides total taxes. Total taxes are deducted from gross wages to compute net pay.

	A	B	C	D	E	F	G	H
1	Don's Restaurant	**********PAYROLL REPORT						
2	---							
3		Hours	Pay	Gross	Income	FICA	Total	Net
4	Employee	Worked	Rate	Wages	Taxes*	Taxes*	Taxes	Pay
5	---							
6	Boxley	24	6.50					
7	Cansler	30	5.95					
8	Curle	20	6.25					
9	Draper	22	5.15					
10	Granacki	35	5.75					
11	Jordan	40	6.45					
12	McCoy	24	4.80					
13	Pipkin	18	5.15					
14	Schelly	26	6.85					
15	Tsai	30	7.25					
16	Wagley	38	6.20					
17	---							
18	Totals		******					
19	---							
20	*Income Tax Rate = 15% and FICA Tax Rate = 7.65%							

Refer to the spreadsheet above to answer the following questions.

1. What is the gross wages amount for Jordan?

   $ _____

2. What is the income taxes amount for Pipkin?

$ _____

3. What is the FICA taxes amount for Draper?

$ _____

4. What is the total taxes amount for Boxley?

$ _____

5. What is the net pay amount for Granacki?

$ _____

6. How many total hours were worked by all employees?

_____

7. How many employees had net pay greater than $100.00?

_____

8. How many employees had total taxes greater than $40.00?

_____

9. How many employees worked exactly 40 hours?

_____

10. What was the total net pay for all employees?

$ _____

UNIT 5 SPREADSHEET APPLICATION 2:

DEPRECIATION COMPUTATION

The following spreadsheet is used to compute the depreciation for
several assets. Totals are computed for the cost, straight-line,
declining-balance, and difference columns. Straight-line depreciation
is computed by dividing the cost amount by the class life of the asset.
The 200-percent-declining-balance depreciation amount is
computed by multiplying the straight-line rate by the value 2 times
the cost amount. The difference is computed by subtracting the
straight-line amount from the declining-balance amount.

	A	B	C	D	E	F	G
1	Don's Pizza		DEPRECIATION COMPUTATION				
2	---						
3				Class	Straight	Declining	
4	#	Asset	Cost	Life	Line	Balance	Difference
5	---						
6	1	Car-A1	14,500	5			
7	2	Car-A2	17,680	5			
8	3	Computer	3,475	5			
9	4	Furniture-A1	4,980	7			
10	5	Land Improv.	25,700	15			
11	6	Machine-A1	6,450	7			
12	7	Small Tools	800	3			
13	8	Truck-A1	14,800	5			
14	9	Truck-A2	15,225	5			
15	10	Truck-A3	15,780	5			
16	11	Truck-A4	16,200	5			
17	12	Truck-A5	16,800	5			
18	---						
19		Totals	******				

Refer to the spreadsheet above to answer the following questions.

1. What is the straight-line depreciation amount for Car-A2?

    $ _____

2. What is the straight-line depreciation amount for small tools?

    $ _____

3. What is the straight-line depreciation amount for Truck-A4?

    $ _____

4. What is the declining balance depreciation amount for Furniture-A1?

    $ _____

5. What is the declining balance depreciation amount for Truck-A2?

    $ _____

6. What is the declining balance depreciation amount for Computer?

    $ _____

7. What is the total cost of the assets?

    $ _____

8. What is the total straight-line depreciation for all assets?

    $ _____

9. What is the total difference in depreciation amounts for Machine-A1?

    $ _____

10. What is the total difference in depreciation amounts for all assets?

    $ _____

UNIT 5 SELF-TEST

ACCOUNTING AND FINANCIAL MATHEMATICS

1. Marilyn Harrison works the following numbers of hours from Monday to Friday respectively during the week: 9, 8, 10, 10, and 8. Assuming a regular rate of $9.60 and an overtime rate of 1.5 times the regular rate for hours in excess of 40, what are her (a) regular earnings, (b) overtime earnings, and (c) gross earnings for the week?

    (a) $ _384.00_

    (b) $ _72.00_

    (c) $ _456.00_

2. Kim Romero produced 3,000 units during the week. If she is paid $0.08 for each of the first 2,000 units produced and $0.10 for each unit produced in excess of 2,000 units, what were her gross earnings? $ _260.00_

3. Odella McKinnon produced 900 units during the week. She is paid $6.25 per hour plus $0.10 per unit produced. What are her gross earnings if she worked 40 hours? $ _340.00_

4. Darren Feldman earned $425.50 last week. If the FICA rate is 8.75%, what amount will be withheld from his paycheck for this tax?

    $ _____

5. Felton Greason earned $18,750 last year. Based on an income tax withholding rate of 18%, what was his tax liability?

    $ _____

6. Jan Klodzinski earned $32,425 last year. Based on an income tax withholding rate of 15% on the first $22,750 and a rate of 28% on income in excess of $22,750, what was his tax liability?

    $ _____

7. Assume that a personal exemption of $2,450 is allowed for each dependent and a standard deduction of $6,350 for John and Joan McKinley. They are filing a joint return with a total of 4 personal exemptions. Their gross income is $32,876. What is their taxable income?

    $ _____

8. Bill McDonald is single. He earned $600 last week. Assume that $115 was withheld for income taxes, that the FICA rate is 7.65%, and that $8 was withheld for union dues. What was his net pay?

    $ _____

9. A crafts store in Dover County has a true value of $269,000. If property is assessed at 25% of its true value, what is the assessed valuation of the property?

   $ _____

10. Abbey Curland owns a business with an assessed value of $320,500. If the property tax is set at $2.75 per $100 of assessed value, how much property tax must be paid?

    $ _____

11. William Vaught owns a house with an assessed value of $175,500. If the tax rate is 0.056, how much in property taxes must be paid?

    $ _____

12. The Briar Store's inventory records provide the following information: Beginning balance on April 1 was 25 units @ $5.20; 10 units purchased on April 10 @ $5.30; and 15 units purchased on April 18 @ $5.40. There were 10 units on hand on April 30. What is the value of the ending inventory under each of the following methods: (a) FIFO, (b) LIFO, and (c) average cost?

    (a) $ _____

    (b) $ _____

    (c) $ _____

13. During the last fiscal year, the House of Gifts had a beginning inventory of $36,000, purchases of $200,000, and an ending inventory of $28,000. Indicate the amount of (a) merchandise available for sale, (b) cost of goods sold, and (c) the merchandise turnover ratio. Round answers to two decimal places.

    (a) $ _____

    (b) $ _____

    (c) _____

14. A particular computer cost $48,000 with an estimated useful life of 5 years and no disposal value. What is the depreciation during the first year under the (a) straight-line and (b) 200-percent-declining-balance methods?

    (a) $ _____

    (b) $ _____

15. A delivery truck cost $17,800 with an estimated life of 5 years and no disposal value. Using the straight-line method, what is the book value at the end of (a) the first year and (b) the second year?

(a) $ _____

(b) $ _____

16. An automobile cost $12,800 with an estimated life of 5 years and no disposal value. Using the 200-percent-declining-balance method, what is the book value at the end of (a) the first year and (b) the second year?

(a) $ _____

(b) $ _____

17. A truck costing $15,500 is purchased on July 1. The asset fits into the 5-year class life. Under the MACRS method, what will the depreciation be on December 31 of (a) the first year and (b) the second year?

(a) $ _____

(b) $ _____

18. An analysis of the balance sheet of Drake's Catering Service yields the following information. Compute the information requested below.

Current Assets	$120,000
Property-Plant-Equipment	$225,000
Current Liabilities	$80,000
Long-Term Liabilities	$150,000
Owner's Equity	$115,000

(a) Working Capital $ 40,000 (120,000-80,000)

(b) Current Ratio   1.5 (120,000 ÷ 80,000)

(c) Assets to Capital Ratio   _____

(d) Capital to Liabilities Ratio   _____

19. Bob Zack Plumbers had income last year of $260,500 and income this year of $325,625. What is the company's (a) amount of increase in income and (b) percent of increase?

(a) 65,125.00 (325,625 - 260,500)

(b) 25% (65,125 ÷ 260,500)

20. Net sales for Ron Lewton Popcorn Supplies for last year were $350,000. The cost of goods sold was $269,500. What percent of net sales is represented by cost of goods sold?

_____

UNIT 6

Business Finance

Just as you have personal financial decisions to make, a business has financial decisions on a much larger scale. Have you ever made a purchase from a business and made arrangements to pay the seller over a period of time at a specified rate of interest? Of course, there was a due date involved when you were expected to pay the seller. A typical business finance computation would involve determining this due date and computing how much interest you must pay for the privilege of paying over a period of time. Businesses can charge simple interest or compound interest for this privilege. For a buyer, understanding and being able to compute interest using these two methods is critical.

A business must also make purchases and pay interest. Typical purchases a business might make are annuities, interest-bearing notes, and insurance coverage. Included in this unit are activities relating to these topics as well as to computing simple and compound interest. These are real-life business finance activities that you may encounter.

COMPUTING SIMPLE INTEREST

Performance Objectives

1. Define interest, principal, rate, time, and future value.
2. Use the simple interest formula to determine interest due on loans and investments for months and years.
3. Compute banker's ordinary interest amounts.
4. Compute exact interest amounts.
5. Determine interest amounts by using tables and shortcut methods.
6. Determine maturity values for loans and investments.

Businesses and individuals borrow money for a variety of purposes, such as expanding operations, purchasing additional plant and equipment, and obtaining additional cash to operate the business. The amount borrowed (principal), plus the fee for using the money (simple interest), is paid at the end of a specified period of time. Promissory notes and trade acceptances are the most common commercial paper used as evidence for short-term loans of one year or less. Material in this chapter illustrates how simple interest is computed on money borrowed from individuals, banks, and other lending agencies.

SIMPLE INTEREST FORMULA

The diagram shown in Figure 24.1 indicates the relationship between *interest* (the amount charged for use of money), *principal* (the amount borrowed), *rate* (the percent charged for use of money), and *time* (the length the money is borrowed). This formula can also be stated as $I = P \times R \times T$.

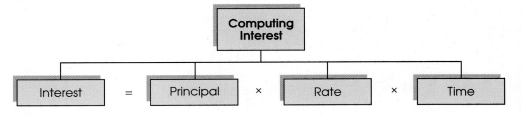

Figure 24.1 Computing Interest

The formula shown in Figure 24.2 can be used to compute the interest amount charged for the use of borrowed money. This formula is basic to all interest computations.

Interest = Principal x Rate x Time
or
I = P x R x T

Figure 24.2 Simple Interest Formula

The *principal* represents the amount of the loan. The *rate* is always expressed as a percent or as a decimal based on the fee charged for using the money for one year. The *time* is always expressed in years or as a fraction of 1 year. These three factors are illustrated in Model 24.1.

Simple interest:
An amount paid for using money for a specified period of time.

Interest formula:
$I = P \times R \times T$ or
$P \times R \times T = I$
if using a calculator.

Interest:
Amount charged for using money.

Principal:
The amount borrowed or invested.

Rate:
The percent charged for the use of money.

Time:
The period of time that money is borrowed or invested, usually stated in terms of days, months, or years.

MODEL 24.1

Computing simple interest

Problem: Floyd Carter borrowed $400.00 with repayment to be made in 1 year. The interest rate was 8%. What was the interest amount?

Solution: Principal x Rate x Time = Interest

$400.00 x 0.08 (8%) x 1 = $32.00

Apply Your Skills

Ray Hemeri invested $2,500 in a savings account that pays 6% simple interest. How much interest will Ray earn for a 2-year period?

$ ___300.⁰⁰___

The interest on this same loan will be $16 for six months (6÷12 or 1/2 of a year) or $64 for two years as shown in Model 24.2. If the time of the loan is expressed in months, the number of months should be placed over 12 since 12 months is equivalent to 1 year.

MODEL 24.2

Time examples:

4 years : T = 4

45 days: T = 45 ÷ 365

3 months: T = 3 ÷ 12

Simple interest formula for a period stated in months or years

P	x	R	x	T	=	I
$400	x	0.08	x	1 ÷ 2	=	$16 (6 months)
$400	x	0.08	x	2	=	$64.00 (2 years)

Apply Your Skills

Karen Butterini borrowed $6,000 from a financial institution that charges 7% simple interest. How much interest will Karen owe after 3 months?

$ ___105.⁰⁰___

A calculator is often used to compute interest.

If an electronic calculator is used, the fractional part of a year can be converted to a decimal to obtain the same results. The calculation of interest on this same loan for six months using a decimal value is shown in Model 24.3.

Simple interest formula for a period stated as a decimal

P	x	R	x	T	=	I
$400	x	0.08	x	0.5	=	$16.00

Apply Your Skills

Martina Kapon borrows $3,000 from a financial institution that charges 8% interest. How much interest will she owe after 6 months?

$ _120.00_

Calculation of interest for a loan with a principal of $600, a rate of 9%, and a time (or due date) of 8 months is shown in Model 24.4.

Procedure for using the simple interest formula

Step 1 Determine the principal, interest, rate, and time of the loan.
Step 2 Substitute the amounts from Step 1 into the interest formula.

$$I = P \times R \times T \quad (\text{or } P \times R \times T = I)$$
$$I = \$600 \times 0.09 \times 8 \div 12$$

Step 3 Compute the interest.

P	x	R	x	T			I
$600.00	x	0.09	x	8 ÷ 12 =	$432.00 ÷ 12 =	$36.00

Apply Your Skills

Compute the interest on a $6,000 loan for 7 months at an 8% simple interest rate.

$ _280.00_

To further illustrate, a loan for $620 due in 6 months with a 12% interest rate will earn interest amounting to $37.20, as shown below.

P	x	R	x	T	=	I
$620.00	x	0.12	x	6÷12	=	$37.20

COMPUTING ORDINARY AND EXACT INTEREST

Some businesses, banks, and other institutions base the time for loans on a *banker's year* of 360 days if the time of the loan is stated in terms of days. A month is considered to be 30 days or 1/12 of a year. This method is often referred to as the banker's method because some banks compute interest on the basis of a 360-day year. The interest computed by this method is called *ordinary interest.*

not Ordinary Interes.

Banker's year:
Uses a 360-day year and exact time. Most banks use 365 days for computing interest on savings accounts.

475

The same basic interest formula (I = P X R X T) is used to compute ordinary interest. For example, assume that a loan for $450 is due in 45 days with an interest rate of 10%. Using the same steps as in Model 24.4, the interest amount is computed as shown in Model 24.5.

MODEL 24.5

Exact interest: Interest is computed based on a 365-day year.

Computing banker's ordinary interest

Step 1 The principal is $450.00, the interest rate is 10%, and the time is 45 days.

Step 2 I = P X R X T

I = $450.00 X 0.10 X 45 ÷ 360

Step 3 $450.00 X 0.10 X 45 ÷ 360 = $2,025.00 ÷ 12 = $5.625 (rounded to $5.63)

Note: The final interest amount is rounded to the nearest cent.

Apply Your Skills

Compute the interest amount for a $9,000 loan for 90 days at an 8% interest rate. The banker's year is used relative to the time factor.

$ _____

In a second example, interest on a 90-day, $1,400 loan with a 12% interest rate is computed as follows:

P X R X T = I

$1,400.00 X 0.12 X 90 ÷ 360 = $42.00

Since the loan bears interest, the borrower will pay the original principal plus interest when the loan is due in 90 days. Therefore, the amount to be repaid is $1,442.00 ($1,400.00 + $42.00).

The procedure for computing *exact interest* is the same as the procedure for computing ordinary interest, except that 365 days are used as the basis for one year. The federal government and Federal Reserve Banks make interest computations on this basis. Most bank loans are now based on a full 365-day year. The same loan in Model 24.5 earns interest based on a 365-day year as shown in Model 24.6.

MODEL 24.6

Computing exact interest

P x R x T = I

$450.00 x 0.10 x 45 ÷ 365 = $2,025 ÷ 365 = $5.55 (rounded)

Apply Your Skills

(a) Compute the exact interest for a $9,000 loan for 90 days at an 8% interest rate.
(b) Was this amount more or less than the amount computed while using a banker's year in Apply Your Skills Model 24.5?

(a) $ _____

(b) _____ More _____ Less

Using the ordinary-interest method, interest was computed to be $5.63, a difference of 8 cents from the interest computed using the exact-interest method. Interest will always be slightly lower when the exact-interest method is used. Unless otherwise directed, use the ordinary-interest method for problems in this chapter.

You may now complete Performance Application 24.1.

THE 60-DAY, 6% METHOD

A shortcut method for computing ordinary simple interest is called the 60-day, 6% method. The basic principle is that when the time is 60 days and the interest rate is 6%, the interest can be determined simply by moving the decimal two places to the left in the principal amount. Therefore, the interest on a $620.00 loan due in 60 days with a 6% interest rate is $6.20. This can be proven by using the basic interest formula.

$$P \quad \times \quad R \quad \times \quad T \quad = \quad I$$
$$\$620.00 \times \quad 0.06 \quad \times \quad 60 \div 360 = \quad \$6.20$$

Notice that the final computation after cancellation involves multiplying the principal amount by 1% (0.01). This is why moving the decimal point two places to the left in the principal amount provides the correct amount of interest. This method is popular because the solution can often be determined mentally without the aid of a calculator or paper and pencil.

By using logic, the interest amount for interest rates that are multiples of 6% and time periods that are multiples of 60 days can be easily determined. For example, interest on the above loan for 120 days at the same 6% interest rate can be determined by multiplying $6.20 by 2 ($12.40) because the number of days is doubled (60 x 2 = 120). Likewise, an interest rate of 9% is 1½ times 6% (9 ÷ 6 = 1½). The interest amount is determined by moving the decimal two places to the left ($6.20) and multiplying the resulting amount by 1½ ($6.20 x 1½ = $9.30). Solve the problems in Model 24.7 mentally and test your knowledge of this shortcut method by comparing your answers to the ones provided below the problems.

Exact time:
The number of days a loan or investment is used.

The 60-day, 6% method does not provide exact interest based on a 365-day year, but can be useful for estimating interest.

MODEL 24.7

Sample problems and solutions using the 60-day, 6% method

Problems: (a) $300.00 at 9% for 60 days $ _____

            (b) $400.00 at 6% for 30 days $ _____

            (c) $650.00 at 6% for 180 days $ _____

            (d) $1,350 at 8% for 30 days $ _____

            (e) $400.00 at 7 1/2% for 72 days $ _____

Solutions: (a) $4.50, (b) $2.00, (c) $19.50, (d) $9.00, (e) $6.00.

Apply Your Skills

Use the short-cut method to compute interest amounts for the following loans.

    (a) $4,000 at 6% for 60 days $ _____

    (b) $400 at 6% for 90 days $ _____

    (c) $900 at 9% for 60 days $ _____

    (d) $800 at 6% for 75 days $ _____

The terms of the loan dictate whether the interest formula or short-cut method is most appropriate. Regardless of the terms, the shortcut method can be used to provide an estimate to indicate whether or not the computed interest amount is a reasonable answer. Because of the possibility of error, two computations are usually made to ensure that the interest amount is correct.

USING A TABLE TO COMPUTE SIMPLE INTEREST

Many financial institutions use a computer software program or a table to compute interest amounts and maturity values. An example of a table that can be used to compute simple exact interest is shown in Figure 24.3. Find the number of days in the left column, then move across until you are in the column with the appropriate interest rate at the top. This particular table shows interest for $100. Multiply this amount by 5 if the amount is $500, by 10 if the amount is $1,000, and so forth.

Rate Day	Interest per $100					
	8.50%	9.00%	9.50%	10.00%	10.50%	11.00%
1	0.023288	0.024658	0.026027	0.027397	0.028767	0.030137
2	0.046575	0.049315	0.052055	0.054795	0.057534	0.060274
3	0.069863	0.073973	0.078082	0.082192	0.086301	0.090411
4	0.093151	0.098630	0.104110	0.109589	0.115068	0.120548
5	0.116438	0.123288	0.130137	0.136986	0.143836	0.150685
6	0.139726	0.147945	0.156164	0.164384	0.172603	0.180822
7	0.163014	0.172603	0.182192	0.191781	0.201370	0.210959
8	0.186301	0.197260	0.208219	0.219178	0.230137	0.241096
9	0.209589	0.221918	0.234247	0.246575	0.258904	0.271233
10	0.232877	0.246575	0.260274	0.273973	0.287671	0.301370
11	0.256164	0.271233	0.286301	0.301370	0.316438	0.331507
12	0.279452	0.295890	0.312329	0.328767	0.345205	0.361644
13	0.302740	0.320548	0.338356	0.356164	0.373973	0.391781
14	0.326027	0.345205	0.364384	0.383562	0.402740	0.421918
15	0.349315	0.369863	0.390411	0.410959	0.431507	0.452055
16	0.372603	0.394521	0.416438	0.438356	0.460274	0.482192
17	0.395890	0.419178	0.442466	0.465753	0.489041	0.512329
18	0.419178	0.443836	0.468493	0.493151	0.517808	0.542466
19	0.442466	0.468493	0.494521	0.520548	0.546575	0.572603
20	0.465753	0.493151	0.520548	0.547945	0.575342	0.602740
21	0.489041	0.517808	0.546575	0.575342	0.604110	0.632877
22	0.512329	0.542466	0.572603	0.602740	0.632877	0.663014
23	0.535616	0.567123	0.598630	0.630137	0.661644	0.693151
24	0.558904	0.591781	0.624658	0.657534	0.690411	0.723288
25	0.582192	0.616438	0.650685	0.684932	0.719178	0.753425
26	0.605479	0.641096	0.676712	0.712329	0.747945	0.783562
27	0.628767	0.665753	0.702740	0.739726	0.776712	0.813699
28	0.652055	0.690411	0.728767	0.767123	0.805479	0.843836
29	0.675342	0.715068	0.754795	0.794521	0.834247	0.873973
30	0.698630	0.739726	0.780822	0.821918	0.863014	0.904110

Figure 24.3 Simple Interest Table Using Exact Interest Per $100

Using a table to compute simple interest

MODEL 24.8

Refer to Figure 24.3 to compute simple interest on a $1,000 loan for 20 days at 10%.

The interest on a $100 loan for 20 days at 10% interest will be $0.547945. Multiply this amount by 10 for a $1,000 loan.

0.547945 x 10 = $5.48 (rounded)

- -

Apply Your Skills

Use the simple interest table shown in Figure 24.3 to compute interest on a $1,000 loan at 10% for 30 days. What is the interest amount?

$ _____

DETERMINING THE DUE DATE

The time when a loan is due is usually stated in terms of days, months, or years. For example, a 30-day loan dated July 15 will be due on August 14. The 16 days remaining in July, plus 14 days in August, account for 30 days. In other words, you must compute the exact due date based on the number of days in each specific month involved.

If the due date is expressed in terms of months, the due date will be the same day of the month as the date of the loan. For example, a one-month loan dated July 15 will be due on August 15. Since some loans contain a provision for penalty if not paid on or before the due date, it is important to accurately determine the due date.

Due date:
The day that payment of the loan balance is required.

COMPUTING MATURITY VALUE

$$MV = P(1 + RT)$$

MV = Maturity value
P = Principlal
R = Interest rate
T = Time in years

Interest applies to money that may be borrowed from an individual, a bank, or other financial institution. Interest also applies to investments that may be made with a financial institution. In a sense, an investment indicates that the investor has let the institution borrow money. Examples of this type of investment include opening a savings account at a bank and purchasing a bond from an investment service.

The typical procedure is to borrow or invest money for a given period of time at a given interest rate. The amount of money that is due at the end of the period equals the original amount borrowed or original investment plus interest earned. For example, $1,000 borrowed at a 6% interest rate for 2 years will earn $120 ($1,000 x 0.06 x 2 = $120). The maturity value will be $1,120, which includes the original principal plus earned interest. A formula can be used to compute the maturity in one step as follows: MV = P(1 + RT) where MV = maturity value, P = principal, R = rate, and T = time expressed in years. This formula can be used to determine maturity value without having to first determine the interest. Of course, the principal can be subtracted from the maturity value to then compute interest if desired.

To use this formula, first multiply the rate by the time and then add 1. Then multiply this amount by the principal amount. This procedure is illustrated in Model 24.9.

MODEL 24.9

Determining maturity value

Problem: Mutsumi Sakai invested $4,000 in a savings account that paid 6% simple interest. After 4 years, what is the maturity value?

Solution: MV=P(1 + RT)   P = $4,000   R = 6% or 0.06   T = 4
MV = $4,000(1 + 0.06 x 4) = $4,960 (see steps below)

Step 1 0.06 x 4 = 0.24
Step 2 1 + 0.24 = 1.24
Step 3 $4,000 x 1.24 = $4,960

Apply Your Skills

City Office Supply borrowed $8,000 for a term of 5 years with a 9% simple interest rate. What will the maturity value for the loan be (using the formula)?

$ _____

FINDING UNKNOWN FACTORS IN SIMPLE INTEREST FORMULA

Examples given earlier in this chapter assumed computation for the interest amount each time. In other words, the interest amount was the unknown factor each time. Actually, any of the four factors can be computed if the three other factors are known. This relationship is illustrated in Figure 24.4.

Rate unknown	Interest unknown
$\text{Rate} = \dfrac{\text{Interest}}{\text{Principal} \times \text{Time}}$	$\text{Interest} = \text{Principal} \times \text{Rate} \times \text{Time}$
Principal unknown	Time unknown
$\text{Principal} = \dfrac{\text{Interest}}{\text{Rate} \times \text{Time}}$	$\text{Time} = \dfrac{\text{Interest}}{\text{Principal} \times \text{Time} \times \text{Rate}}$

Figure 24.4 Solving for Unknown Factors

The examples in Model 24.10 are provided to illustrate each of these formulas.

MODEL 24.10

Solving for unknown factors - Simple Interest Formula

Rate unknown

Interest: $60
Principal: $600
Time: 2 years
Rate: Unknown

$\text{Rate} = \dfrac{\$60}{\$600 \times 2} = \dfrac{\$60}{\$1,200}$

$= 0.05 \text{ or } 5\%$

Interest unknown

Interest: Unknown
Principal: $600
Time: 2 years
Rate: 5%

$\text{Interest} = \$600 \times 0.05 \times 2$

$= \$60$

Principal unknown

Interest: $60
Principal: Unknown
Time: 2 years
Rate: 5%

$\text{Principal} = \dfrac{\$60}{0.05 \times 2} = \dfrac{\$60}{0.1}$

$= \$600.00$

Time unknown

Interest: $60
Principal: $600
Time: Unknown
Rate: 5%

$\text{Time} = \dfrac{\$60}{\$600 \times 0.05} = \dfrac{\$60}{\$30}$

$= 2 \text{ years}$

Apply Your Skills

Supply the missing factor for each of the following:

	Interest	Principal	Rate	Time
(a)	$ _____	$6,000	6%	6 months
(b)	$90	$ _____	5%	2 years
(c)	$90	$600	_____	3 years
(d)	$224	$800	7%	$ _____

You may now complete Performance Application 24.2.

PERFORMANCE APPLICATION 24.1

1. Use the formula for computing interest, I = P x R x T, to find the interest for each of the following loans using a 360-day year and a 365-day year. (Round the answers to the nearest cent.)

Loan	Ordinary Method 360-Day Year	Exact Method 365-Day Year
$600.00 at 10% for 30 days	$ 5.⁰⁰	$ 4.93
$900.00 at 8% for 75 days	$ 15.⁰⁰	$ 14.79
$850.00 at 12% for 90 days	$ 25.5	$ 25.13
$1,250.00 at 12% for 72 days	$ 30.⁰⁰	$ 29.59
$2,400.00 at 9% for 45 days	$ 27.⁰⁰	$ 26.63

2. Use the ordinary-interest method to compute interest on the following loans.

Loan	Ordinary Interest
$840.00 at 9% for 84 days	$ 17.64
$700.00 at 7½% for 72 days	$ 105.0
$2,484.00 at 15% for 2 months	$ 621
$600.00 at 10½% for 7 months	$ 3675
$24,600.00 at 8% for 5 months	$ 820

3. Examine the following promissory note. Use the ordinary interest formula to compute the interest that will be due for the loan. How much interest will be due?

$ _____

PROMISSORY NOTE

Ninety (90) days after current date, I promise to pay to the order of Brad Yahonna the sum of Eight hundred fifty and no/100 dollars ($850.00) plus interest at an annual rate of nine (9) percent.

Date: _____

Signed: _____

PERFORMANCE APPLICATION 24.2

1. Use the 60-day, 6% method to compute interest for each of the
    following loans. Check your answers by using the interest formula.

Loan	60-Day 6% Method	Formula Method
$960.00 at 6% for 60 days	$_____	$_____
$620.00 at 6% for 90 days	$_____	$_____
$480.00 at 18% for 60 days	$_____	$_____
$540.00 at 18% for 30 days	$_____	$_____
$850.00 at 12% for 60 days	$_____	$_____
$960.00 at $7\frac{1}{2}$% for 60 days	$_____	$_____
$540.00 at 6% for 180 days	$_____	$_____
$740.00 at 9% for 75 days	$_____	$_____
$865.00 at 9% for 120 days	$_____	$_____
$1,449.00 at $4\frac{1}{2}$% for 180 days	$_____	$_____

2. Evaluate the dates and due dates of the following loans to determine the number of days for each loan. (Assume that February is not in a leap year.)

Date	Due Date	Number of Days
January 1	February 15	_____
March 4	May 16	_____
July 23	October 12	_____
May 4	July 15	_____
November 7	December 7	_____
January 9	April 15	_____
April 13	July 21	_____
June 3	August 15	_____
February 4	March 28	_____
March 15	May 30	_____

3. Evaluate the date and time to maturity for the following loans to determine the due date. (Assume that February is not in a leap year.)

Date	Time	Due Date
August 16	75 days	_____
April 3	30 days	_____
July 16	72 days	_____
January 3	90 days	_____
March 13	45 days	_____
April 18	3 months	_____
September 14	45 days	_____
November 21	4 months	_____
February 3	6 months	_____
February 8	120 days	_____

PRACTICE TEST FOR CHAPTER 24

COMPUTING SIMPLE INTEREST

Complete each of the following problems and then compare your answers with the ones on page 650.

1. Jose Garcia borrowed $5,400 at the company credit union with the stipulation that the funds would be repaid in 2 years and a 7.5% simple interest rate would be charged. What were the (a) interest earned and (b) maturity value for the loan?

    (a) $ _____

    (b) $ _____

2. A customer at Deerfield National Bank obtained a 75-day, $5,000 loan that carried a 7% interest rate. The bank calculates exact interest. What was the interest earned by the loan?

    $ _____

3. Examine the following promissory note. How much interest (using a banker's year) will be earned?

    $ _____

Promissory Note

Thirty (30) days after current date, I promise to pay to the order of Joe Ellis the sum of Nine hundred and no/100 dollars ($900.00) plus interest at an annual rate of eight (8) percent.

Date: _____

Signed: _____

---

4. Using the shortcut method, what is the interest earned on a 90-day, 6%, $5,600 loan?

    $ _____

5. A 90-day promissory note was dated March 20. What was the due date?

    _____

24.1 Martha Wetzel sold a used automobile to Cecil Cranfield for $8,500 under the following agreement: a $3,000 down payment with the balance secured by an 18-month promissory note as indicated below. What are the (a) due date, (b) interest earned, and (c) maturity value for the note? Cecil could have borrowed the money from a local bank for a 9% interest rate. Martha agreed to reduce the price by $100 if full payment was received at the time of sale. (d) How much could Cecil save by borrowing the funds to fully pay for the automobile at the time of purchase instead of making the promissory note?

(a) _____

(b) $ _____

(c) $ _____

(d) $ _____

$5,500.⁰⁰   October 5   19--

Eighteen months   after date I promise to pay

to the order of Martha Wetzel

Five thousand five hundred   Dollars

at First National Bank

Value received plus interest at 8.5 per cent per annum

No. 45   Due April 5, 19--   Cecil Cranfield

CONNECTIONS

24.2 The chart shown below indicates interest rate yields on 30-year treasury bonds for selected years. What would the interest earned on a $75,000 bond be for the first year, assuming the bonds paid annual simple interest and were purchased during each of the years indicated below? (d) Call a local investment firm in your area and request information about the current rate. How much would the same amount earn in 1 year at the current rate?

(a) 1963: $ _____

(b) 1968: $ _____

(c) 1978: $ _____

(d) Current $ _____

Falling yields

The yield on 30-year Treasury bonds:

Year	Yield in February
1958	3.32%
1963	4.01%
1968	5.29%
1973	6.89%
1978	8.12%
1983	11.18%
1988	8.42%
Monday	6.93%

Source: USA TODAY research

CONNECTIONS

24.1 Carla Duheime listed a condo for sale. Potential buyers made the following offers: (1) $120,000 with a $40,000 down payment and the remainder due in 5 years and secured by a 7% promissory note; (2) $110,000 with the full amount due on the date of sale. Carla has an opportunity to put the funds into an investment that pays 8% simple interest with a 5-year maturity date. What total funds will Carla have at the end of 5 years under (a) the first offer and (b) the second offer? (c) Which offer should Carla accept to have the most funds after 5 years?

(a) $ _____

(b) $ _____

(c) offer 1 _____   offer 2 _____

24.2 Ward and Janice Harder decided to purchase new bedroom furniture. City Furniture offered furniture for $6,500 with total payment, but no interest, due in 6 months. Crosstown Furniture offered the same furniture for $6,300 with an 8.5% interest rate and the total payment due in 180 days. Which offer required the lowest total payment after 6 months?

_____ City Furniture

_____ Crosstown Furniture

DECISIONS

COMPUTING SIMPLE INTEREST
Chapter Review and Quick Reference

Topic	Main Point	Typical Example	Text Page
Simple interest based on years	Use the simple interest formula. **Interest** = **P**rincipal x **R**ate x **T**ime	$800 @ 8.5% for 2 years I = P x R x T I = $800 x 0.085 x 2 I = **$136**	473
Simple interest based on months	Use the simple interest formula. **Interest** = Principal x **R**ate x **T**ime	$4000 @ 8% for 6 months I = P x R x T I = $4,000 x 0.08 x 6 ÷ 12 I = **$160**	474
Ordinary interest based on banker's year	The simple interest formula is used, but the number of days is based on a 360-day year. T = No. of days ÷ 360	$600 @ 5% for 75 days I = P x R x T I = $600 x 0.05 x 75 ÷ 360 I = **$6.25**	476
Exact interest	The simple interest formula is used, but the number of days is based on a 365-day year—or 366 days for a leap year. T = No. of days ÷ 365	$600 @ 5% for 75 days I = P X R X T I = $600 X 0.05 x 75 ÷ 365 I = **$6.16**	476

Topic	Main Point	Typical Example	Text Page
Due date	The due date is the date that the loan will need to be paid or the investment will pay the amount due.	A 3-month loan is dated March 3. The loan payment is due on **June 3**.	479
Maturity valueFinding the rate	The maturity value equals principal plus interest earned. The interest can be computed and then added to the principal or the following formula can be used to compute the maturity value: MV = P(1 + RT)	$800 @ 6% for 2 years **Step 1** Find interest I = P x R x T I = $800 x 0.06 x 2 = $96 **Step 2** Find maturity value MV = P + I = **$896** or MV = P(1 + RT) MV = $800(1 + 0.06 x 2) = **$896**	480
Finding the principal	The basic formula is used: I = PRT R = I ÷ P x T	$800 for 2 years earns $96 interest. What is the rate? R = $96 ÷ ($800 x 2) = $96 ÷ $1,600 = **0.06** or **6%**	481
Finding the time	The basic formula is used: I = PRT P = I ÷ R x T	A 6% loan earns $96 interest over 2 years. What is the principal? P = $96 ÷ (0.06 x 2) = $96 ÷ 0.12 **$800**	481
	The basic formula is used: I = PRT T = I ÷ P x R	An $800 loan @ 6% earns $96 interest. What is the time? T = $96 ÷ ($800 x 0.06) = $96 ÷ $48 = **2**	

Chapter 25

DISCOUNTING NOTES

Performance Objectives

1. Illustrate format for a promissory note.
2. Determine discount period for notes.
3. Determine discount and proceeds for a non-interest-bearing note.
4. Determine discount and proceeds for an interest-bearing note.
5. Determine discount and proceeds for treasury bills.

Promissory note:
An unconditional promise made in writing by one party to another to repay a loan.

A promissory note is a negotiable instrument, which means that the note can be transferred to a bank or other third party in much the same manner as a check. A major difference is that notes usually bear interest. Interest to be earned between the date the note is passed on to a third party and the maturity date must be accounted for. The bank will deduct a specific interest charge from the maturity value of the note because it will have to wait until the maturity date to receive payment for the loan. In these instances, the deduction for interest is commonly called *discount* or *bank discount*, although it is not a discount in the same sense that a retail store discounts merchandise. Material in this chapter shows you how to compute discounts on notes.

USING A PROMISSORY NOTE

Businesses and individuals normally sign a legal document in order to borrow money. The *promissory note*, as defined by the Uniform Commercial Code, is an unconditional promise made in writing by one party to another. This instrument is called a *negotiable promissory note* if it may be sold to a third party. A brief introduction to the use of promissory notes was provided in Chapter 24. A more detailed use of the instrument is provided in this chapter.

The same basic formula previously used to compute simple interest, Interest = Principal X Rate X Time, will be also used in this chapter. The *principal* represents the amount borrowed and the term represents the length (*time*) money is borrowed. The *value received* will indicate the annual interest rate. In addition, the *current date* indicates the date the note was issued. The *maturity date* indicates the date the loan and interest are due, if it is interest bearing, for payment. The *maker* is the person or business responsible for payment. The *payee* is the person or business to receive payment. An example of a promissory note, with parts indicated, is shown in Figure 25.1.

Maturity date:
The day proceeds are due. Sometimes called ***due date***.

Maker:
The person or business to repay the loan.

Payee:
The person or business to receive repayment for a loan.

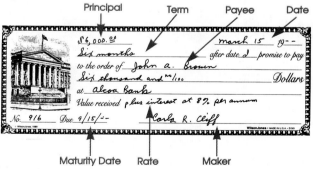

Figure 25.1 Promissory Note

DETERMINING DISCOUNT PERIOD

Businesses frequently accept promissory notes, trade acceptances, or installment sales contracts when selling merchandise. The customer agrees to pay the amount at some future time. In order to get money immediately, the business often trades the document to the bank for cash. The bank will charge a fee to reimburse the business for the period of time that the document must be held until the payment due date. This procedure is called *discounting commercial paper* or *notes*.

The due date and discount period must be determined prior to computing the discount amount. Discussion in this chapter relates to discounting of commercial paper by banks. However, other lending agencies and individuals may use the same procedures when discounting notes or other types of commercial paper. Notes will also be used in examples even though other types of commercial paper may be discounted in a similar manner.

The due date will normally be listed as a specific date or as a certain period of time from the date of the note, such as due in 30 days or due in 5 months. When a due date is stated in months, the due date will be on the same day of the month as the date of the note. For a 2-month loan dated July 8, the due date is September 8.

The diagram shown in Figure 25.2 displays a time line for discounting a note. The top portion indicates the period of time the note was discounted. The bottom portion indicates the full maturity date and value of the note.

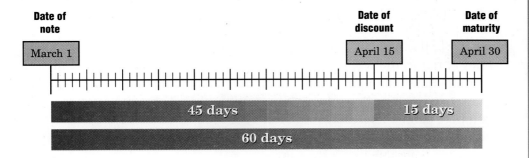

Figure 25.2 Discounting a Note

Assume that a note with a due date of May 18 is discounted on March 13. Computation of the discount period is shown in Model 25.1.

Nondiscounted note:
No interest or fee is subtracted on the date of the note.

Discounted note:
The interest or fee is deducted on the date of the note.

Term:
The length or time of the loan.

MODEL 25.1

Determining the discount period

Step 1 Determine the due date.
May 18 (in this example)

Step 2 Determine the discount date.
March 13 (in this example)

Step 3 Determine the number of days between the due date and the discount date.

Days in March	=	18
Days in April	=	30
Days in May	=	18
Discount period =		66 days

Apply Your Skills

A note with an October 16 maturity date was discounted on September 3. What was the discount period?

Face value:
The amount borrowed.

Bank discount:
The bank's charge on a promissory note.

Proceeds:
The actual amount received by the maker.

DISCOUNTING A NON-INTEREST-BEARING NOTE

The *maturity value* of a note is the total amount of money that will be paid on the due date. *Face value* is the amount of the note without considering interest earned on the note. If the note bears interest, the maturity value equals face value plus interest. In the case of a non-interest-bearing note, the face value and the maturity value are the same and no interest is earned.

Assume that the Perez Office Supply Store has a non-interest bearing note with a face value of $640.00 and a due date of September 15. In order to obtain cash, the store sells the note to the First National Bank on August 16 (30 days prior to the due date.). The bank will not pay the store the full amount (640.00) but it will charge a fee called the *bank discount*. This fee is usually stated as a percentage of the maturity value. The same formula used to compute simple interest (I = P X R X T) is used to compute the bank discount. The amount received (called *proceeds*) by the store equals the maturity value less the bank discount.

To further illustrate this example, the steps shown in Model 25.2 are taken to compute bank discount and proceeds. Assume that the bank uses a 12% discount rate.

Computing bank discount and proceeds for a non-interest-bearing note

MODEL
25.2

Step 1 Determine the maturity value.

$640.00 (in this example)

Step 2 Compute the bank discount using the simple interest formula.

Maturity value X Discount rate X Discount period = Bank discount

     $640.00   X   0.12   X   30 ÷ 360   = $6.40

Step 3 Compute proceeds by subtracting the discount from the maturity value.

Maturity value - Discount = Proceeds

    $640.00   - $6.40   = $633.60

Non-interest-bearing note:
A note that does not bear interest in addition to the face value.
MV = face value

Apply Your Skills

Perez Office Supply Store had a $4,000 non-interest-bearing note due on April 30 that was discounted at the bank on March 1 at a 9% discount rate. What were the (a) discount period and (b) proceeds from the note?

(a) _____

(b) $ _____

As the above example shows, the Perez Office Supply Store will receive $292.50 from the bank on March 1 in return for the note. On the maturity date (April 30), the bank will collect the maturity value ($300.00). If the person who originally purchased the merchandise does not pay the bank when the note becomes due on April 30, the Perez Office Supply Store must pay the bank the maturity value and attempt to collect from the customer. This provides the bank protection from bad debts.

Remember that the main advantage for a person or business selling a note to the bank is to receive proceeds immediately rather than wait until the due date to collect the maturity value

DISCOUNTING AN INTEREST-BEARING NOTE

The face value of a note may bear interest. For this type of note, interest must be computed and added to the face value to compute the maturity value. Except for this computation (Step 1), the procedure for discounting an interest-bearing note is similar to the procedure used to discount a non-interest bearing note in Model 25.2. To illustrate, assume that on May 1 McGuire's Dairy accepts a 90-day note (due date of July 30) with a face value of $500 and an interest rate of 12%. On May 11, the note is sold to the bank with a discount rate of 15%. The bank discount and proceeds on May 11 are computed as shown in Model 25.3.

Interest-bearing note:
A note that earns interest in addition to the face value.
MV = face value + interest

MODEL 25.3

Computing bank discount and proceeds for an interest-bearing note

Step 1 Determine the maturity value, including interest.

P   x   R   x   T   =   I
$500   x   0.12   x   90 ÷ 360   = $15.00
P   +   I   =   MV
$500.00 + $15.00 = $515.00 (maturity value)

Step 2 Determine the discount period.

May 11 to July 30 = 80 days

Step 3 Compute the bank discount by multiplying the maturity value by the discount rate by the time.

MV   x   R   x   T   =   Bank discount
$515.00   x   0.15   x   80 ÷ 360   = $17.17 (rounded)

Step 4 Compute the proceeds by subtracting the bank discount from the maturity value.

Maturity value   -   Discount   =   Proceeds

$515.00   - $17.17   = $497.83

Apply Your Skills

The Nashika Tool Company accepted a 90-day, $600 note bearing interest at a 6% rate with a due date of November 30. On October 31, the note was sold to the bank with a 10% discount rate. What were the (a) bank discount and (b) proceeds?

(a) $ _____

(b) $ _____

Treasury bill:
A loan from the federal government as evidenced by a treasury bill, which is for 13, 26, or 52 weeks.

Governmental agencies also lend money to individual citizens and to businesses. For example, the federal government may issue treasury bills in minimum units of $10,000. In these instances, the government will discount the treasury bill prior to issue. In order to purchase a one-year $10,000 treasury bill bearing 6% interest, the purchaser would first deduct the interest ($10,000 x 0.06 x 1 = $600) from the value of the treasury bill ($10,000 - $600 = $9,400). Therefore, the purchaser would pay $9,400 for the treasury bill and receive proceeds of $10,000 one year later on the maturity date.

Discounting treasury bills

Problem: O.J. Burnside purchased a 26-week, $20,000 treasury bill that paid a 6.5% interest rate. How much will Mr. Burnside have to pay for the treasury bill?

Solution: **Step 1** Find the discount (interest).

Principal x	Rate	x Time	= Interest
$20,000 x	0.065	x 26/52	= $650

Step 2 Find the proceeds.

Maturity value	-	Discount	= Proceeds
$20,000	-	$650	= $19,350.00

Apply Your Skills

City Investment sold 1-year $40,000 treasury bills to a client on March 1. The discount is 7%. How much will the client (a) pay on March 1 and (b) receive as proceeds 1 year later?

(a) $ _____

(b) $ _____

Performance Application 25.1

1. Determine the maturity date and discount period for each of the following notes.

Date of Note	Length of Note	Discount Date	Maturity Date	Discount Period
February 11	30 days	February 14		
April 18	60 days	May 15		
June 3	75 days	July 8		
August 8	80 days	October 15		
May 7	90 days	July 1		

2. Determine the maturity date and discount period for each of the following notes.

Date of Note	Length of Note	Discount Date	Maturity Date	Discount Period
May 16	2 months	May 23		
February 3	3 months	March 1		
July 16	2 months	July 31		
January 28	4 months	February 26		
November 18	3 months	January 3		

3. Find the (a) bank discount and (b) proceeds for the following non-interest-bearing note. A note with a maturity value of $2,400 is discounted 60 days prior to the due date at a 10% discount rate.

    (a) $ _____

    (b) $ _____

4. Find the (a) bank discount and (b) proceeds for the following non-interest-bearing note. A note with a maturity value of $3,624.72 is discounted 75 days prior to the due date at a 12% discount rate.

    (a) $ _____

    (b) $ _____

5. The Pineira Novelty Shoppe accepts a non-interest-bearing note with a date of May 15 and a maturity date of July 29. The face value is $900. The note is discounted on June 14 with a 6% discount rate. What are the (a) length of the note, (b) discount period, (c) discount amount, and (d) amount of proceeds?

    (a) _____

    (b) _____

    (c) $ _____

    (d) $ _____

6. Tom Carlton Builders accepts a non-interest-bearing note with a due date of November 15 and a face value of $1,450. The note is sold to the bank on October 16 with a 12% discount rate. What are the (a) discount period, (b) discount amount, and (c) amount of proceeds?

    (a) _____

    (b) $ _____

    (c) $ _____

PERFORMANCE APPLICATION 25.2

1. The Apex Supplies Company holds an 80-day interest- bearing note with an interest rate of 9%, a face value of $824, and a due date of September 30. On July 22, the note is discounted at the bank for a discount rate of 12%. What are the (a) discount period, (b) discount amount, and (c) proceeds for the note?

   (a) _____

   (b) $ _____

   (c) $ _____

2. Kevin McClain received a 60-day, 6% note from Blanche Madoza for $1,800. The note is dated February 15. He discounted the note at the bank on April 1 at 12%. What are the (a) discount period, (b) discount, and (c) proceeds for the note?

   (a) _____

   (b) $ _____

   (c) $ _____

3. Adam O'Connor receives a 120-day, 10% note from Samuel Dover for $3,600. The note is dated July 31. He discounts the note at the bank on September 30 at 9%. What are the (a) discount period, (b) discount, and (c) proceeds for the note?

   (a) _____

   (b) $ _____

   (c) $ _____

4. Rita Olive purchases farm equipment from the Northside Equipment Center on April 20. She gives an 8% interest-bearing promissory note for $25,000 due in 90 days. On May 20, the Northside Equipment Center discounts the note at the bank with a discount rate of 12%. (a) How much will the Northside Equipment Center receive from the bank on May 20? (b) How much will Rita Olive have to pay the bank when the note comes due? (c) On what date will Rita Olive have to pay the note?

(a) $ _____

(b) $ _____

(c) _____

5. Study the following interest-bearing note to determine (a) what the proceeds will be if the note is discounted on April 20 at 12% and (b) what the maturity value of the note will be on June 4.

(a) $ _____

(b) $ _____

INTEREST-BEARING NOTE

$8,800.00   Memphis, Tennessee   March 4, 19--

Three months after the above date, I promise to pay to the order of Oren Goldstein the sum of Eighty-eight hundred and no/100 dollars ($8,800.00) plus interest at the rate of 9 percent.

Signed: _____
                    Daryl Sparks

PRACTICE TEST FOR CHAPTER 25

DISCOUNTING NOTES

Complete each of the following problems and then compare your answers with the ones on page 651.

1. What are the (a) bank discount and (b) proceeds for a non-interest-bearing note with a $3,600 maturity value that was discounted 90 days prior to the maturity date at a 10% discount rate? (Use a 360-day year.)

   (a) $ _____

   (b) $ _____

2. What is the discount period for a note with an August 17 maturity date that was discounted on July 3?

   _____

3. A 6-month, 9% interest-bearing note dated April 1 for $8,600 was received. The note was discounted at the bank on August 20 at 10%. What were the (a) discount period, (b) discount, and (c) proceeds for the note on August 20? (Use a 360-day year.)

   (a) _____

   (b) $ _____

   (c) $ _____

4. Brenda McQuire purchased $30,000 in 1-year treasury bills with a 7.5% discount rate. What were the proceeds from the purchase?

   $ _____

5. Daryl Quarles borrowed $8,000 from City Bank. He signed a promissory note on August 15 that had an 8.5% interest rate and a 9-month term. What were the (a) face value and (b) maturity value for the note?

   (a) $ _____

   (b) $ _____

25.1 The newspaper article shown below describes a sale of short-term treasury securities by the federal government. What were the discount and proceeds from the Monday sale of (a) 3-month and (b) 6-month bills?

	Discount	Proceeds
(a)	$ _____	$ _____
(b)	$ _____	$ _____

Short-term rates fall as ARM rises

WASHINGTON (AP) – Interest rates on short-term Treasury securities fell in Monday's auction to the lowest level in three weeks.

The Treasury Department sold $12 billion in three-month bills at an average discount rate of 3.07 percent, down from 3.14 percent last week. Another $12 billion was sold in six-month bills at an average discount rate of 3.19 percent, down from 3.30 percent last week.

The rates were the lowest since May 24 when three-month bills sold for 3.06 percent and the six-month bill rate averaged 3.19 percent.

In a separate report, the Federal Reserve said the average yield for one-year Treasury bills, the most popular index for making changes in adjustable rate mortgages, rose to 3.61 percent last week from 3.58 percent.

CONNECTIONS

25.2 The chart shown below indicates the growth history of a $10,000 investment in the fund from December 1978 to June 1993. Assume that Margo Ogren invested $10,000 into the fund shown below in 1978. Based on her original investment, what was the (a) total percentage increase and (b) average annual increase based on her original $10,000 investment? (c) Why do you feel that the average annual rate of increase based on the original $10,000 investment is so high?

(a) _____

(b) _____

(c) _____

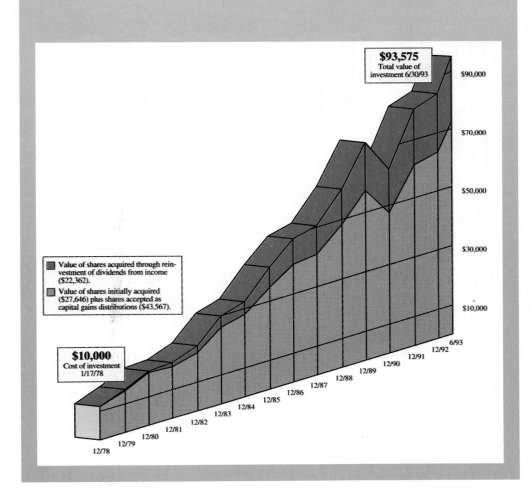

$93,575
Total value of
investment 6/30/93

$90,000

$70,000

$50,000

$30,000

Value of shares acquired through rein-
vestment of dividends from income
($22,362).

Value of shares initially acquired
($27,646) plus shares accepted as
capital gains distributions ($43,567).

$10,000

$10,000
Cost of investment
1/17/78

6/93
12/92
12/91
12/90
12/89
12/88
12/87
12/86
12/85
12/84
12/83
12/82
12/81
12/80
12/79
12/78

CONNECTIONS

25.1 Paulette Rassoul has narrowed her $30,000 investment to one of the following: (1) Citywide Investments offered a bond that has an 8.5% discount rate. (2) Countrywide Investments offered an interest-bearing bond with an 8.25% interest rate. Both bond types have a 10-year maturity date. Which investment will pay Paulette the most interest?

_____ Citywide Investments

_____ Countrywide Investments

25.2 Sabrina Panchikai currently has $23,000 in a checking account that offers a 4.5% interest rate. She also has $30,000 invested in a mutual fund that has been paying a 7.5% interest rate. A friend with an excellent credit record offered to borrow $45,000 from Sabrina, which will be secured with a 9% promissory note. Sabrina decided to withdraw $30,000 from the mutual fund and $15,000 from her checking account. (a) How much **extra** income per month will she earn from the note? (b) What are two factors that Sabrina should consider before making a final decision?

(a) $ _____

(b) _____

_____

DECISIONS

DISCOUNTING NOTES
Chapter Review and Quick Reference

Topic	Main Point	Typical Example	Text Page
Promissory note	A promissory note is an unconditional written promise to repay a loan on a specified date and at a specified interest rate.	After 30 days from April 1, 19-- , I promise to pay Joe Ellis the sum of $400 plus interest at a 6% rate. Signed _____	494
Discount period	The discount period is the period of time a note is discounted prior to the maturity date.	A note dated September 30 is discounted on September 10. The discount period is 20 days—September 10 to 30.	495
Discount and proceeds for a non-interest-bearing note	**Step 1** Find discount. Discount = Maturity value x Discount rate x Time **Step 2** Find proceeds. Proceeds = Maturity value - Discount	Maturity value: $800 Discount period: 60 days Discount rate: 6% **Step 1** Discount $800 x 0.06 x 60 ÷ 360 = **$8**. **Step 2:** Proceeds $800 - $8 = **$792**.	497

Topic	Main Point	Typical Example	Text Page
Discount and proceeds for an interest-bearing note	**Step 1** Find the maturity value. MV = Face value + Interest **Step 2** Find the discount. Discount = MV x Discount rate x Time **Step 3** Find the proceeds. Proceeds = Maturity value - Discount	Face value: $400 Interest rate: 6% Term: 90 days Discount term: 30 days Discount rate: 8% **Step 1** Maturity value $400 x 0.06 x 90 ÷ 360 = $6 $400 + $6 = **$406** **Step 2** Discount $406 x 0.08 x 30 ÷ 360 = **$2.71** (rounded) **Step 3** Proceeds $406 - $2.71 = **$403.29**	498
Treasury bills	Treasury bills are discounted from the face value at the time of purchase. **Step 1** Find the discount. Discount = Maturity value x Discount rate x Time **Step 2** Find the proceeds. Proceeds = Face value - Discount	Face value: $4 billion Term: 26 weeks Discount rate: 4% **Step 1** Discount $4,000,000,000 x 0.04 x 26 ÷ 52 = **$80,000,000** **Step 2** Proceeds $4,000,000,000 - 80,000,000 = **$3,920,000,000**	499

Chapter **26**

COMPUTING
COMPOUND
INTEREST

Performance Objectives

1. Define the concept of future value.
2. Compare and contrast compound and simple interest rates.
3. Compute compound value and interest earned based on an annual, semiannual, and quarterly basis.
4. Use an interest table to determine compound values.
5. Compute effective interest rate.

Interest is normally expressed either as simple interest (as in Chapter 25), in which the principal does not change over the life of the loan, or as *compound interest*. With compound interest, the principal changes at the end of each time period because the interest for the period is added to the principal amount. Common time periods are daily, monthly, quarterly, semiannually, and annually. Interest on deposit accounts and many other accounts with banks and other financial institutions is often computed using compound interest methods. In this chapter, you will learn how compound interest is computed. An understanding of the theory of compound interest is important as a basis for making an investment or business decision.

FORMULA METHOD FOR COMPUTING COMPOUND INTEREST

The same basic interest formula used to compute simple interest (I = P X R X T) is used to compute compound interest. The sum of the principal and interest for one period becomes the principal in the formula for the next period. This process is repeated each period, with the interest being added to the principal from the previous period each time.

The interest earned is called *compound interest*. The difference between the final sum and the original principal is the compound interest for the loan. A given compound interest rate will yield a greater interest amount than the corresponding simple interest rate because the principal increases each period with compound interest. Likewise, more frequent compounding will yield a greater amount of interest. See Figure 26.1.

Savings accounts and most other investment accounts use compound interest.

Compound interest: *The amount of the original loan principal less the compound interest.*

Compound value - Principal = Compound interest

Period: *The length of time between compound computations, such as a day or week.*

Future value: *The value of a loan or investment at the end of the compound periods (also called **compound amount**).*

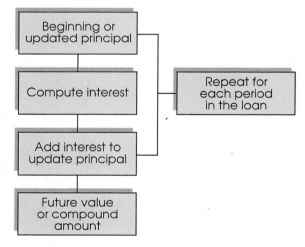

Figure 26.1 Determining Future Value—Compound Interest

Computing compounded interest

Problem: A deposit of $200 is placed into an account that bears interest, compounded annually, for 2 years at an interest rate of 8%. What is the compounded principal after 2 years?

Solution: **Step 1** Compute the interest for the first period.

Principal x Rate x Time = Interest
$200   x 0.08 x   1   = $16

Step 2 Find the new principal after 1 year.

Old principal + interest = New principal
$200   + $16   = $216

Step 3 Compute the interest for the second period.

New principal x Rate x Time = Interest
$216   x 0.08 x   1   = $17.28

Step 4 Find the new principal after 2 years.

Old principal + Interest = New principal
$216.00   + $17.28   = $233.28

Rule of 72:

A general rule is that invested funds will double in value relative to the number of times the interest rate divides into 72. For example, an investment will double in value after 6 years if invested at 12%— 72 divided by 12. This is only an estimate.

Apply Your Skills

What is the future value of a $2,000 investment placed into an account for 2 years that earns a 10% interest rate, compounded annually?

$ _2420.00_

The process is repeated for additional periods. Remember that the interest is added to the principal from the previous period and that this increased principal is used in computing the interest for the next period. In another example, assume that $1,000 yields interest at a 10% rate compounded annually for 3 years.

Step 1 $1,000.00 x 0.10 x 1 = $100.00 (interest for first year)

Step 2 $1,000.00 + $100.00 = $1,100.00 (principal after first conversion)

Step 3 $1,100.00 x 0.10 = $110.00 (interest for second year)

Step 4 $1,100.00 + $110.00 = $1,210.00 (principal after second conversion)

Step 5 $1,210.00 x 0.10 = $121.00 (interest for third year)

Step 6 $1,210.00 + $121.00 = $1,331.00 (principal after third conversion)

The 3 years' compounded interest, computed by subtracting the final sum from the original principal, is $331.00 ($1,331.00 - $1,000). This compares to $300.00 computed using simple interest procedures.

MODEL 26.2

Computing simple interest

Problem: Rosie Howard borrowed $1,000.00 at a 10% simple interest rate for 3 years. What is the interest amount for the 3 years?

Solution: Principal x Rate x Time = Interest
$1,000 x 0.10 x 3 = $300

Apply Your Skills

What is the future value of an $8,750 investment that earns interest for 5 years at a 7% simple interest rate?

$ _____

Typical compound periods: daily, weekly, monthly, quarterly, and annually.

Here is the reason for the difference in simple and compound interest amounts. In compound interest, the principal plus interest is computed each period, resulting in a larger principal amount each period. Simple interest, however, uses only the original principal amount for the full time. The difference in this example is $31.00 ($331.00 - $300.00). As the time increases, the difference will become even greater.

Semiannual means that interest is compounded every 6 months.

The frequency of conversion is also an important factor. For example, assume that two investments, each with an original principal of $1,000, have interest rates of 12%. However, one investment has a conversion period semiannually (every 6 months), while the second investment has a conversion period quarterly (every 3 months). At the end of 1 year, the principal will be $1,123.60 for the first investment and $1,125.51 for the second investment, as computed in Models 26.3 and 26.4.

MODEL 26.3

A calculator or computer is very useful for computing compound interest. Most financial institutions use computers and related software programs.

Computing interest compounded semiannually

First Investment (Interest Compounded Semiannually for 1 Year)

Principal: $1,000   **Rate:** 12%   **Time:** 1 year

Step 1 $1,000.00 x 0.12 x 6 ÷ 12 = $60.00 } First 6 months
Step 2 $1,000.00 + $60.00 = $1,060.00
Step 3 $1,060.00 x 0.12 x 6 ÷ 12 = $63.60 } Second 6 months
Step 4 $1,060.00 + $63.60 = $1,123.60

Apply Your Skills

Brian Suboh made a $1,500 investment that paid a 6% interest rate, compounded semiannually. What was the future value of the investment after 18 months?

$ _1639.09_

Computing interest compounded quarterly

Second Investment (Interest Compounded Quarterly for 1 Year)

Principal: $1,000   **Rate:** 12%   **Time:** 1 year

Step 1	$1,000.00 x 0.12 x 3 ÷ 12 = $30.00	} First quarter
Step 2	$1,000.00 + $30.00 = $1,030.00	
Step 3	$1,030.00 x 0.12 x 3 ÷ 12 = $30.90	} Second quarter
Step 4	$1,030.00 + $30.90 = $1,060.90	
Step 5	$1,060.90 x 0.12 x 3 ÷ 12 = $31.827	} Third quarter
Step 6	$1,060.90 + $31.827 = $1,092.727	
Step 7	$1,092.727 x 0.12 x 3 ÷ 12 = $32.78181	} Fourth quarter
Step 8	$1,092.727 + $32.78181 = $1,125.50881	

Apply Your Skills

Darlene Elston made a $10,000 investment that paid an 8% interest rate, compounded quarterly. What was the value of the investment after 6 months?

twice (2)

$ _10,104.00_

Notice that the principal sum equals $1,125.51 (rounded) when interest is compounded quarterly and $1,123.60 (Model 26.3) when interest is compounded semiannually—a difference of $1.91. This illustrates that the more frequently interest is compounded, the higher the compound interest amount will be. Most financial institutions use computers to make the computation, which permits easy determination of interest even if it is compounded on a daily basis. However, individuals need to understand how compound interest is computed even if the computer or compound interest tables (explained in the next section) are used.

DETERMINING EFFECTIVE INTEREST RATE

The *effective rate* or true rate of interest is higher than the *nominal rate* due to the compounding of interest each period. The effective rate is computed by dividing the compound interest by the amount of the original principal.

MODEL 26.4

Quarterly means that interest is compounded 4 times a year.

Remember that time uses 1 year as a basis. Therefore, the time for 6 months is stated as 6 ÷ 12 and for a quarter is stated as 3 ÷ 12.

Use of computers has made daily compounding of interest practical.

Daily means that interest is compounded each day. Many loans use a 360-day year. Time for 1 day: 1/360.

Effective rate:
The true rate of interest.

MODEL 26.5

Compound interest ÷ Principal = Effective rate

Note: Basic percentage formula applies here.

Amount (Interest) ÷ Base (Principal) = Rate (Effective rate)

Determining effective rate of interest

Problem: A $1,000 investment pays 10% interest, compounded semiannually for 1 year. What is the effective rate of interest for the investment?

Solution: **Step 1** Find the compound amount (Figure 26.3).

Periods: 2   Rate: 5%   Table amount: 1.102 500

Compound amount = 1.1025 x $1,000 = $1,102.50

Step 2 Find the compound interest.

Compound amount	- Principal	=	Compound interest
$1,102.50	- $1,000	=	$102.50

Step 3 Find the effective rate.

Compound interest	÷ Principal	=	Effective rate
$102.50	÷ $1,000	=	10.25%

Apply Your Skills

JoAnn DeFriese made a $2,000 investment at City Bank, which paid an 8% interest rate, compounded quarterly. What was the effective annual rate of interest?

The effective rate is directly affected by the number of periods that interest is compounded—more periods means a higher effective rate. The amounts in Figure 26.2 illustrate the future value and effective rate of increase for a $1,000 investment at the end of 5 years with an 8% interest rate. This example highlights the importance of knowing exactly how often compounding occurs before making investments. Notice that a simple interest rate produces a lower amount compared to compound rates.

Periodic Compounding	Future Value	Effective Rate of Increase
Simple interest	$1,400.00	40.00%
Daily	$1,500.10	50.01%
Quarterly	$1,485.95	48.59%
Semiannually	$1,480.24	48.02%
Annually	$1,469.33	46.93%
Principal: $1,000	Period: 5 years	Nominal rate: 8%

Figure 26.2 Determining Future Value and Effective Increase Rates

You may now complete Performance Application 26.1.

TABLE METHOD FOR COMPUTING COMPOUND INTEREST

Computation of compound interest can be simplified by the use of tables. Financial institutions have tables that show the amount that $1.00 will equal at varying rates of interest for extended periods of time up to 100 years or more. The table in Figure 26.3 shows how $1.00 will increase for 1 to 30 periods at varying rates of interest from 2% to 10%. Remember that a table used by a financial institution will have smaller increments of interest rates and cover longer periods of time; however, the procedure is similar to the one described here.

Periods	2%	3%	4%	5%	6%	7%	8%	9%	10%	Periods
1	1.020 000	1.030 000	1.040 000	1.050 000	1.060 000	1.070 000	1.080 000	1.090 000	1.100 000	1
2	1.040 400	1.060 900	1.081 600	1.102 500	1.123 600	1.144 900	1.166 400	1.188 100	1.210 000	2
3	1.061 208	1.092 727	1.124 864	1.157 625	1.191 016	1.225 043	1.259 712	1.295 029	1.331 000	3
4	1.082 432	1.125 509	1.169 859	1.215 506	1.262 477	1.310 796	1.360 489	1.411 582	1.464 100	4
5	1.104 081	1.159 274	1.216 653	1.276 282	1.338 226	1.402 552	1.469 328	1.538 624	1.610 510	5
6	1.126 162	1.194 052	1.265 319	1.340 096	1.418 519	1.500 730	1.586 874	1.677 100	1.771 561	6
7	1.148 686	1.229 874	1.315 932	1.407 100	1.503 630	1.605 781	1.713 824	1.828 039	1.948 717	7
8	1.171 659	1.266 770	1.368 569	1.477 455	1.593 848	1.718 186	1.850 930	1.992 563	2.143 589	8
9	1.195 093	1.304 773	1.423 312	1.551 328	1.689 479	1.838 459	1.999 005	2.171 893	2.357 948	9
10	1.218 994	1.343 916	1.480 244	1.628 895	1.790 848	1.967 151	2.158 925	2.367 364	2.593 742	10
11	1.243 374	1.384 234	1.539 454	1.710 339	1.898 299	2.104 852	2.331 639	2.580 426	2.853 117	11
12	1.268 242	1.425 761	1.601 032	1.795 856	2.012 196	2.252 192	2.518 170	2.812 665	3.138 428	12
13	1.293 607	1.468 534	1.685 074	1.885 649	2.132 928	2.409 845	2.719 624	3.065 805	3.452 271	13
14	1.319 479	1.512 590	1.731 676	1.979 932	2.260 904	2.578 534	2.937 194	3.341 727	3.797 498	14
15	1.345 868	1.557 967	1.800 944	2.078 928	2.396 558	2.759 032	3.172 169	3.642 482	4.177 248	15
16	1.372 786	1.604 706	1.872 981	2.182 875	2.540 352	2.952 164	3.425 943	3.970 306	4.594 973	16
17	1.400 241	1.652 848	1.947 901	2.292 018	2.692 773	3.158 815	3.700 018	4.327 633	5.054 470	17
18	1.428 246	1.702 433	2.025 817	2.406 619	2.854 339	3.379 932	3.996 019	4.717 120	5.559 917	18
19	1.456 811	1.753 506	2.106 849	2.526 950	3.025 600	3.616 528	4.315 701	5.141 661	6.115 909	19
20	1.485 947	1.806 111	2.191 123	2.653 298	3.207 135	3.869 684	4.660 957	5.604 411	6.727 500	20
21	1.515 666	1.860 295	2.278 768	2.785 963	3.399 564	4.140 562	5.033 834	6.108 808	7.400 250	21
22	1.545 980	1.916 103	2.369 919	2.925 261	3.603 537	4.430 402	5.436 540	6.658 600	8.140 275	22
23	1.576 899	1.973 587	2.464 716	3.071 524	3.819 750	4.740 530	5.871 464	7.257 874	8.954 302	23
24	1.608 437	2.032 794	2.563 304	3.225 100	4.048 935	5.072 367	6.341 181	7.911 083	9.849 733	24
25	1.640 606	2.093 778	2.665 836	3.386 355	4.291 871	5.427 433	6.848 475	8.623 081	10.834 706	25
26	1.673 418	2.156 591	2.772 470	3.555 673	4.549 383	5.807 353	7.396 353	9.399 158	11.918 177	26
27	1.706 886	2.221 289	2.883 369	3.733 456	4.822 346	6.213 868	7.988 061	10.245 082	13.109 994	27
28	1.741 024	2.287 928	2.998 703	3.920 129	5.111 687	6.648 838	8.627 106	11.167 140	14.420 994	28
29	1.775 845	2.356 566	3.118 651	4.116 136	5.418 388	7.114 257	9.317 275	12.172 182	15.863 093	29
30	1.811 362	2.427 262	3.243 398	4.321 942	5.743 491	7.612 255	10.062 657	13.267 678	17.449 402	30

Figure 26.3 Compound Interest Table

Using an interest table to determine the compound amount:

1. Find the number of periods.

2. Find the amount under the appropriate percent column.

3. Multiply the amount by the principal.

An examination of the interest table shows that $1.00 will amount to $1.628895 if compounded for 10 periods at an interest rate of 5%. This is found by going vertically to find the period (10), then horizontally to find the amount under the 5% heading. In another example, $1.00 will increase to $4.660957 if left for 20 periods at a compound interest rate of 8%. As before, go vertically to 20 and then horizontally to the figure below the 8% heading to determine the amount ($4.660957).

To compute the amount that a specific figure will increase, simply multiply the figure from the table by the amount. For example, $500 will increase to $814.45 (rounded) if left for 10 periods at a compound interest rate of 5%. The figure for $1.00 ($1.628895) was located. Then the amount was multiplied by $500 ($500.00 x $1.628895).

To further test your knowledge, compute the amount that $850 will increase to in 12 periods at a compound interest rate of 9%, as shown in Model 26.6.

MODEL 26.6

*Table conversion example: A 5-year loan paying an 8% rate, compounded quarterly, would equal 20 periods and a 2% rate. Note: 4 x 5 = **20** and 8% ÷ 4 = **2%**. Therefore, the table value would be **1.485947**.*

To convert periods and rates to the table, multiply the number of years by the times per year that the amount is compounded and divide the interest rate by the number of times per year the amount is compounded.

Computing compounded value and compound interest

Problem: John Wilfong borrowed $850.00. Using the table method, if the amount is computed for 12 periods at 9% interest, what are the compounded value and compound interest for the loan?

Solution: **Step 1** Find the compounded value at the end of 12 periods.

Table value for

9%, 12 periods	x	Principal	=	Compounded value
$2.812665	x	$850.00	=	$2,390.77 (rounded)

Step 2 Find the amount of compound interest.

Compounded value	-	Original principal	=	Compound interest
$2,390.77	-	$850.00	=	$1,540.77

Apply Your Skills

Pauline Goodner invested $10,000 into a fund that paid 12% interest, compounded quarterly. What was the value of the investment after 7 years?

$ _____

Since interest rates are normally stated as annual rates, adjustments must be made if interest is computed for periods of time other than 1 year. For example, assume that interest is compounded quarterly (4 times per year) for 2 years at a 12% rate. The number of periods will be 8 (2 x 4), and the interest rate will be 3% each period (12 ÷ 4). Therefore, $1.00 compounded quarterly with a compound interest rate of 12% will increase to $1.266770. This is determined by going vertically to 8 in the table, then horizontally under the 3% heading.

Likewise, $1.00 will increase to $1.628895 if compounded semiannually at an interest rate of 10% for 5 years. Go vertically to period 10, then horizontally under the 5% heading. Using this same procedure, $350 will increase to $570.11 ($350.00 x $1.628895) under these same terms. Remember to adjust the number of periods and interest rate to fit the situation.

You may now complete Performance Application 26.2.

PERFORMANCE APPLICATION 26.1

1. Compute the compound interest for each of the following loans. (Round final answers to two decimal places.)

Loan	Compound Interest
$100.00 for 2 years at 6%, compounded annually	$ _12.36_
$1,400.00 for 2 years at 5%, compounded annually	$ _143.50_
$2,000.00 for 3 years at 10%, compounded annually	$ _662.00_
$1,000.00 for 18 months at 8%, compounded semiannually	$ _124.86_
$875.00 for 1 year at 12%, compounded semiannually	$ _108.15_
$1,000.00 for 9 months at 8%, compounded quarterly	$ _61.21_

(handwritten working)
1020
1040.40
1061.208

9207.50
983.15

1040
1081.60
1124.864

106.00
1470
2200
2420
2662

2. Carl Gallegos invested $5,000 into an account that pays 8% interest, compounded semiannually. At the end of 18 months, what are the (a) compound interest and (b) compounded amount?

(a) $ _616.32_
(b) $ _5616.32_

(handwritten working)
200
5200
208
5400
216.32

3. Sue Yoshida can earn $320.00 in interest by loaning $2,000.00 to a friend at 8% interest for 18 months. If the money is invested for 8 months at 8%, compounded semiannually, how much *more* will she earn with this investment than she would earn from the loan to her friend?

   $ _____

4. Jean Harlowe invested $4,000 for 2 years at 9% interest, compounded semiannually. What are the (a) compound interest and (b) compounded amount for this investment?

   (a) $ _368.10_

   (b) $ _4368.10_

   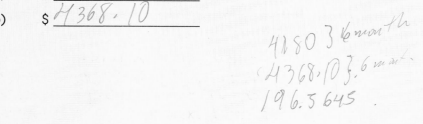

5. Loretta Spitzer invested $4,750.00 for 18 months at 8% interest, compounded semiannually. What will the compounded amount be after (a) 6 months, (b) 12 months, and (c) 18 months?

   (a) $ _4940_

   (b) $ _5137.60_

   (c) $ _5343.10_

PERFORMANCE APPLICATION 26.2

1. Use the compound interest table in Figure 26.3 to find the compounded amount and compound interest for each of the following loans. Round answers to two decimal places.

Loan	Compounded Amount	Compound Interest
$785.00 for 5 years at 7%, compounded annually	$ _____	$ _____
$658.00 for 14 years at 9%, compounded annually	$ _____	$ _____
$1,685.00 for 9 years at 10%, compounded semiannually	$ _____	$ _____
$1,260.00 for 10 years at 12%, compounded semiannually	$ _____	$ _____
$1,950.00 for 6 years at 12%, compounded quarterly	$ _____	$ _____
$1,650.00 for 5 years at 8%, compounded quarterly	$ _____	$ _____

2. George Stevens has an opportunity to invest $1,000 at 8% interest, compounded semiannually, or at 9%, compounded annually. Both terms are for 15 years. (a) Which investment will yield the most compound interest? (b) How much will the better investment earn in excess of the other investment?

   (a) _____

   (b) $ _____

3. Ronda Andes makes a $1,000 investment at the beginning of each year for 3 years. If interest is compounded semiannually at a 10% rate on each investment, how much will be available at the end of the third year?

   $ _____

4. The City National Bank pays 8% interest, compounded quarterly, to investors. If Inez Cortesi invests $3,200.00, how much will she have at the end of 5 1/2 years?

   $ _____

5. Harold Beaty invested $3,000 in a savings certificate when his daughter Rachel was born. If the certificate yields interest at 9%, compounded annually, how much will be available when Rachel is 18 years old?

   $ _____

6. Marcia Evans invested $1,000 into an account that paid an 8% interest rate, compounded quarterly. What was the effective interest rate?

   _____

PRACTICE TEST FOR CHAPTER 26
COMPUTING COMPOUND INTEREST

Complete each of the following problems and then compare your answers with the ones on page 651. Use tables in Chapter 26 as needed.

1. What is the future value for a $5,000 investment that earns a 10% interest rate, compounded annually, after 2 years?

   $ _____

2. Bill Woods invested $3,000 into an account that paid a 6% interest rate, compounded semiannually. LaVon Cofer invested $3,000 into an account that paid a 6% simple interest rate. How much greater than LaVon's will Bill's investment be after 2 years?

   $ _____

3. What is the future value of a $6,000 investment that pays a 5% interest rate, compounded quarterly, after 1 year?

   $ _____

4. Quenton Lane invested $10,000 into an account that pays an 8% interest rate, compounded quarterly. What is the future value of the account after 6 years?

   $ _____

5. Tommy Butler invested $10,000 into an account that pays an 8% interest rate, compounded semiannually. Duey Brackstone invested $10,000 into an account that pays an 8% interest rate, compounded quarterly. What was the effective interest rate for the investments made by (a) Mrs. Butler and (b) Mr. Brackstone?

   (a) _____

   (b) _____

26.1 The chart shown below indicates the average annual cost for a middle-income family to raise a child born in 1992 to the age of 17. Assume that instead of being used to raise a child, the funds were invested each year into an investment that paid an 8% interest rate, compounded annually. What would the (a) compound amount and (b) total interest be after 17 years? (Round each computation to two decimal places.)

(a) $ _____

(b) $ _____

A look at statistics that shape our lives

Raising the kids

Middle-income couples who had babies in 1992 will spend an average of $128,670 by the time the baby is 18. Average costs per year:

$6,810
$6,865
$7,540
$8,000

ages 0 – 5   6 – 11   12 – 14   15 – 17

Source: Family Economics Research Group of the U.S. Dept. of Agriculture
(Figures do not include college expenses)

By Nick Galifianakis, USA TODAY

26.2 The chart shown below indicates the average funeral costs in 1992. Assume that these costs will double by the year 2002. Approximately what amount would have to be invested into an account with an 8% interest rate, computed semiannually, in order to have the account grow to a future value in 10 years sufficient to cover the funeral costs for one person? (Hint: Use Figure 26.3 to find the desired amount.)

$ _____

A look at funeral costs

The federal government requires funeral homes to provide itemized lists of funeral costs. That helps families cut funeral costs by forgoing some services. Here's a list of average funeral costs in 1992:

Item	Cost
Casket (8-gauge steel, sealer, velvet interior)	$1,958
Concrete grave vault	$751
Staff costs, overhead	$716
Embalming	$263
Use of chapel for wake or memorial service	$201
Use of chapel for funeral service	$191
Hearse, local rates	$124
Limousine	$100
Transfer of remains to funeral home	$97
Makeup, hairstyling	$92
Total	**$4,493**

Source: National Funeral Directors Association

CONNECTIONS

DECISIONS

26.1 Laquita Johnson considered several investment opportunities for her $10,000 inheritance. Fund A offered an 8% interest rate, compounded quarterly. Fund B offered an 8.5% simple interest rate. Fund C offered an 8% interest rate, compounded semiannually. Which fund offered the highest return on her investment after 6 years?

_____ Fund A

_____ Fund B

_____ Fund C

26.2 Roscoe and Debbie Sankar have twin daughters who are 7 years old. They decided to invest $20,000 into a fund that paid a 10% interest rate, compounded semiannually. Their desire is to accumulate a $60,000 account balance by the time the daughters are 18 years old. (a) Will the investment provide the desired account balance? (b) If not, how much will the couple be short of their goal?

(a) _____ Yes

_____ No

(b) $ _____

COMPUTING COMPOUND INTEREST AND FUTURE VALUE
Chapter Review and Quick Reference

Topic	Main Point	Typical Example	Text Page
Compound interest (annually)	Interest is computed each period and then added to the principal. The updated principal is then used to determine interest for the next period. **Compound interest cycle each period:** P I = P x R x T P + I	Principal: $1,000 Rate: 8%, compounded annually for 2 years Interest = P x R x T Compound value = I + P **First year** $1,000 x 0.08 x 1 = **$80** $1,000 + $80 = **$1,080** **Second year** $1,080 x 0.08 x 1 = **$86.40** **Value after 2 years** $1,080 + $86.40 = **$1,166.40**	513
Simple interest	The initial principal is used for the length of the loan or investment. **Interest amount:** I = P x R x T **Value:** Value = Principal + Interest amount	Principal: $1,000 Rate: 8% simple interest I = P x R x T **Interest amount:** $1,000 x 0.08 x 2 = **$160** **Value after 2 years:** $1,000 + $160 = **$1,160**	514

Topic	Main Point	Typical Example	Text Page
Compound interest (quarterly)	The time is divided into a portion of a year—3÷12 for quarterly. The interest amount computed each period is added to the principal to compute an updated principal. This process is repeated until all computations for all periods have been completed.	Principal: $1,000 Rate: 8%, compounded quarterly. **First quarter:** $1,000 x 0.08 x 3 ÷ 12 = **$20** $1,000 + $20 = **$1,020** **Second quarter:** $1,020 x 0.08 x 3/12 = **$20.40** $1,020 + $20.40 = **$1,040.40**	515
Interest amount	The interest amount is the difference between the original principal and the compound value. Compound amount = Table value x Principal Compound interest = Compound amount - Original principal	A $1,000 investment at 8% compounded quarterly. Based on the data in Figure 26.3, the following computation is for 4 periods at a 2% interest rate. **Compound amount:** 1.082432 x $1,000 = **$1,082.43** **Compound interest:** $1,082.43 - $1,000 = **$82.43**	516

Topic	Main Point	Typical Example	Text Page
Effective rate	The effective rate is the true interest rate earned on the original principal. Effective rate= Compound interest ÷ Original principal	The compound interest computed above will be used here. **Effective rate:** $82.43 ÷ $1,000 = 0.08243 or **8.24%** (rounded)	516
Compound interest tables	Compound interest tables can be used to more easily compute compound interest. The table provides the future value of the loan or investment.	Principal: $1,000 Rate: 8%, compounded quarterly for 5 years Periods: 20 (5 x 4) Rate per period: 2% (8% ÷ 4) **Step 1** Find the number of periods in the left column: **20** **Step 2** Find the percent column: **2%** **Step 3** Multiply the value at the intersection by the principal 1.485947 x $1,000 = **$1,485.95** (rounded)	517

Chapter **27**

PRESENT VALUE AND ANNUITIES

Performance Objectives

1. Show how financial information can be used as a basis for planning and making decisions.
2. Use the present value table to determine the current worth of money to be received in the future.
3. Use the present value of an annuity table to determine the current worth of a series of periodic payments to be received in the future.
4. Use the amount of annuity at compound interest table to determine the future value of a series of periodic investments.
5. Use the sinking fund table to determine the periodic investment that must be made in order to accumulate a specified sum of money in the future.

Individuals and businesses use financial information as a basis for planning and making decisions. It helps them to answer questions such as these: Is the value of money likely to go up or down in the future? What amount must be paid periodically to retire a debt? How will periodic deposits accumulate over a period of time? Information such as this is essential for operating and budgeting. This chapter shows how this information is computed and provides specific ways in which it can be used.

COMPUTING PRESENT VALUE OF MONEY

Inflation, fluctuating interest rates, and other economic conditions make money received in the future worth less than it is today. For example, a dollar buys less today than a dollar bought 30 years ago. Likewise, a dollar will buy less in 30 years than it buys today. This process determines computed present value of money to be received at some future date. For example, $1.00 to be received in 3 years may have a computed present value of only $0.82.

The information shown in Figure 27.1 indicates the present value of $1,000 to be received at various times, assuming a 5% interest rate. For example, the present value of $1,000 is only $952.38 if received one year from now or $907.03 if received two years from now. Notice that longer periods of waiting to receive the money makes the present value lower. Procedures for making these computations are illustrated later in this chapter.

> **Present value:** The current value of a sum of money to be received some time in the future.
>
> Present value factors:
> 1. Number of periods
> 2. Interest rate
> 3. Amount

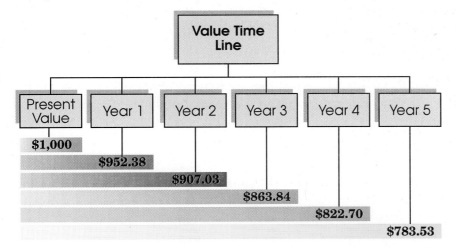

Figure 27.1 Present Value of $1,000

Most financial institutions use computers or tables to determine present value amounts. The table in Figure 27.2 shows the present value of $1.00 for 1 to 30 periods with percentages ranging from 2% to 10% in increments of 1%. For example, the present value of $1.00 to be received in 10 periods at a percentage of 5% is $0.613913. In the table, this is found by going vertically to period 10, then horizontally to under the 5% heading.

Periods	2%	3%	4%	5%	6%	7%	8%	9%	10%	Periods
1	0.980 392	0.970 874	0.961 538	0.952 381	0.943 396	0.934 580	0.925 926	0.917 431	0.909 091	1
2	0.961 169	0.942 596	0.924 556	0.907 029	0.889 996	0.873 439	0.857 339	0.841 680	0.826 446	2
3	0.942 322	0.915 142	0.888 996	0.863 838	0.839 619	0.816 298	0.793 832	0.772 183	0.751 315	3
4	0.923 845	0.888 487	0.854 804	0.822 702	0.792 094	0.762 895	0.735 030	0.708 425	0.683 013	4
5	0.905 731	0.862 609	0.821 927	0.783 526	0.747 258	0.712 986	0.680 583	0.649 931	0.620 921	5
6	0.887 971	0.837 484	0.790 315	0.746 215	0.704 961	0.666 342	0.630 170	0.596 267	0.564 474	6
7	0.870 560	0.813 092	0.759 918	0.710 681	0.665 057	0.622 750	0.583 490	0.547 034	0.513 158	7
8	0.853 490	0.789 409	0.730 690	0.676 839	0.627 412	0.582 009	0.540 269	0.501 866	0.466 507	8
9	0.836 755	0.766 417	0.702 587	0.644 609	0.591 898	0.543 934	0.500 249	0.460 428	0.424 098	9
10	0.820 348	0.744 094	0.675 564	0.613 913	0.558 395	0.508 349	0.463 193	0.422 411	0.385 543	10
11	0.804 263	0.722 421	0.649 581	0.584 679	0.526 788	0.475 093	0.428 883	0.387 533	0.350 494	11
12	0.788 493	0.701 380	0.624 597	0.556 837	0.496 969	0.444 012	0.397 114	0.355 535	0.318 631	12
13	0.773 033	0.680 951	0.600 574	0.530 321	0.468 839	0.414 964	0.367 698	0.326 179	0.289 664	13
14	0.757 875	0.661 118	0.577 475	0.505 068	0.442 301	0.387 817	0.340 461	0.299 246	0.263 331	14
15	0.743 015	0.641 862	0.555 265	0.481 017	0.417 265	0.362 446	0.315 242	0.274 538	0.239 392	15
16	0.728 446	0.623 167	0.533 908	0.458 112	0.393 646	0.338 735	0.291 890	0.251 870	0.217 629	16
17	0.714 163	0.605 016	0.513 373	0.436 297	0.371 364	0.316 574	0.270 269	0.231 073	0.197 845	17
18	0.700 159	0.587 395	0.493 628	0.415 521	0.350 344	0.295 864	0.250 249	0.211 994	0.179 859	18
19	0.686 431	0.570 286	0.474 642	0.395 734	0.330 513	0.276 508	0.231 712	0.194 490	0.163 508	19
20	0.672 971	0.553 676	0.456 387	0.376 889	0.311 805	0.258 419	0.214 548	0.178 431	0.148 644	20
21	0.659 776	0.537 549	0.438 834	0.358 942	0.294 155	0.241 513	0.198 656	0.163 698	0.135 131	21
22	0.646 839	0.521 893	0.421 955	0.341 850	0.277 505	0.225 713	0.183 941	0.150 182	0.122 846	22
23	0.634 156	0.506 692	0.405 726	0.325 571	0.261 797	0.210 947	0.170 315	0.137 781	0.111 678	23
24	0.621 721	0.491 934	0.390 121	0.310 068	0.246 979	0.197 147	0.157 699	0.126 405	0.101 526	24
25	0.609 531	0.477 606	0.375 117	0.295 303	0.232 999	0.184 249	0.146 018	0.115 968	0.092 296	25
26	0.597 579	0.463 695	0.360 689	0.281 241	0.219 810	0.172 195	0.135 202	0.106 393	0.083 905	26
27	0.585 862	0.450 189	0.346 817	0.267 848	0.207 368	0.160 930	0.125 187	0.097 608	0.076 278	27
28	0.574 375	0.437 077	0.333 477	0.255 094	0.195 630	0.150 402	0.115 914	0.089 548	0.069 343	28
29	0.563 112	0.424 346	0.320 651	0.242 946	0.184 557	0.140 563	0.107 328	0.082 155	0.063 039	29
30	0.552 071	0.411 987	0.308 319	0.231 377	0.174 110	0.131 367	0.099 377	0.075 371	0.957 309	30

Figure 27.2 Present Value of $1.00 Table

The present value under the same conditions can be found by multiplying $0.613913 by $500 ($0.613913 x $500.00 = $306.96). This is interpreted to mean that $500 to be received in 10 years with an interest rate of 5%, compounded annually, has a present value of $306.96. Determination of proceeds when compound interest is to be computed in a period less than 1 year requires an adjustment. In this example, semiannual interest computation for 10 years will require 20 periods (every 6 months for 10 years) and an interest rate of 2½% (one-half the annual rate since interest is computed at 6-month intervals). Interest compounded quarterly under the same conditions results in using 40 periods and an interest rate of 1¼%.

To prove your answer, consider the following example: Mary Jane Collins will receive $300 in 5 years with a 6% compound interest rate (compounded annually). To determine the present value, multiply $300 by $0.747258 ($300.00 x $0.747258 = $224.1774 rounded to $224.18). To prove this answer, use the value of $1.00 in the compound interest table in Chapter 26. The horizontal value across from 5 periods and under the 6% heading is $1.338226. Multiply this value by $224.18 ($224.18 x $1.338226) to yield a value of $300.00 (rounded). This shows the close relationship between future value and present value. In other words, $224.18 has a future value of $300.00 (5 periods and a compound interest rate of 6%), and $300.00 (due in

5 periods and a compound interest rate of 6%) has a present value of $224.18. Computation of present value using the present value of $1.00 table is illustrated in Model 27.1.

Computing present value

Problem: Francis Hertz is scheduled to receive the sum of $800 in three years. Assuming that the interest rate is 8%, what is the value of the sum today?

Solution: **Step 1** Locate the number of periods (see Figure 27.2) in the present value of $1.00 table (**3**).

Step 2 Move across the table horizontally to the column headed by 8% (**0.793 832**).

Step 3 Multiply the table value by the amount to be received as follows:

Table value x Future amount = Present value
0.793832   x $800   = $635.07

- -

Apply Your Skills

Norfleet Turner is scheduled to receive $1,500 in 10 years. Assume a 6% interest rate. What is the present value of the $1,500?

$ _____

MODEL 27.1

Compound discount: *The difference between present and future values.*

The difference between present and future values is the interest earned, called *compound discount.*

You may now complete Performance Application 27.1.

COMPUTING PRESENT VALUE OF AN ANNUITY

Discussion in the previous section related to a single amount that was invested today in order to receive an amount of money at some time in the future. The present value of a future amount was computed. *Annuity* indicates a series of investments made at regular intervals. For example, what single sum must be invested today in order to earn a specified annuity in the future?

Remember that an annuity is a series of regular payments. If $1.00 is to be received in 1 year, what single sum must be invested? If $1.00 is needed at the end of each of the next 2 years, what single sum must be invested? To illustrate this procedure, assume that $1.00 is desired at the end of each of the next 3 years. The present value of $1.00 table can be used to compute the present value assuming a 6% compound interest rate for each of these three $1.00 amounts, as shown in Figure 27.3.

Annuity: *A series of payments over a period of time.*

Remember that annuity indicates a series of payments or investments.

Present value of $1.00 in 3 periods	$0.839619
Present value of $1.00 in 2 periods	$0.889996
Present value of $1.00 in 1 period	$0.943396
Total needed to receive $1.00 for each of the next 3 periods	$2.673011

Figure 27.3 Computing Present Value of an Annuity

Figure 27.3 shows that $2.673011 invested today will provide an annuity of $1.00 for each of the next 3 periods. As shown above, the present value of each $1.00 receipt was computed separately using the present value of $1.00 table. A separate table, the present value of an annuity of $1.00, shown in Figure 27.4, can provide this figure more easily. Go vertically to period 3, then horizontally to under the 6% heading. This amount ($2.673012) is the same amount shown above in Figure 27.3 (with a slight difference due to rounding). Use of this table makes it easier to compute the present value of annuities.

Periods	2%	3%	4%	5%	6%	8%	10%	Periods
1	0.980392	0.970874	0.961539	0.952381	0.943396	0.925926	0.909091	1
2	1.941561	1.913470	1.886095	1.859410	1.183393	1.783265	1.735537	2
3	2.883883	2.828611	2.775091	2.723248	2.673012	2.577097	2.486852	3
4	3.807729	3.717098	3.629895	3.545951	3.465106	3.312127	3.169865	4
5	4.713460	4.579707	4.451822	4.329477	4.212364	3.992710	3.790787	5
6	5.601431	5.417191	5.242137	5.075692	4.917324	4.622880	4.355261	6
7	6.471991	6.230283	6.002055	5.786373	5.582381	5.206370	4.868419	7
8	7.325481	7.019692	6.732745	6.463213	6.209794	5.746639	5.334926	8
9	8.162237	7.786109	7.435332	7.107822	6.801692	6.246888	5.759024	9
10	8.982585	8.530203	8.110896	7.721735	7.360087	6.710081	6.144567	10
11	9.786848	9.252624	8.760477	8.306414	7.886875	7.138964	6.495061	11
12	10.575341	9.954004	9.385074	8.863252	8.383844	7.536078	6.813692	12
13	11.348374	10.634955	9.985648	9.393573	8.852683	7.903776	7.103356	13
14	12.106249	11.296073	10.563123	9.898641	9.294984	8.244237	7.366687	14
15	12.849264	11.937935	11.118387	10.379658	9.712249	8.559479	7.606080	15
16	13.577709	12.561102	11.652296	10.837770	10.105895	8.851369	7.823709	16
17	14.291872	13.166119	12.165669	11.274066	10.477260	9.121638	8.021553	17
18	14.992031	13.753513	12.659297	11.689587	10.827603	9.371887	8.201412	18
19	15.678462	14.323799	13.133939	12.085321	11.158116	9.603599	8.364920	19
20	16.351433	14.877475	13.590326	12.462210	11.469921	9.818147	8.513564	20

Figure 27.4 Present Value of an Annuity of $1.00 Table

Present value of an annuity

Problem: An annuity of $200 is desired for each of the next 10 years. The interest rate is 5%. What investment is needed today to provide the desired annuity?

Solution: **Step 1** Find the number of periods **(10)**.

Step 2 Move horizontally under the column headed by 5% to locate the table value **(7.721735)**.

Step 3 Multiply the table value by the annuity amount to compute the investment needed (present value).

Table value x   Annuity amount = Present value
7.721735   x $200   = $1,544.35

Apply Your Skills

Marsha Dudenbostel decided to invest sufficient funds in order for her son to receive $300 per quarter for the next 5 years. The compound interest rate is 12%. What investment will be needed?

$ _____

For another example, assume that Danny Nash desires to receive $200 per quarter for the next 5 years. If the compound interest rate is 12%, the single sum that must be invested today is $2,975.495 ($200.00 x $14.877475). This rounds to $2,975.50.

You may now complete Performance Application 27.2.

COMPUTING ANNUITY INVESTMENTS

Investors often place a regular amount into an account. When the amount is deposited, it immediately begins to earn interest and earns compound interest for the duration of the annuity. The table in Figure 27.5 shows how periodic deposits will accumulate over a period of time.

Number of Interest Periods	2%	3%	4%	6%	8%
1	1.020000	1.030000	1.040000	1.060000	1.080000
2	2.060400	2.090900	2.121600	2.183600	2.246400
3	3.122608	3.183627	3.246464	3.374616	3.506112
4	4.204040	4.309136	4.416323	4.637093	4.866601
5	5.308121	5.468410	5.632976	5.975319	6.335929
6	6.434283	6.662462	6.898295	7.393838	7.922803
7	7.582969	7.892336	8.214226	8.897468	9.636628
8	8.754628	9.159106	9.582795	10.491316	11.487558
9	9.949721	10.463879	11.006107	12.180795	13.486563
10	11.168715	11.807796	12.486351	13.971643	15.645488
11	12.412090	13.192030	14.025806	15.869941	17.977127
12	13.680331	14.617790	15.626838	17.882138	20.495297
13	14.973938	16.086324	17.291911	20.015066	23.214920
14	16.293417	17.598914	19.913588	22.275970	26.152114
15	17.639285	19.156881	20.824531	24.672528	29.324283
16	19.012071	20.761588	22.697512	27.212880	32.750226
17	20.412312	22.414435	24.645413	29.905653	36.450244
18	21.840559	24.116868	26.671229	32.759992	40.446263
19	23.297370	25.870375	28.778079	35.785591	44.761964
20	24.783317	27.676486	30.969202	38.992727	49.422921
25	32.670906	37.553042	43.311745	58.156383	78.954415
30	41.379441	49.002678	58.328335	83.801677	122.345868
40	61.610023	77.663298	98.826536	164.047684	279.781040
50	86.270990	116.180773	158.773767	307.756059	619.671768
60	116.332570	167.945040	247.510313	565.115872	1353.470359
70	152.977469	237.511886	379.862077	1026.008100	2937.686480
80	197.647397	331.003909	573.294776	1852.395885	6357.890263
90	252.099789	456.649371	861.102667	3329.539698	13741.853705
100	318.476951	625.506362	1287.128653	5976.670142	29682.276961

Figure 27.5 Amount of Annuity of $1.00 at Compound Interest Table

As an example, Ramone Ruiz decides to invest $500 per year into an annuity that pays 6% compound interest. To compute the amount in the fund after 10 years, go vertically to period 10 then horizontally to the 6% heading. Multiply the figure at the intersection by $500 to compute the value of the annuity after 10 years, as shown in Model 27.3.

This table assumes investments at the **beginning** of each period.

MODEL 27.3

The value **13.971643** is found in the table on row 10, column 5.

An annuity can indicate that a lump sum has been invested in order to provide a series of income payments in the future. Also, a series of investments can be deposited to provide a specific lump sum on a future date.

Computing value of annuity

Problem: Ramone Ruiz invests $500 per year into an annuity that pays 6% compounded interest. What is the value of the annuity after 10 years?

Solution:

Periodic investment	x	Table value	=	Annuity value
$500	x	$13.971643	=	$6,985.82 (rounded)

Apply Your Skills

Brandon Hall decided to deposit $60 per quarter for 15 years into an annuity at 12% compound interest for his son's education. At the end of 15 years, how much will Brandon have available for his son's education?

$ _____

The chart shown below indicates the difference between amount invested and the value of the annuity.

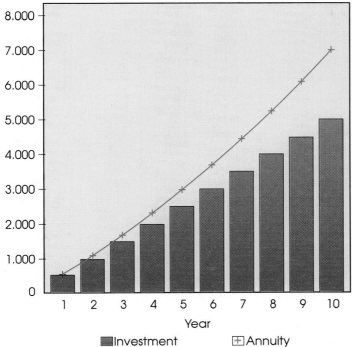

Figure 27.6 Value of an Annuity Investment

COMPUTING SINKING FUND AMOUNTS

A *sinking fund* involves the systematic accumulation of funds by investing a certain sum of money at the end of each period. A sinking fund differs from an annuity in two ways. First, deposits are made into a sinking fund at the end of each period, whereas deposits are made into an annuity at the beginning of each period. Therefore, interest is earned during the first period for an annuity investment. Secondly, in a sinking fund the accumulated amount is known, but the periodic deposit must be computed. With an annuity the periodic deposit is known, but the final accumulated amount must be computed.

A business may use a sinking fund to determine periodic amounts needed to pay off a bond issue in 15, 20, or 30 years. Other typical uses of a sinking fund are to determine periodic amounts needed to replace a building in 50 years, to replace a piece of equipment in 15 years, or to have a specific pension fund reserve available by a specified date. The sinking fund table in Figure 27.7 can be used to make computations for sinking funds in this chapter.

Sinking fund:
Accumulation of funds by investing funds at the end of each period.

The sinking fund table indicates the periodic investment that must be made in order to accumulate a certain sum of money at the end of the term.

Annuity That Amounts to $1 at Compound Interest (Sinking Fund Table)					
Number of Periods	2%	3%	4%	6%	8%
1	1.000000	1.000000	1.000000	1.000000	1.000000
2	0.495050	0.492611	0.490196	0.485437	0.480769
3	0.326755	0.323530	0.320349	0.314110	0.308034
4	0.242624	0.239027	0.235490	0.228592	0.221921
5	0.192158	0.188355	0.184627	0.177396	0.170457
6	0.158526	0.154598	0.150762	0.143363	0.136315
7	0.134512	0.130506	0.126610	0.119135	0.112072
8	0.116590	0.112456	0.108528	0.101036	0.094015
9	0.102515	0.098434	0.094493	0.087022	0.080080
10	0.091327	0.087231	0.083291	0.075868	0.069030
11	0.082178	0.078078	0.074149	0.066793	0.060076
12	0.074560	0.070462	0.067552	0.059277	0.052695
13	0.068118	0.067030	0.060144	0.052960	0.046522
14	0.062602	0.058526	0.054670	0.047585	0.041297
15	0.057826	0.053767	0.049941	0.042963	0.036830
16	0.053650	0.049611	0.045820	0.038952	0.032977
17	0.049970	0.045953	0.042199	0.035445	0.029629
18	0.046702	0.042709	0.038993	0.032357	0.026702
19	0.043782	0.039814	0.036139	0.029621	0.024128
20	0.041157	0.037216	0.033582	0.027185	0.021852
25	0.031220	0.027428	0.024012	0.018227	0.013679
30	0.024650	0.021019	0.017830	0.012649	0.008827
40	0.016556	0.013262	0.010524	0.006462	0.003860
50	0.011823	0.008866	0.006550	0.003444	0.001743
60	0.008768	0.006133	0.004202	0.001876	0.000798
70	0.006668	0.004337	0.002745	0.001033	0.000368
80	0.005161	0.003112	0.001814	0.000573	0.000170
90	0.004046	0.002256	0.001208	0.000318	0.000079
100	0.003203	0.001647	0.000808	0.000177	0.000036

Figure 27.7 Sinking Fund Table

The Richards Manufacturing Company purchased a piece of equipment with an estimated life of 10 years and an estimated replacement cost of $18,500. The company decided to make annual deposits into a sinking fund with a compound interest rate of 8%. To compute the amount of periodic deposit needed, go vertically to period 10, then horizontally to under the 8% heading. The figure at the intersection is multiplied by $18,500 to compute the periodic deposits needed, as shown in Model 27.4.

MODEL 27.4

Computing sinking fund amounts

Problem: The Richards Manufacturing Company needs to know the amount that should be deposited annually into a sinking fund for 10 years, at 8% interest, to accumulate $18,500. What amount should be deposited annually?

Solution: Amount to accumulate x Table value =   Deposit needed

$18,500   x $0.069030 = $1,277.06 (rounded)

Apply Your Skills

Tower Broadcasting Company purchased a building under an agreement that requires a $100,000 payment at the end of 15 years. The assumed interest rate is 4%. What annual amount must be deposited in order to assure that the $100,000 payment will be available at the end of 15 years?

$ _____

In a second example, Central Church has a $15,000 bond issue due in 15 years. To compute the semiannual deposits into a 12% compound interest sinking fund needed to pay off the issue, multiply the figure obtained from the sinking fund table by $15,000 ($15,000.00 x 0.012649 = $189.74). Therefore, the church will make a $189.74 deposit at the end of each 6-month period in order to have funds available at the end of 15 years to pay off the bond issue.

SUMMARY OF TABLES

Typical tables for present value, future value, annuity, and sinking fund investments are presented in this chapter. The appropriate table for each application must be selected. The following general overview of the purpose of each table is given as a reference and review.

1. *Amount of $1.00 at compound interest:* This table shows what $1.00 invested today will amount to in the future.

2. *Present value of $1.00 at compound interest:* This table shows what must be invested today to have $1.00 in the future. Stated a different way, the table shows what $1.00 to be received in the future is worth today.

3. *Amount of annuity of $1.00 at compound interest:* This table shows how periodic deposits will accumulate over a period of time.

4. *Annuity that amounts to $1.00 at compound interest:* This table is also called a sinking fund table. This table shows what must be deposited periodically over a specified period of time to amount to $1.00.

You may now complete Performance Application 27.3.

With a sinking fund, you know the amount you desire to accumulate. Then you determine the periodic investment needed to reach the desired amount.

PERFORMANCE APPLICATION 27.1

1. Waldo Breckheimer can have access to $600 in 10 years. If money is worth 6%, compounded annually, how much is the amount worth today?

   $ _____

2. Cheryl Hawks will receive an inheritance of $8,500.00 in 13 years. If money is worth 5%, compounded annually, how much is the amount worth today?

   $ _____

3. Clyde Holder holds a non-interest-bearing note that will be due in 7 years. If money is worth 9%, compounded annually, how much is the amount worth today if the face value is $750.00?

   $ _____

4. Elizabeth Bottoms is due to receive a bonus of $2,500 in 3 years. If money is worth 10%, compounded semiannually, how much is the bonus worth in today's value?

   $ _____

5. Carol Moduar is scheduled to receive $7,850 in 6 years. If money is worth 8%, compounded quarterly, how much is the amount worth today?

   $ _____

6. Billy Braden's Body Shop did a job for $360 due in 6 months. If money is worth 12%, compounded annually, how much is the bill worth today?

   $ _____

7. Opal Venne is offered $2,800 today or $3,000 in 5 years. If money is worth 8%, compounded annually, (a) which choice should be made and (b) what is the difference in present value of the two amounts?

   (a) $ _____

   (b) $ _____

8. Stephen Trombley is given an option of paying $6,800 today or $7,300 in 3 years. If money is worth 7%, compounded annually, (a) which choice will result in the lower present value and (b) what is the difference in present value of the two amounts?

   (a) $ _____

   (b) $ _____

9. Franz Viertbauer will receive $840 in 36 months. If money is worth 6%, compounded annually, how much is (a) the amount today and (b) the amount of compound interest?

   (a) $ _____

   (b) $ _____

10. Montie Walker loans a friend $600 for 1 year with no interest charge. If money is worth 8%, compounded annually, (a) How much less than the $600 loaned today is the present value of the money to be received in 1 year? (b) Why will Montie receive less in real terms even though the full $600 loan is repaid?

   (a) $ _____

   (b) _____

PERFORMANCE APPLICATION 27.2

1. Compute the present value of each of the following annuities. Use the tables in the text of this chapter, as needed, to compute the answers.

Annuity	Present Value
$300.00 every 3 months for 4 years at 8%, compounded quarterly	$_____
$100.00 every 6 months for 5 years at 12%, compounded every 6 months	$_____
$680.00 every 3 months for 5 years at 12%, compounded quarterly	$_____
$3,600.00 each year for 20 years at 6%, compounded annually	$_____
$3,800.00 every 6 months for 9 years at 8%, compounded semiannually	$_____
$2,700.00 every 6 months for 7 years at 10%, compounded semiannually	$_____

2. Lynn Mitchell will enter college next year. Her estimated annual costs are $7,800 per year for 4 years. Lynn works in a department store to pay half of her expenses. How much must her parents invest if Lynn is to receive the remainder in four equal amounts each year and the interest is compounded quarterly at a rate of 8%?

    $ _____

3. Andy Hall desires to provide his daughter Sandy an income of $3,500 every 3 months for 4 years. If the prevailing interest rate is 8%, compounded quarterly, what amount must be invested?

    $ _____

4. David Guthrie purchased a small business from Linwood Heilberg under an agreement that the seller was to receive $6,500 every 6 months for 8 years. If money is worth 8%, compounded semiannually, what amount must David invest to provide the income for the seller?

$ _____

5. Porter Hart signs a professional football contract. As a signing bonus, he is given an option of $80,000 cash now or a bonus of $7,000 per year for 13 years. If money is worth 8%, compounded annually, (a) Which offer is better? (b) How much difference in present value terms is there between the two options?

(a) $ _____

(b) $ _____

PERFORMANCE APPLICATION 27.3

1. Robert and Linda Hendrix placed $200 each quarter into an account earning 8% interest, compounded quarterly, when their son Bryant was born. When Bryant is 5 years old, (a) what amount will be in the account and (b) what amount of interest will have been earned?

   (a) $ _____

   (b) $ _____

2. The Bellbrook Electric Service placed $6,000 each year into an account earning 8% interest, compounded annually, to provide funds for machinery replacement in 14 years. (a) What amount will be in the fund in 14 years? (b) How much of this amount will represent interest earned?

   (a) $ _____

   (b) $ _____

3. The Max Line Furniture Center decided to set aside $3,000 every 6 months to provide donation funds for a youth community center scheduled to open in 3 years. If money is worth 12%, compounded semiannually, how much will be available for donation to the youth center in 3 years?

   $ _____

4. The Chickasaw Lumber Company invested $6,200 each year for the past 9 years into an account paying 8% interest, compounded annually. The purpose of the account was to have funds available to purchase an adjoining lot. Today, the lot is available for a cash price of $93,250.00. (a) What amount is currently in the fund? (b) What amount of additional money will be needed to purchase the lot?

   (a) $ _____

   (b) $ _____

5. The Youth Clubs of America issued $80,000 worth of 11-year non-interest-bearing bonds. What amount must be set aside at the end of each year in order to retire the bonds when they become due? Assume that money placed in the sinking fund draws interest at 6%, compounded annually.

$ _____

6. United Teleconferencing Services plans to purchase additional satellite connections that are available for $2,600,000 with 50% due immediately and the balance due in 10 years. A provision is added that a reduction amounting to $100,000 will be provided if the loan is paid within 6 years. (a) If money is worth 6%, compounded annually, how much must be placed in a sinking fund each year to retire the loan in 10 years? (b) If money is worth 8%, compounded annually, how much must be placed in a sinking fund each year to retire the loan in 6 years?

(a) $ _____

(b) $ _____

7. Creative Hair Styles plans to replace all of its equipment in 5 years. The estimated replacement cost is $46,500. If money is worth 8%, compounded quarterly, how much must be placed into a sinking fund each quarter in order to have sufficient funds to replace the equipment?

$ _____

8. The Gossett Custom Auto Shop will need $95,000 in an employees' pension fund in 3 1/2 years. If money is worth 6%, compounded semiannually, how much must be invested into a sinking fund each 6 months in order to have the necessary funds available?

$ _____

PRACTICE TEST FOR CHAPTER 27
PRESENT VALUE AND ANNUITIES

Complete each of the following problems and then compare your answers with the ones on page 651.

1. Don Montesi is scheduled to receive the sum of $12,000 in 18 years. Assume an 8% annual interest rate. What is the value of the sum today?

   $ _____

2. Brad Smith decided to make an investment that will pay a $500 annuity every 6 months for the next 8 years. Assume a 10% annual interest rate. What investment must Brad make to provide the desired annuity?

   $ _____

3. Thomas McInnish began investing $2,000 each year into an annuity 20 years ago. Assume a 6% interest rate. What is the value of the annuity investment after 20 years?

   $ _____

4. First Church has a $90,000 bond issue that must be retired in 20 years. Assume a 6% interest rate. What annual amount must be deposited in order to have sufficient funds to retire the bond issue?

   $ _____

5. Jerry Mathis is given an opportunity to receive $40,000 today or $50,000 in 5 years. Assume a 7% interest rate. Which opportunity has the highest worth relative to today's value?

   _____ $40,000 today   _____ $50,000 in 5 years

CONNECTIONS

27.1 Four years ago, Hugh Posnack began investing $1,200 per quarter into an annuity at a compound interest, annual rate of 8%, compounded quarterly. How much additional funding does Hugh need in order to purchase the automobile, based on the price indicated?

$ _____

#M7827 $25,388

27.2 The table shown below indicates a recommended amount that persons in various categories should have saved in order to retire without a decrease in their standard of living. Bernard and Carol Rabafais have $200,000 annual earnings and are 65 years old. The couple has worked for 30 years. In order to accumulate the amount indicated in the table for persons in their category, what annual amount should have been invested each working year? Assume a 6% annual interest rate.

$ _____

HOW MUCH SHOULD YOU HAVE SAVED?

The minimum needed besides Social Security and a company pension to retire at 65

By age	35	45	55	65
Married couple earning $200,000	$100,100	$321,500	$727,200	$1,273,700
Single man earning $50,000	$6,330	$36,110	$95,700	$172,210
Single woman earning $50,000	$35,650	$72,850	$126,800	$189,960

FORTUNE TABLE / SOURCE: B. DOUGLAS BERNHEIM FOR MERRILL

CONNECTIONS

27.1 Phillip and Bernice Raffel have one child, a son. The couple decided to begin an annuity fund when their son was 3 years old in order to provide for his college education. The couple estimated that a college education would cost $98,000. The couple invested $750 every 3 months into an annuity that had an 8% annual interest rate, compounded quarterly. (a) Will sufficient funds be available for the college education when their son is 18 years old? (b) If not, how much will the fund be short of the amount needed?

(a) _____ Yes   _____ No

(b) $ _____

27.2 Catherine Smith, owner of Paramount Delivery Service, believes that her fleet of trucks will need replacing in 5 years for an estimated $80,000. She decided to deposit $7,000 every 6 months into a sinking fund in order to have sufficient funds to replace the trucks. Assume a 6% annual interest rate. (a) Will Catherine have sufficient funds available to replace the trucks? (b) What was the minimum deposit needed in order to have sufficient funds to replace the trucks?

(a) _____ Yes   _____ No

(b) $ _____

DECISIONS

PRESENT VALUE AND ANNUITIES
Chapter Review and Quick Reference

Topic	Main Point	Typical Example	Text Page
Use of tables	Tables are often used to determine amounts relating to present value and annuities.	**Procedures** 1. Find the row containing the number of periods on the left. 2. Find the column containing the interest rate. 3. Multiply the value at the intersection of the row and column by the amount.	532
Present value of a sum of money	Use the **present value of $1.00 table** to determine the present value of a sum to be received in the future.	What is the present value of $500 to be received in 10 years if the interest rate is 5%? Table value x Amount = Present value .613913 x $500 = **$306.96**	533
Present value of an annuity	Use the **present value of an annuity of $1.00 table** to determine the series of payments to expect from an investment today.	$500 is desired for each of the next 10 years. What investment is necessary to provide $500 each year for 10 years if the interest rate is 5%? Table value x Amount = Needed investment 7.721735 x $500 = **$3,860.87**	534

Topic	Main Point	Typical Example	Text Page
Annuity investments	Use the **amount of annuity of $1.00 at compound interest table** to determine the future value of a series of investments.	$500 is invested each year for 10 years. What will the future worth of $500 invested each year for 10 years be if the interest rate is 6%? Table value x Amount = Future worth 13.971643 x $500 = **$6,985.82**	536
Sinking fund	Use the **sinking fund table** to determine the amount of each of a series of payments needed to accumulate a sum of money.	$5,000 is needed in 10 years. What amount is needed each year to accumulate $5,000 if the interest rate is 6%? Table value x Amount = Series value .075868 x $5,000 = **$379.34**	538
Payments or investments made at intervals of less than 1 year	1. Multiply the number of years by the number of times per year to determine the total number of periods. 2. Divide the annual interest rate by the number of times per year to determine the periodic interest rate.	An amount is invested quarterly for 10 years at a 12% interest rate. Periods = 4 x 10 = **40** Interest rate = 12 ÷ 4 = **3** Then use the table in the normal manner: 40 periods and a 3% interest rate.	532

Chapter *28*

|NSURANCE

Performance Objectives

1. Define terms relating to various types of insurance coverage: life, property, and automobile.
2. Compute insurance premiums for various coverages.
3. Compute cash surrender value for life insurance coverage.
4. Compute recovery amounts for property damage.
5. Compute insurance premiums for automobile insurance.

Have you ever wondered who pays for losses due to an earthquake, fire, flood, or accident? Unexpected events can cause financial loss to a business or individual. Possibilities of fire, burglaries, car accidents, deaths, health problems, and damage to goods being shipped are typical purposes for which businesses and/or individuals often purchase insurance. *Insurance* provides protection against losses when these or similar events occur. Within legal guidelines, insurance companies set *premiums* to be charged for providing this protection. A *policy* outlines items covered and the amount of coverage provided under certain specified conditions. Typical computations relating to life and property (fire) insurance are presented in this chapter.

LIFE INSURANCE

Life insurance is designed to provide financial support for the person designated as beneficiary in the policy when the insured person dies. The beneficiary is often a family member who may be left in a weak financial condition if the policyholder dies unexpectedly. In some instances, companies purchase life insurance to provide protection in the event that a valuable executive dies.

There are several different types of life insurance coverage, as illustrated in Figure 28.1. The most common types are term, straight life (also called *whole life* or *ordinary life*), limited payment life, and endowment. With all insurance policies, the premium amounts are based on the amount of the face value, age of the insured person, and type of coverage.

Term insurance is in effect for a specified period of time, such as 5 years. Unless the insured person dies within the term of the policy coverage, the beneficiary receives nothing and the protection ends. This type of policy usually pays the greatest benefits for the lowest premiums.

Straight life provides protection throughout the insured person's life, as long as premiums continue to be paid.

Limited payment life policies require that premiums be paid only for a limited number of years or until the insured person reaches a certain age, such as 65 years. Insurance is then provided (often at a reduced face value) for the remainder of the life of the insured.

Endowment life provides protection for a specified number of years. At the end of this time, the insured person can usually have the option of receiving a specified amount of cash or lifetime periodic income payments from the insurance company.

*A **policy** is a written contract that describes types and amounts of coverage provided.*

***Term insurance** is the least expensive type of insurance coverage, but must be renewed or dropped at the end of the period.*

***Term insurance** covers a specified period of time, such as 3 years.*

***Limited payment life** provides permanent life coverage.*

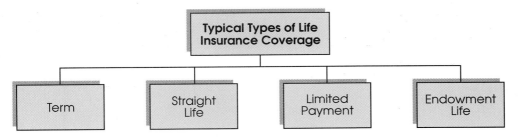

Figure 28.1 Common Types of Life Insurance Coverage

COMPUTING PREMIUMS

The amount charged for premiums varies from company to company and depends on factors such as the age, sex, and health of the insured person. The table in Figure 28.2 shows typical annual premiums for persons in various age groups with straight life, 20-payment life, 20-year endowment, and 10-year term policies.

Age	Straight Life Premium	20-Payment Life Premium	20-Year Endowment Premium	10-Year Term Premium
21	$13.65	$28.70	$45.13	$4.20
22	13.95	29.20	45.28	4.24
23	14.27	29.72	45.44	4.26
24	14.65	30.27	45.63	4.30
25	15.03	30.83	45.83	4.35

Figure 28.2 Annual Premiums for $1,000 Life Insurance Policy

Notes: (a) Multiply the annual rate by 54% for semiannual premiums.
           (b) Multiply the annual rate by 28% for quarterly premiums.

A comparison of premiums for different types of coverage for a person 25 years old is shown in Figure 28.3.

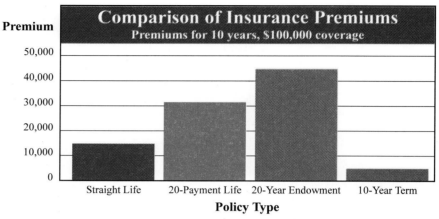

Taken at Age 25

Figure 28.3 Comparison of Insurance Premiums

To compute the premium due, as shown in Model 28.1, find the age category for the insured person and then multiply the premium for the type of policy desired by the number of thousands of dollars in coverage needed (Rate X Base = Amount).

MODEL 28.1

Computing insurance premium

Problem: Mark Cammack is 23 years old and desires a straight life policy for $15,000. Using the table in figure 28.2 compute his premium.

Solution:

Premium rate per $1,000 of coverage	x	Base number of $1,000's	=	Amount of premium
$14.27	x	15	=	$214.05

- -

Apply Your Skills

James Brown is 25 years old and desires a 20-year payment life policy for $30,000. What is his annual premium?

$ _____

If payments are made quarterly, the annual premium ($214.05) is multiplied by 28% ($214.05 X 0.28 = $59.934, rounded to $59.93). For Model 28.1, the premium for $15,000 of straight life coverage is $214.05 if paid annually and $59.93 if paid quarterly.

In a second example, if a 24-year-old student takes out a 10-year term policy with a face value of $30,000, the annual premium is $129.00 ($4.30 X 30 = $129.00).

CASH SURRENDER VALUE

To receive cash or for other reasons, persons may surrender (cancel) a policy prior to the end of the period of the policy. With the exception of term policies, many policies provide for a *cash surrender value*, which is the amount the insurance company will pay the insured person on the surrender of the policy. Insured persons can usually borrow up to an amount equal to the surrender value without surrendering the policy. However, this amount must be repaid— usually with interest on the loan. The table in Figure 28.4 shows typical surrender values for various lengths of time that policies have been in force.

Cash surrender value is the amount that is provided to the insured person if the policy is dropped.

Policy Issued at Age 20			
Policy Life	Straight Life	20-Payment Life	20-Year Endowment
5 years	$ 28.00	$ 72.00	$ 140.00
10 years	76.00	195.00	315.00
15 years	153.00	371.00	520.00
20 years	248.00	502.00	1,000.00
25 years	362.00	672.00	1,000.00
30 years	520.00	795.00	1,000.00

Figure 28.4 Typical Surrender Values per $1,000

Using the table in Figure 28.4, consider the problem in Model 28.2.

Computing cash surrender value

MODEL 28.2

Problem: Brenda Fekula has a $5,000 face value straight life policy that has been in force for 15 years. Using the above table, what is the cash surrender value of her policy?

Solution:

Cash surrender value per $1,000 in face value	x	Number of $1,000's	=	Cash surrender value
$153.00	x	5	=	$765.00

- -

Apply Your Skills

Donna Pervis has a $40,000 face value straight life policy that has been in force for 20 years. What is the cash surrender value of her policy?

$ _____

To further illustrate, a person with a $7,000 face value 20-payment life policy that has been in force for 25 years can collect a cash surrender value of $4,704.00 ($672.00 x 7).

Remember that premiums and cash surrender values vary depending on the rates set by the insurance company and the background of the insured person. Males typically pay a higher premium than females because the life expectancy of a female is higher than the life expectancy of a male. Persons in dangerous occupations may be required to pay a higher premium also.

You may now complete Performance Application 28.1.

PROPERTY INSURANCE

Property insurance provides protection against loss of or damage to property.

Protection against loss or damage of property is called *property insurance.* Coverage includes fire, marine, liability, and casualty insurance. The premiums for property insurance depend on several factors, such as the location of the property, the amount of coverage desired, and the nature of risk related to the coverage. Premium rates are quoted by the number of dollars per $1,000 of insurance coverage. Most owners of real property carry fire insurance coverage. Therefore, fire insurance is discussed in this chapter.

Coverage in case of fire may include a payment for loss up to a certain amount, such as $80,000, or it may include full replacement cost, which means that the property lost to fire will be replaced at current replacement costs.

COINSURANCE

Coinsurance determines the distribution of loss between the insured and the insurer.

A typical coinsurance percentage is 80%.

Another typical feature is a *coinsurance clause* that distributes the loss between the insured and the insurance company. If a coinsurance clause is in effect, the insured agrees to carry a policy for a stated percentage of the value, such as 80%. Property valued at $100,000 must be insured for $80,000 ($100,000.00 x .80). If the insured carries at least $80,000 worth of insurance, the full amount of losses up to the face value will be recovered. If the property is not insured for the full 80% ($80,000 in this example), only a fraction of coverage will be recovered. Assume that the person in Model 28.3 carries a policy for $60,000. This is 75% ($60,000 ÷ $80,000 = .75) of the 80% coinsurance coverage. Thus, a loss of $30,000 will be covered for $22,500.

MODEL 28.3

Computation of coinsurance recovery amount

Insurance carried	÷	Coinsurance percent	x	Property value	x	Amount of loss	=	Recovery amount
$60,000	÷	(0.80	x	$100,000.00)	x	$30,000	=	$22,500.00

Apply Your Skills

A building valued at $80,000 is insured for $32,000 under an 80% coinsurance clause. A $7,000 loss occurs. What is the recovery amount?

$ _____

The loss and recovery amounts are illustrated in Figure 28.5.

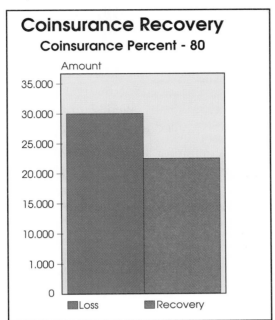

Figure 28.5 Coinsurance Recovery at 80%

COMPUTING PREMIUMS

Fire insurance premiums are usually stated as a certain amount per $1,000 of coverage, such as $3.40 per $1,000 of coverage. A building covered for $80,000 will have an annual premium of $272.00, as computed in Model 28.4.

Premium is the charge by the insurer for coverage.

MODEL 28.4

Computing annual premium

Problem: An office building is insured for $80,000. What is the annual premium?

Solution:

Number of $1,000's	x	Rate per $1,000	=	Annual premium
80	x	$3.40	=	$272.00

Apply Your Skills

The Executive Sports Center is located in an area that has a rate structure of $4.25 per $1,000 for buildings and contents. The building is insured for $90,000, and its contents are insured for $45,000. What is the premium for the building and contents? (Round answer to nearest dollar.)

$ _____

The usual practice for fire insurance coverage is to round the final annual premium computed to the nearest whole dollar. Location, amount of coverage, and type of coverage determine the rate structure to be used for fire insurance.

Rates may be paid annually or at intervals more or less often than once each year. Due to administrative costs, the premium will usually be increased if it is paid more often than once each year (called *short rate*) or be decreased if it is paid several years in advance (called *long rate*).

Assume that the annual premium for a policy is $380. The short rate is 56% of the annual premium for payment at 6-month intervals. The long rate is 181% of the annual premium for payment at 2-year intervals. A 6-month policy will carry a premium of $212.80 rounded to $213.00 ($380.00 x 0.56). If the premium is paid 2 years in advance, the premium for the 2 years of coverage will be $687.80 rounded to $688.00 ($380.00 x 1.81).

A short rate situation may also occur if a policy is canceled prior to its expiration date. In this event, the short rate will be charged. For example, assume that a policy with an annual premium of $278 is canceled 6 months prior to *expiration date* (the end of the period covered by the policy). The short rate schedule for paying at 6-month intervals will be applied to determine the refund. If this rate is $145.00 for premiums paid at 6-month intervals, the refund will be $133.00 ($278.00 - $145.00).

MOTOR VEHICLE INSURANCE

Vehicle insurance: Protection in an accident against bodily injury, property damage, comprehensive, and collision damages.

Property damage covers damage that your vehicle may do to another vehicle or object.

Some states require that all motor vehicles carry insurance protection. Premiums for this type of insurance can be fairly high for individuals and businesses. The exact premium depends on several factors such as age of driver, driving history, area of the country, use of vehicle, and sex of driver. Motor vehicle insurance coverage usually includes bodily injury, property damage, medical payments, comprehensive, and collision coverage as shown in Figure 28.6.

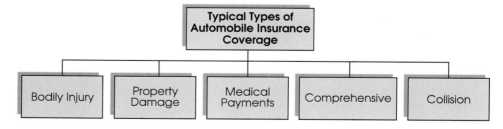

Figure 28.6 Typical Types of Automobile Insurance Coverage

Property damage (also called *liability*) *insurance* provides protection against accidents resulting in property damage to other vehicles when the insured person is at fault for the accident. This type of insurance is often purchased in units of $5,000.

Bodily injury coverage is stated in terms of *minimum/maximum* coverage, such as 25/50, which means the insurance company will pay up to $25,000 for the injury or death of one person or a total of $50,000 for injury or death of all persons involved in the accident.

Comprehensive insurance provides protection against damages caused by fire, theft, vandalism, rocks in the road, falling limbs from trees, storms, and other risks.

Collision insurance provides protection against the insured's vehicle when the insured is at fault for the accident or the other driver is at fault but does not have insurance coverage. A *deductible* is usually part of this coverage, which means that the insurance company will pay for damages above a specified amount, such as $100.

Some states have *no-fault insurance* protection statutes, which declare that each party in the accident will pay damages to that party's vehicle regardless of who is at fault in the accident. The coverage normally only covers up to a stated amount.

The *premium,* as with other types of insurance, is the amount charged by the insurance company (the insurer) to the vehicle owner (the insured). A *policy* is a written contract that describes types of coverage and amounts charged. A typical premium notice is shown in Figure 28.7.

Bodily injury *covers your liability for other persons' injuries or death caused by your vehicle.*

Comprehensive damage *covers items such as falling objects, theft, storms, and vandalism.*

Collision insurance *covers the insured's vehicle in case of an accident.*

Deductible *applies to damages before insurance coverage begins.*

No-fault insurance *permits persons to submit claims up to a specified amount to their insurance company regardless of responsibility for the accident. This feature is not required in all states.*

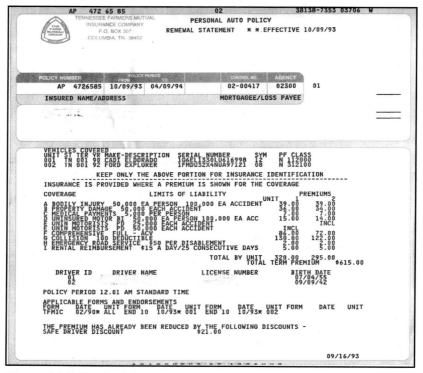

Figure 28.7 Typical Premium Notice

COMPUTING PREMIUMS

Premiums are based on a number of factors, as indicated above. A sample of typical base rates is shown in Figure 28.8.

Coverage Type	Pleasure Use	Business Use
Bodily injury	$140	$170
Property damage	120	140
Age	160	180
Number of Accidents	160	190

Figure 28.8 Premium Base Rates

Coverage limits, deductible amount, age and sex of the driver, driving record, and use of vehicle are typical factors that affect the final premium. For example, premiums are normally reduced when the insured reaches 25 years of age. Selected factors and their effects are shown below. Multiply the index by the base premium to obtain the actual premium when referring to Figure 28.9.

Factor	Index	Factor	Index
Age		**Number of Accidents**	
18	1.78	0	0.75
20	1.66	1	1.20
22	1.58	2	1.50
25	1.40	3	2.25
55	1.45	4	3.80
Bodily Injury		**Property Damage**	
25/50	0.90	25	1.00
50/100	1.15	50	1.10
100/200	1.30	100	1.20

Figure 28.9 Selected Factors Affecting the Premium Base Rate

Computing premiums using indexes is illustrated in Model 28.5.

Computing vehicle insurance premiums

MODEL 28.5

Problem: Pamela Burrows is 20 years old and uses her vehicle for pleasure. She has not incurred any accidents during the past three years and desires insurance coverage of 50/100 for bodily injury and 100 for property damage. What is her premium?

Solution:

Insurance Factor	Base Premium	x Index	=	Premium
Age (20)	$ 160	x 1.66	=	$ 265.60
Bodily injury (50/100)	140	x 1.15	=	161.00
Property damage (100)	120	x 1.20	=	144.00
Number of accidents (0)	160	x 0.75	=	120.00
Total premium				$ 690.60

Apply Your Skills

Bogart Card Shop placed a vehicle into service that will be driven for business purposes by Juan Marcel, who is 25 years old. Juan had 1 accident during the previous 3 years. The shop desires 100/200 bodily injury coverage and 100 property damage coverage. What is the premium for the vehicle?

$ _____

You may now complete Performance Application 28.2.

PERFORMANCE APPLICATION 28.1

Use the tables in the text of this chapter, as needed, to answer the following questions.

1. Charlene Bodine purchased a straight life policy at age 22 with a face value of $36,000. What is the amount of her annual premium?

    $ _____

2. Harry Maynard purchased a 20-year endowment life insurance policy with a face value of $48,000 at age 23. What is the amount of his annual premium?

    $ _____

3. Reginald Moore purchased a 10-year term life insurance policy with a face value of $80,000 at age 21. What is his semiannual premium?

    $ _____

4. Geneva Miller purchased a 20-payment life insurance policy with a face value of $75,000 at age 25. What is her quarterly premium?

    $ _____

5. Isaac Morris purchased a life insurance policy with a face value of $90,000 at age 21. What is his premium for (a) a straight life policy and (b) a 10-year term policy?

    (a) $ _____

    (b) $ _____

6. Pauline McQueen, age 23, is undecided about whether to purchase a 20-payment life or a 10-year term policy. She desires $65,000 coverage. If she pays annual premiums for 5 years, how much will be saved in premiums during the 5 years?

    $ _____

7. Dalton Frazier, age 21, and Walter Garcia, age 25, each purchased a 20-payment life insurance policy with a face value of $76,000. After 20 years of annual payments, how much will (a) Dalton and (b) Walter pay in total premiums?

   (a) $ _____

   (b) $ _____

8. Albert Gandy, age 25, and Edward Regan, age 25, each purchased a life insurance policy with a face value of $85,000. Albert purchased a straight life policy, and Edward purchased a 20-year endowment policy. After 10 years of annual payments, what is the difference in total premiums paid by the two men?

   $ _____

9. Freda Vaughn has a straight life policy with a face value of $36,000 that was purchased 20 years ago when she was 20 years old. What is the cash surrender value of the policy today?

   $ _____

10. Claudette Minns has a 20-payment life policy with a face value of $42,000 that was purchased 30 years ago when she was 20 years old. What is the cash surrender value of the policy today?

    $ _____

11. Phillip Hughes purchased a 20-year endowment life insurance policy at age 23. The policy has a face value of $40,000 and was purchased 20 years ago. What are the (a) total premiums paid and (b) cash surrender value of the policy?

    (a) $ _____

    (b) $ _____

12. Linda Rainey purchased a straight life policy at age 24. The policy has a face value of $60,000 and was purchased 15 years ago. What are the (a) total premiums paid and (b) cash surrender value of the policy?

    (a) $ _____

    (b) $ _____

PERFORMANCE APPLICATION 28.2

1. The McCall Development Corporation has a building valued at $200,000. Under an 80% coinsurance clause, the company carries $120,000 coverage. A fire causes $70,000 in damages. How much of the loss will the company recover?

   $ _____

2. Professional Sporting Goods, Inc., has a building valued at $120,000. Under an 80% coinsurance clause, the company carries $72,000 coverage. A fire causes $18,000 in damages. How much of the loss will the company recover?

   $ _____

3. Cedar Lake Nurseries decided to insure a building valued at $90,000 for $46,800 under an 80% coinsurance clause. Weather damage covered by the policy amounts to $6,000. How much of the loss will the company recover?

   $ _____

4. The Loving Care Pet Shop purchased a building with a value of $75,000 that is insured for up to 80% of its value. A fire caused $16,787 in damages. How much of the loss will the company recover?

   $ _____

5. Sabrina Worley purchased a home with a value of $85,000. Under an 80% coinsurance clause, she insured the house for $68,000. For a covered loss of $18,570, how much will she recover?

   $ _____

6. Travis Johnston acquires a building with a value of $87,000. Its contents are valued at $22,000. He purchased a policy under a 90% coinsurance clause with a face value of $46,980 for the building and $11,880 for the contents. A fire caused $6,000 damages to the building and $7,600 damages to the contents. How much will be recovered for the loss (a) to the building and (b) to the contents?

   (a) $ _____

   (b) $ _____

7. The Hill Hardware Store purchased an insurance policy with a face value of $90,000 on an office building and a second policy with a face value of $120,000 on a warehouse building. If the annual insurance premiums are $3.45 per $1,000 in coverage on the office building and $3.60 per $1,000 in coverage on the warehouse, how much are the annual premiums on the (a) office building and (b) warehouse? Round answers to the nearest dollar.

(a) $ _____

(b) $ _____

8. The Portsmouth Family Center purchased a new building with a value of $92,000. They decided to insure the building for the full value. The Ashmore Insurance Company offers coverage on a 3-year policy for an annual premium of $3.50 per $1,000 in coverage, and the Eastland Insurance Company offers coverage for an annual premium of $3.62 per $1,000 in coverage. Over a 3-year period, (a) What will the total premium be for a policy with the Ashmore Insurance Company? (b) What will the total premium be for a policy with the Eastland Insurance Company? (c) What will be saved during the 3 years if the Ashmore Insurance Company is chosen?

(a) $ _____

(b) $ _____

(c) $ _____

9. The Anderson Appliance Center purchased a policy with a face value of $120,000 on its building and $70,000 on the building contents. If insurance premiums are $3.80 per $1,000 in coverage, what will the premium be for (a) the building, (b) the contents, and (c) both the building and its contents?

(a) $ _____

(b) $ _____

(c) $ _____

10. Jerry Bradstone is 18 years old with no accidents during the past three years. He drives his vehicle for pleasure and desires 50/100 bodily injury coverage and 100 property damage coverage. What is the amount of his premium?

$ _____

PRACTICE TEST FOR CHAPTER 28

INSURANCE

Complete each of the following problems and then compare your answers with the ones on page 651. Use tables in the text, as appropriate, for computing solutions.

1. Charlene Carroll purchased a straight life policy with a $72,000 face value at age 22. What is the annual premium?

   $ _____

2. Yvonne Davidson purchased a 20-payment life policy with a $150,000 face value at age 25. What is her quarterly premium?

   $ _____

3. Marge McQueen, age 23, is undecided about whether to purchase a 20-payment life or a 10-year term policy. She desires $130,000 coverage. What will her savings in premiums be for the term policy over the first 5 years?

   $ _____

4. Dave's Hair Salon decided to insure a building valued at $240,000. Under an 80% coinsurance clause, the salon carries $144,000 coverage. A fire causes $36,000 in damages. How much of the loss will the salon recover?

   $ _____

5. Bart Utley purchased the following pleasure-use automobile coverage: bodily coverage, 25/50, and property damage, 50. He is 18 years old and has no previous accidents on his record. What is his premium?

   $ _____

CONNECTIONS

28.1 The advertisement shown below indicates term insurance monthly rates for selected age categories. Notice that the rates vary according to age, tobacco use, and sex due to differences in life expectancies. Use data in the table to compute term insurance rates for $100,000 coverage for the following persons.

(a) Male, smoker, 30 years old.

$ _____

(b) Female, smoker, 30 years old.

$ _____

(c) Male, smoker, 44 years old.

$ _____

(d) Male, nonsmoker, 44 years old.

$ _____

(e) Female, non-smoker, 23 years old.

$ _____

(f) Male, nonsmoker, 27 years old.

$ _____

AM LIFE Insurance Company of America

Issue Age	NON-TOBACCO USE Monthly Rates $10,000 Male	Female	$50,000 Male	Female	$100,000 Male	Female	$250,000 Male	Female
20	7.10	6.60	10.90	9.70	11.50	11.40	18.75	18.55
21	7.10	6.60	10.90	9.70	11.50	11.40	18.75	18.55
22	7.10	6.60	10.90	9.70	11.50	11.40	18.75	18.55
23	7.10	6.60	10.90	9.70	11.50	11.40	18.75	18.55
24	7.10	6.60	10.90	9.70	11.50	11.40	18.75	18.55
25	7.10	6.85	10.90	9.70	11.50	11.40	18.75	18.55
26	7.13	6.91	10.90	9.70	11.50	11.40	18.75	18.55
27	7.18	6.97	10.90	9.70	11.50	11.40	18.75	18.55
28	7.24	7.03	10.90	9.70	11.50	11.40	18.75	18.55
29	7.31	7.11	10.90	9.70	11.50	11.40	18.75	18.55
30	7.40	7.20	10.95	9.70	11.50	11.40	18.75	18.55
31	7.50	7.31	11.05	9.85	11.50	11.40	18.75	18.55
32	7.62	7.44	11.15	10.10	11.50	11.40	18.75	18.55
33	7.76	7.58	11.25	10.35	11.50	11.40	18.75	18.55
34	7.92	7.73	11.50	10.65	11.50	11.40	18.75	18.55
35	8.10	7.90	11.80	11.00	11.50	11.40	18.75	18.55
36	8.31	8.08	10.21	11.40	11.80	11.60	19.38	18.96
37	8.54	8.28	10.63	11.80	10.25	11.80	20.42	19.59
38	8.80	8.49	11.13	10.21	10.67	10.09	21.46	20.21
39	9.09	8.72	11.71	10.63	11.17	10.59	22.71	21.46
40	9.40	8.95	12.34	11.05	11.67	11.34	23.96	23.13
41	9.73	9.18	13.00	11.46	12.25	11.67	25.21	23.96
42	10.07	9.40	13.71	11.88	12.84	12.25	26.25	25.21
43	10.44	9.65	14.50	12.30	13.59	12.67	27.71	26.25
44	10.88	9.94	15.34	12.80	14.25	13.00	29.38	27.30
45	11.40	10.30	16.25	13.34	15.34	13.34	31.05	28.13
46	10.04	10.77	17.21	13.96	16.50	14.00	33.13	28.96
47	10.65	11.32	18.21	14.63	17.84	14.67	35.00	30.00

Issue Age	TOBACCO USE Monthly Rates $10,000 Male	Female	$50,000 Male	Female	$100,000 Male	Female	$250,000 Male	Female
20	8.15	7.00	13.96	11.80	16.59	16.09	34.38	31.25
21	8.20	7.04	13.96	11.80	16.59	16.09	34.38	31.25
22	8.26	7.11	13.96	11.80	16.59	16.09	34.38	31.25
23	8.33	7.19	13.96	11.80	16.59	16.09	34.38	31.25
24	8.41	7.28	13.96	11.80	16.59	16.09	34.38	31.25
25	8.50	7.40	13.96	11.80	16.59	16.09	34.38	31.25
26	8.58	7.53	14.05	11.84	16.59	16.09	34.38	31.25
27	8.66	7.69	14.17	11.92	16.59	16.09	34.38	31.25
28	8.75	7.86	14.30	12.00	16.59	16.09	34.38	31.25
29	8.89	8.05	14.46	12.13	16.59	16.09	34.38	31.25
30	9.10	8.25	14.67	12.30	16.59	16.09	34.38	31.25
31	9.39	8.47	14.84	12.42	16.84	16.09	35.00	31.25
32	9.73	8.70	14.96	12.59	17.09	16.09	35.63	31.25
33	10.13	8.94	15.17	12.75	17.42	16.09	36.25	31.25
34	10.55	9.21	15.50	13.05	17.67	16.09	36.88	31.25
35	11.00	9.50	16.05	13.55	17.92	16.09	37.30	31.25
36	11.45	9.81	16.80	14.25	18.59	16.42	38.96	32.30
37	11.92	10.14	17.67	15.13	19.59	16.84	41.25	33.34
38	10.35	10.49	18.75	16.17	20.59	17.17	43.75	34.38
39	10.81	10.86	20.25	17.25	21.92	18.17	46.88	36.67
40	11.34	11.25	21.67	18.34	23.17	19.50	50.00	39.80
41	11.94	11.66	23.67	19.46	24.84	20.34	53.96	41.67
42	12.60	10.07	25.96	20.71	26.42	21.42	57.71	44.17
43	13.31	10.44	28.50	21.96	28.34	22.42	61.67	46.46
44	14.05	10.83	31.17	23.17	30.50	23.25	66.67	48.75
45	14.80	11.25	33.75	24.38	33.25	24.00	72.09	50.63
46	15.55	11.71	36.30	25.42	35.42	25.00	76.05	51.88
47	16.30	12.20	38.88	26.38	37.84	26.00	80.00	53.55

28.2 The chart shown below indicates benchmark rates for term life insurance provided by one insurance company. What is the premium for the following persons?

(a) Don Nelson, male, 35 years old, preferred risk:

$ _____

(b) Beverley Holder, female, 25 years old, standard risk:

$ _____

(c) Ricardo Martinez, male, 45 years old, standard risk:

$ _____

(d) Cynthia Blackwell, female, 25 years old, preferred risk:

$ _____

Benchmark Rates for Term Life

These rates aren't rock-bottom but are a good benchmark for a fair value. These are first-year premiums for $100,000 annual renewable term insurance from USAA Life (800-555-8000),which sells policies over the phone. A preferred risk is generally a healthy nonsmoker.

Age	Preferred		Standard	
	Female	Male	Female	Male
25	$119	$128	$150	$153
35	130	132	178	191
45	206	221	303	381
55	401	474	704	889

CONNECTIONS

28.1 Harold Yount is a male who is 25 years old. He decided to purchase $300,000 term insurance coverage. He is a healthy nonsmoker. His wife, Belinda, is also 25 years old, healthy, and a nonsmoker. The couple decided to budget $60 per month for term insurance premiums. (a) Can they purchase the desired coverage for this amount? (b) If the answer is no, what monthly premium will be required? The monthly rate is 10% of the annual rate (see Figure 28.2).

(a) _____ Yes _____ No

(b) $ _____

28.2 Brandon Insurance Co. offered Donna Hutson, age 55, $300,000 term insurance coverage for $1,748 with a 40% discount for being a nonsmoker and a 2% discount for paying the premium one time per year instead of monthly payments. City Insurance Co. offered insurance for $401 per unit of $100,000 with no additional discounts. Which insurance company offered the lower premium?

_____ Brandon Insurance Co.

_____ City Insurance Co.

DECISIONS

INSURANCE
CHAPTER REVIEW AND QUICK REFERENCE

Topic	Main Point	Typical Example	Text Page
Premiums	Premiums, charges for life insurance, are based on factors such as age, smoking habits, and type of insurance. Use the **annual premiums for $1,000 life insurance policy table.**	What is the charge for a person who is 22 years old for $30,000 coverage on a straight life policy? Premium amount x No. of units = Annual premium $13.95 x 30 = **$418.50**	555
Surrender value	Some policies pay a sum if the policy is dropped prior to the end of the term. Use the **typical cash surrender values per $1,000 table.**	What is the cash surrender value for a $30,000 20-payment life policy, issued at age 20, that has been in force for 10 years? Table amt. x No. of units = Cash surrender $195 x 30 = **$5,850.00**	557
Coinsurance	Coinsurance is a procedure to distribute property losses between insurer and insured. The coinsurance percent is often 80.	Property is valued at $50,000. The coverage carried is $30,000. The coinsurance percent is 80. A $10,000 loss occurs. What recovery amount is possible? **Step 1** Find portion of loss covered. Percent x Value = Loss covered 0.80 x $50,000 = **$40,000** **Step 2** Find the percent of recovery. Insurance carried ÷ Loss covered = Recovery percent $30,000 ÷ $40,000 = **0.75** **Step 3** Find the recovery amount. Loss x Recovery percent = Recovery amount $10,000 x 0.75 = **$7,500**	558

Topic	Main Point	Typical Example	Text Page
Auto insurance premiums	Coverage is available to insure against loss as a result of accidents. Base rates are affected by factors such as driving record, coverage amount, type of auto, age and sex of driver, and purpose of the auto.	Veronica Bailey is 22 years old, uses her vehicle for pleasure, and desires coverage as follows: 50/100 bodily injury and 50 property damage. She has no previous accidents. What is her premium? Factor Base x Index = Premium Age $160 x 1.58 = $ 252.80 BI 140 x 1.15 = 161.00 PD 120 x 1.10 = 132.00 No. 160 x 0.75 = 120.00 Total $ 665.80	562

Read the following conversation between a customer and a customer service banker and answer the questions.

Customer: I need some help understanding the compound interest on this savings account. Can you help me?

Banker: Certainly. With compound interest, principal increases each period. For this reason your money will grow faster in an account that earns compound interest as opposed to simple interest.

Customer: I see. Can you give me an example?

Banker: Well, if you invest $1,000 in an account that earns 10% simple interest each month, you will have $1,100 at the end of six months. If that $1,000 is generating the same percent of interest compounded quarterly, you will have $1,103.82 after the same length of time. It may not seem like a big difference, but it adds up over time.

Customer: Hmm. Why the difference if the rate is the same?

Banker: Because the effective rate is higher than the nominal rate.

Customer: Oh. So which type of periodic compounding generates the most interest? Daily, quarterly, semiannually, or annually?

Banker: The effective rate decreases with more frequent periods, so an account that earns annually compounded interest will yield the most interest income.

1. The banker provided correct information with one exception. Can you find the error?

2. Define effective rate and nominal rate for the customer.

3. The customer would like to know how to compute interest compounded semiannually. Can you supply an answer?

4. Which terms will generate more interest for the customer's $2,000.00 deposit—1% compounded quarterly or 1.25% compounded semiannually?

COMMUNICATIONS

UNIT 6 SPREADSHEET APPLICATION 1:

SIMPLE INTEREST

The following spreadsheet is used to determine the interest due and amount needed to repay various loans. Totals and averages are also computed. The following formula is needed to compute the interest due:

Principal x Interest Rate x Days ÷ 365

The amount repaid is computed by adding the interest due to the principal for each loan. The total for each column should be computed, except Columns C and D. The average for each column can be computed by dividing the total of values in the column by 10 (since there are 10 values in each column).

Refer to the spreadsheet above to answer the following questions:

	A	B	C	D	E	F	G
1	Dalton Finance Co.			SIMPLE INTEREST			
2	----						
3	Loan		Interest	No. of	Interest	Amount	
4	Number	Principal	Rate	Days	Due	Repaid	
5	----						********
6	X-347	800.00	0.080	90			********
7	X-348	1,250.00	0.100	120			Compute
8	X-349	650.00	0.090	85			Exact
9	X-350	2,500.00	0.085	75			Interest
10	X-351	3,200.00	0.125	65			********
11	X-352	1,400.00	0.120	195			********
12	X-353	3,600.00	0.105	225			********
13	X-354	900.00	0.145	115			********
14	X-355	4,520.00	0.095	480			********
15	X-356	3,750.00	0.120	150			
16	----						
17	Totals						
18	----						
19	Averages						

1. What was the interest due for Loan X-349?

   $ _____

2. What was the interest due for Loan X-352?

   $ _____

3. What was the interest due for Loan X-355?

   $ _____

4. What was the amount repaid for Loan X-348?

   $ _____

5. What was the amount repaid for Loan X-354?

   $ _____

6. What was the amount repaid for Loan X-356?

   $ _____

7. What was the average length of the loans?

   _____

8. What was the average amount repaid?

   $ _____

9. What was the total amount repaid?

   $ _____

10. How many loans had interest due amounts greater than $1,000?

   _____

UNIT 6 SPREADSHEET APPLICATION 2:

NOTE PROCEEDS

The following spreadsheet is used to determine the maturity value and proceeds for various loans that are discounted prior to their maturity date. The interest for each loan should be computed and added to the loan amount to compute the maturity value. The discount for each loan should be computed and subtracted from the maturity value to compute the proceeds. Totals for each column, except Columns C and F, should be computed. Averages for each column should be computed. The maturity value and proceeds for the first loan are shown in the spreadsheet. **Include** these amounts while computing totals and averages.

Refer to the spreadsheet above to answer the following questions:

	A	B	C	D	E	F	G	H
1	Dalton Finance Co.				NOTE PROCEEDS			
2	--							
3	Loan	Loan		Loan	Maturity	Discount	Discount	
4	Number	Amount	Rate	Time	Value	Rate	Time	Proceeds
5	--							
6	Y-101	800.00	0.09	150	829.59	0.08	95	812.32
7	Y-102	600.00	0.10	225		0.08	100	
8	Y-103	500.00	0.08	300		0.06	150	
9	Y-104	400.00	0.08	420		0.06	250	
10	Y-105	600.00	0.12	90		0.10	60	
11	Y-106	1,200.00	0.10	100		0.10	30	
12	Y-107	600.00	0.15	200		0.12	75	
13	Y-108	700.00	0.09	325		0.10	90	
14	Y-109	300.00	0.11	400		0.12	280	
15	Y-110	500.00	0.12	600		0.10	150	
16	--							
17	Totals							
18	--							
19	Averages							

1. What is the maturity value for Loan Y-102?

   $ _____

2. What is the maturity value for Loan Y-108?

   $ _____

3. What is the proceeds amount for Loan Y-109?

   $ _____

4. What is the proceeds amount for Loan Y-110?

   $ _____

5. What is the total loan amount?

   $ _____

6. What is the total maturity value?

   $ _____

7. What is the average maturity value?

   $ _____

8. What is the average proceeds?

   $ _____

9. How many loans had maturity values less than $600.00?

   _____

10. How many loans had proceeds greater than $600.00?

   _____

UNIT 6 SELF-TEST
BUSINESS FINANCE

1. Using the ordinary method, what is the amount of interest for a 9%, 84-day loan for $1,680?

   $ _____

2. Using the ordinary method, what is the amount of interest for an 8%, 75-day loan for $1,800?

   $ _____

3. Using the ordinary method, what is the amount of interest for an 8%, 5-month loan for $12,300?

   $ _____

4. Using the exact method, what is the amount (rounded to two decimal places) for a 9%, 72-day loan for $675?

   $ _____

5. A 60-day promissory note is dated June 15. What is the due date for the loan?

   _____

6. A note dated August 13 is paid on November 3. How many days elapsed between the two dates?

   _____

7. A 60-day note dated April 19 is discounted on May 13. How many days are in the discount period for the note?

   _____

8. A 90-day note dated September 28 is discounted on October 11. How many days are in the discount period for the note?

   _____

9. Find the (a) bank discount and (b) proceeds for the following non-interest bearing note: a note with a maturity value of $1,200 discounted 90 days prior to the due date at a 9% discount rate.

   (a) $ _____

   (b) $ _____

10. June Berkshire discounted a note with a maturity value of $800 at a 6% discount rate 60 days prior to the due date. What are the (a) discount and (b) proceeds for the note?

    (a) $ _____

    (b) $ _____

11. Arthur Simmons accepted a 120-day, 10% interest-bearing note from Harriet Crowe for $1,800. The note was dated August 31. He discounted the note at the bank on September 30 at 6%. What are the (a) discount period, (b) discount, and (c) proceeds for the note?

    (a) _____

    (b) $ _____

    (c) $ _____

12. Johnny Watkins invested $5,000 into an account that pays 8%, compounded semiannually. At the end of 18 months, what are the (a) compound interest and (b) compounded amount?

    (a) $ _____

    (b) $ _____

13. The Kirk Driswald Decorating Service loaned $4,000 to a customer at 5% interest for 2 years. If the interest is compounded annually, what are the (a) compound interest and (b) compounded amount after 2 years?

    (a) $ _____

    (b) $ _____

14. The Good Vision Optical Center borrowed $3,000 at 8% interest, compounded quarterly. At the end of 9 months, what are the (a) compound interest and (b) compounded amount?

    (a) $ _____

    (b) $ _____

15. Ann Hewlett invested $9,400 for 18 months at 8% interest, compounded semiannually. What is the compounded amount after (a) 6 months, (b) 12 months, and (c) 18 months?

    (a) $ _____

    (b) $ _____

    (c) $ _____

UNIT 7

Statistics, Graphs, Stocks, and Bonds

Have you ever looked at a report that contained pages of numbers showing financial activities over a period of time? Looking at these numbers can be time consuming and confusing. Would a graphic representation, such as a pie chart or bar graph, make it easier for you to see the broad picture? Statistical analysis and graphic representation are widely used to improve understanding and simplify what might otherwise be overwhelming to the reader. Businesses use these methods to present the results of their business activity to shareholders and employees who have an interest in the business.

Many businesses have profit-sharing plans and sell stocks and bonds to the public to help provide working capital to keep the business in operation. This unit includes simple statistical analysis and graphic representation, as well as financial computations relating to buying and selling stocks and bonds, paying dividends on stocks, and discounting bonds. These activities present real-life situations you can relate to as a potential business owner, employee, or stockholder.

Chapter 29

SIMPLE STATISTICS AND GRAPHS

Performance Objectives

1. Define and use terminology relating to simple statistics.
2. Compute the mean, median, and mode from ungrouped data.
3. Determine frequency distributions for a grouped data set.
4. Define and illustrate basic terminology and function of graphic representation of data.

Data must be analyzed in order to provide useful information for making business decisions. *Business statistics* is the area of business mathematics in which data is collected, tabulated, summarized, and presented numerically in a way that can be easily interpreted and understood. For example, a listing of each individual sale made during the day by a drug store is not nearly as useful as one figure that shows total sales for the day. Basic business statistics are fun and invoke fairly simple computations. This chapter shows you several basic statistical techniques that are typically used in business situations.

Statistics can be used to compare one value, such as a business expenditure, with another value. A 20.8 share of the television audience watching a particular program, for example, can affect advertising budgets for that program.

Statistics: *the use of numbers to describe numerical data to provide information.*

MEASURES OF CENTRAL TENDENCY

The mean, median, and mode are often used to compute one value that is representative of a set or group of values. These three statistics are also known as *measures of central tendency*.

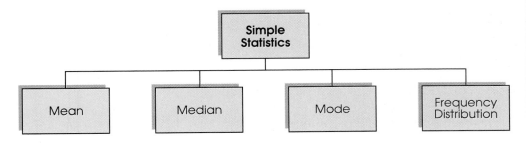

Figure 29.1 Simple Statistics

MEAN

The *mean*, which is also called the *average*, is computed by finding the sum of a group of values and then dividing the sum by the number of values in the group. The mean is a misleading value when only a small number of values are used or when a few very high or a few very low values can distort the mean value computed. Calculation of the mean is shown in Model 29.1.

Mean: *the sum of a group of values divided by the number of values in the group. Also called **average**.*

MODEL 29.1

Total of values ÷ Number of values = Mean

Computing the mean

Problem: The Village Hardware Store had the following sales for the past 5 days respectively: $7,000, $9,000, $7,000, $8,000, and $10,000. What is the mean sales for the week?

Solution: **Step 1** Find the sum of the values.

$7,000 + $9,000 + $7,000 + $8,000 + $10,000 = $41,000

Step 2 Find the mean (or average) sales.

Sum of values ÷ Number of values = Mean
$41,000 ÷ 5 = $8,200

Apply Your Skills

Five employees taking an employment test earned the following scores: 85, 90, 80, 95, and 70. What was the mean score?

The mean, or average, sales for the week were $8,200. An examination of the sales will show on which days sales were above average and on which days sales were below average. Another use of the mean is to compare one week's average sales with average sales for other weeks in the month or the year.

MEDIAN

Median: the middle value in a group of values arranged from smallest to highest or vice versa.

The *median* is the middle point in a series of values. To compute the median, the values must be arranged in order from low to high or from high to low. The median value is determined by adding 1 to the number of values in the group and then dividing by 2. Half of the values should fall above the median value, and half of the values should fall below the median value. For example, the median value for a series containing 11 values is 6. The median in a series containing 14 values is 7.5 (halfway between the seventh and eighth values). These computations are shown below.

$(11 + 1) \div 2 = 6$

$(14 + 1) \div 2 = 7.5$

Consider the steps for calculating the median in Model 29.2.

Computing the median

MODEL 29.2

Problem: The Village Hardware Store had the following sales for the past 5 days respectively: $7,000, $9,000, $7,000, $8,000, and $10,000. What is the median sales figure for the week?

Solution: **Step 1** Average the values in the group from high to low.

1. $10,000
2.   9,000
3.   8,000
4.   7,000
5.   7,000

Step 2 Determine the median point.

(No. of values + 1) ÷ 2 = Median point
(5 + 1)   ÷ 2 = 3

Step 3 Find the corresponding value in the range in Step 1 to locate the median sales value.

The third value is $8,000.

If the group has an even number of values, the median is the average of the two middle numbers.

Apply Your Skills

Five employees taking an employment test earned the following scores: 85, 90, 80, 95, and 70. What was the median?

_____

MODE

The *mode* is the specific value that occurs most frequently in a series of values. The usual practice to determine the mode is to arrange the values from highest to lowest and then visually scan the list to determine the single value that occurs most frequently. If there are two values in the same series that occur with equal frequency, the series is *bimodal* (which means that there are two modes). The mode is the least useful of the statistics discussed in this chapter. Model 29.3 illustrates finding the mode in a series of values.

Mode: *the value in a group of values that occurs most frequently.*

A group that has two modes is classified as **bimodal.**

MODEL 29.3

Computing the mode

Problem: The Village Hardware Store had the following sales for the past 5 days respectively: $7,000, $9,000, $7,000, $8,000, and $10,000. What is the mode of this sales distribution?

Solution: **Step 1** Arrange the values in order from highest to lowest as in Step 1 of Model 29.2.

Step 2 Scan the range of values to determine the value that occurs most frequently.

Notice that the fourth and fifth values are $7,000 in this group. No other value occurs more than one time. Therefore, the mode in this example is $7,000.

- -

Apply Your Skills

Shirley Moore worked the following hours last week: Monday, 8; Tuesday, 7; Wednesday, 5; Thursday, 8; and Friday, 6. What was the mode?

Largest value - Smallest value = Range

Range: *the difference between the lowest and highest value in a group of values.*

Grouped data: *an arrangement of data frequencies in specific intervals.*

Frequency distribution: *a listing of how many times each value appears in a group of values.*

RANGE

The *range* is the difference between the lowest value and the highest value in the group. After arranging the values in order from highest to lowest, determine the range by subtracting the lowest value from the highest value. The range for the daily sales used in Model 29.3 is $10,000.00 - $7,000.00 = $3,000.00. This statistic is often used because it shows the difference between values at the two extreme positions in the series.

You may now complete Performance Application 29.1.

FREQUENCY DISTRIBUTIONS FOR GROUPED DATA

The values in the preceding section were ungrouped, with each value listed separately. In working with a large number of values, it often becomes more practical to arrange values into categories or groups.

FREQUENCY DISTRIBUTION

When a large number of values is used, the values are placed into classes with an interval representing the low point and high point of each category. The ranges of the various class widths are normally equal. To illustrate this statistic, the ages of employees who work for American School Products Company will be used. Ages and method for computing the frequency distribution are shown in Model 29.4.

Arranging a frequency distribution

Ungrouped data:

21	48	32	32
25	24	33	54
35	45	52	37
50	53	64	39
65	51	28	43
44	53	27	31

Step 1 In this ungrouped data, the lowest age is 21 and the highest age is 66. Therefore, the range is 45 (66 - 21 = 45).

Step 2 Determine class width by dividing the range by the number of classes desired. Arbitrarily, the number of classes desired for this grouping is 5.
$45 \div 5 = 9$ (class width)

Step 3 Arrange the categories into classes beginning with the lowest value (21). The number of values determined in Step 1 should be included in each interval.

Interval	Tally
21-29	/////
30-38	//////
39-47	////
48-56	///////
57-65	//

Step 4 Look at each value to determine the class category. In the tally column, add 1 to the tally for a class each time a value falls into that class. This tally is shown in Step 3.

MODEL 29.4

Class width is determined by dividing the range of the values by the number of classes desired for the group.

Frequency: *the number of times a value appears in a group of values or in an interval if data is grouped.*

Class width: *the range of the interval.*

Apply Your Skills

Use the data in the box to indicate the interval and tally for the data set.

Interval **Tally**

_____ _____

_____ _____

_____ _____

_____ _____

_____

57	53	80	53	85	90
65	70	60	90	75	65
85	92	88	70	84	91
72	74	89	77	83	58

The frequency distribution table organizes and gathers data so that possible patterns can be seen. This data can then be shown visually. The three most popular graphic forms for presenting data are the line graph, bar graph, and circle graph. In this chapter, you will learn how to construct these graphs.

CONSTRUCTING LINE GRAPHS

The *line graph* is the oldest and most widely used form of graph. This graph is very useful for showing how values change over a period of time. A grid with a vertical and a horizontal axis is normally used, with the time periods placed on the horizontal axis at the bottom of the grid. Value categories are placed on the vertical axis at the left on the grid. Values for each corresponding time period are plotted on the grid with a dot. The dots are then connected to form the line on the graph. The title of the graph is usually placed either above or below the grid.

For example, enrollment of students at Meadows Junior College of Business for the past 5 years is shown in Figure 29.2.

Year	Enrollment
19Y1	1,980
19Y2	2,965
19Y3	4,115
19Y4	3,971
19Y5	4,852

Figure 29.2 Meadows Junior College Enrollment for the Years 19Y1 to 19Y2

This data is plotted on the grid shown in Model 29.5. To reduce the range of values on the graph, the data shown in the example is plotted in hundreds. For example, 1,980 is plotted on the grid slightly below 20. Businesses normally reduce values to hundreds, thousands, millions, and so forth in order to reduce the range for plotting purposes and still show an accurate graphic representation of the data.

Constructing a line graph for student enrollment

MODEL 29.5

Meadows Junior College

Student Enrollment in Hundreds of Students for the Years 19Y1 to 19Y5

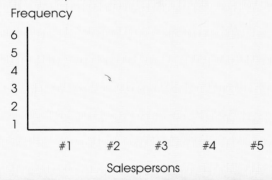

Line graph: *A line that connects a series of data points and is used to show trends or changes over a period of time.*

Apply Your Skills

The following number of auto sales were made by salespersons at City Auto Center: #1, 4 sales; #2, 3 sales; #3, 5 sales; #4, 3 sales; #5, 5 sales. Construct a line chart to show a picture of these sales.

Frequency

6
5
4
3
2
1

#1   #2   #3   #4   #5

Salespersons

CONSTRUCTING BAR GRAPHS

The *bar graph* is used to show the relationship and comparison between items of the same kind. The width of each bar should be equal, with the space between the bars about 1/2 to 1 times the width of the bar. The length or height of the bar is used to represent the value.

A grid similar to the one used for depicting the line graph, with a vertical and horizontal axis, can be used to depict a bar graph. The bars in the graph can run vertically or horizontally, depending on the way the graph is arranged. When different bars are used to show different values, color or shading should be used to represent each type of value. When time is a factor in the graph, the periods should be on the horizontal axis.

The same enrollment data pertaining to the Meadows Junior College of Business will be used for the bar graph in Model 29.6, except that in this example the data will be divided by sex of students.

MODEL 29.6

Bar graph: *Used to compare or to show relationships.*

Constructing a bar graph for student enrollment

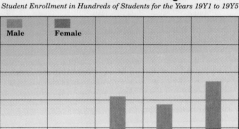

Meadows Junior College
Student Enrollment in Hundreds of Students for the Years 19Y1 to 19Y5

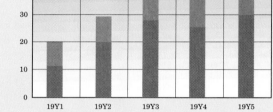

Apply Your Skills

The following number of auto sales were made by salespersons at City Auto Center: #1, 4 sales; #2, 3 sales; #3, 5 sales; #4, 3 sales; and #5, 5 sales. Construct a bar chart to show a picture of these sales.

Frequency

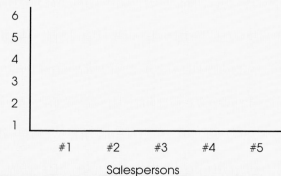

Constructing a Circle Graph

A circle graph (often called a pie chart because of its design) is used to show how segments relate to the whole. The entire circle (360° of the circumference) represents the whole (100%). The value of each segment is usually converted to a percent of the whole, with the total of all segments equaling 100%. The circle is then divided into segments (slices) depending on how the percentage or the degrees of the segment relate to the whole. For example, a segment representing 25% will take one fourth of the circle, as shown in the circle graph in Model 29.7.

The table in Figure 29.3 presents the sources of income for Midland State College. This table is represented by a circle graph in Model 29.7 that depicts the income by segment. Notice that the amount for each item is converted to a percent (rounded to two decimal places).

Source	Amount	Percentage
Fees	$33	33.67
State	25	25.51
Sports	16	16.33
Grants	12	12.24
Donations	6	6.12
Miscellaneous	6	6.12
TOTALS	98	99.99

Figure 29.3 Midland State College Sources of Income for the Year 19Y1 (in millions of dollars)

Notice that the final percent does not equal 100 due to rounding. The final percent is often adjusted so that the total will equal 100.

Circle graph:
Used to show how segments relate to the whole or how some quantity is divided. Also called **pie chart.**

Each percent represents 3.6°.

MODEL 29.7

A pie chart is always a circle that contains 360° or 100%.

The total of the percents should equal 100.

Constructing a circle graph for sources of income

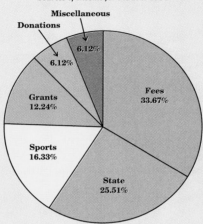

MIDLAND STATE COLLEGE
Sources of Income for the Year 19Y1

Miscellaneous
Donations
6.12%
6.12%
Grants
12.24%
Fees
33.67%
Sports
16.33%
State
25.51%

Apply Your Skills

The following number of auto sales were made by salespersons at City Auto Center: #1, 4 sales; #2, 3 sales; #3, 5 sales; #4, 3 sales; and #5, 5 sales. Construct a pie chart to show the portion of total sales represented by each salesperson.

PERFORMANCE APPLICATION 29.1

Round each answer to two decimal places.

1. The Middle States Savings and Loan Association evaluates employees once each year. Overall ratings of 1 to 100 are possible. The ratings below are for four different locations. Compute the mean, median, mode, and range for each location.

Location A	Location B	Location C	Location D
89	92	60	65
72	75	76	82
93	89	95	91
76	67	82	67
65	94	77	54
70	73	76	89
72	88	82	97
95	67	91	66
	95	73	91
	79	82	78
		70	88
		76	93
			75
			89
			97

Location	Mean	Median	Mode	Range
A				
B				
C				
D				

2. There are 45 employees working for the Middle State Savings and Loan Association included in the above evaluations. Compute the (a) mean, (b) median, (c) mode, and (d) range for all employees combined.

(a) _____

(b) _____

(c) _____

(d) _____

3. The Diebold Mobile Catering Service has several trucks. On Monday of last week, the following miles were recorded by the various trucks in the fleet: 132, 176, 180, 96, 120, 176, and 135. What are the (a) mean, (b) median, and (c) mode mileage for the fleet?

(a) _____

(b) _____

(c) _____

4. Seven employees of the Brewer Photo Center make the following weekly salaries respectively: $278, $275, $264, $278, $286, $290, and $310. What are the (a) mean, (b) median, and (c) mode salary for the employees?

(a) $ _____

(b) $ _____

(c) $ _____

5. La Filipina Jewelry had the following daily sales during six days last week: $4,678, $5,289, $4,672, $4,738, $5,389, and $5,432. What are the (a) mean and (b) median daily sales?

(a) $ _____

(b) $ _____

6. Dyson's Cabinet Shop had the following numbers of employees absent each day during the past 11 working days: 7, 8, 6, 9, 5, 6, 7, 10, 3, 4, and 1. What are the (a) mean and (b) median absentee rates?

(a) _____

(b) _____

Performance Application 29.2

1. The age-adjusted death rates per 100,000 population for 19Y1 for selected causes of death are listed in the following table. Use the following bar graph to prepare a graph to compare Indian and Alaskan death rates (white bar) with death rates of all races (dark bar). Include a legend.

DEATH RATES PER 100,000 POPULATION
Indian/Alaskan Natives vs. All Races for 19Y1

Cause of Death	Indian and Alaskan Natives	All Races
Vehicle Accidents	79.3	23.7
Other Accidents	61.4	20.0
Homicide	25.5	10.4
Diabetes	22.8	10.0
Suicide	21.8	11.9
Pneumonia	23.1	11.4

DEATH RATES PER 100,000 POPULATION
Indian/Alaskan Natives vs. All Races for 19Y1

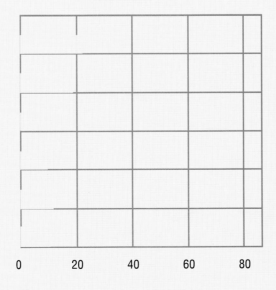

2. Data in the following table indicates a hypothetical breakdown of families in the United States by income level. Display this data in a circle graph.

FAMILY INCOME
Percentages by Income Levels

Income	Percentage
Less than $5,000	5.6
$5,000 to $9,999	11.9
$10,000 to $19,999	29.7
$20,000 to $34,999	35.2
$35,000 or more	17.6

FAMILY INCOME
Percentages by Income Levels

PRACTICE TEST FOR CHAPTER 29
SIMPLE STATISTICS AND GRAPHS

Complete each of the following problems and then compare your answers with the ones on page 652.

1. Security Tax Services employs 14 tax accountants who earned $514,290 last year. What was the average salary?

   $ _____

2. A survey of 10 customers at Neighbor's Restaurant revealed the following ages: 24, 18, 34, 28, 55, 28, 30, 35, 40, and 26. What was the median age? _____

3. Review the data shown in problem 2 above. What was the mode? _____

4. Ages of a sampling of 50 students attending City College were grouped into categories, as shown below. What was the mean age for the students in the survey? _____

Interval	Midpoint	Frequency
18-20	19	18
21-23	22	12
24-26	25	10
27-29	28	8
30-32	31	2

5. Review the data shown in problem 4 above. What was the median age?

   _____

6. A survey of 20 persons was conducted to determine the number of years that remains before they will make a new car purchase.

Number of Years	Men	Women	Total
1	3	2	5
2	2	1	3
3	4	3	7
4	2	3	5

   Prepare a chart showing total number of persons planning new car purchases during the next 4 years. You pick which type of chart is most appropriate.

29.1 The chart shown below indicates health-care costs for the three largest U.S automakers. What are the (a) average of the three cost figures and (b) the range of cost per car for the three automakers?

(a) $ _____

(b) $ _____

A look at statistics that shape your finances

Automakers' health-care costs

Chrysler, which has the oldest workforce of the Big Three, pays more per car for employees' health care than its Detroit rivals.

Chrysler $1,100

GM $929

Ford $529

Source: Ernst & Young   By Marcia Staimer, USA TODAY

29.2 The chart shown below indicates the areas of the body where orthopedic surgeons most often operate. Prepare a circle chart to display this information. Use **Other** as a category representing 16 percent.

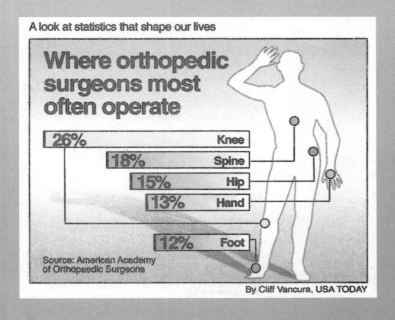

A look at statistics that shape our lives

Where orthopedic surgeons most often operate

26% Knee
18% Spine
15% Hip
13% Hand
12% Foot

Source: American Academy of Orthopaedic Surgeons

By Cliff Vancura, USA TODAY

29.1 A review of wages for employees at Bob's Body Shop revealed the following hourly wage rates: $9.25, $11.30, $9.20, $12.74, $7.50, $8.90, $15.45, $9.75, and $10.95. Daren McCloud currently earns $10.75 per hour at Clara's Body Shop. He is offered a job at Bob's Body Shop and promised a wage rate that is equivalent to the average wage rate at the shop. Which job will offer Daren the higher wage rate?

_____ Bob's Body Shop

_____ Clara's Body Shop

29.2 The chart shown below indicates the kinds of athletic shoes purchased by persons selected in a survey. Conduct a survey of 50 persons in your school and/or neighborhood who purchase athletic shoes. Construct a bar chart to display your results. Let #1 represent basketball, #2 represent cross training, and so forth in the chart. Were the results from your survey representative of the results indicated in the chart below?

_____ Yes _____ No

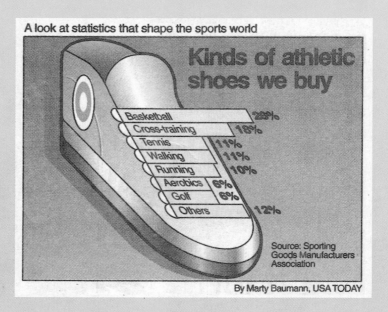

A look at statistics that shape the sports world

Kinds of athletic shoes we buy

Basketball	23%
Cross-training	18%
Tennis	11%
Walking	11%
Running	10%
Aerobics	6%
Golf	6%
Others	12%

Source: Sporting Goods Manufacturers Association

By Marty Baumann, USA TODAY

DECISIONS

SIMPLE STATISTICS AND GRAPHS
Chapter Review and Quick Reference

Topic	Main Point	Typical Example	Text Page
Statistics	Statistics uses one value to represent a group of values.	Examples include mean, median, and mode.	585
Mean, also called average	The mean is the sum of a group of values divided by the number of values in the group.	Series: 30 + 40 + 40 + 50 + 60 = 220 (sum of values) Number of values: 5 Mean = 220 ÷ 5 = **44**	585
Median	The median is the number in the middle position in a series of values.	Series: 30 40 40 50 60 Median equals the number of values plus 1 and then divided by 2: 5 + 1 = 6 ÷ 2 = 3. Therefore, the median is the third number in the series or **40**.	586
Mode	The mode is the number that occurs most frequently in a series of values.	Series: 30 40 40 50 60 Mode equals **40** since this value occurs two times and all other values occur only one time.	587
Graphs	Graphs are used to provide a pictorial representation of data.	Typical graphs include line, bar, and circle (or pie) charts	590

Chapter *30*

STOCKS AND
BONDS

Performance Objectives

1. Read stock listings for stock exchanges.
2. Illustrate terminology relating to stock investments.
3. Compute stock dividends on preferred and common stock issues.
4. Compute rate of return on stock investments.
5. Read and interpret bond listings.
6. Determine the cost for buying and selling bonds.
7. Determine bond premium and discount.
8. Determine rate of return on bond investments.

STOCKS

Ownership in a corporation is represented by *certificates of stock* (shares) held by individuals who have invested in the corporation. A typical stock certificate is shown in Figure 30.1. A fairly small number of persons may hold stock in some corporations, while several thousand persons may hold stock in other corporations. When a company is incorporated, ownership is evidenced by shares of stock that are issued or sold to people who invest in the business. The board of directors may decide to pay *dividends* to stockholders or retain earnings from profitable operation of the business. Shares of stock in many larger corporations can be bought and sold on the New York or American Stock Exchange (NYSE or AMEX), which are listed in most newspapers. Material in this chapter shows computations relating to ownership in corporations.

Stock certificate: *A document indicating stock ownership.*

Dividends: *A distribution of income to owners of stock.*

THIS CERTIFIES THAT

Is the owner of

Shares of the Capital Stock of

transferable only on the books of the Corporation by the holder hereof in person or by Attorney upon surrender of this Certificate properly endorsed.

IN WITNESS WHEREOF *the said Corporation has caused this Certificate to be signed by its duly authorized officers and its Corporate Seal to be hereunto affixed this _____ day of _____ A.D. 19___*

Figure 30.1 Sample Stock Certificate Form

BUYING CORPORATION STOCK AT MARKET PRICE

The most widely used method for investors to buy stock is to go to a stockbroker, who will discuss the purchases and provide information about various stocks. After a stock is chosen, the broker will issue an order for the agent at the stock exchange to purchase shares of stock at a specified rate when it is available at that price or to purchase the stock at the current rate.

Stockbroker: *A person who can assist with trading stock.*

***Stock:** A unit of ownership in a corporation that can be bought or sold.*

Stock is auctioned at the exchange, so the price fluctuates depending on the demand for the stock. Most transactions relate to stocks in companies that are members of the New York Stock Exchange or the American Stock Exchange. A section of the daily rates listing from the New York Stock Exchange is shown in Figure 30.2. In addition, about 12% of the stock sold in the two exchanges is sold over the counter. As many as 80 to 100 million shares of stock may be sold daily.

NEW YORK STOCK EXCHANGE ISSUES

52-Week High	52-Week Low	Stock	Div	Yld %	P/E	Sales 100s	High	Low	Last	Chg
		A								
15 1/8	11 7/8	AAR	.48	3.5	24	79	13 7/8	13 5/8	13 7/8	+ 1/4
41	26 5/8	AbtLab	.84h	2.2	20	15700	39 1/8	38 1/8	38 3/4	+ 3/4
8 5/8	6 3/8	Abex	...	...	...	766	8 3/8	8	8 1/8	− 1/8
15 1/2	11 5/8	^Abtibi	.40p	2.6	92	1129	15 3/4	15 1/2	15 5/8	+ 1/8
24 3/8	19	AMBInd	.60	2.6	14	716	23 1/4	22 3/4	23 1/8	+ 1/4
18	12	Acpls	...	...	9	193	15 7/8	15 3/8	15 3/8	− 3/8
28 3/4	20 3/4	AceLtd	.56h	2.3	...	1451	25 1/4	24 3/4	24 3/4	− 1/2
11 3/8	8	ACMIn	.90	9.7	q	943	9 3/8	9 1/8	9 1/4	+ 1/8
8 3/4	6 3/8	ACMOp	.66	9.3	q	222	7 1/4	7 1/8	7 1/8	...
10 3/8	7 1/4	ACMSc	.90	10.9	q	2530	8 3/8	8 1/8	8 1/4	...
9	5 3/4	ACMSp	.75	11.1	q	1132	6 7/8	6 5/8	6 3/4	...
12 5/8	7 5/8	ACMMD	1.26	12.9	q	537	9 7/8	9 3/4	9 3/4	− 1/8
10	7 3/8	ACMM	1.08	12.5	q	798	8 3/4	8 1/2	8 5/8	...
12 1/4	8 1/2	ACMMSI	.90	7.7	...	286	11 3/4	11 5/8	11 5/8	+ 1/8
26	9 7/8	AcmeC	.48	1.8	14	1047	26	25	26	+ 7/8
23 1/2	6 1/2	AcmeE	...	...	54	436	21 3/4	21 1/4	21 1/2	+ 1/8
34 1/2	24 5/8	Acorda	.72h	2.3	15	90	30 7/8	30 5/8	30 7/8	+ 3/8
13 3/4	7 3/4	ActvaG	...	...	...	489	9 1/8	8 7/8	9	...
18 3/8	10 1/8	Acuson	...	...	25	441	11 7/8	11 5/8	11 3/4	+ 1/8
17 3/4	15 3/8	AdaEx	.48h	2.7	...	537	17 5/8	17 3/8	17 5/8	+ 1/4
25	12 3/4	AdmiF n	.55e	2.2	...	320	25	24 5/8	24 5/8	− 3/8
12 1/4	9 3/8	ADT	...	...	17	2422	12	11 5/8	11 3/4	− 1/4
37 5/8	22 1/4	AdvMD	.01 i	0.0	11	15411	36	34 7/8	35 5/8	− 1/8
6 3/8	5	Advest	...	...	34	576	6 3/8	6 1/8	6 3/8	+ 1/8
21 3/8	15	Advo	.10	0.5	17	1082	20 3/4	20 3/8	20 3/4	− 1/8
13 7/8	8 1/4	Advocat n	...	...	14	22	11 3/4	11 5/8	11 5/8	
80 1/2	51	Aegon	2.57e	3.4	12	152	76 5/8	76 1/8	76 1/2	...
4 3/4	3 3/8	AeroFlx	...	...	7	656	4	3 3/4	4	+ 1/8
27	25	AETCap pf	2.38	8.8	...	222	27	26 7/8	27	...
60 1/4	42 1/4	AetnLf	2.76	4.6	12	3038	60 1/4	59 3/8	59 1/2	− 3/4
42 3/4	31 5/8	AFLAC	.52h	1.3	13	3204	40 3/8	39 5/8	40 3/8	+ 1/2
39 3/4	24	^Agco s	.04	0.1	6	2900	39 7/8	38 5/8	39 1/4	+ 5/8
78	47 3/4	Agco pfA	1.63	2.1	...	36	78	76	77	+ 1/2
14 3/4	8 1/4	AgEgML	.10	0.8	42	538	12 1/4	12	12 1/4	+ 1/8
19 1/4	14 1/2	AgreRty n	1.80	11.4	13	74	15 3/4	15 5/8	15 3/4	+ 1/8
23 5/8	15 1/4	Ahman	.88	3.9	15	19830	23 5/8	22 3/4	22 3/4	+ 1/8
26 7/8	24 1/2	Ahman pfB	2.40	9.3	...	28	25 7/8	25 5/8	25 3/4	...
26	22 1/8	Ahman pfC	2.10	8.2	...	49	25 1/2	25 3/8	25 1/2	+ 1/8
52 1/8	39 3/4	^Ahman pfD	3.00	5.8	...	743	52 1/4	51 1/2	51 5/8	+ 3/4
36 3/8	24	Ahold x	.16e	0.5	19	41	34 1/2	33 7/8	34 1/2	+ 5/8
3	15/32	vjAileen	...	...	...	343	9/16	1/2	1/2	...
52 1/4	**41**	**^AirPrd**	**.98**	**1.8**	**19**	**6295**	**54 1/4**	**52**	**54 1/4**	**+2 1/8**
38 3/8	18	AirFrt	.30	1.6	12	343	18 7/8	18 3/4	18 3/4	− 1/4
29 7/8	**19 5/8**	**Airgas**	...	...	**27**	**1740**	**26 1/2**	**24 3/4**	**26 1/4**	**+1 1/2**
17	10 7/8	Airlese	1.88	13.1	11	45	14 3/8	14 1/4	14 3/8	...
30 5/8	23 1/8	AirTch	...	...	...	8323	27 3/8	26 7/8	26 7/8	− 1/4
33 5/8	24 1/8	AKStel pf n	2.15	7.4	...	1203	29 1/8	28 7/8	29	+ 1/4
33 1/4	19 3/4	AKStel	...	...	2	1748	27 5/8	27 1/8	27 1/4	− 1/4
22 1/2	18 1/4	AktiSv pf	1.84	8.5	...	56	21 5/8	21 1/2	21 5/8	...
24	12 5/8	ALPhar	.18	1.0	...	222	18 7/8	18 7/8	18 7/8	...
25 3/8	22	AlaP pfA	1.90	7.6	...	27	25	25	25	− 1/4
23 1/4	18	AlaP pfB	1.70	7.4	...	20	23	22 7/8	22 7/8	− 1/8
23 1/2	18 3/8	AlaP pfC	1.60	7.0	...	21	23	22 3/4	22 3/4	− 1/2
24 3/4	20 1/32	AlaP pfD	1.48e	6.6	...	4	22 1/4	22 1/4	22 1/4	+ 1/8
25 1/2	21 7/8	AlaP pfH	1.90	7.6	...	8	24 7/8	24 7/8	24 7/8	− 1/8
18	13 1/8	AlakAir	...	...	18	623	16 3/4	16 3/8	16 3/4	+ 3/8
22 3/8	16 1/8	Albnyln	.35	1.6	23	2316	22 3/8	21 7/8	22	− 3/8
17 5/8	12 1/4	Albemar	.20	1.4	17	1150	14 7/8	14 1/8	14 5/8	+ 3/8
31 7/8	19 3/8	AlbCul	.32	1.0	17	275	30 7/8	30 3/4	30 3/4	− 1/8
28	17 3/4	AlbCulA	.32	1.2	14	211	26 1/2	25 3/4	25 3/4	− 3/8
32 1/2	25 3/4	Albtsn s	.52h	1.7	18	3319	30 7/8	30 3/8	30 1/2	− 3/8
29 1/8	21 7/8	^Alcan	.30	1.0	24	4031	29 1/4	28 7/8	29	+ 1/4
24 1/2	15 3/8	Alcatel	.41e	2.4	...	408	17 5/8	17 3/8	17 3/8	− 1/2
73 3/4	53	AlcoSd x	1.04	1.4	49	642	72 5/8	72	72 1/4	+ 5/8
82 7/8	62 1/8	AlcoSd pf	2.38	2.9	...	5	82 1/8	82 1/8	82 1/8	+1 1/8
43	24	AlexBr	.70	1.7	10	1339	42	41	41 5/8	− 1/4
26	14	^AlexAlx	.10	0.4	...	596	26 7/16	26	26 1/4	+ 1/4
58 1/8	48 7/8	^Alexdrs	...	...	...	24	58 1/2	58 1/8	58 1/2	+ 1/2
13 5/8	11 1/8	AlAmT s	1.14	9.1	...	325	12 5/8	12 3/8	12 1/2	...
159 1/2	138 7/32	AlegCp	...r	...	21	5	155 7/8	155 3/4	155 7/8	...
23	17 1/4	AlgLud s	.48	2.2	53	3748	22 1/8	21 7/8	21 7/8	− 1/8
24 3/8	19 3/4	AlgPw	1.64	6.9	13	3614	23 7/8	23 1/2	23 7/8	+ 1/4
25 3/4	15 3/4	AlenG s	.20	0.8	21	400	24 3/4	24 3/8	24 3/4	− 1/8
30 7/8	21 5/8	Alergn	.48h	1.8	15	1719	26 3/4	26 3/8	26 1/2	− 1/8

52-Week High	52-Week Low	Stock	Div	Yld %	P/E	Sales 100s	High	Low	Last	Chg
19 1/2	16 1/4	AptInM n	1.66	8.7	...	381	19 1/4	18 7/8	19	...
10	7 7/8	Apex	.66o	7.2	...	97	9 3/8	9 1/4	9 1/4	...
95 1/2	**84 1/2**	**^AppPw pfC**	**7.40**	**7.7**	...	**83**	**99 9/16**	**91**	**95 3/4**	**+6 3/4**
5 5/8	2 1/8	ApplMg	...	...	...	3189	5 1/2	5 1/8	5 1/2	+ 1/4
27	19	AppldP A	.12	0.4	17	127	27	26 7/8	26 7/8	...
30 3/4	22 1/8	Aptargp	.24	0.8	17	61	30 3/8	30 1/8	30 3/8	+ 1/8
26 7/8	21 1/2	Aquarn	1.62	7.2	12	115	22 3/4	22 3/8	22 1/2	− 1/4
10 3/8	6 1/4	AquilaG	.05	.0.5	18	142	9 5/16	9 1/4	9 1/4	− 1/8
11 1/8	6 7/8	^Aracrz s	.36e	3.2	...	1254	11 1/4	11	11	...
9 7/8	7 1/4	ArborPrp	.70	8.6	35	65	8 1/4	8	8 1/8	...
27	21 3/8	Arcadn	2.42	9.0	28	409	26 7/8	26 5/8	26 3/4	+ 1/8
21 1/8	14 21/32	ArchDn s	.10y	0.5	13	11196	18 3/4	18 1/4	18 5/8	+ 1/4
51	41 1/4	ArcCh	2.50	5.2	13	236	47 7/8	47 3/8	47 7/8	+ 3/8
22 5/8	14	Argent	.76e	4.4	...	352	17 1/2	17 1/4	17 1/4	+ 1/8
16 3/4	7 1/2	ArgFd	.27p	2.0	q	735	13 1/2	13 1/8	13 1/4	+ 1/8
27 5/8	24 3/4	AzPS un n	2.50	9.1	...	58	27 1/2	27	27 3/8	+ 1/8
23 3/4	19 3/8	AriP pfW	1.81	7.9	...	10	22 7/8	22 5/8	22 7/8	...
27 1/2	24 5/8	ArkPL pf	2.40	9.3	...	110	26 1/4	25 3/4	25 3/4	− 1/2
7 1/2	5 1/4	Armco	...	...	8	1786	7 1/8	6 7/8	7 1/8	+ 1/8
56 1/4	47 1/2	Armc pfB	3.63	6.7	...	1	54	54	54	...
24 1/2	19 3/4	Armc	2.10	8.7	...	17	24 1/8	23 7/8	24 1/8	...
56 1/4	36	ArmWI	1.44h	2.8	11	1882	52	51 1/4	51 5/8	+ 1/2
47 1/8	33 3/4	ArrowE	...	...	18	2610	46 1/2	45 1/2	46 1/4	+ 1/4
7 1/4	3 1/4	Artra	...	...	...	215	4 1/4	4 1/8	4 1/8	− 1/4
27	19 3/4	Arvin	.76	3.2	...	438	23 3/4	23 1/2	23 5/8	− 1/8
53 3/4	41 1/2	ASA	2.00	4.6	q	684	43 5/8	43 1/8	43 5/8	+ 3/8
34 7/8	23 11/16	Asarco	.80h	2.9	11	1534	27 3/8	27 1/8	27 3/8	+ 3/8
31 1/4	22 1/2	AshCoal	.46	1.7	11	27	26 7/8	26 7/8	26 7/8	− 1/8
39 7/8	31 1/4	Ashland	1.10	2.9	15	1320	37 1/2	37	37 3/8	− 1/8
64 7/8	53	Ashland pf	3.13	5.1	...	55	61	60 3/8	61	+ 1/8
22 1/2	12 1/8	AsiaPc	3.12e	18.3	q	259	17	16 3/4	17	+ 1/8
8 5/8	7 1/2	AsPacRIH n	...	...	...	867	8 3/8	8 3/8	8 3/8	+ 1/8
12 1/8	11 1/4	AsiaPlp n	...	...	...	665	11 5/8	11 3/8	11 1/2	...
14 3/8	8 7/8	AsiaTgr	.21e	1.7	...	582	11 7/8	11 3/4	11 3/4	...
3 1/4	1 5/8	AsstInv	.32a	13.5	4	305	2 1/2	2 3/8	2 3/8	− 1/8
23 7/8	17	AssocEs n	1.72h	8.2	17	88	21	20 5/8	21	+ 1/4
27 3/4	19 3/4	ATTCap	.40	1.6	11	595	25 1/2	25 1/8	25 1/2	+ 3/8
57 1/8	47 1/4	AT&T	1.32	2.6	17	18877	51 5/8	51	51 1/4	+ 3/8
7 1/2	5 1/4	AtalSos	.15 i	2.1	10	60	7 1/8	7 1/8	7 1/8	+ 1/8
36 3/4	29 1/8	AtltaGs	2.08	6.0	42	173	34 3/4	34 1/2	34 5/8	− 1/8
25 5/8	21 3/4	AtltaGs pf	1.93	7.8	...	8	24 3/4	24 3/4	24 3/4	− 1/4
19 5/8	16	AtlEng	1.64	8.4	15	730	18 1/2	18 1/4	18 3/8	+ 1/8
117 7/8	97 5/8	AtRch	5.50	4.8	17	2569	115 3/8	114 3/8	115	+ 1/4
32	22 5/8	AtRchN n	2.23	8.3	...	1317	27	26 3/4	26 7/8	...
280	234 1/2	AtRch pfC	2.80	1.0	...	1	274 1/2	274 1/2	274 1/2	+1 1/2
7 5/8	1 1/4	Atlas	...	...	...	125	1 3/4	1 5/8	1 3/4	+ 1/8
19 3/4	15 7/8	ATMOS s	.92	4.9	20	123	19	18 5/8	18 7/8	+ 3/8
24 7/8	14 1/2	Augat	.16	0.8	15	360	20 1/4	20	20 1/8	+ 1/8
26 1/2	23 1/4	AusNZI pf	2.28	8.6	...	77	26 1/2	26 3/8	26 3/8	− 1/8
20	15 1/8	AusNZI n	.46e	2.4	9	11	19 3/8	19 1/4	19 3/8	...
11 1/8	7 3/8	Austr	.03p	0.3	q	150	8 1/2	8 3/8	8 1/2	− 1/8
17 1/8	11 7/8	AuthFit s	...	...	26	83	16 3/8	16	16 1/8	+ 1/8
3 5/8	1 1/2	AutSec	...r	...	...	279	1 3/4	1 5/8	1 5/8	...
56	49 3/4	AutoDt	.60	0.9	24	2967	64	63 1/2	63 5/8	− 1/8
29	21 5/8	AutoZon s	...	...	29	2583	25	24 5/8	24 3/4	− 1/4
23 7/8	17 3/4	AvalnPr n	1.44	7.2	18	82	20 1/4	19 7/8	20 1/8	+ 1/8
18 1/4	13 3/8	Avemco	.44	2.5	14	45	17 3/4	17 3/8	17 1/2	...
42 3/4	28 1/8	^AveryD	1.08	2.5	20	685	43 1/8	42 1/2	43 1/8	+ 3/4
15 1/2	5 7/8	Aviall	.04	0.5	15	1899	7 7/8	7 5/8	7 7/8	+ 1/4
15 3/8	30 3/4	Avnet	.60	1.4	15	1669	44 1/4	43 5/8	44 1/8	− 1/8
53/8	54	Avon	2.00	3.1	17	1208	64 3/8	63 5/8	63 3/4	− 1/4
15 3/4	10 1/8	Aydin	...	...	15	39	15 5/8	15 1/2	15 1/2	− 1/8
10	5 3/8	Aztar	...	...	27	1027	9 7/8	9 5/8	9 3/4	− 1/8
		B								
5 1/2	3 1/2	Bairnco	.20	4.4	6	397	4 1/2	4 3/8	4 1/2	+ 1/8
7 1/2	13 3/8	BakrF	.40a	2.5	q	254	15 7/8	15 5/8	15 3/4	+ 1/8
3 3/4	16 3/4	BakHgh	.46	2.0	25	12369	23 1/2	22 7/8	23 1/8	− 1/4
9 7/8	21 1/4	Baldor s	.48	1.6	20	65	29 3/8	29 1/8	29 3/8	+ 1/8
6 7/8	24 3/8	Ball	.60	1.8	12	894	32 1/2	32	32 1/2	+ 1/2
3 3/4	8 1/2	BalMedPr	.06e	0.5	21	198	11 1/2	11 1/4	11 1/2	+ 1/4
1 1/8	5 1/4	BallyEnt	...	...	54	3205	11 1/8	10 3/4	10 3/4	− 1/4
5	20 3/4	BaltG	1.52	6.1	14	3335	24 3/4	24 1/4	24 3/4	+ 3/8
2	55	BaltG pfB	4.50	7.8	...	z10	58	58	58	...
8	24 1/8	BancOn s	1.36	4.2	14	9749	32 3/8	31 3/4	32 1/4	+ 3/8
7 1/2	24 1/4	BncBil pf	2.44	9.2	...	79	26 5/8	26 1/2	26 1/2	− 1/4
6 1/4	22 5/8	BncBil pfB	2.25e	8.9	...	89	25 5/8	25 1/4	25 1/4	+ 1/8

Figure 30.2 New York Stock exchange composite Listing of Transactions

The listing often gives the open price, highest and lowest prices, and the last price for the daily sales of the various stocks.

In Figure 30.2, the names of the companies are abbreviated. Other headings are P-E (price to earnings) Ratio (the last sales price divided by earnings for the past 12 months), Sales (shown in hundreds of shares sold during the day), Close (the price per share at the end of the day), and Net Chg. (change from the day before). Dividends paid are listed at an annual rate next to the name of the stock.

Notice that the price quotation for stock is always given in halves, fourths, or eighths of a dollar. For example, 50½ is equal to $50.50, and 19⅜ is equal to $19.375 per share. If the closing price for Heinz Corporation stock is 46¾, the cost for purchasing 20 shares will be $935.00 ($46.75 × 20 = $935.00). Similarly, the cost for purchasing 30 shares of Kimberly Clark stock listed at 89⅜ will be $2,681.25 ($89.375 × 30 = $2,681.25).

Figure 30.3 includes guidelines for reading stock exchange listings.

HOW TO READ NYSE, AMEX

These composite tables for the New York Stock Exchange and the American Stock Exchange reflect trades on the New York, Philadelphia, Boston, Midwest, Cincinnati and Pacific stock exchanges and trades reported by the National Association of Securities Dealers.

Each NYSE and Amex stock is identified by a company abbreviation followed by the annual dividend per share. **Sale hds** is the number of shares sold; it must be multiplied by 100 unless preceded by **z**. **PE** is the company's price-to-earnings ratio, derived from dividing the company's stock price per share by the profit per share for the previous four quarters. **Last** refers to the stock's final price per share. **Chg.** is the change between the final price and previous day's final price.

NYSE & AMEX footnotes

a – Also extra or extras. b – Annual rate plus stock dividend. c – Liquidating dividend. e – Declared or paid in preceding 12 months. i – Declared or paid after stock dividend or split up. j – Paid this year, dividend omitted, deferred or no action taken at last dividend meeting. k – Declared or paid this year on accumulative issue with dividends in arrears. r – Declared or paid in preceding 12 months plus stock dividend. t – Paid in stock in preceding 12 months, estimated cash value on ex-dividend or ex-distribution date. x – Ex-dividend or ex-rights. y – Ex-dividend and sales in full. z – Sales in full.

pf – Preferred. pp – Holder owes instalments(s) of purchase price. rt – Rights. un – Units. wd – When distributed. wi – When issued. wt – Warrants. ww – With warrants. xw – Without warrants. vj – In bankruptcy or receivership or being reorganized under the Bankruptcy Act, or securities assumed by such companies.

Figure 30.3 Guidelines for Reading the NYSE and AMEX

Many of the stocks listed do not represent companies that are well known to the general public, but a listing of the ten most active stocks in the New York Stock Exchange corporate trading for a recent date shows listings for several widely known companies (see Figure 30.4).

Stock transactions are listed in the business section of daily newspapers.

Stocks are listed in eighths, halves, or fourths of a dollar, such as 14¼, which is equal to $14.25.

Trade: *A stock purchase or sale.*

MOST ACTIVE SHARES MONDAY

Top stocks by number of shares traded

New York Stock Exchange

	Vol	Last	Chg
HCA Hosp ...	5,710,900	28⅞	+6⅛
ColumHlthcre	3,678,900	28⅞	–1⅜
AMD	2,468,200	26¾	+⅞
IBM	2,414,500	44¼	+⅜
RJR Nab	2,280,300	4½	—
PhilipPet	2,202,900	36⅞	+1¾
Marriot wi	2,035,400	7⅝	+⅝
Safeway	1,836,300	18⅛	–⅜
WalMart s	1,764,700	24¾	—
Belden n	1,748,800	14⅞	–¼

American Stock Exchange

	Vol	Last	Chg
EngySvc	1,836,100	3⅝	+1/16
SPDR n	1,038,500	46 7/32	+1/16
EchoBay	804,500	10½	+¼
Roadmstr	526,700	4 1/16	+¼
US Biosci	404,400	10½	+⅛
ChartMed	388,900	23	—
RoyalOak g	382,000	4 3/16	+1/16
NY Times	336,300	25¼	—
Hillhaven	335,000	3 9/16	+⅛
ICH Cp	262,000	5⅞	–⅝

NASDAQ

	Vol	Last	Chg
Intel s	3,544,900	72¾	—
SynOpt s	3,159,100	22½	–1
Novell s	3,113,700	18	–¼
SunMic	2,986,600	23⅛	+1
Fonar	2,954,300	3	–½
US Hlth	1,914,900	48	+1¼
AppleC	1,721,800	22¾	—
Lotus	1,627,200	47¼	+½
SpecTch	1,620,800	6 3/16	+1/16
Legent	1,600,100	24¼	+2¾

Figure 30.4 Most Active Shares on Stock Exchanges

On this particular day, HCA Hospital Corporation was the company with the most active stock on the New York Stock Exchange (NYSE) with 5,710,900 shares of stock being sold. These rates indicate exchanges of stock from previous owners to new owners. The price represents market value with little or no relationship to the original price paid for the stock.

The DOW provides a composite picture indicating the overall prosperity of the stock exchange. As indicated in Figures 30.5, the DOW constantly changes even on a daily basis. Prices of individual stocks can also fluctuate several dollars per share during one day's trading. Stock can then be sold at a later date. A stockbroker's fee is also assessed for selling the stock.

LEADING GAINERS MONDAY

New York Stock Exchange

	Last	Chg	Pct
HCA Hosp	29	+6¼	+27.5
Hanson wt	2	+⅜	+23.1
KimmEnv	2¾	+½	+22.2
MHI Group	2¼	+¼	+12.5
OEC Med	8¼	+⅞	+11.9
Wainoco	4¾	+½	+11.8
EQK Rty	2⅞	+¼	+9.5
HospitStaf	2⅞	+¼	+9.5
Hlthtrust	24¾	+2⅛	+9.4
Marriot wi	7⅝	+⅝	+8.9

American Stock Exchange

	Last	Chg	Pct
Calton n	2¼	+7/16	+24.1
Davstar wt	2⅝	+⅜	+16.7
Portage	2¼	+¼	+12.5
Helionetics	4⅛	+7/16	+11.9
Crowley Mil	7¾	+¾	+10.7
EZ Serv	3 9/16	+5/16	+9.6
Softnet	4⅜	+⅜	+9.4
IncOpporRT	15¾	+1¼	+8.6
WolfHow B	8¼	+⅝	+8.2
TejonRnch	17	+1¼	+7.9

NASDAQ

	Last	Chg	Pct
ComCentrl	3⅝	+1 3/16	+48.7
WashBcp	11⅛	+3⅝	+48.3
MechanicTech.....	2½	+¾	+42.9
TideMrkBc	2½	+¾	+42.9
Metricom	20¼	+4½	+28.6
ParkwayCo	14	+3	+27.3
Strober	4¼	+⅞	+25.9
Cygnus	8¼	+1½	+22.2
BioImg	2⅛	+⅜	+21.4
WashFdlDC	4¼	+¾	+21.4

LEADING LOSERS MONDAY

New York Stock Exchange

	Last	Chg	Pct
WabanInc	12⅞	–1⅜	–9.6
Rymer	2⅜	–¼	–9.5
AppldMag	6¼	–⅝	–9.1
MarkIV	23⅝	–2⅛	–8.3
UnitCp	4⅜	–⅜	–7.9
PolicyMgmt	24	–1⅞	–7.2
HilbRogal	12½	–⅞	–6.5
LifeReCorp n.......	23⅜	–1⅝	–6.5
Safeway wt	3⅞	–¼	–6.1
DataGenl	9¾	–⅝	–6.0

American Stock Exchange

	Last	Chg	Pct
AdvMedicTc	1 13/16	–⅜	–17.1
PlymRub B	6⅛	–¾	–10.9
HarvardIntl	14½	–1¾	–10.8
Sterl Electr	13⅝	–1⅝	–10.7
Belmac	2 13/16	–5/16	–10.0
PageAmer	3⅜	–⅜	–10.0
ICH Cp	5⅞	–⅝	–9.6
vjSunshnJr	4⅞	–½	–9.3
AdvMed pf	7¾	–¾	–8.8
LawrInsGp	5¼	–½	–8.7

NASDAQ

	Last	Chg	Pct
BioLogic	3	–1	–25.0
CAP Rx wt	1⅞	–⅝	–25.0
OpthImg	1⅝	–½	–23.5
EVRO s	2⅞	–¾	–20.7
PMR Cp	5¾	–1½	–20.7
Medarex wt	2	–½	–20.0
BlckHawk wtA.....	1 29/32	–15/32	–19.7
AldenEl	3⅜	–¾	–18.2
BlChipCmp	1¾	–⅜	–17.6
HawkinsEng	2 1/16	–7/16	–17.5

Figure 30.5 Chart Showing Stock Gainers and Losers

SELLING STOCK

The certificate of incorporation shows the maximum number of shares, called *authorized capital stock*, that the corporation has authority to issue to investors. As shares of stock are originally issued, the total number issued is the *outstanding capital stock*. Two broad classifications of capital stock are *common stock* and *preferred stock*. Common stock represents the major portion of shares, with no guarantee of dividends from profits of the corporation. Preferred stock usually has some provision for preference in distribution of dividends and of money from liquidation of the corporation in case it is dissolved. Dividends may be paid in cash (cash dividend) or in additional stock (stock dividend).

The value of the stock as stated on the original stock certificate is the *par value* or *face value* of the stock. Remember from the preceding section that the amount necessary to purchase stock is determined by market conditions and not by the original par value. Stock originally issued for more than its par value is sold for a *premium*, while stock issued for less than its par value is sold at a *discount*.

COMPUTING DIVIDENDS ON STOCK

Dividends on common stock are declared periodically by the corporation's board of directors. This amount is usually stated as a percent of the par value of the outstanding stock or as a certain amount for each share of outstanding stock. Model 30.1 illustrates computation of a dividend.

Share: A unit of stock.

Common stock: Ownership right in the corporation that carries voting rights—usually one vote per share owned.

Preferred stock: Stock that has preferential rights to dividends.

Dividends are often issued on a quarterly basis.

Computing dividends on one shareholder's stock

MODEL 30.1

Problem: William Dodd has 50 shares of common stock in the Artex Corporation. What are his dividends if the corporation declares a dividend of $2.40 per share?

Solution:

Dividend per share	x	Shares	=	Dividend
$2.40	x	50	=	$120.00

- -

Apply Your Skills

Yvonne Sung purchased 200 shares of common stock in the Bermeil Corporation last year. The company declared a $2.85 per share dividend. How much in dividends will Yvonne receive?

$ _____

A corporation may allocate a specific amount of funds for dividend distribution. The dividend per share is then computed by dividing the dividend distribution by the number of shares of stock outstanding, as shown in Model 30.2.

MODEL 30.2

Computing dividend per share of stock

Problem: The Stanway Corporation decides to declare dividends in the amount of $50,000. If 40,000 shares of stock are outstanding, what is the amount of dividend per share?

Solution:

Dividends	÷	Outstanding shares	=	Dividend per share
$50,000	÷	40,000	=	$1.25

Apply Your Skills

Bernard Corporation allocated $1,500,000 to dividends for the second quarter. There are 600,000 shares of outstanding stock. What is the amount of dividend per share?

$ _____

Preferred stockholders receive dividends first; then common stockholders receive their dividends if funds are available. Model 30.3 illustrates computation of dividends for preferred and common stockholders.

MODEL 30.3

Computing dividends for preferred and common stock

Problem: The Rhodes Corporation has 1,000 shares of preferred stock and 1,000 shares of common stock outstanding. Each share has a par value of $10. A dividend of 5% is declared. However, there is only $750 available for dividends. How much will be distributed to preferred and common stockholders?

Solution: **Step 1** Compute the dividends for preferred stock.

Par value		x Dividend rate	=	Preferred dividends
$10,000 ($10 x 1,000)	x	0.05 (5%)	=	$500

Step 2 Compute the amount left for common stock.

Dividends available	−	Preferred dividends	=	Amount for common stock
$750	−	$500	=	$250

Apply Your Skills

Marta Corporation has 2,000 shares of preferred stock and 3,000 shares of common stock outstanding. Each share has a $10 par value. A 6% dividend, based on par value, was declared. The company allocated $2,500 to dividends. How much will be distributed to (a) preferred and (b) common stockholders?

(a) $ _____

(b) $ _____

COMPUTING RATE OF RETURN ON STOCKS

People who buy and sell stock intend to make a profit on their transactions. They plan for the sales price plus dividends to be high enough to cover brokerage fees, cost of the stock, and a fair rate of return on their investment. The *rate of return* is determined by dividing the amount of the gain by the cost of the transaction. This percent represents the overall rate of return relative to profit on the stock transaction. It does not correspond to an annual rate. For example, in this chapter brokerage fees and taxes are not considered, so the computations are simpler. In reality, they would be additions to the cost of the stock. Model 30.4 illustrates computation of rate of return.

Rate of return: The gain resulting from sale of a stock. Includes price increase and dividends.

Computing rate of return on stocks

MODEL 30.4

Problem: James Dunavent purchased 100 shares of stock at 62½ and kept the stock for 2 years. Dividends of $4.25 per share were paid each year. He sold the stock for 72¼ . What is his rate of return?

Solution: **Step 1** Multiply the annual dividend per share by the number of years to compute the gain from dividends per share.

$4.25 x 2 = $8.50 (gain per share from dividends)

Step 2 Subtract the purchase price from the selling price to compute the loss or gain from sales of stock.

$72.25 - $62.50 = $9.75 (gain on sale of stock)

Step 3 Add the gain from dividends to the gain (or loss) from sale of stock to compute the total gain (or loss).*

$8.50 + $9.75 = $18.25 (total gain per share)

Step 4 Divide the total gain (or loss) by the purchase price to compute the rate of return.**

$18.25 ÷ $62.50 = 29.2% (rate of return)

* If a loss on sale of stock is incurred, the loss will be deducted from the dividends (computed in Step 1) in Step 3.

** If a total loss is incurred, the rate will represent a negative return in Step 4.

Apply Your Skills

Rita Duff purchased 20 shares of stock at 18 1/4 and kept the stock for 2 years. Dividends of $3.20 per share were paid each year. She sold the stock for 15½ . What was her rate of return?

_____

You may now complete Performance Application 30.1.

BONDS

Bond: A written agreement to pay an amount at some time in the future.

Maturity date: The day that the face value of the bond will be paid.

Face value: Usually some denomination of $1,000. Also called **par value.**

Corporations may issue stock to persons who then become part owners. However, a way to raise large amounts of capital without expanding ownership is to borrow money by issuing bonds. A *bond* is a written agreement to pay an amount *(face value)* at some time in the future *(maturity date).* In addition, the corporation or governmental agency issuing the bond normally pays a stated rate of interest based on the face value of the bond. Like stocks, bonds are often bought and sold on the major security exchanges. In this chapter, you learn about computations needed for corporate borrowing of money by issuing bonds. Figure 30.6 illustrates a typical bond.

UNITED STATES OF AMERICA
STATE OF MISSISSIPPI

BEARER
SPECIMEN

YAZOO COUNTY

GENERAL OBLIGATION ROAD AND BRIDGE BOND
SERIES 1983

DOLLARS
5000

RATE	MATURITY	DATE OF ORIGINAL ISSUE	CUSIP
8.70%	DUE JUNE 1, 1998	JUNE 1, 1983	985369 HW 0

Yazoo County, in the State of Mississippi (hereinafter refered to as the "County"), a body politic existing under the Constitution and Laws of the State of Mississippi, acknowledges itself indebted and, for value received, hereby promises to pay the bearer the principal sum of

FIVE THOUSAND DOLLARS

on the date specified above, upon the presentation and surrender hereof, and to pay interest thereon from the date hereof at the rate per annum specified above. Such interest shall be payable on June 1, 1984 and semiannually thereafter on June 1 and December 1 in each year, until the principal hereof shall have been paid, upon presentation and surrender of the interest coupons appertaining hereto as they severally become due. Both principal of and interest on this bond are payable in lawful money of the United States of America at Bank of Morton, Morton, Mississippi.

Bonds maturing in the years 1994 through 2003, inclusive, are subject to redemption prior to their respective maturities at the election of the County on June 1, 1993, or any interest payment date thereafter, either as a whole or in part (in inverse order of maturity and by lot if less than all of the maturity is to be redeemed), upon not less than thirty (30) days prior notice, at the principal amount thereof plus accrued interest to date of redemption.

This bond is one of a series of three hundred forty (340) bonds of like date, tenor and effect except as to number, rate of interest and date of maturity, numbered consecutively from one (1) through three hundred forty (340), inclusive, aggregating the authorized sum of One Million Seven Hundred Thousand Dollars ($1,700,000) (the "Bonds"), issued to raise money for the purpose of constructing, reconstructing, and repairing roads, highways and bridges, and acquiring the necessary land, including land for road building materials, and rights-of-way therefor.

This bond is issued under the authority of the Constitution and statutes of the State of Mississippi, including Sections 19-9-1 through 19-9-31, Mississippi Code of 1972, and by the further authority of proceedings duly had by the Board of Supervisors of the County, including a Bond Resolution adopted May 2, 1983.

The Bonds are and will continue to be payable as to principal and interest out of and secured by an irrevocable pledge of the avails of a direct and continuing tax to be levied annually without limitation as to time, rate or amount upon all the taxable property within the geographical limits of the County. The County covenants and agrees that it will apply the proceeds of the Bonds to the purpose above set forth, and that so long as any of the Bonds or any of the interest coupons appertaining thereto is outstanding and unpaid, it will levy annually a special tax upon all taxable property within the geographical limits of the County adequate and sufficient to provide for the payment of the principal of and the interest on the Bonds as the same falls due.

IT IS HEREBY CERTIFIED, RECITED AND REPRESENTED that all conditions, acts and things required by law to exist, to have happened and to have been performed precedent to and in the issuance of the Bonds, in order to make the same legal and binding general obligations of Yazoo County, Mississippi, according to the terms thereof, do exist, have happened, and have been performed in regular and due time, form and manner as required by law. For the performance in apt time and manner of every official act herein required and for the prompt payment of this bond, both principal and interest, the full faith and credit of Yazoo County, Mississippi, are hereby irrevocably pledged.

IN WITNESS WHEREOF, Yazoo County, Mississippi, has caused this bond to be executed in its name by the facsimile signature of the President of its Board of Supervisors and countersigned by the manual signature of the Clerk of its Board of Supervisors, thereunto duly authorized, and the Seal of the County to be affixed hereto, and has caused the interest coupons hereto attached to be executed by the facsimile signatures of said officers, all as of the first day of June, 1983.

COUNTERSIGNED:

Clerk of the Board of Supervisors
of Yazoo County, Mississippi

YAZOO COUNTY, MISSISSIPPI

BY:

President of the Board of Supervisors
of Yazoo County, Mississippi

Figure 30.6 A Bond

ISSUING BONDS

Bonds are used for long-term borrowing of money. Maturity dates are the dates when the bonds will be paid by the issuer and usually extend to ten years or longer. In addition to corporate bonds, many local and state governmental agencies issue *municipal bonds*. The federal government also issues *treasury bonds* to borrow money. Interest earned on some governmental bonds is tax exempt from federal income taxes, which helps to make them an attractive investment.

Many bonds are bought and sold on security exchanges for a commission. While the face value is usually in multiples of $1,000, the actual *market price* or *quoted price* of the bond may be higher (sold at a *premium*) or lower (sold at a *discount*) than the face value.

The basic reason for issuing bonds is to borrow money. Investors then buy the bonds and hold them until their maturity or until they are redeemed by the issuer. During this period of time, the investor usually earns interest.

Corporate bond: A bond issued by a corporation.

Municipal bond: A bond issued from a municipal agency.

Premium: A price that is higher than the bond face value.

Discount: A price that is lower than the bond face value.

READING BOND QUOTATIONS

Bonds may be auctioned or sold to investors on the local level. For example, a church may announce a bond issue and make the bonds available to local investors. However, many large bond issues available to general investors are sold on a national exchange.

A typical listing from the New York Exchange is shown in Figure 30.7 The first column shows the name of the corporation issuing the bonds, the original rate of interest, and the maturity date. For example, the first listing (InldStl) shows that the bond pays 9.5% interest and matures in the year 2000.

Bonds	Cur Yld	Vol	High	Low	Close	Net Chg
InldStl $9^1/_2$00	12.	65	$79^7/_8$	79	79	$-^7/_8$
Intrfst $9^3/_8$99	11.	2	85	85	85	...
Intrfst $7^3/_4$05	cv	46	96	95	96	-1
IBM $9^1/_2$86	9.8	265	$98^1/_4$	$97^1/_4$	$97^3/_8$	$-^7/_8$
IBM $9^3/_8$04	11.	455	$88^1/_4$	$87^3/_4$	88	$-^3/_8$
IntHrv 4.8s91	9.0	2	$53^1/_8$	$53^1/_8$	$53^1/_8$	...
IntHrv $8^5/_8$95	15.	173	$56^1/_2$	$55^1/_2$	$56^1/_2$	$+^9/_8$
IntHrv 9s04	16.	143	56	$55^1/_4$	$55^1/_2$	$+^1/_2$
IntHrv 18s02	19.	194	$94^5/_8$	$93^1/_2$	$93^1/_2$	$-1^7/_8$
InHvC $8^5/_8$91	13.	17	$64^1/_4$	63	$64^1/_4$	$+1^1/_4$
InHvC $7^1/_8$94	14.	13	$52^7/_8$	$52^3/_4$	$52^3/_4$	$+^1/_8$
InHvC 9s84	9.9	23	$91^3/_8$	$90^1/_2$	$91^1/_8$	$-^1/_4$
InHvC 8.35s86	11.	99	$73^5/_8$	$73^1/_4$	$73^1/_4$	$-^3/_4$
InHvC $13^1/_8$88	16.	60	$84^1/_2$	$84^1/_8$	$84^1/_2$	$-^1/_4$
IPap 8.85s95	10.	5	$85^1/_2$	$85^1/_2$	$85^1/_2$	...
IPap $4^1/_4$96	cv	6	160	160	160	$+4$
IntTT 8.9s95	11.	10	$84^3/_4$	$84^1/_8$	$84^3/_4$	$-^1/_4$
IntTT $8^5/_8$00	cv	1	156	156	156	...
Intnr $10^5/_8$90	11.	12	$98^1/_2$	$98^1/_2$	$98^1/_2$	$-1^1/_8$
Intnr $17^1/_2$91	14.	10	123	123	123	$+1$
IntrBk $5^1/_2$87	cv	50	$73^3/_4$	$73^1/_4$	$73^3/_4$	$+^1/_2$
JnM 7.85s04f	.	41	$68^1/_8$	$67^1/_2$	$67^1/_2$	...
JnM 9.7s85f	..	12	84	84	84	$-^3/_4$
JonsLI $6^3/_4$94	11.	20	63	$62^1/_8$	$62^1/_2$	$+^5/_8$
JoneL $6^3/_4$94	11.	4	$62^3/_8$	$62^3/_8$	$62^3/_8$	$-^5/_8$
JoneL $9^7/_8$95	13.	4	80	79	79	$-3^3/_4$
K mart 6s99	cv	43	$101^1/_2$	$100^1/_2$	101	$+^1/_4$
K mart $9^7/_8$85	9.9	5	$99^1/_4$	$99^1/_4$	$99^1/_4$	$-^1/_4$
Kane $9^1/_2$90	11.	10	84	83	83	...
Kellog $8^5/_8$85	8.8	3	$98^1/_8$	$98^1/_8$	$98^1/_8$	...
KimCl $5^7/_8$91	8.0	1	$73^3/_4$	$73^3/_8$	$73^3/_8$	$+^1/_4$
I TV 5s88	6.8	99	$74^1/_8$	74	74	$-^1/_8$

Figure 30.7 New York Exchange Listing for Bonds

Current yield shows the actual interest rate if the bond is purchased at the current price. *Volume* shows current sales in units of $1,000. *High* and *Low* show the highest and lowest prices, as percentages of face value, paid for the bond issue during the day. *Close* shows the price at the end of the day as a percentage of face value. *Net Chg* shows the difference (plus or minus) between the closing price for the current day and the closing price for the preceding day.

In the first listing (InldStl), the current yield is 12%, with $65,000 in bonds being sold during the day. The high, low, and closing prices are 79.125, 79, and 79 respectively. This shows that the price of the bond ranged from $790.00 to $791.25 during the day, with a closing price of $790.00 (0.79 x $1,000) for each $1,000 bond issue purchased. The current closing price is 0.375 lower than the closing price from the preceding day.

The name of the company issuing bonds is abbreviated in the newspaper listing. Some of the abbreviations, such as IBM, are generally recognized. A security broker provides information about companies to help investors choose bonds for maximum security. For a commission, the broker provides advice and handles the transaction to purchase the bond issue. Broker fees vary on bond sales, but a set fee (such as $5.00 per $1,000 bond) for each bond purchased or sold is typical.

PURCHASING BONDS

A fixed rate of interest is specified for each bond. If the bond is purchased between interest dates, the purchaser ordinarily pays the accrued interest since the last payment date. For purposes of computing accrued bond interest, all 12 months are counted as having 30 days, and the year is counted as having 360 days. Model 30.5 illustrates calculation of the accrued interest period, and Model 30.6 illustrates calculation of the accrued interest amount.

MODEL 30.5

Computing accrued interest period

Problem: A bond with a semiannual interest payment date of June 30 is sold on September 15. What is the accrued interest period?

Solution:

June 30 to August 31	=	60 days
August 31 to September 15	=	15 days
Total days of accrued interest	=	75 days

Apply Your Skills

A bond with a semiannual interest payment date of December 31 is sold on February 14. What is the accrued interest period?

Computing accrued interest

MODEL 30.6

Problem: The Belz Corporation issued 20 $1,000 bonds bearing interest at 12%. If the accrued interest period is 75 days, what is the accrued interest to be paid by the purchaser?

Solution: Face value × Interest rate × Accrued interest = Accrued
period   interest

$20,000.00 ×   0.12   ×   75 ÷ 360   = $500.00

Apply Your Skills

The Danz Corporation issued 40 $1,000 bonds bearing interest at 8%. If the accrued interest period is 45 days, what is the accrued interest?

$ _____

Remember that each full month counts as having 30 days regardless of the actual number of days in the month.

Other costs of the bond purchase include the market value and broker's commission. These costs are considered in Models 30.7 and 30.8.

Computing full bond purchase price

MODEL 30.7

Problem: Suzanne Morrison purchased 4 $1,000 bonds at 102, plus accrued interest from January 15 to March 30 at 9%. The broker's commission is $5.00 per $1,000 bond issue. What is the full bond purchase price?

Solution: **Step 1** Compute the accrued interest period.

January 15 to March 15 is 60 days, and March 15 to March 30 is 15 days.

60 + 15 = 75 days (accrued interest period)

Step 2 Multiply the face value by the interest rate by the time to compute the accrued interest.

$4,000.00 × 0.09 × 75 ÷ 360 = $75.00 (accrued interest)

Step 3 Multiply the face value by the price quotation to compute the market price.

$4,000.00 × $1.02 = $4,080.00 (market price)

Step 4 Multiply the number of issues by the rate per $1,000 to compute the broker's commission.

4 × $5.00 = $20.00 (broker's commission)

Step 5 Add the accrued interest, market price, and commission to compute the bond purchase price.

$75.00 + $4,080.00 + $20.00 = $4,175.00 (bond purchase price)

Proceeds: The amount that will actually be received for the sale of a bond.

Bonds are rarely sold on their issue date, so accrued interest is normally computed.

Apply Your Skills

Vicki Robertson purchased 5 $1,000 bonds at 103, plus accrued interest for 45 days at 8%. The broker's commission is $6 per $1,000 bond issue. What is the full bond purchase price?

$ _____

In Model 30.7, Ms. Morrison will pay $4,175.00 to purchase the bonds on March 30. Since she will receive interest for the full period on the next interest payment date, the accrued interest ($75.00) will be received back on that date. After deducting the commission, the broker will submit the remainder to the seller. Therefore, the *proceeds to the seller* will be $4,155.00 ($4,175.00 - $20.00).

Some bonds are purchased at a discount. In Model 30.8, Beverley Cafer purchased 2 $1,000 bonds at 88, plus accrued interest from April 2 to July 2 at 12%. The broker's commission is $5.00 per $1,000 bond issue.

MODEL 30.8

Purchasing bonds at a discount

Step 1 Accrued interest period is 90 days.
Step 2 $2,000 x 0.12 x 90 ÷ 360 = $60.00 (accrued interest)
Step 3 $2,000 x 0.88 = $1,760.00 (market price)
Step 4 2 x $5.00 = $10.00 (broker's commission)
Step 5 $60.00 + $1,760.00 + $10.00 = $1,830.00 (bond purchase price)

The proceeds to the seller will be $1,820.00 ($1,830.00 - $10.00).

Apply Your Skills

Brad Frolick purchased 3 $1,000 bonds at 92, plus accrued interest at 6% for 60 days. The broker's commission is $5 per $1,000 bond issue. What is the bond purchase price?

$ _____

COMPUTING RATE OF RETURN ON BONDS

Yield: Annual earnings divided by the current closing price.

Computation of interest is based on the face value (also called *par value*) of the bonds. Therefore, a bond purchased at 100 will show a rate of return equal to the annual rate of interest. However, bonds are sold at market value, which seldom equals the face value. Bonds sold at a premium will show a rate of return that is less than the stated rate of interest, while bonds sold at a discount will show a rate of return that is higher than the stated rate of interest. The rate of return on the investment is called the *yield* of the bond issue.

ANNUAL RATE OF RETURN

The rate of return is expressed as a percentage, such as a 7.8% annual rate. The rate of return is computed by dividing annual interest by total cost for the bond issue, as shown in Model 30.9.

Computing rate of return on bonds purchased at a discount

Problem: LaVon Finiello purchased 2 $1,000 bonds at 90. The bonds pay an 8% interest rate. A total commission of $10 is charged. What is the rate of return?

Solution: **Step 1** Compute the market value.

Face value x Price quotation = Market value
$2,000   x $0.90   = $1,800.00

Step 2 Compute the total cost.

Market value + Commission = Total cost
$1,800.00   + $10.00   = $1,810.00

Step 3 Compute the interest earned.

Face value   x Interest rate = Interest earned
$2,000.00   x 0.08   = $160.00

Step 4 Compute the rate of return.

Interest earned ÷ Total cost = Rate of return
$160.00   ÷ $1,810.00 = 0.0883977 or 8.84%

Apply Your Skills

Sang Baek purchased 3 $1,000 bonds at 95. The bonds pay a 7% interest rate. A $25 commission is charged. What is the rate of return? _____

Notice that the rate of return is higher than the stated interest because the bonds were purchased at a discount. The rate of return is computed as shown in Model 30.10.

MODEL 30.10

Computing rate of return on bonds purchased at a premium

Problem: Arlene Alexander purchased 3 $1,000 bonds at 105. The bonds pay an 8% interest rate. A commission of $15 is charged by the broker. What is the rate of return?

Solution:
Step 1 $3,000.00 x $1.05 = $3,150.00 (market value)
Step 2 $3,150.00 + $15.00 = $3,165.00 (total cost)
Step 3 $3,000.00 x 0.08 = $240.00 (interest earned)
Step 4 $240.00 ÷ $3,165.00 = 0.0758 or 7.58% (rate of return, rounded)

Apply Your Skills

Edgar Roark purchased 4 $1,000 bonds at 106. The bonds pay a 7% interest rate. A $30 commission is charged. What is the rate of return? _____

Since the rate of return is lower than the stated interest rate, the bonds were purchased at a premium.

You may now complete Performance Application 30.2.

PERFORMANCE APPLICATION 30.1

Unless otherwise specified, preferred stock will not earn dividends above the stated rate.

1. Determine the amount of dividends that will be paid for each of the following stocks:

Shares	Par Value	Rate of Dividend	Total Dividend
200	20	5%	$
400	100	7%	$
700	30	4%	$
1,500	8	8%	$
2,000	50	6%	$

2. Equidor Parts, Inc. issued dividends of $1.75 per share on its 4,000 shares of outstanding stock. What amount was paid in dividends?

   $ _____

3. The Marshall Micro Concepts Corporation had earnings of $62,000 during the past year. If 20,000 shares of stock are outstanding, what were the earnings per share?

   $ _____

4. The Miller Appliances Company has 800 shares of preferred stock, par value $10, and 500 shares of common stock, par value $12. A dividend of 5% is declared based on availability of dividends. A total of $600 is available for dividends. How much will be received by (a) preferred stockholders and (b) common stockholders?

   (a) $ _____

   (b) $ _____

5. Safety Hospital Management, Inc. has 2,000 shares of 6% preferred stock, par value $100 per share, and 1,000 shares of common stock, par value $80. During the year, profits were $20,000. If a 6% dividend is declared for both types of stock, how much will (a) be paid to preferred stockholders, (b) be paid to common stockholders, and (c) remain in retained earnings?

    (a) $ _____

    (b) $ _____

    (c) $ _____

6. Glynda Wilfong purchased 75 shares of common stock 4 years ago at 60½ . Annual dividends have averaged $.50 per share. If she sells the stock today for 75¾ what is her rate of return?

    _____

7. Lea Ann Goss purchased 50 shares of common stock 2 years ago at 30¼ . Dividends during the first year were $2.80 per share, and second-year dividends were $3.20 per share. If she sells the stock for 42½ , what is her rate of return?

    _____

8. What is the rate of return on stock purchased 5 years ago at 25¼ and selling today for 35½ with annual dividends of $2.20 during the past 5 years?

    _____

9. What is the rate of return on stock purchased 1 year ago at 40½ and selling today for 36¼ with annual dividends of $1.75 during the past year?

    _____

PERFORMANCE APPLICATION 30.2

1. Answer the following questions based on the following newspaper listing of bonds sold on the American Exchange.

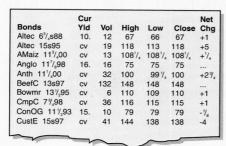

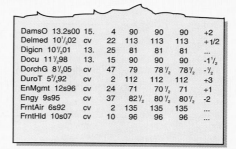

Bonds	Cur Yld	Vol	High	Low	Close	Net Chg
Altec 6 3/4s88	10.	12	67	66	67	+1
Altec 15s95	cv	19	118	113	118	+5
AMaiz 11 3/4 00	cv	13	108 1/4	108 1/4	108 1/4	+1/4
Anglo 11 7/8 98	16.	16	75	75	75	...
Anth 11 1/4 00	cv	32	100	99 1/4	100	+2 3/4
BeefC 13s97	cv	132	148	148	148	...
Bowmr 13 1/2 95	cv	6	110	109	110	+1
CmpC 7 3/4 98	cv	36	116	115	115	+1
ConOG 11 1/2 93	15.	10	79	79	79	-1/8
CustE 15s97	cv	41	144	138	138	-4
DamsO 13.2s00	15.	4	90	90	90	+2
Delmed 10 1/2 02	cv	22	113	113	113	+1/2
Digicn 10 1/2 01	13.	25	81	81	81	...
Docu 11 1/2 98	13.	15	90	90	90	-1 1/2
DorchG 8 1/2 05	cv	47	79	78 1/2	78 1/2	-1/2
DuroT 5 3/4 92	cv	2	112	112	112	+3
EnMgmt 12s96	cv	24	71	70 1/2	71	+1
Engy 9s95	cv	37	82 1/2	80 1/2	80 1/2	-2
FrntAir 6s92	cv	2	135	135	135	...
FrntHld 10s07	cv	10	96	96	96	...

(a) What rate of interest do bonds offered by AMaiz pay?

____

(b) What is the maturity date for bonds offered by Anth?

____

(c) What is the current yield being paid for bonds offered by Docu?

____

(d) How many issues of bonds were sold by CustE?

____

(e) What was the highest quote during the day for bonds offered by ConOG?

____

(f) At the close of the day, what was the quote for bonds offered by Engy?

_____

(g) How much did bonds offered by DamsO change from the close of the previous day?

_____

(h) At the close of the day, how much money will be required to purchase $10,000 in bonds from Frontier Airlines?

_____

(i) Which company sold the highest volume of bonds during the day?

_____

(j) Based on the closing quote for the day, how much money will be required to purchase $8,000 in bonds from Bowmr?

$ _____

2. Eight bonds from a recent newspaper listing are shown in the following table. Complete the table to show the annual rate of return for the purchase of the $1,000 bonds. Assume a commission of $5.00 per $1,000 for each bond. (Round rate of return to two decimal places.) The discount or premium is not amortized.

Bond	Number Purchased	Price	Interest Rate	Market Value	Total Cost	Annual Interest	Rate of Return
1	4	88	6%	$_____	$_____	$_____	_____
2	6	92	$8\frac{1}{2}\%$	$_____	$_____	$_____	_____
3	5	94	8%	$_____	$_____	$_____	_____
4	3	104	10%	$_____	$_____	$_____	_____
5	2	102	5%	$_____	$_____	$_____	_____
6	8	106	12%	$_____	$_____	$_____	_____
7	1	96	9%	$_____	$_____	$_____	_____
8	7	101	4%	$_____	$_____	$_____	_____

PRACTICE TEST FOR CHAPTER 30
STOCKS AND BONDS

Complete each of the problems shown below and then compare
your answers with the ones on page 652.

1. Bearden Corporation stock listed for 37³/₈. What is the cost of
   200 shares? $ _____

2. Brownstone Center has 1,200 shares of preferred stock, par
   value $10, and 1,000 shares of common stock, par value $20. A
   7% dividend based on par value was declared. A total of
   $1,000 is available for dividends. How much will common
   stockholders receive? $ _____

3. Stock was purchased 5 years ago at $40 and sells today for
   $48. There was a $1.50 per share annual dividend for the past 5
   years. What was the rate of return? _____

4. Janis Williams purchased 4 $1,000 bonds on July 1 with an
   annual interest payment due on July 31. The interest rate is 8%.
   What is the (a) accrued interest period and (b) accrued
   interest amount? (a) _____ (b) $ _____

5. Randy McPherson purchased 5 $1,000 bonds at 108 with a $5
   commission per $1,000 bond issue. What is the purchase price?

   $ _____

6. Michelle Reihi purchased 8 $1,000 bonds on April 7, which was
   60 days after the interest payment date. The bonds were
   purchased at 88 with an 8% interest rate and a $45
   commission. What is the purchase price?

   $ _____

7. Margo Pierce purchased 15 $1,000 bonds, maturing in 10 years,
   at 90. The bonds pay a 9% interest rate. What is the amortized
   rate of return? _____

8. Barry Smith purchased 7 $1,000 bonds, maturing in 20 years, at
   105. The bonds pay a 6% interest rate. What is the amortized
   rate of return? _____

30.1 The chart shown below indicates the 52-week high and low prices for selected stocks relating to high technology areas. Assume that you purchased 100 shares of each of the following stocks at its lowest point and sold the stock at its highest point. How much would have been earned on each sale?

(a) Oracle Systems $ _____

(b) Hewlett Packard $ _____

(c) Intel $ _____

(d) Microsoft $ _____

A month of sunny days

Wednesday's high-technology surge was the latest move in the group's month-old rally.

Company	Wednesday cls., chng.	52-week high / low	Change from 4/19
Oracle Sys.	$ 42 $\frac{7}{8}$, + 2 $\frac{1}{4}$	42$\frac{7}{8}$ / 14	+31%
Sybase	$ 69 $\frac{5}{8}$, + 1 $\frac{7}{8}$	70$\frac{3}{4}$ / 21	+31%
Cisco Sys.	$ 55 $\frac{3}{8}$, + 2 $\frac{1}{8}$	55$\frac{1}{2}$ / 19$\frac{3}{4}$	+29%
Hewl.-Pack.	$ 87 $\frac{1}{2}$, + 2 $\frac{3}{4}$	88$\frac{7}{8}$ / 50$\frac{1}{4}$	+19%
Cabletron	$ 103, + 3	103$\frac{5}{8}$ / 42$\frac{1}{8}$	+18%
Compaq	$ 57 $\frac{1}{8}$, + 1 $\frac{3}{4}$	58$\frac{1}{2}$ / 23$\frac{1}{8}$	+15%
Motorola	$ 80 $\frac{1}{8}$, + 2 $\frac{1}{8}$	80$\frac{3}{8}$ / 37$\frac{1}{8}$	+13%
Intel	$ 104 $\frac{1}{2}$, + 3 $\frac{1}{4}$	121$\frac{1}{4}$ / 46$\frac{1}{2}$	+7%
Microsoft	$ 92 $\frac{1}{2}$, + 4	95 / 65$\frac{1}{2}$	+6%
S&P 500	**447.57, +7.25**	**456.33 / 400.96**	**unch.**

Source: USA TODAY research

CONNECTIONS

30.2 The Coffee County government issued bonds with income free of state and federal income taxes. The bonds pay a 5% interest rate. Neeman Corporation issued bonds that pay a 9% interest rate, but are not free of state and federal income taxes. Harry Younger is in the 28% federal income tax bracket and 2% state income tax bracket. Which plan will result in the highest net income, after taxes, for Mr. Younger?

_____ Coffee County

_____ Neeman Corporation

CONNECTIONS

30.1 Assume that you have $10,000 to invest in the purchase of stocks. Review stock listings in your daily newspaper to select the desired stocks. Review the stock listings one week later. (a) How much did you gain or lose on your investment? (b) What was your percentage of gain or loss on an annual basis? (c) If you had $10,000 to invest, what type of investment do you feel would be best for you? Why?

(a)   Gain or (loss) $ _____

(b)   Percentage gain or (loss)   _____

(c)   _____

_____

_____

30.2 Herman Hecker can purchase 7 $1,000 bonds from Ram Corporation at 104 with a 7% interest rate. The commission charge is $45. He can also purchase 7 $1,000 10-year bonds from Heinz Corporation at 98 with a 5% interest rate. The commission charge is $45. Which investment will offer the highest rate of return?

_____ Ram Corporation

_____ Heinz Corporation

DECISIONS

STOCKS AND BONDS
Chapter Review and Quick Reference

Topic	Main Point	Typical Example	Text Page
Stock purchase	Stocks can be bought and sold through stock brokers.	100 shares were purchased at 27 3/4. Price x No. of shares = Cost $27.75 x 100 = **$2,750**	605
Reading stock listings	Stock listings are in the business sections of most daily newspapers.	WalMart: Vol, 3,400,000; Last, 25¾ ; and Chg, +3/8. This is read as **WalMart stock sold 3,400,000 shares during the day, with the price at the end of the day at $25.75, which was $0.375 more than the day before.**	606
Dividends	Dividends are earnings that are distributed to stockholders.	XYZ Corp. declares a $1.75 per share dividend. Don owns 100 shares. Per share dividend x No. of shares = No. of Dividends $1.75 x 100 = **$175**	609
Rate of return	Total increase in price and dividends divided by original cost.	Stock costing $10 has earned $4 dividends and is now selling for $12. Increase: $4 + $2 = $6 Rate of return: Increase ÷ Cost = Rate of return $6 ÷ $10 = **60%**	611

Topic	Main Point	Typical Example	Text Page
Bond quotation	Bonds are quoted as a percent of $1,000, such as 88.	A bond is quoted as 88. The purchase price is then $1,000 x 0.88 = $880 per unit purchased.	613
Accrued interest period	The period of time that interest has been earned but not yet paid is the accrued interest period.	A bond paying semiannual interest on December 31 and June 30 was purchased on July 30. Interest will accrue from June 30 to July 30, a period of 30 days.	614
Accrued interest	Interest that has been earned but not yet paid on the bond purchase date is accrued.	A bond paying 6% interest on June 30 was purchased on July 30. Face value x Interest rate x Time = Accrued interest $1,000 x 0.06 x 30 ÷ 360 = **$5**	615
Purchase price	The price of a bond includes premium or discount and commission fees.	A $1,000 bond is purchased at 102 with $25 broker fees. Face value x Premium = Market value $1,000 x 1.02 = **$1,020** Market value + Broker fees = Purchase price $1,020 + $25 = **$1,045**	615
Rate of return	The yield on the investment is the rate of return.	A $1,000 bond with a $1,045 purchase price earns a 6% interest rate. Face value x Interest rate = Interest $1,000 x 0.06 = **$60** Interest ÷ Purchase price = Return rate $60 ÷ $1,045 = **5.74%**	617

Read the graph and analysis shown and answer the questions.

Analysis: Industry average stock prices rose from $30.375 per share in the first quarter to $34.25 per share by the second quarter. Prices hit a plateau at $34.50 in the third quarter, then climbed to a high of $40.625 in the fourth quarter. In comparison, our stock price rose gradually from $20.25 in the first quarter to $25.625 in the second quarter. Prices jumped to $45.375 in the third quarter, surpassing the industry average by a margin of roughly $10 per share. Our stock resumed a gradual climb in the fourth quarter to a current stock price of $48.25.

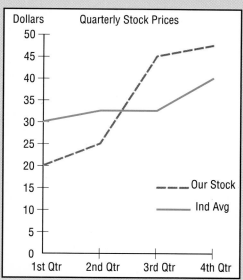

1. Find the mean stock price for the year for "our stock."

2. Define the following terms: industry average, share, plateau, surpass, margin

3. Chart the following information for Company X on the line graph and write an analysis of the data.

Company X	Stock Price
1st Qtr	23.25
2nd Qtr	26.375
3rd Qtr	32.375
4th Qtr	33.625

4. Create a bar graph showing the information in the line graph.

COMMUNICATIONS

UNIT 7 SPREADSHEET APPLICATION 1:
BOND COST

The following spreadsheet is used to compute the market value, commission, and total cost for a series of bond issues. The face value is multiplied by the price quotation to compute the market value. The commission equals $10 per $1,000 of face value. Total cost equals the market value plus the commission. To check your computations, total cost for the first bond (ID Number 1782Q) should be $4,360.

	A	B	C	D	E	F	
1	Teek State Bank		BOND COST				
2	--						
3	ID	Face	Price	Market		Commission	Total
4	Number	Value	Quotation	Value	($10 per 1,000)		Cost
5	--						
6	1782Q	4,000	108				
7	1436Q	3,000	105				
8	2431Q	5,000	96				
9	3254Q	5,000	102				
10	7832Q	2,000	95				
11	1087R	12,000	97				
12	2142R	8,000	92				
13	4356R	7,000	112				
14	5632R	13,000	94				
15	7831R	6,000	91				
16	2048Y	5,000	112				
17	3154Y	3,000	106				
18	4127Y	7,000	96				
19	8010Y	10,000	94				

Refer to the spreadsheet above to answer the following questions:

1. What is the market value for ID Number 3254Q?

   $ _____

2. What is the market value for ID Number 7831R?

   $ _____

3. What is the market value for ID Number 4127Y?

$ _____

4. What is the commission for ID Number 4356R?

$ _____

5. What is the total cost for ID Number 2431Q?

$ _____

6. What is the total cost for ID Number 2048Y?

$ _____

7. What is the ID Number of the bond with the highest total cost?

_____

8. How many bonds were sold for a premium?

_____

9. How many bonds were sold for a discount?

_____

10. How many bonds had a market value greater than $10,000?

_____

UNIT 7 SELF-TEST

STATISTICS, GRAPHS, STOCKS, AND BONDS

1. Employees who work for Copeland's Photo Shop earned the following salaries last week: $303, $310, $320, $308, $310, $314, and $340. What are the (a) mean, (b) median, and (c) mode salaries for the employees?

   (a) $ _____

   (b) $ _____

   (c) $ _____

2. The 5 cabs in the Urban Cab Company's fleet were driven the following numbers of miles last week: 162.6, 150.5, 148.3, 139.4, and 154.7. What are the (a) mean and (b) median miles driven for the fleet?

   (a) _____

   (b) _____

3. Scores made on the final exam by advanced accounting students at Waverly Junior College are shown below grouped by interval category. What are the (a) mean, (b) median, and (c) modal class for the test?

   (a) _____

   (b) _____

   (c) _____

Scores	Frequency
73– 79	4
80– 86	5
87– 93	7
94–100	4

4. Furniture and appliance sales (in millions of dollars) for the past 12 months in a large city were as follows: January, 6.5; February, 10.2; March, 10.4; April, 10.1; May, 11.3; June, 11.5; July, 12.2; August, 11.4; September, 10.1; October, 11.3; November, 11.5; and December, 12.5. Use the following chart to prepare a line graph to show sales for each month. Let each block on the graph represent $10,000,000.

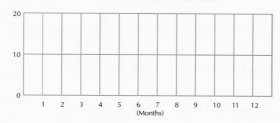

FURNITURE AND APPLIANCE SALES
in Millions of Dollars for the Year 19Y1

5. Use the same furniture and appliance sales data provided in Problem 4 above to construct a bar graph. Let each block on the graph represent $5,000,000. Use the following chart to prepare the bar graph.

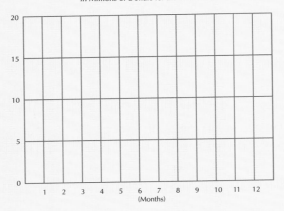

FURNITURE AND APPLIANCE SALES
in Millions of Dollars for the Year 19Y1

6. The Kraft Equipment Company issues 4,600 shares of its stock, which has a par value of $5.00. The stock is issued for $6.00 per share. What is the total (a) par value, (b) issue price, and (c) premium for the stock?

    (a) $ _____

    (b) $ _____

    (c) $ _____

7. What is the total cost of the following stock purchases: 30 shares @ 15½, 80 shares @ 20⅞, and 20 shares @ 10¼?

    $ _____

8. Michelle Goldstein owns 200 shares of stock with a par value of $15. The board of directors declared a 7% cash dividend. What amount did she receive in dividends?

    $ _____

9. Marjorie Lowell purchased 20 shares of common stock 2 years ago for 40¼. Dividends were $3.50 per share each year. If she sells the stock for 45½, what is the rate of return (rounded to two decimal places)?

    _____

10. Marshall Electronics, Inc. has 20,000 shares of 5% preferred stock outstanding with a par value of $30 and 20,000 shares of common stock outstanding with a par value of $10. If $40,000 is available for dividends, what amount will be paid to holders of common stock?

$ _____

11. On January 16, Lamar O'Toole purchased 6 $1,000 bonds with an annual interest payment date of January 1. The interest rate is 12%. What are the (a) accrued interest period, and (b) accrued interest amount for the bond issue?

(a) _____

(b) $ _____

12. Kristen Cohen purchased 4 $1,000 bonds at 104 with a commission of $5.00 per $1,000. What is the purchase price of the bonds?

$ _____

13. Theodore Ashe purchased 12 $1,000 United Steel 8s20 bonds at 105 in 1995. What is the amortized rate of return (rounded to two decimal places)?

_____

14. Caroline Bisno purchased 8 $1,000 bonds in 1995. She chose Kane 9½ 15 at 89. (a) What total amount will she pay for the bonds? (b) How much of the discount should be amortized each year? (c) Taking the discount into account, what is the actual annual interest rate?

(a) $ _____

(b) $ _____

(c) _____

INTRODUCTION TO ALGEBRA

You have already used some of the basic principles of algebra to solve business problems while solving problems in this text. For example, you used a basic percentage formula (Amount = Base x Rate) in several chapters relating to merchandising mathematics. In an algebra format, the formula would be stated as A = BR. For another example, the basic interest formula (Interest = Principal x Rate x Time) is also stated in an algebra format as I = PRT. A letter is used as a *variable* or an *unknown factor* in the equation. The variables BR are read as B times R.

When all factors in a formula are known except for one, the other factor can be determined by using algebra concepts. Algebra uses letters of the alphabet to represent values. The basic interest formula can be used to determine various factors as shown below.

$$P = \frac{I}{R \times T} \qquad R = \frac{I}{P \times T} \qquad T = \frac{I}{P \times R}$$

Figure A.1 Algebra Forms for Interest Formula

The above formulas were derived from the basic interest formula, I = P x R x T, by using the principles of algebra. Basic rules, with examples, for using algebra are presented below. Notice that the goal is to isolate the formula until a single letter appears on the left of the equal sign.

After each of the basic rules is illustrated, opportunities will be provided to apply your skills to reinforce understanding of the process. The answers will be provided. First, solve the problem. Then compare your answer with the one provided.

BASIC ALGEBRA RULES

1. Each value on the left and right of the equal sign must be equivalent.

   A = 4 + 3   Therefore, the value of A is 7.

   B = 8 ÷ 2   Therefore, the value of B is 4.

   X = 3 X 7   Therefore, the value of X is 21.

Apply Your Skills

   X = 5 + 3 + 8   X = _____

   X = 2 X 5 + 8   X = _____

2. A value can be added to or subtracted from one side as long as the same value is added to or subtracted from the other side.

   A + 3 = 7 + 8   Subtract 3 from both sides as follows.

   A + 3 - 3 = 7 + 8 - 3   Therefore, A = 12.

   A - 3 = 12 - 2   Add 3 to both sides as follows.

   A - 3 + 3 = 12 - 2 + 3   Therefore, A = 13.

Apply Your Skills

   X + 4 = 3 + 6   X = _____

   X - 3 = 7 + 2   X = _____

   X - 7 = 12   X = _____

3. A value can be divided into one side as long as the same value is divided into the other side. Notice that cancellation can be used during this process.

   4A = 12 Divide both sides by 4 as follows.

   4A = 12 Therefore, A = 3.

   4 = 4

5X = 20   X = _____

3X = 21   X = _____

4. The order of arithmetic operations is performed from the left to the right side of the equation with multiplication and division operations being performed first, followed by addition and subtraction operations.

X = 2 + 3 X 5   The first operation performed will be multiplication (3 X 5 = 15). Then, the second operation performed will be addition (15 + 2). Therefore, X = 17.

Apply Your Skills

X = 17 - 2 X 5 + 8   X = _____

X = 8 + 21 ÷ 3 + 5   X = _____

X = 28 - 10 ÷ 2 x 4   X = _____

5. Parentheses can be used to change the order of operations. All operations within parentheses are performed in the order presented in #4 above, followed by operations outside the parentheses in the order presented in #4 above.

X = 2 + (3 + 2) X 4

The first operation performed will be addition within parentheses (3 + 2 = 5). The second operation performed will be multiplication (5 X 4 = 20). The third operation performed will be addition (2 + 20 = 22). Therefore, X = 22.

Apply Your Skills

X = 5 x (4 + 3)   X = _____

X = 28 ÷ (4 + 3) + 10   X = _____

X = 32 ÷ (5 + 3) x 3   X = _____

6. A value can be multiplied by values on one side as long as the same value is multiplied by values on the other side. Notice that cancellation can be used during this process.

$$\frac{X}{3} = 5 \text{ becomes } \frac{3X}{3} = 5 \times 3$$

The value 3 is then canceled on the left side to isolate X. Therefore, X = 15.

Apply Your Skills

$$\frac{X}{7} = 3 \qquad \textbf{X} = \underline{\hspace{1cm}}$$

$$\frac{X}{5} = 4 \qquad \textbf{X} = \underline{\hspace{1cm}}$$

$$5X = 30 \qquad \textbf{X} = \underline{\hspace{1cm}}$$

$$4X = 28 \qquad \textbf{X} = \underline{\hspace{1cm}}$$

ALGEBRA CONCEPTS

The previous examples illustrate that the equation is the central concept to algebra. In an equation, both sides of the equal sign are equal. For the equation A = 2 + 6 ÷ 2, this concept makes the value of A be 5.

Several basic rules that guide algebra concepts are outlined in Figure A.2.

1.	Both sides of the equation must be equal.
2.	The equation should be simplified until a single variable appears on one side of the equation.
3.	The same number can be added to each side of the equation.
4.	The same number can be subtracted from each side of the equation.
5.	The same number can be divided into each side of the equation.
6.	The same number can be multiplied by each side of the equation.
7.	A hierarchical order exists as follows:
	(a) operations are performed from left to right.
	(b) multiplication and division occur first.
	(c) addition and subtraction occur next.
	(d) parentheses can be used to change the order of computation.
8.	Multiplication operations involving variables do not normally have an operation sign. For example, 4x means 4 times x.

Figure A.2 Algebra Concepts

CHECKING ALGEBRA SOLUTIONS

The computed value can be substituted for the variable in the formula to assure that both sides of the equation are equal. If the two sides are not equal after substitution for the variable, a mistake has occurred. For example, the equation

$$\frac{X}{2} = 12$$

can be solved by multiplying both sides by the value 2 and then using cancellation to isolate the variable X.

$$\frac{X}{2} = 12 \quad \text{becomes} \quad \frac{2X}{2} = 12 \times 2 \quad \text{or} \quad X = 24$$

If the value 24 is substituted for the variable X in the original formula, the result will be as follows:

$$\frac{24}{2} = 12 \quad \text{The equation is equal since 24 divided by 2 equals 12.}$$

BUSINESS APPLICATIONS

Algebra can be used to solve business applications that require a formula and that have all factors known except one.

BASIC INTEREST FORMULA

The basic interest formula discussed earlier in this lesson took the form of **I**nterest = **P**rincipal x **R**ate x **T**ime or I = PRT. If the rate (R) is unknown and the other three factors are known, this variable can be isolated by dividing both sides of the equation by PT and then using cancellation as indicated below:

$$I = PRT \quad \text{becomes} \quad \frac{I}{PT} = \frac{PRT}{PT} \quad \text{becomes} \quad \frac{I}{PT} = R$$

Assume that I = $6, P = $100, and T = 1. These values can then be substituted in the formula to compute **R** or the rate as follows.

$$R = \frac{6}{100 \times 1} = \frac{6}{100} = 0.06 \text{ or } 6\%.$$

Apply Your Skills

I = $25   R = 5% or 0.05   T = 2   P = ?

$$I = PRT \quad \text{or} \quad \frac{I}{RT} = \frac{PRT}{RT} \qquad P = \frac{I}{RT}$$

$$P = \frac{\$25}{0.05 \times 2} = \frac{\$25}{0.1} = \mathbf{\$250}$$

PERCENTAGE FORMULA

The basic formula, **A**mount = **R**ate x **B**ase or A = RB, can also be used to derive formulas relative to solving for other unknown factors in this formula. For example, assume that the rate is unknown and the base and amount are known. Both sides of the equation can be divided by the base to isolate the rate as shown below.

$$A = RB \quad \text{becomes} \quad \frac{A}{B} = \frac{RB}{B} \quad \text{becomes} \quad \frac{A}{B} = R \quad \text{or} \quad R = \frac{A}{B}$$

Assume that the amount = 20 and the base = 200. These amounts can then be placed into the derived formula as shown below to compute the rate.

$$R = \frac{A}{B} \qquad R = \frac{20}{200} = 0.01 \text{ or } 10\%$$

Merchandise inventory formula

The formula for computing inventories and turnovers is Beginning inventory + Purchases = Ending inventory + Cost of goods sold. Algebra letters can be used (the first letter of each word) to shorten the formula as follows: B + P = E + C. If any three factors are known, the fourth factor can be computed. Assume that the cost of goods sold (C) is unknown, but that the other factors are as follows: B = $200, P = $75, and E = $50. The first step is to use a derived formula to isolate the unknown factor as indicated below.

B + P = E + C

The variable E (ending inventory) can be isolated by subtracting C (cost of goods sold) from both sides of the equation.

B + P - C = E + C - C becomes B + P - C = E or E = B + P - C

Values are then substituted for variables in the formula.

E = $200 + $75 - $50 = $225.

Therefore, the ending inventory as represented by the variable E equals $225.

As illustrated by these business applications, algebra concepts can be very valuable and easy to use to solve business problems that utilize a formula to make a computation.

PERFORMANCE APPLICATION

1. Solve each of the following equations.

   (a) X = 4 + 3   X = _____

   (b) X = 23 - 14 + 4   X = _____

   (c) X = 8 x 7   X = _____

   (d) X = 24 ÷ 6   X = _____

   (e) X = 8 + 3 x 4   X = _____

   (f) X = 7 + 2 x 6 - 2   X = _____

   (g) X = 3 x 2 + 6   X = _____

   (h) X = 3 x (2 + 6)   X = _____

   (i) X = 3 x 2 x 4 ÷ 3   X = _____

   (j) X = 4 x (5 - 2) +   X = _____

2. Solve each of the following equations.

   (a) A = 3   B = 2   X = A + B   X = _____

   (b) A = 2   B = 4   X = AB   X = _____

   (c) A = 3   B = 4   X = A + B - 2   X = _____

   (d) A = 3   B = 2   X = 3 x (A + B)   X = _____

   (e) A = 5   B = 2   X = 15 - (A + B) + 4   X = _____

   (f) A = 2   B = 3   X = 13 + (A + B) x 2   X = _____

3. Solve each of the following equations.

   (a) A = 4   B = 2 C = 6   X + A = B + C   X = _____

   (b) A = 7   B = 4 C = 9   X + A = B + C   X = _____

   (c) A = 4   B = 16 C = 7   X - A = B - C   X = _____

   (d) A = 18   B = 7 C = 5   X - C = A - B   X = _____

   (e) A = 4   B = 2   X = AB   X = _____

   (f) A = 6   B = 2   X = A ÷ B   X = _____

   (g) A = 2   B = 4 C = 6   X = ABC   X = _____

4. Solve each of the following equations.

I = PRT   P = $4,000   R = 6%   T = 2   I = _____
I = PRT   I = $15   R = 5%   T = 1   P = _____
I = PRT   I = $20   P = $400 T = 1   R = _____

5. John Simpson borrowed $600 at the bank. He will repay the amount in 2 years. The interest amount will be $48. What rate of interest did the bank charge? What derived formula can be used to compute the answer? Basic formula: I=PRT

   Rate: _____

   Derived formula: _____

6. Jenny Bottoms purchased a stereo system that originally cost $800. Jenny was given a $200 discount amount. What rate of discount was Jenny given? What derived formula can be used to compute the answer? Basic formula: A = BR

   Rate: _____

   Derived formula: _____

7. Sarah Fieldstone signed a promissory note to borrow $800 at the bank. The interest rate will be 8%. The interest on the loan will be $192. What was the length of time for the loan? What derived formula can be used to compute the answer? Basic formula: I = PRT

   Time: _____

   Derived formula: _____

8. City Center has offered a television for a $90 discount, which was a 25% discount from the original base price. What was the original base price? What derived formula can be used to compute the answer? Basic formula: A = BR

   Base price: $ _____

   Derived formula: _____

Answers

CHAPTER 1

Apply Your Skills 1.1

(a) Three hundred forty-five
(b) One thousand three hundred eighty-two
(c) Four hundred twenty-five and eighty-four hundredths
(d) Twenty-seven dollars and fifty-three cents
(e) Fourteen and two-tenths percent

Apply Your Skills 1.2

(a) 7 and 3
(b) 4 and 6

Apply Your Skills 1.3

13,292

Apply Your Skills 1.4

(a) 400
(b) 3,000
(c) 8.3
(d) 4.25
(e) $28

Apply Your Skills 1.5

(a) 4,017
(b) 4,000

Apply Your Skills 1.6

(a) 32.99
(b) 33

Apply Your Skills 1.7

(a) 513
(b) 211
(c) 292
(d) 364
(e) 264
(f) 388
(g) 1,016

Apply Your Skills 1.9

$2,462.08

Apply Your Skills 1.10

(a) $1,307
(b) $1,300

Practice Test

1. $ 732.94
2. (a) 78.908
   (b) 78.9
3. (a) $4,440.55
   (b) $4,400
4. $127,000
5. $ 4,000

Apply Your Skills 2.1

$21,480

Apply Your Skills 2.2

(a) $1,874.25
(b) $1,800

Apply Your Skills 2.3

Yes

Apply Your Skills 2.4

$12

Apply Your Skills 2.5

24

Apply Your Skills 2.6

(a) $12,345.30
(b) $15,000

Apply Your Skills 2.7

No

Apply Your Skills 2.8

8 hours

Practice Test

1. (a) $429
   (b) $400
2. 1,026 miles
3. $853
4. (a) $656.25
   (b) $600

Apply Your Skills 3.1

$133.35 amount due
$16.65 change due

Apply Your Skills 3.2

50
45
37
49
46

Apply Your Skills 3.3

$470.55 total

Practice Test

1. $261.35
2. $2,759.40
3. Timothy Brumberg
4. $4,499.95 (regular price)
   $4,274.95 (discount price)
5. (a) $9,025
   (b) $9,014.75

Apply Your Skills 4.1

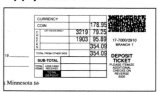

Apply Your Skills 4.2

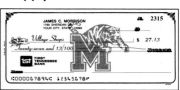

Apply Your Skills 4.3

Apply Your Skills 4.4

Practice Test

1. a
2. $975
3. $1,696
4. $3,650
5. $8,274.50

Answers

CHAPTER 5

Practice Test

1. a. 17/18
   b. 17/4
   c. 79/8
   d. 241/8
   e. 85/2
   f. 211/4
   g. 7 1/4
   h. 4 3/8
   i. 5 2/9
   j. 29 2/3
   k. 19 3/7
   l. 54 3/4
2. a. 4
   b. 1
   c. 1
   d. 6
   e. 21
   f. 16
3. a. 1/3
   b. 1/4
   c. 1/6
   d. 1/3
   e. 3/16
   f. 5/12
   g. 3/4
   h. 3/5
   i. 5/8
4. a. 16
   b. 36
   c. 30
   d. 48
   e. 21
   f. 40
   g. 90
   h. 72
5. a. 1 1/6
   b. 3/8
   c. 7/12
   d. 10/21
   e. 1 23/36
   f. 77/96
   g. 17/26
   h. 1 19/30
   i. 1 1/24
6. a. 5 5/6
   b. 14 1/6
   c. 24 1/16
   d. 89 1/24
   e. 19 17/24
   f. 26 1/12

7. a. 1/6
   b. 1/12
   c. 1/4
   d. 5/54
   e. 1/3
   f. 10
   g. 25
   h. 3/4
   i. 27/119
8. a. 39 7/8
   b. 38
   c. 88
   d. 279
   e. 25 2/3
   f. 108

CHAPTER 6

Apply Your Skills 6.1

0.7 Seven-tenths   7/10
0.08 Eight-hundredths
     8/100
0.075   Seventy-five
     thousandths   75/1000
0.0075   Seventy-five ten-
     thousandths   75/10000
3.4 Three and four-tenths   3
     4/10

Apply Your Skills 6.2

0.4 = 4/10 or 2/5   0.25 =
     25/100 or 1/4
0.75 = 75/100 or 3/4 0.62 =
     62/100 or 31/50

Apply Your Skills 6.3

3.25 = 3 25/100 or 3 1/4
25.35 = 25 35/100 or 25 7/20
5.450 = 5 450/1000 or 5 9/20

Apply Your Skills 6.4

3/5 = 0.6
3/4 = 0.75
13/65 = 0.2

Practice Test

1. Thirty-seven hundredths
2. Thousandths
3. (a) 0.35
4. 35/100 or 7/20
5. 0.875

CHAPTER 7

Apply Your Skills 7.1

38.745

Apply Your Skills 7.2

20.17

Apply Your Skills 7.3

(a) 12.308
(b) 163.8542

Practice Test

1. 23.25 hours
2. 66.6 gallons
3. 1.6 tons
4. 10.7 ounces
5. $556.31

CHAPTER 8

Apply Your Skills 8.1

14.00096

Apply Your Skills 8.2

$301.00

Apply Your Skills 8.3

0.02 inches

Apply Your Skills 8.4

$1,147.50

Apply Your Skills 8.5

(a) 348.92
(b) 2782.3
(c) 3400.

Apply Your Skills 8.6

(a) $362.50
(b) $10.76

Practice Test

1. 87.7984
2. 643.
3. $359.34
4. $160.00
5. $1,207.43

CHAPTER 9

Apply Your Skills 9.1

4.5% or 4.5 percent

Apply Your Skills 9.2

0.285

Apply Your Skills 9.3

70% or 70 percent

Apply Your Skills 9.4

351

Apply Your Skills 9.5

$276,000

Apply Your Skills 9.6

640

Practice Test

1. (a) $3,612.50
   (b) $46,112.50
2. $600.00
3. (a) $11,240
   (b) $5,213
4. (a) $2,925.00
   (b) $3,575.00
5. (a) $216,000
   (b) $259,200

CHAPTER 10

Apply Your Skills 10.1

27

Apply Your Skills 10.2

$44,000

Apply Your Skills 10.3

40 percent

Apply Your Skills 10.4

10 percent

Apply Your Skills 10.5

25 percent

Apply Your Skills 10.6

$20.00

Practice Test

1. $19,530
2. $2,592.50
3. 6.5%
4. (a)   130
   (b) 1,755
5. 8%

CHAPTER 11

Apply Your Skills 11.1

21%

Apply Your Skills 11.2

$2,874.40

Apply Your Skills 11.3

(a) $9.00
(b) $7.09
(c) $9.16

Apply Your Skills 11.4

(a) $920
(b) $13.80

Apply Your Skills 11.5

$120

Apply Your Skills 11.6

(a) $1,800
(b) $7,800
(c) $216.67

Apply Your Skills 11.7

19.46% (rounded)

Apply Your Skills 11.8

$18

Apply Your Skills 11.9

$18

Practice Test

1. (a) $97.50
   (b) $102.50
2. (a) $1,008.00
   (b) $84.00
3. $10.50
4. $2.00
5. (a) $1,000.00
   (b) 25.26 % (rounded)

CHAPTER 12

Apply Your Skills 12.1

$1,298.50

Apply Your Skills 12.2

$24,750.00

Apply Your Skills 12.3

$17,550.00

Apply Your Skills 12.4

$1,046.25

Practice Test

1. $808.65
2. (a) $357,075.00
   (b) $339,825.00
3. (a) $10,725.00
   (b) $1,239,275.00
4. 28
5. (a) $1,197.00
   (b) $ 297.00

CHAPTER 13

Apply Your Skills 13.1

(a) May 13
(b) June 27

Apply Your Skills 13.2

(a) September 10
(b) October 19

Apply Your Skills 13.3

(a) $77.18
(b) $1,852.32

Apply Your Skills 13.4

$1,157.53

Apply Your Skills 13.5

(a) $34.73
(b) $1,160.78

Practice Test

1. January 2
2. December 10
3. (a) October 11
   (b) November 10
4. (a) $490.00
   (b) $24,010
5. $7,272.65

CHAPTER 14

Apply Your Skills 14.1

(a) $840.00
(b) $1,560.00

Apply Your Skills 14.2

(a) 0.80
(b) $2,760.00

Apply Your Skills 14.3

$1,224.00

Apply Your Skills 14.4

0.352 (35.2%)

Apply Your Skills 14.5

(a) 0.24 (24%)
(b) $1,800.00
(c) $5,700.00

Apply Your Skills 14.6

(a) 0.388 (38.8%)
(b) $3,104.00
(c) $4,896.00
(d) $4,406.40

Apply Your Skills 14.7

28 percent

Apply Your Skills 14.8

31.6 percent

Practice Test

1. Metro Sports Center
2. (a) $739.20
   (b) $1,900.80
3. 0.316 (31.6%)
4. (a) 0.43 (43%)
   (b) $5,375.00
   (c) $7,125.00
5. (a) $10,327.50
   (b) $9,707.85

CHAPTER 15

Apply Your Skills 15.1

(a) $3.50
(b) $12.25

Apply Your Skills 15.2

(a) $4.90
(b) 0.35 or 35%

Apply Your Skills 15.3

(a) $800
(b) $2,400

Apply Your Skills 15.4

(a) $200
(b) 0.20 or 20%

Apply Your Skills 15.5

$16

Practice Test

1. (a) $510
   (b) $1,785
2. (a) $19.60
   (b) 0.35 or 35%
3. $1,000
4. (a) $270,000
   (b) $75,000
5. (a) 0.25 or 25%
   (b) 0.20 or 20%

CHAPTER 16

Apply Your Skills 16.1

$11.50

Apply Your Skills 16.2

(a) $1.59
(b) $6.36

Apply Your Skills 16.3

13.49 percent

Apply Your Skills 16.4

(a) $78.00
(b) $66.30

Practice Test

1. $6.86
2. (a) $2,625
   (b) $14,875
3. Product A
4. 15%
5. 17%

CHAPTER 17

Apply Your Skills 17.1

$34.75

Apply Your Skills 17.2

$3,000

Apply Your Skills 17.3

$611.00

Practice Test

1. $170.95
2. $288.91
3. $16,868.60
4. $320.00
5. (a) $3,400.00
   (b) $5,007.50

CHAPTER 18

Apply Your Skills 18.1

$582.75

Apply Your Skills 18.2

(a) $560.00
(b) $126.00
(c) $686.00

Apply Your Skills 18.3

$731.85

Apply Your Skills 18.4

$750.00

Apply Your Skills 18.5

$71,250.00

Practice Test

1. (a) $30,900.00
   (b) $1,188.46
   (c) $594.23
2. $456.95
3. (a) $568.00
   (b) $149.10
4. $786.75
5. (b) Supervisory position

CHAPTER 19

Apply Your Skills 19.1
$11,155.00
Apply Your Skills 19.2
$ 7,350.00
Apply Your Skills 19.3
(a) Itemize deductions
Apply Your Skills 19.4
$69,750.00
Apply Your Skills 19.5
$12,415.00

Apply Your Skills 19.6
(a) Taxes due
(b) $356.00
Apply Your Skills 19.7
(a) $132.00
(b) $164.00
Apply Your Skills 19.8
$2,864.93
Apply Your Skills 19.9
$707.93

Apply Your Skills 19.10
$135.00
Apply Your Skills 19.11
(a) $175.00
(b) $259.00
Practice Test
1. $12,250.00
2. $ 4,380.00
3. $ 7,361.00
4. $ 3,978.00
5. $166.00

CHAPTER 20

Apply Your Skills 20.1

2.9%

Apply Your Skills 20.2

$2,925.00

Apply Your Skills 20.3

$8,000.00

Apply Your Skills 20.4

$6,908.00

Practice Test

1. 3.5%
2. (a) $133,000.00
   (b) $95,000.00
3. (a) $76,500.00
   (b) $2,868.75
4. $61,200.00
5. $3,840.00

■ CHAPTER 21

Apply Your Skills 21.1

$629.00

Apply Your Skills 21.2

$630.00

Apply Your Skills 21.3

$695.00

Apply Your Skills 21.4

$575

Apply Your Skills 21.5

$ 382.50
   300.00
   478.50
   134.24
   225.00
   227.40
$1,747.64

Apply Your Skills 21.6

(a) $218,000.00
(b) $176,000.00

Apply Your Skills 21.7

4.4

Practice Test

1. $1,900.50
2. $1,918.00
3. $1,880.60
4. $ 797.00
5. 0.66

■ CHAPTER 22

Apply Your Skills 22.1

$6,250.00

Apply Your Skills 22.2

(a) $3,600.00
(b) $1,200.00

Apply Your Skills 22.3

(a) $8,000.00
(b) $6,000.00

Apply Your Skills 22.4

(a) $2,799.00
(b) $7,799.00

Apply Your Skills 22.5

(a) 20% (0.20)
(b) $16,000.00
(c) $64,000.00

Apply Your Skills 22.6

(a) $0.017
(b) $2,125.00

Apply Your Skills 22.7

(a) 5-year class
(b) $537.60
(c) $1,993.60
(d) $806.40

Practice Test

1. (a) $2,400.00
   (b) $9,200.00
2. (a) $3,200.00
   (b) $6,800.00
3. (a) $3,360.00
   (b) $5,040.00
4. (a) $1,440.00
   (b) $10,760.00
5. (a) $4,480.00
   (b) $6,720.00

■ CHAPTER 23

Apply Your Skills 23.1

$50,000

Apply Your Skills 23.2

5.17 (rounded)

Apply Your Skills 23.3

1.83 (rounded)

Apply Your Skills 23.4

1.77 (rounded)

Apply Your Skills 23.5

1.56 (rounded)

Apply Your Skills 23.6

1.77 (rounded)

Apply Your Skills 23.7

0.08 or 8%

Apply Your Skills 23.8

0.7739 or 77.39% (rounded)

Apply Your Skills 23.9

0.325 or 32.5%

Practice Test

1. (a) 2.59 (rounded)
   (b) 2.1
2. (a) 0.8
   (b) 2.25
   (c) 0.8
3. (a) $13,847.00
   (b) 0.0400 or 4% (rounded)
4. (a) 0.75 or 75%
   (b) 0.5 or 50%
5. (a) $21,760.00
   (b) 0.085 or 8.5%

■ CHAPTER 24

Apply Your Skills 24.1

$300

Apply Your Skills 24.2

$105.00

Apply Your Skills 24.3

$120.00

Apply Your Skills 24.4

$280.00

Apply Your Skills 24.5

$180.00

Apply Your Skills 24.6

(a) $177.53 (rounded)
(b) Less

Apply Your Skills 24.7

(a) $40.00
(b) $6.00
(c) $13.50
(d) $10.00

Apply Your Skills 24.8

$8.22 (rounded)

Apply Your Skills 24.9

$11,600.00

Apply Your Skills 24.10

(a) $180.00
(b) $900.00
(c) 5%
(d) 4 Years

Practice Test

1. (a) $810.00
   (b) $6,210.00
2. $71.92 (rounded)
3. $6.00
4. $84.00
5. June 18

CHAPTER 25

Apply Your Skills 25.1

43 days

Apply Your Skills 25.2

(a) 60 days
(b) $60.00

Apply Your Skills 25.3

(a) $5.08
(b) $603.92

Apply Your Skills 25.4

(a) $37,200.00
(b) $40,000.00

Practice Test

1. (a) $90
   (b) $3,510
2. 45 days
3. (a) 90 days
   (b) $209
   (c) $8151
4. $27,750
5. (a) $8,000
   (b) $8,510

CHAPTER 26

Apply Your Skills 26.1

$2,420.00

Apply Your Skills 26.2

$11,812.50

Apply Your Skills 26.3

$1,639.09

Apply Your Skills 26.4

$10,404.00

Apply Your Skills 26.5

8.24%

Apply Your Skills 26.6

$22,879.28

Practice Test

1. $6,050.00
2. $16.53
3. $6,305.67
4. $16,084.37
5. (a) 8.16%
   (b) 8.24%

CHAPTER 27

Apply Your Skills 27.1

$837.59

Apply Your Skills 27.2

$4,463.24

Apply Your Skills 27.3

$10,076.70

Apply Your Skills 27.4

$4,994.10

Practice Test

1. $3,002.99
2. $5,418.89
3. $77,985.45
4. $2,446.65
5. $40,000 today

CHAPTER 28

Apply Your Skills 28.1

$924.90

Apply Your Skills 28.2

$9,920.00

Apply Your Skills 28.3

$3,500.00

Apply Your Skills 28.4

$573.75 (rounded to $574)

Apply Your Skills 28.5

$869.00

Practice Test

1. $1,004.40
2. $1,294.86
3. $16,549.00
4. $27,000.00
5. $662.80

Answers

CHAPTER 29

Apply Your Skills 29.1

84

Apply Your Skills 29.2

85

Apply Your Skills 29.3

8

Apply Your Skills 29.4

Interval	Tally
53-60	/////
61-68	//
69-76	/////
77-84	////
85-92	////////

Apply Your Skills 29.5

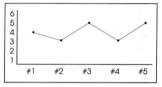

Apply Your Skills 29.6

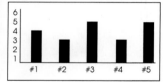

Apply Your Skills 29.7

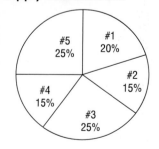

Practice Test

1. $36,735
2. 29 (halfway between 28 and 30)
3. 28
4. 22.84 or 23 (rounded)
5. 22.75
6. Responses will vary

CHAPTER 30

Apply Your Skills 30.1

$570

Apply Your Skills 30.2

$2.50

Apply Your Skills 30.3

(a) $1,200
(b) $1,300

Apply Your Skills 30.4

58.39% (rounded)

Apply Your Skills 30.5

45 days

Apply Your Skills 30.6

$400 (rounded)

Apply Your Skills 30.7

$5,320

Apply Your Skills 30.8

$2,805

Apply Your Skills 30.9

7.30% (rounded)

Apply Your Skills 30.10

6.56% (rounded)

Practice Test

1. $7,475
2. $160
3. 38.75%
4. (a) 30 days
   (b) $26.67 (rounded)
5. $5,425
6. $7,191.67
7. 10.53% (rounded)
8. 5.61% (rounded)

INDEX

NOTES